*A Sketchbook of...*

# The Border Wars

# of the Upper Ohio Valley:

# 1769-1794

*Conflicts and Resolutions*

*by*

## William Hintzen

Precision Shooting, Inc.
222 McKee Street
Manchester, CT 06040

D0813239

ISBN #0-9670948-0-1 (softcover)
ISBN #1-931220-06-9 (hardcover)

First Edition: April, 1999
Second Edition: April, 2001

# A Dedicatory

## To All of Boyhood's Heroes:

Randolph Scott, Gene Autry, Roy Rogers, and the rest,
Not the least of whom was Lewis Wetzel;

And to all the other Ghosts and Spirits
Who roamed Freeman's Woods with me,
In those Golden, Olden Days gone by.

This book is respectfully dedicated
by the author.

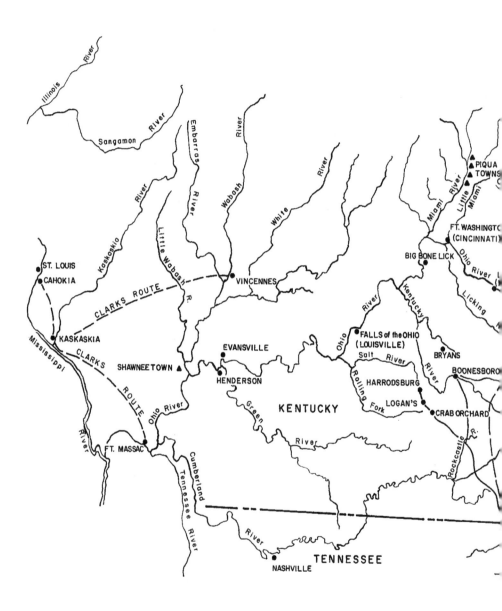

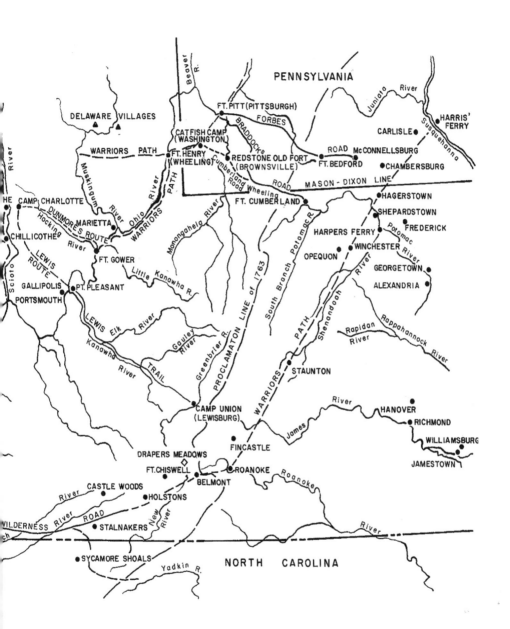

Cover Painting...

## "THE DEFENDER
### *Lewis Wetzel, a study*"

is an original work by noted artist Lee Teter of Wyoming, and is reproduced here with his kind permission.

# Table of Contents

MAPS for:

*A Sketchbook of the Border Wars*

(Note: All maps are the work of artist Charles S. Kovach, to whom the author extends his deep thanks).

## The Final Resting Places

## The Illustrations

# Prologue:
## The American Pioneer

*A Sketchbook of the Border Wars* is the story of that Trans-Allegheny movement of the American pioneer in the quarter-century from 1769 to 1794. It embraces the area of the present United States from western Pennsylvania to the Mississippi, and from the Great Lakes southward into Tennessee. The story of this westward movement begins with the emigration of the Zane family from the South Branch of the Potomac River, from their home near Moorefield, in present Hardy County, West Virginia, to the mouth of Wheeling Creek in the panhandle of that state, and it concludes with Wayne's victory over the confederated Indian tribes at Fallen Timbers.

In the quarter century with which this volume deals there were four major disasters for the American colonists, balanced against one victory:   Crawford's Expedition of May and June, 1782;   then, only two months later, in August, the defeat of the Kentuckians at the Blue Licks. The last two were the humiliating military campaigns of Generals Josiah Harmar in 1790, and of Arthur St. Clair in 1791. But opposed to these three, and outweighing them all in the final analysis, was the one ultimate victory — that of General Anthony Wayne, "Mad" Anthony they called him, at the Battle of Fallen Timbers, in August of 1794.

Throughout this book will be found the phrase: *at about this time.* One of the more unfortunate aspects of our knowledge of the Border Wars is that there is such a great deal of confusion about who did what, and when and where they did it. We are often frustrated by the lack of specific records detailing the activities of those men and women who lived in the 200-year distant past, and by the innumerable conflicts in the testimony of those who described those happenings. Perhaps it would be as well if we keep in mind the following lines written by Alpheus Favour, who once remarked on the discrepancies which are found in the accounts of names, dates, and events in the life of one of the preeminent mountain men, Old Bill Williams, but which apply equally well to those earlier and no less adventuresome men and women from the frontiers of North Carolina, Virginia, and Pennsylvania, such as the Zanes, the Boones, and the Wetzels, all of whom, like the mountain men, were born and bred backwoodsmen.

*"There is, however, much of truth in all these accounts, and after all, what does it matter? It is undoubtedly a fact that many of these adventures, or similar exploits ...., did occur in the manner related, if not in the life of Williams, then as the experiences of other mountain men. In those days truth outran fiction. The dates may he moved about because of fault in memory;  names of persons may not have been set down with accuracy in the recitals, or places may have been mislocated. The life of that day and time has been correctly portrayed in the main. The wonder is not that we do not have more, but rather that we have as much as we do, when we consider that most of these men were out of touch with those who wrote down happenings. The majority of their comrades could not read or write. Their associates were men like themselves, or Indians, and each day they had more important matters to attend to than that of keeping a reckoning of their adventures."* [1]

\*     \*     \*

With the conclusion of the French and Indian War in 1763, and the ensuing short-lived Rebellion of Pontiac, the western edge of white settlement followed an irregular north-south line from Albany, in New York, southward along the Appalachian ridge. England's long and bloody wars with France for the control of North America had lasted over half a century, and had finally resulted in the expulsion of France, with control of the eastern half of the continent north of Spanish Florida passing to Great Britain[2]. But nearly a century and a half after its first settlement at Jamestown, Virginia, in 1607, the English colonists had as yet pushed only as far west as the crest of the Allegheny Mountains. In another half century, in one of the most remarkable achievements of the American pioneering spirit, their descendants would move across a continent, from the Alleghenies to the Pacific Ocean.

In October, 1758, the Treaty of Easton (Pennsylvania) was negotiated by British Indian agent George Croghan, at the same time that General John Forbes was marching his massive army over the mountains and through the Pennsylvania wilderness toward the French Fort Duquesne at the Forks of the Ohio. At Easton, Croghan, with the blessings of the English ministries, was able to convince the Indians that the land west of the mountains was to be *Indian Land Forever*, even though the King's Proclamation Line, which would proscribe white settlement west of the central ridge of the Appalachian Mountains, was still five years in the future. At the time it made little difference; in the century and a half since 1607 the white man had crossed that mountain range only to peek at what was beyond before scurrying back to the safety of the Atlantic coast. Rare indeed was the English settler who would dare cross the mountains to live in a wilderness surrounded by wild Indians. The time of the American Pioneer was not yet come.

Therefore, in order to prevent future wars involving the Indian nations, a line, the *King's Proclamation Line of 1763,* was established along the crest of the Appalachians, west of which no settlement by the English colonists was to be allowed. A few scattered English forts, such as Niagra, and Pitt (now Pittsburgh) at the Forks of the Ohio, contained a few English settlers, but other than military personnel most of the non-Indians at those posts were traders, licensed by the British Government for that purpose.

As the Iroquois nation claimed dominion of all land north of Virginia as far west as the Forks, and since they had traditionally been aligned with the English, the English government now controlled the Great Lakes/Ohio Valley area as far south as Tennessee, and east to the Atlantic. It was hoped that this boundary limiting the western extent of white settlement would provide a permanent solution to the "Indian Problem" which had plagued both white and red men since nearly the first appearance of Europeans. But proclaiming a line is not the same as enforcing a line;

it was not so easy to dictate to the American, who had managed to get along pretty much on his own in a wilderness that was nearly overwhelming. Although at the moment he still believed that he was reliant on the presence of the English military for protection, he was soon to learn the lessons of independence.

It all began with those few daring or reckless men who had trekked to the Forks of the Ohio with Washington in 1754, where the Allegheny River, coming in from the north, merged with the Monongahela from the south. The next year an army containing a large number of Virginia and North Carolina militia, future settlers, had moved across Virginia and through Maryland, under ill-fated Braddock, to within a few miles of that spot. Among those volunteer militia were Dan Morgan, 18-year-old Daniel Boone, and former Indian trader John Finley. What they saw of that incredible land west of the mountains would make irrelevant any King's Proclamation. The land called to them, irresistibly, and although it was yet to be several years, they would answer. It would be more than a decade before chance threw them all together again, but when the time came, they were ready. It was not until the fall of 1769 when Boone, in the company of Sam Harrod and Michael Stoner, finally crossed the Cumberland Gap and wintered in the mountains of eastern Kentucky.

Nor were they the only men who wanted land of their own; there were thousands of men whose eyes were turned westward, across the mountains. Nor was it greed that drove them, as is now often stated by unknowing writers. Except for the landed gentry, of which there were only a handful, the North American colonist, no matter whether English, French, or Spanish, lived a life not only of quiet desperation, but of ceaseless exceeding drudgery. Life was short, life was hard, and there were few rewards found at the end of it. If a man and his wife worked hard all their lives, paid their debts, and managed to raise a family without the children starving and with not too many of them dying of disease or accident, they could count themselves blessed to die in bed, with nothing more than that to show for their years of unceasing toil.

\*    \*    \*

But West! — *there* was land. Daniel Boone was a poor man with a large family, the son of a poor man with an equally large family, and the land in the west was there for the asking. Boone asked for some, not out of greed, but rather because land was wealth — not in the sense of fine clothes, baubles, and gold and silver in the pocket, but real wealth. It was land that provided a man the freedom to do as he wished, to live where he wanted, to educate his children as he saw fit, to earn his living in the most productive and the most enjoyable manner, to worship however he chose, to have leisure time and the means to enjoy that leisure — *that* was wealth. And the key word in all this is freedom.

Best of all, the land was incredibly cheap. These were poor men, and they had always been poor. For centuries their forefathers in Europe had lived in a feudal society; you were born, you spent your life working another man's land, and then you died. Your children would spend their lives as you had, working the same land for the offspring of the same feudal baron. No matter how hard you strove in life, at the end of your time you would own nothing but the clothes on your back, nor would your children, nor would your children's children.

But in the North American wilderness there was land to own, and more importantly, there was land to pass on to your children. You cleared the forest, planted your crops, and then the land belonged to you and your family. For the English colonist who could look westward to the Mississippi, from the Great Lakes southward, beyond the confluence of the Monongahela and Allegheny, the headwaters of the Ohio, and continuing further south to Spanish Florida — there were literally millions of acres of the most magnificent land imaginable; and it was uninhabited, or inhabited only by bands of Indians, and to the colonists the native Indians were heathen savages who had no claim to the land. Upon the arrival of the first Europeans the North American aborigines were Neolithic tribes that had not yet progressed into the age of metals. Rather than following the European custom of clearing fields to raise crops, and tending herds of cattle, these were hunter-gatherer societies, killing the wild game and moving from place to place as desire or advantage motivated them.

As Europeans these colonists had been familiar with *heathens*; their ancestors had gone on Crusades to fight Holy Wars against them. They were bad enough, but the North American Indians were a breed apart — not only were they not Christians, but when they fought they murdered women and children, sparing not even babies, and they evidenced a great delight in so doing. They took prisoners, sometimes as slaves, but more often than not these unfortunates were taken to provide amusement for the tribe, by means of the most hellish tortures their captors could envision. Even as late as the mid-eighteenth century, European soldiers sent to America could not believe such fantastic stories as they heard. At the Battle of the Monongahela many of Braddock's soldiers, despite being warned, threw down their flintlocks and surrendered to the Indians, foolishly believing that they would be treated as prisoners of war. Not one of them survived their torture.

\*    \*    \*

*But in those days truth outran fiction!* Therefore, as you read this book, always keep in mind that the wonder is not that we do not have more, but rather that we have as much as we do. Most of these men were out of touch with those who wrote down happenings. The majority of their comrades could not read or write. Their associates were men like themselves, or Indians. And, it cannot be overemphasized, each day they had more important matters to attend to than that of keeping a reckoning of their adventures.

To be sure!

# Chapter 1

Opening the Floodgates of Western Expansion:
The Treaty of Fort Stanwix-1768

One of the most important events to occur in the entire history of the border wars took place not in the Ohio Valley, but in the State of New York, in the late fall and early winter of 1767. Sir William Johnson, Superintendent for Indian Affairs, assembled a large conference of the Indian nations to discuss proposed changes in the King's Proclamation line. Although some 3,000 Indian delegates finally convened, by the time most of them had arrived Johnson had already concluded his deal with the Iroquois, the renowned Six Nations, and then proceeded to outline the new boundary line for American settlement. Grudging agreement by the other tribes was finally given in January, 1768.

The new line broke the Appalachian Mountain barrier; according to the British ministries' intentions, the boundary was supposed to swing south from the Mohawk Valley to central Pennsylvania, where it would veer sharply to the left until it reached Fort Pitt, thence down the course of the Ohio River to the mouth of the Kanawha [present Point Pleasant, WV], then in a straight line south-by-southeast back toward the original Proclamation Line, near the Yadkin River. All this would produce no more change than a single prominent westward bulge in the land available for settlement, including those parts of Pennsylvania and Virginia west of the Appalachians.

But the Iroquois were the dominant Indian nation, and in their arrogance they would not be told by the King's ministers what lands they could give away. They insisted that the line not stop at the mouth of the Kanawha, but rather that it extend down the Ohio, cutting across the hunting grounds of both the Shawnee and the Cherokee, all the way to the valleys of the Cumberland and the Tennessee. Johnson, far exceeding his instructions from London, and hoping that these differences could be ironed out later, concurred.

But if the English were going to treat with the Iroquois, then they must also treat with the other major Indian power of the day, the Cherokee in the south, who felt that their claims had not been properly recognized. Thus, John Stuart, the King's superintendent of Indian affairs for the southern department (Johnson's counterpart), negotiated the Treaty of Lochaber in 1770. By this treaty, oftentimes appropriately enough referred to as the Treaty of Hard Labor, the Cherokee ceded all claim to their lands, from a line running almost due south from the mouth of the Kanawha on the Ohio to a point on the Holston River in eastern Tennessee. But the following year, when the commissioners from Virginia and the Cherokee Nation ran the line, they followed it from the Holston to the head of the Kentucky river, instead of to the mouth of the Kanawha. This line, however, being acceptable to the Cherokee, it was then necessary to determine the real limits of the boundaries, as land grants to the officers of the French and Indian War were waiting to be located, and the question was raised as to whether any of the grants in eastern Kentucky would be valid. The only recourse was to send government surveyors into Kentucky; since Kentucky was no more than the western arm of Virginia, it was up to the Colonial Governor of Virginia to order out the surveying teams.

The fly in all this ointment was that Kentucky was claimed, if by anyone, by the Shawnee. A treaty had been made with the Iroquois, another with the Cherokee, but the Shawnee had not given anyone permission to cross their lands. Trouble was brewing.

\*       \*       \*

As just one example of the intentions of the English colonists in North America in relation to this land grant, a petition was presented to King George III in June of 1769, requesting permission to purchase an immense tract of land within the limits of the area which had been ceded by the Iroquois at Fort Stanwix. The ultimate goal of this purchase would be the founding of a new colony, the fourteenth, to be called *Vandalia*, and with its seat of government located at the mouth of the Kanawha. The wheels of government move exceedingly slow, however, and although the petition was finally approved, it was not until late October of 1773. By that time a rebellion was beginning to take shape in the Massachusetts colony, and that rebellion would squelch the establishment of Vandalia.

\*       \*       \*

The major results of the Fort Stanwix treaty were manifold. The Iroquois League had gained two major points: they had deflected white settlement southward, away from their homeland, which was their primary goal, and at the same time they had reaffirmed their prestige by demonstrating their continuing dominance over the other Indian tribes.

The land companies were given the opportunity to obtain immense acreages of wilderness, which could be sold at enormous profit, with the assurance that the Iroquois would neither complain nor interfere.

Johnson's maneuverings had avoided an Indian war, which would have meant considerable expense, either for the English government or for the suffering colonies, probably both.

Johnson and Croghan gained most of all; the power of the Indian Department had declined steadily over the past several years, but Johnson received a gift of 200,000 acres from the Iroquois, and Croghan received 100,000 acres, plus confirmation of an earlier grant made to him of 200,000 acres on the Ohio.

With so many winners, there had to be losers, and the losers in this particular deal were the other Indian tribes inhabiting the Upper Ohio Valley, none of them powerful enough to oppose the mighty Iroquois. The three major tribes who claimed joint control of the present state of Ohio and, by extension, of Kentucky, were the Shawnee, the Delaware, and the Wyandot, or *Huron*, as the French called them.

The Shawnee were originally a southern tribe, from the region of the Carolinas, but following continuous wars with the Cherokee they moved northward, passing through Kentucky and into the Ohio Valley. But in 1672 they were forced to flee the valley to escape the Iroquois League; it was more than a half century later, in 1728, when they returned again, locating in the unoccupied valley of the Scioto. After the French and Indian War most of them withdrew to the upper waters of the two Miami Rivers, Little and Great, where they were living as of 1768, in towns upon the Mad River, known as the Mac-a-chack, and upon the parent streams in the Scioto Valley, at Chillicothe and Upper and Lower Piqua, between the present Chillicothe and Circleville, Ohio. Having previously fled from the Iroquois, the Shawnee could not oppose them at Fort Stanwix in 1768, although they were soon made aware that this treaty would allow a flood of white emigrants to pour into what they had long considered to be their personal private hunting grounds of Kentucky.

Until the seventeenth century the Delaware nation had previously lived along the Delaware River. Displaced by the infamous Walking Purchase from their Minisink lands on the Delaware, they were driven west by the Iroquois, first to the Allegheny region of Pennsylvania and then, in 1724, to a previously unoccupied region, the valley of the Muskingum in eastern Ohio. By the Treaty of Fort Stanwix, the Delaware were forced to give up their hunting grounds between the Alleghenies and the Ohio, as were the Mingo. Of the several Delaware clans the Munsee, sometimes called the Wolf tribe, were the northern and most warlike division. In 1780, upon their disaffection with the Americans, the Delaware war faction drew further back, to the region of the Scioto and the Sandusky Rivers. Here they were in close alliance with the Shawnee and the Wyandot.

The Wyandot had previously lived in Canada, in the territory east of Georgian Bay, where they had carried on a long and bloody war with the Iroquois until 1649, when they were utterly defeated. Nearly destroyed, they were driven from their ancient seat upon Lake Simcoe, Canada; they fled westward and, placing themselves under French protection, they finally located on the Detroit and Sandusky Rivers, where they arrived about 1690, in an uninhabited country, and settling about Detroit early in the eighteenth century; here they had ever since made their homes. Gradually they straggled eastward along the southern shore of Lake Erie, then southward along the waters of the Sandusky and Mad Rivers. During the French and Indian War they remained loyal to the French, taking part in Braddock's Defeat, and afterwards they joined Pontiac's Conspiracy. As their towns lay in western Ohio, they remained aloof during Dunmore's War, but throughout the Revolution they were under the influence of the British at Detroit.

In addition to these three there was one other tribe of consequence, known as the Mingo, who are usually considered to be "Ohio Valley Iroquois". They were probably the tribe which had previously been known to the English as the Susquehannocks or Conestogas. That tribe had been conquered by the Iroquois about 1675, and the remnant was incorporated into their League. In the eighteenth century the Mingo were mainly wanderers from the New York Iroquois stock.

These so-called "Ohio tribes", then, were all immigrants from the north, the south, and the east. Before the latter part of the seventeenth century not one of the tribes had continuously lived in, nor could they, by any stretch of the imagination,

7

claim proprietary right to ownership of the land known as the Ohio Country. The concept of buying, owning, and selling land was totally foreign to the Indian; the whites would negotiate a treaty, at the conclusion they would "pay" the Indians for the "purchase", and then they would "claim" the land. But they might as well, as the Indians always said, try to *buy* the air that they breathed; how could you buy air, or land, and not allow anyone else the use of that air, or that land? The supposed payments for ownership of land were nothing more to the Indians than their customary presents, or bribes, which they had always received from the white man.

When the Zane brothers came out to Wheeling Creek in 1769, and settled on the left (east) side of the Ohio[3], they were well within the boundaries which had been established by treaty the preceding year. It was the Proclamation Line which had retarded development west of the mountains following the French and Indian War, but the treaty of Fort Stanwix relocated that line, and it was this official change in the legal status of the western lands that gave the tremendous impetus to the westward movement.

It was six years later, in 1775, when the power of the Iroquois was beginning to diminish, that the other tribes began to realize that they no longer needed to be told by the Iroquois where they could live, or what lands the Iroquois could cede to the whites. The Shawnee and Wyandot, and later the Wolf clan of the Delaware, led by the famous chiefs Pipe and Wingenund, therefore, refused to honor the right of the Iroquois to give away those lands on which these tribes had been living for the past half century. The leader of hostility toward the whites were the Shawnee, but it was not so much the settlement along the eastern banks of the Ohio that bothered this tribe; there had been settlements to the east since 1754, when the French had established Fort Duquesne at the Forks of the Ohio. Rather it was the sudden intrusion into and settlement of the *Kaintuck* lands, which the Shawnee had come to regard as their personal hunting grounds, that worried them so. The paleface had always lived toward the rising sun — there were English (formerly French) settlements to the north, as at Niagra, Detroit, and Michilimackinac. But the Indians were accustomed to these and, importantly, it was from these posts that they received presents, as a matter of course, and trade goods (and rum) in return for their furs. These northern posts were vital to the Indian culture; they could no longer rely on the bow and arrow and stone knives for survival. To the west were the relatively unimportant forts of Ouiatenon on the Wabash and, lower down, Post St. Vincent. These two French settlements had been handed over to the English in 1763, but they were still basically French in custom, and thus could be ignored.

In 1773 Daniel Boone had attempted to bring a party of settlers, including his family, into Kentucky; but they had been driven back before they had even entered the Promised Land, albeit more by a chance meeting of Indians than by design. Boone's oldest son, James, had been killed by those Indians. The next year surveyors had entered Kentucky and had begun their work for the land grants; but they too had withdrawn, under orders from the Royal Governor of Virginia, when they ran into Indian war parties, in whose honor the ensuing war would be named.

The Cherokee had signed away their claims to the Kentucky lands at the Treaty of Hard Labor; five years later they would once more sell the identical land (what fools these white men were!) to Col. Richard Henderson at Sycamore Shoals. Before the ink was hardly dry Boonesborough, Logan's Station (alternately known as St. Asaph's), and Harrod's Town, or Harrodsburg were established, all legally within the bounds of the various treaties, and now the whites were pouring into the Shawnee hunting preserve. Through the Cumberland Gap and along Boone's Wilderness Road, along Braddock's old road of 1755 and the slightly newer Forbes Road of 1758 to Fort Pitt, and down the Ohio from Pitt — an increasing flood of pioneers was moving westward, and the flood tide could only continue to rise. So now in 1775, with this sudden influx into Kentucky, the Shawnee were surrounded. It was as impossible to stop the newcomers as it was to stop the ocean's tide; the only alternative was to drive them out. Nor did they hesitate. Indeed, the Shawnee had barely had time to return from Fort Pitt, where they had signed yet another peace treaty in October of 1775, before they attacked.

Boone had arrived at the site of future Boonesborough in early April; in August he had gone back to North Carolina to get his wife, Rebecca, and his daughter, Jemima, and had returned with them in September; as he proudly said, "My wife and daughter being the first white women that ever stood on the banks of the Kentucke River."

Less than three months later the Shawnee arrived. They had come to spy out the settlement, and if they did not know about him then, they would soon learn that Daniel Boone was a most formidable opponent. The attack on a harmless, unarmed man and two boys caught outside the fort was something that no Indian raiding party could ever resist, but it was premature. Better if they had not attacked at all, for the only result was to warn the settlers what they could expect of peace treaties made with Indians.

## Chapter II

The Great Boone, and the Kentucky Wilderness

In the roll call of names of all the great American pioneers, none stands out more, nor is today better known, than that of Daniel Boone. Indeed, not only among revolutionary-period figures, but of famous men in American history, in his own way Boone fits in as one of the great leaders of their times, along with Washington, Franklin, and Jefferson; Lincoln, Grant, and Lee; Eisenhower, Patton, and MacArthur.

Boone was born on November 2, 1734, just east of Reading, in present Berks County, Pennsylvania. The family homestead is now a state park, and although the cabin in which Daniel was born is no longer standing, the original Boone stone house which replaced it can still be visited. His parents, Squire and Sarah Morgan Boone, were Quakers. Squire was undoubtedly a stern father; with so many children it was necessary. Being Quakers they were permitted to marry only other Quakers, but in 1742, when Daniel was not quite eight, his older sister Sarah was "treated for marrying out"; in other words, for marrying a "worldling". Even worse was soon to be discovered, as the women in the community who were able to count to nine found out, when Sarah's baby was born. Six years later Daniel's older brother Israel was also "testified against" for marrying out, although this time there was no hint of scandal. Squire Boone may have been strict, but even in those early days the old man had definite ideas about personal freedom and independence. He insisted that his children had the right to marry whomever they wished. Although the Society of Friends tried to show him the error of his ways, to "bring him to a sense of his out-goings", Squire's beliefs were so strong that the situation became unpleasant; he was "disowned", so it was time to move on. Other families had found reason to leave Berks County, many of them moving south into the Shenandoah and Cumberland Valleys. One of those of note was John Lincoln, who moved from Berks County to Virginia at about this time. John's son, Abraham, would later take his own son, Thomas, and head west for Kentucky; there Thomas's son, another Abraham, would be born in 1809, and from Kentucky they would later move north to Indiana.

In the spring of 1750 Squire pulled stakes from relatively safe Pennsylvania and moved his family to the wild frontier, finally settling along the Yadkin River in pres-ent Davidson County, North Carolina. He could hardly have chosen a better loca-tion to suit his sixth son; Daniel loved hunting and the outdoors from the day he was old enough to leave the cabin and enter the forest, which was never more than a few paces from his doorstep. To the end of his days, and to the dismay of his chil-dren and grandchildren (unless they were allowed to go along, of course) he would pack up his gear and set off for the wild lands; accompanied or alone, it made no difference to Boone. He loved the solitude of the deep woods as perhaps no other man has ever enjoyed it. One day the renowned Caspar Mansker, exploring the Green River country of Kentucky, heard an unearthly caterwauling coming from the depths of the forest. Even such an experienced woodsman as Mansker was unable to identify such a noise as he had never heard before; he crept nearer and nearer, with the utmost caution, wondering what kind of strange creature could make such an unearthly sound. Or perhaps it was some new kind of Indian decoy. But it was not a strange creature, he discovered; it was only Daniel, stretched out full length on the ground, under the leafy trees, and singing at the top of his lungs from pure happiness.

One of the Boones' nearby neighbors on the Yadkin were the Bryans, and one of the Bryan girls was named Rebecca, or Becky as everyone called her. She was several years younger than Daniel, and she caught his eye, but Daniel had no time for dalliance. He was off to the wars.

As with many other young men, the beginning of the French and Indian War promised excitement and relief from the monotony and drudgery of farm life. When recruiting for Braddock's Expedition began early in 1755 Daniel signed on as a teamster, and in this capacity he accompanied the army of nearly two thousand regular soldiers and militia toward the French fort of Duquesne, where the Allegheny River came down from the north to join the Monongahela flowing up from the south, at the renowned Forks of the Ohio. Braddock, although enjoying a solid reputation on the continent, had no experience with North American bush fighting, nor any knowledge of his Indian enemy, nor had he any desire, at his age, to learn new techniques. It was all cut and dried. He would move his army against the fort, somewhere in the wilderness. Wherever it was he would find it, besiege it, and then, after what was deemed a proper interval of face-saving time for the French commander, he would accept their surrender.

The French commander at Duquesne concurred; his small force stood no chance whatsoever against the British behemoth which was crawling ever closer. Unfortunately for Braddock, one of the French officers disagreed. A subordinate officer named Beaujeau requested permission to take a force of soldiers and Indians and, if nothing more, at least delay the ultimate disaster. At first the commander refused, it was suicide, he said, but at last he relented and Beaujeau was off to assemble his force, only to find that the Indians also had no desire to commit suicide. Finally able to assemble about 800 men, and even so still outnumbered by better than two to one, Beaujeau set up an ambush across a ravine that the British would have to cross.

The rest is history, how on July 9, 1755, Braddock's army stumbled into the trap, and then, in the best manner of European battlefield tactics, stood in formation to be slaughtered at the bloody Battle of the Monongahela. Eventually Braddock was shot off his horse; rumor circulated that it was one of his own militiamen who had done that, and the troops broke, no troops could stand that type of horror. As the troops began pouring back through the wagon train Boone and the other teamsters cut the traces on their horses, jumped on, and rode for their lives.

Back home Daniel and Rebecca Bryan were married on August 14th, 1756, and there in the valley they tried to settle down to a life of farming, hunting, trapping, and raising a family. But the war would not go away, and in 1758 Daniel and Becky went to Culpeper County, Virginia, where Daniel again signed on with an English army heading for the Forks of the Ohio, this time under General John Forbes, and this time they were successful. As successful as General Wolfe the next year, on the Plains of Abraham outside the walls of Quebec, which brought about the downfall of the French in the New World.

With the war over, and Boone "getting along in years" (by the close of 1767 he was now well into his thirties), it looked as if Boone would never again roam the wilderness. But farming and raising a family in North Carolina, even with the yearly breaks of fall hunting and trapping, was not the way Boone had intended to spend his life. And then 1768 opened with the news of the Fort Stanwix Treaty; prospects in the now-opened *Kaintuck* lands seemed bright, although still distant.

And then one day in the late winter or early spring of 1769 Fate beckoned to Daniel Boone. On that particular day Fate was dressed, oddly enough, in a peddler's clothes, and leading a pack horse, and occupying a form which enjoyed the name of John Finley. It was the same John Finley who had been a fellow teamster with Boone fourteen years before, on that fateful July day in 1755, when Braddock and his soldiers had been shot down. It was the same John Finley who had sat around the campfires in the Monongahela wilderness and poured into young Boone's ear tales of land even more magnificent, just a little further west. It was always that way with the true pioneer; just a little further west, just around the next bend in the river, Paradise awaited. Boone had seen the land west of the mountains, and the land was an irresistible lure which he could never forget.

Finley had been in the Indian business for years. By the late 1740s he was an Indian trader at Pitt; in 1752 he and four assistants had floated a canoe load of English trade goods down the Ohio. Met by a party of Indians who invited them to trade, they paddled up the Kentucky River and enjoyed a brisk business until a band of French-Canadian Indians descended upon them, killing three of the assistants. Finley and the other man managed to escape back up to the Forks of the Ohio, but it was incidents such as this that helped pave the way for the French and Indian War.

After the war was over Finley had again floated down the Ohio with another canoe load of trade goods, all the way back to the Kentucky lands, where he had been warmly greeted by the Indians, who were delighted to trade their peltries for his merchandise. Then came the long pull back up the Ohio to Pitt, where he could exchange his furs for hard money. Finley longed to return to the Western Lands, as did Boone, but Boone had a family, and Finley needed companions. It was one thing to be a trader; almost always one could expect to be welcomed by the Indians, but it was quite another to "invade" what the Indians considered their territory, to take the game themselves.

On the first day of May, in 1769, Boone set out on the first of his "long hunts". With him went Finley, John Stuart, Boone's brother-in-law, and three camp-keepers. Daniel's brother Squire would stay home to take care of the family until the crops were in, and would then come to join them sometime in early winter. The six men set up their station camp on June 7th, and things went smoothly enough until almost the end of the year, even though they had unwisely made this base camp quite close to the Warriors' Path. But on December 22nd, Stuart and Boone, out hunting as a pair, were suddenly surprised by a band of mounted Shawnees, returning from a hunting trip. Taken captive, Boone managed to warn the four others as they approached their camp, and the Indians never seemed to know just how many men were in this party. Gathering up everything in sight, including, worst of all, the horses and the rifles and ammunition, the Indians herded Boone and Stuart north toward the Ohio, but released them after a few days, with the admonition never to return, hinting, in their quaint way, that if they were ever to return, the "wasps and yellow jackets will sting you severely."

But neither Boone nor Stuart were afraid of wasps and yellow jackets, not while those insects had possession of their horses, anyway. Rather than heading home, they boldly followed the Indians, plotting how to recover the horses, if nothing more. They finally succeeded in taking four or five, and rode all night, putting considerable distance between them and their former captors. But the next morning, as they paused to rest, the Indians, who had also ridden all night, caught up with them. Fortunately they were more amused than angered by the daring of the whites, courage was always most highly esteemed by the red man. But this time they intended to take them all the way to the Ohio before they released them. A day or two later, however, as the Indians were preparing camp, Boone winked at Stuart. Suddenly the two men grabbed their rifles and ran into the canebrakes, managing to escape. Upon returning to their base camp they found it deserted; without even seeing a hostile Indian the three camp helpers had had enough, and Finley was guiding them back to the settlements.

Boone and Stuart remained, and one day, not long after, they saw two strangers approaching, white or Indian they could not be sure. Amazingly enough, it turned out to be Daniel's brother, Squire, and a companion, Alexander Neeley. Squire was keeping the appointment he had made the previous spring; how he had managed to run down his brother in all the wilderness of Kentucky appears to be a miracle, but neither of the Boones ever considered it anything out of the ordinary.

Hunting and trapping continued throughout the winter, with Daniel and Stuart, whom he considered as close as a brother, working as a pair. One day, sometime probably in March, they split up, Stuart crossing to the south side of the Kentucky River. They agreed to meet a few days later at one of their outlying camps. Daniel showed up on time, and began waiting for his friend and the husband of his sister, but Stuart did not appear. Although Daniel and the other two searched thoroughly, even finding a tree with Stuart's initials carved on it, he was never seen again[4].

It was too much for Neeley. Although men died commonly enough, sometimes violently, for a grown man to be swallowed up in the wilderness, the mystery of his disappearance perhaps never to be explained, without leaving a trace which three experienced woodsmen could find, that played on his nerves. He decided to call it quits, and left the two brothers to go it alone.

By May, with the ammunition that Squire had brought out running low, they realized it was time for Squire to load up the packhorses and head back home; Daniel would remain, all alone, to do what he loved best, exploring a wilderness. It had been a year since he had seen Becky and the children, and it would be another year before he saw them again, but Squire would bring them news of him, and make sure the family was well cared for.

In late July Squire was back; in spite of losing the first portion of their labors to the Indians, the remainder of the trip had proved a success. Squire had sold the furs, provided for the families, paid off all the old debts, and purchased supplies to keep them going for another year in the wilderness. In the fall Squire made another trip home, and upon his return the two brothers spent another winter in Kentucky, this time southward in the Green and Cumberland River areas. By the next March it was time to begin loading up the horses and return home; Daniel had been absent for nearly two years, but was in high spirits. He had already sent back two pack loads of furs, and was returning with a third; perhaps it would be possible now to bring his family out to this paradise. But then in May, nearly home, disaster struck. They were in the Cumberland Gap, preparing their evening meal, when a half dozen warriors materialized. When the Indians departed Daniel and Squire had their lives and the clothes they were wearing, and nothing besides. The work of an entire year was gone, and more, their rifles and horses were also gone, to enrich an Indian family somewhere in the great wilderness.

Daniel was dejected, but nothing could ruin his dream of Kentucky; it haunted his imagination, and so, taking his family this time he moved to Tennessee. For the next two years he probably visited the Cherokee villages, sounding them out about the possibility of their selling their claims to the land. Richard Henderson, a prominent North Carolinian and, through the counsel and encouragement of Boone, soon to become one of the great land speculators, was interested, but he wasn't interested yet. And time, as they said, waits for no man. Kentucky was a wilderness, but not for long. Word had spread about this paradise, and already other adventurers, like the McAfee brothers, were entering Kentucky, to spy out some of the choice land for their own. And with the treaty of Fort Stanwix in hand, now the government surveyors would be moving in, with their instructions to lay out military lands grants for the war veterans.

The McAfee brothers had just returned in mid-August, and they reported that the Delaware and Shawnee seemed peaceable enough. Boone decided not to wait; it was risky, but with a well-armed band of men to protect the families, the first group intent on founding a Kentucky settlement started out in September, 1773. They expected no trouble, and put out no guards. By the time they entered Powell's Valley the entire caravan was stretched out for several miles. It was then, on October 10th, that Daniel decided to send his oldest son, James, back to the William Russell group to get some farm tools. James, trained by his father to follow a trail in the wilderness, had no trouble retracing the path and finding the Russells. He started back with the tools and with one of the Russell boys, Henry, seventeen years old, just about James's age. With them went two young men named Mendenhall, and a couple of slaves. They made camp that night, still too near the settlements to feel they were in any danger.

Just before dawn a party of Cherokees, led by a notorious killer named Big Jim, fired into the camp, hitting both the boys in the legs, and killing all the others except one of the slaves, who managed to hid in a pile of driftwood in the river. While some of the Indians rounded up the horses, the rest decided to amuse themselves by torturing the two helpless teenagers. By the time the Russell party came up a few hours later, the Indians were gone and the boys were dead. Their bodies had been cut to pieces, the palms of their hands slashed where they had tried to turn aside the blades of the Indians' knives. The slave hiding in the driftwood had been forced to listen to their pleas for mercy and to their screams of agony as long as it had lasted, but he was able to identify the perpetrators. Word was immediately sent ahead to the Boones with the sorrowful news, and although Daniel wanted to push on, since they really had no place behind them to return to, the rest of them were all too demoralized now to continue. Rebecca, anguished, sent back a linen sheet in which James should be wrapped; nothing more than that to keep the earth off her first-born child. Then, after the burial service, Boone reluctantly led them back home again, his first great venture a failure.

# Chapter III

## The Zanes: A Remarkable Family

The first Zane to settle in North America was Robert Zane, of Danish ancestry, who arrived in Salem, New Jersey from Dublin in 1673. His first son Nathaniel was born there in 1675, before Robert moved to Philadelphia in 1677. His wife is unknown, but she was possibly an Indian; evidently she died soon after, for in 1679 Robert married Alice Alday. About 1685 he married for a third time; life in the colonies was hard, but especially hard on the women. In 1712 Nathaniel's son William was born, and it is with William Zane and his illustrious children that this story begins to take shape.

Around the year 1740 William moved westward from Philadelphia, across Maryland to what was then the Virginia frontier, where he settled on the South Branch of the Potomac River, in what is now Hardy County, near present Moorefield, West Virginia. There he probably married, since his first child was not born until five years later; there his five sons were born, following at regular two-year intervals. Although his wife's Christian name is unknown, there is a strong possibility that it may have been Catherine; of William Zane's four children who had daughters, all four gave a daughter the name of Catherine. William's five sons were Silas, born in 1745, then Ebenezer in 1747, Jonathan in 1749, Andrew in 1751, and Isaac in 1753. In the same year that Isaac was born Governor Dinwiddie sent young George Washington with a message to the French on Lake Erie, warning them to vacate the property claimed by the English government.

There are no records of the Zane's life on that portion of the Virginia frontier, from the birth of Isaac in 1753 until nearly ten years later. Since war was being waged between the French and the English for control of North America, and since both had gained allies among the numerous Indian tribes, it is almost certain that the Zane family was involved in some way. At about the time that Silas was reaching the age (fifteen) at which he could be called upon for militia duty, an obscure battle took place near the Zane home, known as the Battle of the Trough. Whether Silas, or Will Zane, for that matter, participated in that battle is unfortunately not known. In the same vein, much of the later history of the Zanes has been lost. Unlike the case with Daniel Boone, no one interviewed members of the immediate family while they were still living, nor did anyone paint their portraits, as both Chester Harding and the illustrious painter and naturalist, John James Audubon, painted Boone's. Indeed, in the first major work to be published on the Border Wars, Joseph Doddridge's 1824 *Notes on the Settlement and Indian Wars of the Western Parts of Virginia and Pennsylvania*, there is not a single mention of any of the three attacks on the Zane settlement at Wheeling, (West) Virginia, between 1777 and 1782, although Wheeling was second only to Fort Pitt as the hub of frontier activity. The reason for this omission is given in the author's original preface:

*The various attacks on Wheeling fort [Fort Henry], and the fatal ambuscade near Grave creek [the Foreman Massacre], have been omitted for want of a correct account of those occurrences. These omissions are the less to be regretted as Noah Zane, Esq., has professed a determination to give the public the biography of his father, Col. Ebenezer Zane, the first proprietor and defender of the important*

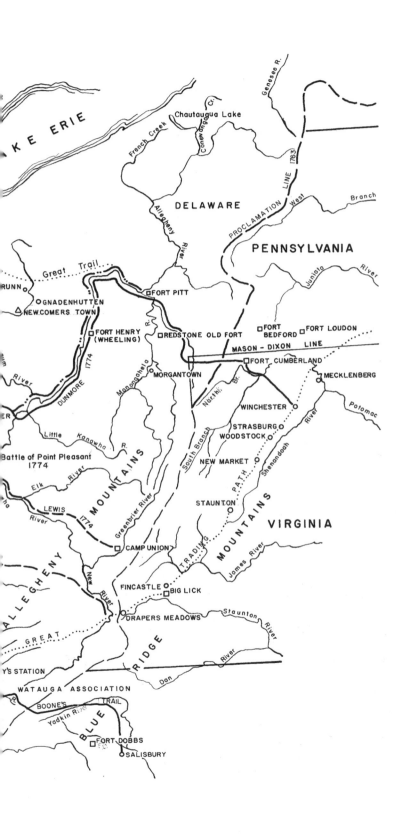

*station at Wheeling .... [and it] will contain an accurate account of all the attacks on Wheeling, as well as all other events of the war which took place in its immediate neighborhood.*

Noah was Ebenezer Zane's oldest son; born in 1778 he lived through the last dozen years of border warfare. About 1830 he also was interviewed by Alexander Scott Withers, while Withers was preparing his book on frontier history. In that work there is a fairly detailed account of the two major sieges of Fort Henry, in 1777 and again in 1782, and this material surely came from Noah Zane's own lips. Unfortunately Noah died suddenly, in 1833, and those important historical materials which he had prepared were inadvertently lost [5].

In 1762, just as the French and Indian War was drawing to a close, the eventual raid on the Zane home occurred; William and his five sons were taken captive and, in an unusual circumstance, not one of the six failed to survive the ordeal of attack, capture, and the brutal journey to the Indian towns, and eventually to Detroit. At that time William was no longer a young man — he was fifty years old, and his sons were not yet all in their teens: Silas was seventeen, Ebenezer fifteen, Jonathan thirteen, and Andrew eleven, while Isaac, the youngest, was only nine. After two years of captivity William and the four oldest boys, all but Isaac, were ransomed in Detroit, and they returned to the South Branch.

But a young Indian princess, the daughter of Chief Tarhe, the Crane, of the Wyandots, had become infatuated with Isaac, and although efforts to obtain his release continued, the Indians steadfastly refused to ransom him. Isaac would spend the rest of his life on the Mad River, first in the Indian town of Wapatomica, and then, after its destruction by Benjamin Logan's army in 1786, in the town which grew up around his cabin, and which was eventually named in his honor — Zanesfield, Ohio. But unlike most of the young white captive boys under similar circumstances, Isaac never became "Indianized", nor did he ever wage war against the whites. Although he had been adopted into the Wyandot tribe, for many years he considered himself an Indian captive. In 1772, at the age of nineteen, he escaped from the Indians and reached his brothers' home on Wheeling Creek. Not long after he was recaptured and returned to his "home" on the Mad River, where he eventually became reconciled to life among the Indians and married Myeerah.

Back from Indian captivity on the South Branch of the Potomac, William Zane's only daughter, Elizabeth, the baby of the family, was born in 1766. When she was only two came the great Indian assembly at Fort Stanwix, and the Zane brothers, like their father before them, longed to move to the frontier. In the summer of 1769, only a few months after the treaty had been signed, Isaac Williams, with Silas, Ebenezer, and Jonathan Zane, now twenty-four, twenty-two, and twenty, respectively, set out to explore the western territory. Williams selected a site near the mouth of Buffalo Creek (now West Liberty, WV), while the Zanes chose a dozen miles lower down, at the mouth of a creek known as *Weelunk*, supposedly from a man's decapitated head having been placed on a pole there[6]. Ebenezer Zane chose as the location for his cabin a spot on the bluff overlooking the river, now located on the east side of

Main Street in the center of the modern city of Wheeling, West Virginia. Silas moved six miles further up the creek, to present Elm Grove, while Jonathan, unmarried and still not having reached his majority, settled in with Ebenezer. The men spent the summer there, making tomahawk improvements, blazing trees with a mark and putting in a small crop of corn. Under Virginia colonial laws this entitled the settler to four hundred acres of land, but more importantly it gave him the right to claim another one thousand adjoining acres as a pre-emption right, paying the Virginia Treasury a few cents per acre.

Returning to the South Branch, Ebenezer brought out his young wife, Elizabeth, and his first-born child, a year-old daughter named Catherine, to the Monongahela country. Leaving them at one of the settlements south of Pittsburgh, probably Catfish Camp (Washington, PA) or Redstone Old Fort (Brownsville, PA) he returned to his improvement, built a cabin for his growing family, and put in another crop of corn. As soon as possible he brought his wife and daughter out to their new home, where they were to spend the remainder of their lives, and where all of his twelve remaining children would be born.

Ebenezer had chosen his wife well; in years to come Elizabeth McColloch Zane, the sister of the famed McColloch brothers, Sam and John, of Short Creek and Van Meter's fort, would become nearly as renowned as her husband, due to her skill as a surgeon and healer. When one considers the lack of physicians in the backwoods, together with the daily privations of life in general, and specifically the lack of medical supplies, it now seems little short of miraculous that any of the pioneers survived. Mrs. Zane's best-known achievement came in 1784 when, with the assistance of Isaac William's wife [7], she saved a well-known pioneer named Thomas Mills from certain death. Mills and three others had been out gigging fish by moonlight, a mile north of Fort Henry, near the northern end of the island. As Mills stood in the bow of the canoe holding a torch aloft, he provided a fair mark for several Indians concealed on the shore. A sudden volley of shots, and Mills received fourteen bullet wounds in the body, one breaking an arm, another a leg. His companions, amazingly enough unharmed, quickly brought him to the settlement, and left him in the care of the Mistresses Zane and Williams. Had he been in military service he would almost certainly have had one or both of the extremities amputated, and then most probably would have died from his treatment. But amputation was almost unheard of in frontier communities, and although everyone despaired of his life, Elizabeth Zane had already treated, many times over, everything from cuts and bruises to childhood illness to snakebite to broken bones to gunshot wounds. With poultices of slippery elm bark and jimson weed, and constant ablution with warm water, not only did the patient recover, but both the arm and the leg were saved. Fifty years after the treatment of his wounds Thomas Mills was a hale and hearty old man of Wheeling.

## CHAPTER 3: THE ZANES: A REMARKABLE FAMILY

From the time of their arrival until the outbreak of the Indian war in 1774, the only incident of note in the life of the Zanes was the escape of Isaac from his Wyandot captivity, and his arrival at his brothers' station on Wheeling Creek. Of this only two specifics have been passed down to us; it was in 1772, and before long he was recaptured.

# Chapter IV

## The Cause of Logan's Lament

Logan, the Mingo Chief
From an old illustration

After the horrors of the rebellion of the great Ottawa war chief Pontiac, the first few years following the Treaties of Fort Stanwix in 1768 and Lochaber in 1770 were a time of relative peace with the Indians, and although there was the occasional attack on an isolated settler's cabin, the Zanes and their neighbors did not live in constant dread of the war whoop, as they would for many years afterward. The killing of James Boone and Henry Russell in October, 1773, was an instance of a party of Indians, quite by chance, running across a defenseless group of whites, and the temptation for torture, scalps, and plunder, was, as usual, too great to be resisted. Still, it signaled the beginning of a conflict as yet undeclared.

Early in 1774, however, a series of retaliatory attacks and counterattacks by red and white men below Fort Pitt, at Pipe Creek and Yellow Creek erupted into a border war along the Ohio which involved principally the Shawnee, but also drew in the other three principal Ohio tribes, the Wyandot, the Mingo, and finally the Delaware.

In March of 1774, a 32-year-old Pennsylvanian named James Harrod, then living on Ten Mile Creek in Washington County, began assembling a group of settlers to descend the Ohio to the mouth of the Kentucky River; they would then ascend that river and the Licking River to locate suitable sites for their new homes. About thirty young men, among them Andrew Zane of Wheeling, collected at the mouth of Grave Creek, a dozen miles below Wheeling. Upon reaching their destination, the future site of Harrodburg, Kentucky, they began clearing the land and making improvements. By June they had completed some forty cabins, and considerable fields of corn had been planted.

In the memorable month of April, 1774, a full year before the shot heard 'round the world was fired, several events occurred along the Ohio that were to prove to be of as great a consequence for the future of the country, although they no longer claim the attention given to those skirmishes in Massachusetts. On April 15th William Butler dispatched from Pittsburgh three of his employees, with two canoes loaded with trade goods, heading for one of the Shawnee towns. On the next day, the 16th, they were attacked by a small band of Cherokee, who waylaid them from the shore. One of the men was killed, another wounded, and the third made his escape. On the 24th, Butler sent out another canoe, as it was necessary for him to procure the furs from the Shawnee; in this canoe were two white men, and two trusty Indians. This led to two other incidents, known as the Captina (Pipe Creek) affair, and the Yellow Creek massacre, which occurred within three days and within about 50 miles of each other, although they were conducted by two separate bodies of men.

At the same time that Harrod's settlers were building new homes, Major Angus McDonald was out surveying military bounty lands in Kentucky for the colony of Virginia; after more than ten years this was the territory which would be used finally to pay off those officers and men who had served in the French and Indian War of 1754-1763. McDonald, a Scotch Highlander, had served in that war, and as a result was himself entitled to 2,000 acres of land. But his surveyors met Indians at almost every turn, and as a result of this and the Indian attacks upon traders and other parties of surveyors, he was forced to retire to the small settlement at Wheeling Creek, 90 miles south of Fort Pitt on the Ohio, whence he sent word to his superior, Lord Dunmore, concerning the state of Indian hostility.

Yet another group had entered Kentucky that same spring of 1774; John Floyd, a recently-appointed deputy sheriff of Fincastle County, had led a small party of surveyors into the bluegrass country shortly before the border began preparing for the Indian war soon to be known as Lord Dunmore's War. A number of other parties, which included Ebenezer Zane and young George Rogers Clark, had been out surveying land for future settlement along the Ohio, some miles south of Wheeling. News reached them that Indians had attacked some of the surveyors in Kentucky, whereupon all of them ascended the Ohio to the Wheeling settlement. Upon receiving news of these incidents, Lord Dunmore, Royal Governor of Virginia, sent two experienced woodsmen to warn the Kentucky surveyors to depart. The names of the two adventurers were Daniel Boone and Michael Stoner; they not only found the surveyors, but they also ran into James Harrod and delivered the same warning to them. All of them had the good sense to heed the warnings, and by summer there were no white men left in the Kentucky wilderness.

On the morning of Wednesday, April 27th, word reached that settlement that two traders from Pittsburgh, with two Indians, were a short distance above Wheeling, and Captain Michael Cresap with a group of men decided to attack and kill the Indians. Despite the strenuous objections of Zane, who warned them that an unprovoked murder could lead to a general Indian war, Cresap's men left in canoes; they returned shortly with the traders, but when asked about the two Indians, they responded by saying only that they had fallen into the river. Zane, however, knew the reason for the blood and the bullet holes in the canoe. Soon after their return, on that same day, fresh news arrived that an Indian had been discovered some miles south of Wheeling, and the same group of men, again led by Cresap, descended the Ohio that afternoon to the mouth of Pipe creek, thirteen miles below Wheeling, for the purpose of killing those Indians. They returned the next day, the 28th, with a fresh scalp, a great deal of property taken from the Indians, and with one of their own men seriously wounded. Although this is usually referred to as the Captina affair, it actually occurred at the mouth of Pipe Creek; Captina is seven miles further south, about 20 miles below Wheeling.

Hearing that a large Indian camp under the leadership of the friendly Mingo Logan was located about 50 miles north of Wheeling, on the Ohio shore where Yellow Creek empties into the Ohio, Cresap's party next decided to attack that camp. Better judgment finally prevailed here, as Logan was widely known to be a peaceful, inoffensive Indian[8], and so the men instead marched overland to Redstone Old Fort (present Brownsville, PA).

Fifty miles to the north, on the east, or Virginia, shore, just opposite the mouth of Yellow Creek, was the settlement of Joshua Baker, known as Baker's Bottom. Baker kept a grog-shop which certain members of Logan's family were in the habit of visiting. On the morning of April 30th, when a number of Indians came across for their customary ration of whisky, one of the visitors was an Indian squaw, reputedly Logan's sister (and the wife of trader John Gibson), who had been given milk for her infant child by Mrs. Baker. Drawing Mrs. Baker aside, she hurriedly whispered that several of the Indians present planned to kill the Baker family before leaving, in retaliation for the murder of the Indians near Wheeling. Mrs. Baker hastily informed a neighbor, Daniel Greathouse, who immediately raised a party of about thirty men, John Sappington, George Cox, Edward King, Nathaniel Tomlinson, and a number of others, and proceeded to Baker's. When they arrived the majority of the men were posted out of sight along the river bank, to prevent a sortie by the Indians across the river, while the five above-named men went inside. They found that Baker himself was absent, and Cox, saying that he would not take part in their Indian-killing scheme, left. One of the warriors, Logan's brother, who had been drinking heavily, had put on Sappington's hat and coat, and was strutting about the room. The owner of the coat, not enjoying the humor of the situation, demanded that he remove said article, but the Indian was too proud and perhaps too inebriated to acquiesce. This appeared to be an opportune time to begin the killing; Sappington grabbed a musket and fired at the Indian, who did not expire quickly enough, and so King took his knife and finished the job. Another warrior was then killed, then two squaws were shot, including Gibson's wife, the other was probably Logan's mother — those two were shot by Greathouse and Sappington.

Logan, hearing the firing from across the river, assumed the worst; soon a large dugout with several warriors started across, but upon nearing the shore they were driven back by a volley from the whites assembled there. Altogether twelve Indians were killed, including Logan's sister, his mother, and a younger brother[9]. Knowing that Michael Cresap had been involved in the murders of the Indians near Wheeling three days before, Logan naturally assumed that he was once again at the head of this party. When he gave his celebrated speech to Gibson in the late fall of that year, he accused Cresap of killing all the members of his family, and the accusation stuck.

The earliest reports of the Yellow Creek Massacre were written barely a week after the event, to George Washington, by two brothers, Valentine and William Crawford, old friends of Washington, whom he had sent west to survey his land claims.

*May 7, 1774*

*Dear Sir: I am sorry to inform you the Indians have stopped all the gentlemen from going down the river. In the first place, they killed one Murphy, a trader, and wounded another; then robbed their canoes. This alarmed the gentlemen very much; and Major Cresap took a party of men and waylaid some Indians in their canoes, who were going down the river, and shot two of them and scalped them. He also raised a party, took canoes and followed some Indians from Wheeling down to the Little Kanawha[10]; when, coming up with them, he killed three and wounded several. The Indians wounded three of his men, only one of whom is dead; he was shot through, while the others were but slightly wounded. On Saturday last, about 12 o'clock, one Greathouse and about twenty men fell on a party of Indians at Yellow creek, and killed ten of them. They brought away one child a prisoner, which is now at my brother William Crawford's.*

*Valentine Crawford, Jacob's Creek*

The next day his brother, William, wrote a more detailed account, ending with an ominous warning:

*May 8, 1774*

*Sir: I suppose by this time various reports have reached you. I have given myself some trouble to acquaint myself with the truth of the matters; but there are some doubts remaining as to certain facts; however, I will give you the best account I can. The surveyors that were sent down the Kanawha, as report goes, were stopped by the Shawanese Indians, upon which some of the white people attacked some Indians and killed several, took thirty horse-loads of skins near the mouth of Scioto; on which news and expecting an Indian war, Mr. Cresap and some other people fell on some other Indians at the mouth of Pipe Creek, killed three and scalped them. Daniel Greathouse and some others fell on some at the mouth of Yellow Creek and killed and scalped ten, and took one child about two months old, which is now at my house. I have taken the child from a woman it had been given to. Our inhabitants are much alarmed, many hundreds having gone over the mountain, and the whole country evacuated as far as the Monongahela, and many on this side of the river are gone over the mountain. In short, a war is every moment expected. We have a council now with the Indians. What will be the event I do not know.*

*I am now setting out for Fort Pitt at the head of one hundred men. Many others are to meet me there and at Wheeling, where we shall wait the motions of the Indians and shall act accordingly.*

*William Crawford*

\*   \*   \*

**In short, a war is every moment expected .... What will be the event I do not know.**

The war came, and the event would be Logan's revenge. On July 12th William Robinson, Thomas Hellen, and Coleman Brown were working in a field near the west fork of the Monongahela, when a sudden burst of gunfire from the edge of the woods dropped Brown. Robinson and Hellen took to their heels, but Hellen was soon overtaken and securely tied. Logan, leader of the band of warriors, shouted to the third man to stop, that he would not be hurt, but Robinson had little faith in Indian promises. He would probably have escaped, but upon glancing over his shoulder, he stumbled and fell over a log, whereupon Logan, true to his word, took him unharmed to the Indian towns. There he was forced to run the gauntlet, but he passed through that ordeal relatively unharmed. He was then tied to the stake for burning, but Logan intervened, as he had promised, and Robinson was adopted into an Indian family, but with an ulterior motive. Logan would be avenged, and everyone was to know of Logan's vengeance.

They would learn of it some two months later, on the 25th of September, at a remote cabin on a remote section of the North Fork of the Holston, on Reedy Creek in present Sullivan County, Tennessee. Inside that cabin, to the horror of their neighbors, were discovered the bodies of popular John Roberts, his wife, and all their young children, save one; all had been killed and scalped the day before. The Roberts were so isolated, and so far from the scene of any Indian attacks, that they no doubt considered themselves quite safe, not seeking the shelter of any of the nearby forts.

Although the men searched the area thoroughly, the oldest child, Jamie Roberts, then ten years old, was nowhere to be found; he was still alive, but he had been carried off into captivity. What the men did find was an Indian war club, purposely left behind, and tied around it was a message from Logan:

*To Captain Cresap —*
*What did you kill my people on Yellow Creek for. The white People killed my kin at Coneestoga[11] a great while ago, & I thought nothing of that. But you killed my kin again on Yellow Creek, and took my cousin prisoner. Then I thought I must kill too; and I have been to war three times since but the Indians is not Angry only myself.*

*July 21st*

The letter had been written by Will Robinson within days of his arrival at the Indian town where he had run the gauntlet. From that time onward it had been carried by Logan until he found what he considered to be an opportune time and place to leave it to its best advantage. The Roberts' cabin on Reedy Creek seemed to be such a place, and such a time, no matter how far from Yellow Creek. John Roberts and his family were the innocent and unfortunate ones, while Robinson was the favored one; had he been unable to read and write, he would have been devoured by flames, albeit very slowly, and another author would have been selected. As it was he later returned to his Virginia home, where he gave a deposition regarding his adventures, after four months of what must have been one of the most unusual cases of Indian captivity on record. The Roberts family, on the other hand, had been offered no such choice.

**Note: For an authentic account of the events leading up to the Yellow Creek massacre, written some years later by two unimpeachable sources, see Appendix C for the Zane and Clark letters.**

# Chapter V

The Building of Fort Fincastle, and
Dunmore's War
(Peace with the Shawnee - Nevermore!)

**"The Indians ... are a Rash Inconsistent peple & inclin'd to Mischiff
& will never consider Consequences tho itt May End in thire Ruen."**
**(George Croghan to Sir William Johnson, ca. 1760)**

The short-lived Indian war known as *Lord Dunmore's War* began unofficially in June of that year when the colonial governor of Virginia, John Murray, fourth earl of Dunmore, viscount Fincastle, received intelligence of those events on the western border, and took appropriate action. Believing an Indian uprising to be imminent, he sent two scouts, Boone and Stoner, to Kentucky to warn not only Harrod and his men, but also any others they encountered of their danger, and to escort them back to safety. Boone had made a trip to Kentucky in 1769, and had attempted a settlement himself only the year before, but had been driven back by an unexpected assault upon his little band of pioneers. Michael Stoner (or Holsteiner), was also an experienced woodsman of the Kentucky lands. In 1767, before any other white man, he had paddled down the Ohio from Pittsburgh, as far west as the Illinois country, and south to the present site of Nashville, Tennessee.

Boone and Stoner found the Harrodsburg men hard at work, and escorted them safely back through the Cumberland Gap; John Floyd and his men came in on August 13th. Upon receiving orders from the governor, McDonald proceeded to assemble 400 militia at Wheeling, and began the construction of Fort Fincastle, later Fort Henry[12]. At the same time Dunmore sent orders to Col. Andrew Lewis to assemble an army of roughly a thousand militia from the *Greenbriar Country*, and to march them westward along the New/Kanawha River, to the mouth of the Kanawha on the Ohio (Point Pleasant, WV), where they would rendezvous with Dunmore's army coming down the Ohio from Pittsburgh.

Leaving Col. William Crawford and a few of the militia to finish the fortification at Wheeling, McDonald proceeded down the Ohio about twenty miles to the mouth of Captina Creek, and from there, on July 26th, began his march westward into the Indian country, guided by Jonathan Zane, Thomas Nicholson, and Tady Kelly. Among the men were Michael Cresap, Daniel Morgan, soon to become one of the most distinguished generals of the Revolution, and the intrepid James Wood.

The goal was Wapatomica, a cluster of Shawnee villages on the Muskingum, about fifteen miles below present Coshocton (near the present town of Dresden, Muskingum County, Ohio). These were the westernmost of the Shawnee towns, and the home of their most warlike members. Earlier in the summer these villages had been abandoned in anticipation of an attack, but since the attack was so long delayed the Shawnee had returned, and were now lying in wait for McDonald's advancing army.

On the second of August the vanguard of the army had approached to within six miles of the river, when it was engaged with warriors who blocked their way. After a skirmish which lasted about half an hour, the Indians retreated, and the army continued on to the Upper Shawnee towns, which they found deserted. The scouts soon discovered the main body of Indians had crossed the river and had set up an ambush, hoping the militia would follow. McDonald refused to do so, however, and as the destruction of the village and the corn in the fields was begun, the Indians sent across messengers asking for a parley. The following morning five warriors appeared, but they notified McDonald that they must advise their chiefs, who were the only ones empowered to negotiate. Accordingly, McDonald sent across one of the five with a message, but after he failed to return, another was sent. When the second one also failed to return, McDonald moved his army against the next series of towns, about two miles further upstream, where another skirmish with a concealed body of Indians took place at a village known as Snake's Town. Pushing those aside, the army continued on to the remainder of the towns, by now abandoned, which were burned and the crops destroyed.

Having taken only seven days' provisions from Captina, the army was now forced to return to Wheeling, there to await their commander, Dunmore himself. The expedition had had only reasonable success, having burned five towns and destroyed some seventy acres of corn still standing in the fields. They had killed several Indians, but altogether less than a half dozen, and taken one prisoner, at a loss of two of their own men killed and six wounded. It was not the severe punishment which they had hoped to inflict on the Shawnee, but now the two major wings of the army were coming.

Around the end of August Dunmore finally arrived at Pitt, only to begin a series of futile negotiations with the Delaware, Mingo, and Shawnee. Knowing that they must strike before Dunmore could affect a union of his half of the Virginian army with Col. Lewis, the Shawnee played for time, asking Dunmore to meet them further down the river, there to negotiate the treaty.

If such a treaty could be obtained with no more bloodshed, and if a show of Royal force was the only cost, then Dunmore was eager to comply; by the end of September the governor had moved his army of 1,200 men down to Wheeling, in two divisions, one moving by land, the other by river. Dunmore floated down the Ohio with 700 of his men, in a grand procession of over a hundred canoes, keelboats and pirogues. Crawford, having in the meantime returned to Pitt, was sent with the other 500 men on a march overland with the cattle to Wheeling, where they arrived on the last day of September. Among the men he picked up there was John Wetzel, who had joined the army with his 16-year-old son, Martin. From there Crawford continued to the mouth of the Hocking River, where his division crossed the Ohio and began building a small stockade, which was named Fort Gower.

Dunmore arrived a few days later, but was greeted only by Crawford's division; there were no Shawnee chiefs to negotiate the proposed treaty, only the friendly Delaware chief White Eyes. Dunmore immediately sent out a messenger, John Montour, son of the famous Delaware interpreter Andrew Montour[13], to find them. He soon returned and informed the governor/general that the Shawnee had gone south, as they put it, "to negotiate with Lewis' army". Realizing the treachery of the Shawnee, Dunmore changed his plans, instead of continuing down the river to Point Pleasant and a union with Lewis' army, he sent orders to Lewis to cross the river at once and begin moving toward the Shawnee towns; he, Dunmore, would move westward at the same time, and the Indians would be caught in a pincer movement.

But on October 10th, before Dunmore could get his army in motion, the sound of gunfire was heard drifting up from the south and, fearing the worst, Dunmore began his march the next day. On the third day into Indian country, a runner arrived from Lewis with the glad tidings of victory at Point Pleasant. Two days later a different type of messenger appeared at Dunmore's camp — the Shawnee were now willing, indeed they were eager, to negotiate. Dunmore pushed on.

Col. Andrew Lewis had assembled 1,100 men at Camp Union (present Lewisburg, WV), at a site known as the Big Levels of the Savannah. Here, in 1763, an earlier settlement had been raided by a Shawnee war party under the chief known as Cornstalk. Beginning the march westward with his men on September 11th, Lewis reached the mouth of the Kanawha (Point Pleasant) on October 6th, just about the same time that Dunmore had arrived at the Hocking. The army had been led a distance of 160 miles, through "trackless wilderness", by one of the frontier's most capable scouts, Matthew Arbuckle. Here a camp was established, and scouts searched the area for word from Lord Dunmore, which was to be awaiting them upon their arrival. The message was soon found in the trunk of a hollow tree, left there by Dunmore's scouts before the arrival of Lewis, supposed to have been Simon Girty, Peter Parchment, and Simon Kenton, who was then known as Simon Butler. Lewis sent north three scouts in the direction of Fort Pitt to obtain further information. But before they could return, messengers arrived from Dunmore on October 9th, informing Lewis that the plan had been changed; Dunmore had descended the Ohio to the Hocking, and he would now march westward. Lewis was directed to begin moving his men across the Ohio, toward Chalagawtha, the Shawnee capital [14], and to commence an envelopment. Immediately preparations were begun to cross the river the following morning, the fateful tenth of October.

But early on the morning of the 10th, just before break of day, two young men named James Mooney and Joseph Hughey had been sent out to hunt for the army; Mooney was a former neighbor of Daniel Boone's on the Yadkin, and had been a member of that ill-fated expedition in 1773. After scouting about three miles upriver they were suddenly fired upon by an advance guard of an Indian army. Hughey was killed by a shot fired by Tavener Ross, a notorious renegade, while Mooney fled back down the river to the camp with the warning. Lewis immediately sent out two detachments of troops, one under Col. William Fleming, the other commanded by his own brother, Col. Charles Lewis.

Cornstalk had succeeded in moving nearly a thousand warriors across the Ohio during the night, and now, half an hour before sunrise, they had almost reached the Virginians' camp. Having lost the element of surprise, the Shawnee now moved rapidly; the Virginians had advanced less than a quarter mile when they were met by a terrific fusillade from the Indians' guns. Falling back, they were met by a reinforcement, and there they dug in. The Shawnee now fell back a short distance themselves and formed a line behind rocks and trees which stretched from the

Kanawha to the Ohio. Lewis' army, as well as his camp, was thus enclosed between the two rivers, with the Indian line of battle in front; there would be no retreat from this position.

The two sides were evenly matched, and although the Virginians were caught between the two rivers, in their favor was the fact that many of them were expert riflemen, accustomed to handling a rifle in the woods. After the battle fewer than thirty-five dead Indians were found, but it was believed that others, probably as many more, had been thrown into the river to prevent them from falling into the hands of the Long Knives. The Battle of Point Pleasant continued all that day, and throughout the day the booming voice of Cornstalk could be heard above the din, exhorting his warriors, "Be strong! Be strong!"

The lines surged back and forth with little advantage gained by either side, until nearly nightfall, when Captains Arbuckle, Matthews, Shelby, and Stuart led a regiment up Crooked Creek, under cover of the bank, with the view of gaining a ridge to the rear of the Indian lines. They were soon observed, but Cornstalk, believing these men to be the reinforcements known to be coming up under Col. William Christian, hastily terminated the battle and withdrew his warriors back across the river. Of the more than one thousand Virginians engaged in this battle, considered at the time to be one of the fiercest ever waged between white and red man, the American force lost seventy-five killed, including Boone's neighbor and fellow pioneer, Jim Mooney, who had fallen after he had saved the army by bringing the first news of the enemy's advance. Another hundred forty had been wounded, totaling nearly a fourth of the entire army incapacitated. Christian's reinforcements from Fincastle County finally arrived at the camp around midnight, after the battle had been decided.

Now facing the realization that they were caught between a movement of two wings of an army, one of which, if not inflicting an outright defeat upon them, had at the least caused them to withdraw from the battlefield, the magnificent Cornstalk drew his warriors together in council and explained the situation. He had been opposed to the war since its beginning; before the battle on the tenth he had proposed sending a flag of truce as an overture for negotiations, but he had been unanimously voted down by the sub-chiefs. Now he rose and presented them with their choices. "We have fought them and been forced to retreat; now they are approaching along two fronts, twice as strong as before. What shall we do?" he asked. "Shall we go out and fight them again?" There was no response, no one rose to offer a solution.

"Shall we kill all our women and children, and then go and fight until we too are slain?"

Again, nothing but silence followed his words.

"Then," said Cornstalk quietly, "since you will not fight, I will go and make peace."

Dunmore received the request for a parley, but continued his march until within eight miles of the Shawnee village on the Scioto. Here his men erected a temporary camp, named Camp Charlotte in honor of the English Queen, and Dunmore sent word that now he was ready to talk. At the same time, while peace negotiations were getting under way, Dunmore sent another message to Lewis to encamp his army, which by now had crossed the river and was advancing quickly toward the Shawnee towns, to await the outcome of the negotiations. But neither Lewis nor the men of his command were in any mood to listen to protestations of peace from an enemy who had just killed and wounded over two hundred of their friends and relatives, not the least of whom was the commander's own brother, Col. Charles Lewis, who had been mortally wounded at the first fire of the battle. Nor had they forgotten the destruction of their settlement on the Big Levels, eleven years before, by this same Shawnee chief. Lewis' army continued its advance, with murder in its heart.

Now thoroughly alarmed, the Shawnee asked Dunmore to halt the movement of Lewis' men, whereupon Dunmore himself visited the camp and ordered Lewis to begin an immediate retreat. Lewis was forced to comply, albeit reluctantly, while Dunmore returned to Camp Charlotte and began negotiations. Cornstalk delivered an oration in which he accused the Virginians of starting the war by the killings of the Indians near Wheeling, and the massacre of Logan's family. Logan himself, although he stated that he would not continue the bloodshed, adamantly refused to attend any formal peace talks.

By November the war was over, and terms had been agreed upon; both sides were to discontinue hostilities, the Indians would surrender all prisoners (those who had not already been tortured to death), and the Shawnee, along with the other Indian tribes, would meet with representatives from the Virginia colonial government the next autumn to sign a lasting treaty of peace, whatever that meant. This, and nothing more.

*   *   *

Over the years there has been an attempt to designate the Battle of Point Pleasant as the *First Battle of the American Revolution.* The basic contention is that Dunmore, aware of the social upheaval in Massachusetts Colony, in the spring of 1774 purposely fomented an Indian War in Virginia in order to distract attention from New England. Included in this line of reasoning is that he intended to allow Lewis' Division to be destroyed by the Indians, thus weakening the Americans if they were to declare independence from Great Britain at some time in the future.

But these arguments cannot be seriously supported. The men of Lewis' Division were fighting for the colonial government of Virginia; by extension then, they were fighting for the King of England, not against him. They were opposed by warriors from the Shawnee Nation, who were not allies of England at the time, and following their defeat at Point Pleasant this tribe was forced into signing articles of peace by Lord Dunmore, Royal Governor of the Colony of Virginia. As of April, 1774, when "Dunmore's Plot" was supposedly hatched, and in spite of the well-named "Intolerable Acts" which had closed the port of Boston, there was no positive indication that rebellion was in the air, and especially not in Virginia. The "Boston Massacre" had occurred four years previously, in March, 1770, while the latest unofficial act of defiance had been the "Boston Tea Party" in December, 1773.

If Lord Dunmore were prescient enough to sniff out a Declaration of Independence two years in the future, then rather than being a little-known Royal Governor in a far-distant colony, he should instead have been crowned King of England, in London, where his services to the British Empire would have been of infinitely greater value as he performed other miracles of prognostication.

### First Interlude:
### Logan's Lament
### When, Where, Why, and Michael Cresap

One of the most influential leaders in the retaliatory killings of settlers had been the man who had suffered most, the Mingo Logan. Still mourning the loss of his family he refused to attend the peace negotiations at Camp Charlotte between Dunmore and the Shawnee leaders. Thereupon Dunmore sent John Gibson, Logan's brother-in-law, to invite Logan personally to come to the camp. Still refusing to come to Camp Charlotte, Logan, in a remarkable speech, declaimed on the causes of his actions, and as soon as he had returned and reported to Dunmore, Gibson entered the officer's tent and wrote down the speech as best as he could remember it; it was then read aloud to the assembled officers:

*I appeal to any white man to say if ever he entered Logan's cabin hungry, and he gave him not meat; if ever he came cold and naked, and he clothed him not. During the course of the last long and bloody war, Logan remained idle in his cabin, an advocate for peace. Such was my love for the whites that my countrymen pointed as they passed, and said, 'Logan is the friend of the white man.' I had even thought to have lived with you, but for the injuries of one man. Col. Cresap, the last spring, in cold blood, and unprovoked, murdered all the relations of Logan, not even sparing my women and children. There runs not a drop of my blood in the veins of any living creature. This called on me for revenge. I have sought it; I have killed many; I have fully glutted my vengeance. For my country I rejoice at the beams of peace; but do not harbor a thought that mine is the joy of fear. Logan never felt fear. He will not turn on his heel to save his life. Who is there to mourn for Logan? Not one!*

The speech was hailed as one of the greatest orations ever delivered; certainly the greatest by an American Indian. Jefferson thought so highly of it he included it in his *Notes on Virginia*. For years it was memorized and recited by schoolchildren, and so the name of Michael Cresap became indelibly linked to that of Logan's. And although Cresap was the leader, on two separate occasions, of men who were involved in the killing of several Indians, he was not responsible for the deaths of the members of Logan's family at Yellow Creek. That singular honor goes to Daniel Greathouse. Whether there was justification for any of the killings, whether the lives of the Bakers were in fact in danger, will probably never be determined. Now there is nothing more than *Might-have-beens*.

*    *    *

## Col. John Gibson

A great deal of controversy was stirred up by the publication of the *Lament*; it was known to all those actually involved that Cresap had had no connection with the Yellow Creek Massacre, and some years afterward, in an attempt to absolve him, the Reverend John Jacob wrote extensively on the subject, influenced no doubt by the fact that he had married Cresap's widow. But rather than trying to place the blame for the massacre of Logan's family where it belonged, i.e., on the Greathouse party, Jacob, in trying to clear Cresap's name, attempted to disprove that Logan had ever made such a speech. Any number of statements have been written during and since Jacob's time, most of them with little or no basis in fact — among them that Logan never gave the speech, it was manufactured by Gibson; the speech was given to Simon Girty, alone, who returned with it to Camp Charlotte and related it to Gibson, who then wrote it down and "elaborated" upon it; the fact that Logan had said, "not even sparing my women and children", when his nephew, Gibson's son, had indeed been spared, was hailed as proof that someone other than Logan had composed the *Lament*, as was Logan's referring to Cresap as a colonel, when he was only a captain. But that was nothing more than an Indian's typical difficulty in distinguishing the niceties of military rank, much as the earlier colonists had referred to Indian chiefs as "kings".

The controversy continues to the present day, but even in the eighteenth century it aroused debate. Gibson no doubt translated the speech into the best English possible[15], as soon as he returned and was able to get his hands on quill and ink, and as well as he could remember it. He himself stated that he was sent by Dunmore to see Logan, and that Logan gave the celebrated speech to him when "the two were alone together". George Rogers Clark, who was present when Gibson returned, also stated that he remembered the speech being presented to the officers at Camp Charlotte, and of Clark's "rallying Cresap" about it, for the Indians' blaming Cresap for every episode that had occurred; in addition Clark recalled that Cresap was quite upset that he had been named as the killer of Logan's family.

Logan had once before named Cresap as the killer of his family; tied to a war club was a letter from Logan asking Cresap why he had killed his family. The war club was found, purposely left behind, in the cabin of a family of slaughtered settlers. The statements themselves which Logan made are in the main truthful, and there really seems to be little basis for the controversy. Gibson, an Indian trader and the brother-in-law of Logan, was the logical choice for Dunmore to send, and unless we consider the unlikely possibility that both George Rogers Clark and John Gibson were inveterate liars, the matter should probably rest there.

George Rogers Clark is one of the better-known American heroes, his conquest of the Old Northwest territory in 1778-79 was at least the equal of any other American victory of the Revolutionary War. As a result of that victory the size of the fledgling United States was doubled — the western border became the Mississippi River, rather than the crest of the Appalachians. His march across and through the flooded plain of the Wabash, in February's freezing weather, was a feat of human endurance now impossible to imagine. His ability to reduce Fort Sackville — defended by English regulars and by English cannon and commanded by none other than Henry Hamilton himself, Governor-General of all Canada, and reducing it with the aid of no more than a hundred wet, cold, hungry, volunteers — must rank as one of the world's great strategic victories. That men would flock to his call for expeditions against the Indians, when no other commander could raise volunteers, speaks just as loudly for the unshakable faith which his contemporaries had in him. All in all, George Rogers Clark's veracity may hardly be doubted.

But John Gibson is not so well known, not well known at all. Sadly, indeed, for he was one of the many fascinating characters involved in the Border Wars. He was born in Lancaster, Pennsylvania, in 1740. After receiving a good education he entered the army in 1758, at the age of 18, serving under Forbes in the successful expedition to take Fort Duquesne. After the conclusion of the French and Indian War he built a trading post at Logstown, Pennsylvania[16]. He was captured there by Indians during Pontiac's Rebellion in 1763, but was saved from the stake by being adopted by a squaw, the sister of Logan. The next year he was freed by Bouquet's Expedition, but he remained at Logstown as a trader. On April 30, 1774, Gibson's wife was killed by the Greathouse party at the infamous Yellow Creek Massacre; their infant child was spared, and was sent to Gibson by Capt. Neville, at Catfish Camp (Washington, PA). Upon the outbreak of the Revolution Gibson commanded the 13th Virginia, and after 1778 he was stationed at Fort Pitt. During General Lachlan McIntosh's campaign in the fall of 1778, he accompanied the army to the Tuscarawas, where Fort Laurens (Ohio) was built. He remained there, as commander of the fort, until its abandonment in 1779, when he returned to Pittsburgh. In 1781 he succeeded Col. Daniel Brodhead as commander of Fort Pitt, and was in turn succeeded by Gen. William Irvine that November. In 1782 he commanded the 7th Virginia Regiment at Fort Pitt.

After the Revolution he held numerous public offices, serving as a judge in Allegheny County, Pennsylvania, then later as Secretary of the Indiana Territory. For nearly a quarter of a century, from the French and Indian War through the end of the Revolution, Gibson had been involved in nearly all the important events swirling around Fort Pitt, and then lived through the "Second War of American Independence" of 1812. After a most extraordinary life, he died at his home in western Pennsylvania in 1822.

# Chapter VI

The Pittsburgh Conference, 1775

Even before Lord Dunmore had left Williamsburg for Fort Pitt, news had come of the death of the Superintendent of Indian Affairs for North America, the extremely capable Sir William Johnson, who had died on July 11, 1774. He had been succeeded by his nephew, Guy Johnson, and even though the Shawnee had agreed to negotiate a treaty, now, with the outbreak of revolution in New England, the New York-central Pennsylvania frontier was terrified at the thought of a horde of thousands of Iroquois warriors sweeping down on the unprotected settlements, leaving nothing but death and destruction in their wake. When they heard that Johnson had called an Indian conference at Oswego, which was attended by some 1,500 Iroquois, it only added to their alarm. In the year between the time that Dunmore and Cornstalk had talked, and the final conclusion of the peace treaty at Pittsburgh, the battles of Lexington, Concord, and Bunker Hill had been fought, Boston was under siege, George Washington had been appointed to command a Continental Army, Benedict Arnold and Ethan Allen, "in the name of the Great Jehovah and the Continental Congress", had captured Fort Ticonderoga, and the United Colonies were on the verge of declaring independence from Great Britain.

But at Oswego all the Indians heard was a series of long-winded speeches urging them to maintain their loyalty to the king, with never a hint of offensive action. It seemed that the mighty Iroquois would remain neutral, and the faint-hearted burghers of Albany must certainly have heaved a mighty sigh of relief.

Scarcely less important than the Treaty of Fort Stanwix was the Indian conference held at Pittsburgh in the fall of 1775[17], agreeable to the conditions at Camp Charlotte. But with such heady and worrisome topics in the east, no one was too concerned about just one more Indian conference, somewhere "out west". After all, the Shawnee had been defeated, hadn't they, and had sued for peace. There were too many other significant problems that needed immediate attention, and it appeared just as likely that the Shawnee could also be kept out of the conflict. Adding to the confusion in the west was the old boundary dispute between Virginia and Pennsylvania, Virginia claiming all the land west of the Monongahela. By this time the dispute had reached the point of arresting each other's magistrates.

But the Pittsburgh Conference was of extreme importance, just because of that declaration which would come in July of 1776. The Americans, primarily as a result of this treaty at Pittsburgh, were able to avoid the outbreak of open hostilities with the Indian nations for well over a year. Indeed, it was not until early in 1777 that it became obvious that the treaty had been discarded by the Indians, who were now flocking to the English cause. And that sixteen-month breathing space, between late 1775 and early 1777, was vital not only to the struggling colonies, but to the equally-struggling westerners. Even though an isolated Indian raid was always possible, there were no large-scale planned invasions, and this allowed the Trans-Allegheny settlements to send, proportionately, a considerable body of men to help in the initial struggles in the eastern theater of the Revolution. At the same time it spared the frontier settlements from the massacres which were always associated with major Indian incursions. In the summer of 1775 the panic which would have been inspired by those Indian raids would probably have caused a precipitous flight of refugees back across the mountains; the American Pioneer was not yet the battle-hardened veteran he was soon to become. By the time the raids began in earnest in 1777 the hardy settlers, those who had stuck it out this long, had become so accustomed to the expectation of daily Indian attack that it now seemed easier to stay and fight than to flee.

This neutrality by the Indians for the first year of the war was also, in part, a matter of necessity. Between September of 1775 and June of 1776 the two-pronged attack of Brig. Gen. Richard Montgomery and Col. Benedict Arnold in Canada, on Montreal and Quebec, respectively, denied to the British the use of the St. Lawrence River. Both the Canadian Governor Guy Carleton, in escaping from Montreal to Quebec, and Lieutenant-Governor Henry Hamilton, attempting to go the opposite direction to his post at Detroit, were forced to assume disguises in order to sneak through the American lines. The St. Lawrence was the only route of transport to the interior; thus, since the Indians could receive no provisions from the English, it was necessary for the braves to remain with their families in order to provide for them.

The news from Lexington and Concord had aroused the eastern seaboard; on the last day of what was to be its last session the Virginia House of Burgesses selected a distinguished group of men as commissioners to travel to Pittsburgh to treat with the Ohio Indians. These were George Washington, Andrew Lewis, John Walker, James Wood, and Adam Stephen. Washington was called away on June 15th by the Continental Congress to become commander-in-chief of the army, and the remaining commissioners recommended to the House that Wood, although only twenty-five years of age, was the man best suited to travel through the wilderness to deliver the information concerning the date and place of the conference to the Indians. James Wood was just one more of those astonishing frontiersmen.

In his journal entry for June 24th, 1775, Wood, after stating that he had been asked by the Virginia House of Burgesses to go to the Indian towns to invite them to a conference, wrote that he had asked the House to advise him:

*"... how far I was to go in an Explanation of the disputes with Great Britain ...."*
And the House moved:

*"... that I should be directed to Explain the whole dispute to the Indians to make them sensible of the Great Unanimity of the Colonies to Assure them of our Peaceable Intentions towards them and that we did not stand in need of or desire any assistance from them or any other Nation ...."*

Starting out from Pittsburgh on July 18th, with interpreter Simon Girty, Wood made an incredible voyage through the wilderness; in 25 days he covered nearly a thousand miles and visited fifteen Indian villages, at which he presented his message from Virginia. Not only did he and his companion suffer the hardships of such a journey, but there was also the fact that his life was often in danger. At one of the Indian towns a squaw warned them that it had been planned to kill them that night, and the two men decamped, spending the night in the forest listening for the footsteps of approaching assassins. Often Wood and Girty saw Indian braves painted black, the most ominous sign of all. The Shawnee had suffered a bitter defeat at Point Pleasant the year before, and their one overriding ambition was revenge. The Mingo were still influenced by the massacre of Logan's family, while the Wyandot were too far away to feel the need to negotiate with the Virginians.

Only the Delaware were peaceably disposed, and not all of those, but they had their reasons. Most important to them was a burning desire finally to escape the humiliation of the domination of the Iroquois. The Delaware had also been profoundly influenced by the message of peace being spread by the Moravian missionaries at the Christian Indian villages on the Tuscarawas, and their principal chief was White Eyes, who was strongly pro-American. To assist the Indians in their negotiations at Pittsburgh would be deputy Indian Agent Alexander McKee, the only representative of the King still left west of the mountains.

As late as March it had been intended that the conference would involve delegates from the Indian tribes and from Virginia, but by June the Continental Congress had assembled in Philadelphia, and Indian matters were no longer in the hands of the Virginians alone. In July Congress also appointed their own commissioners, three in number, who would assist the Virginians. The original three commissioners appointed by the Congress were no less distinguished than those from Virginia: Benjamin Franklin and James Wilson from Pennsylvania, both of whom would be signers of the Declaration of Independence, and Patrick Henry of Virginia. As Franklin was unable to attend, and Henry declined to serve, Lewis Morris of New York (another future signer of the Declaration), and Dr. Thomas Walker of Virginia[18], who had also been a Virginia commissioner at Fort Stanwix, were chosen in their places. These two, then, with Wilson, made up the final group of commissioners: along with the three Congressional selections were the delegates finally selected by Virginia, James Wood, Andrew Lewis, John Walker, and Adam Stephen.

On September 26th the conference previously agreed upon between the Shawnee and Dunmore nearly a year before finally opened in Pittsburgh. The Indian nations, the Iroquois (or Six Nations), Shawnee, Delaware, Wyandot, Mingo, and Ottawa, were well represented by their delegates, which included such noteworthies as Cornstalk for the Shawnee; the Seneca chief Guyashuta; the Delaware's Custaloga, Wingenund, and Pipe; and the Wyandot Half King. As per instructions the American commissioners asked the Indian tribes to remain neutral during this conflict between the American colonists and the English king, and to continue to honor the previous treaties between them. On the 10th of October John Walker addressed the assembled Indian tribes:

*"You must all be sensible that the lands on this side [of] Ohio as far down as the C[h]erokee River [now known as the Tennessee River] was Purchased at the Treaty of Fort Stanwix by Sir William Johnson for the King of England who has since sold it to his children on this continent and which they now Expect to Enjoy in Peace."*

Two days later, on October 12th, Flying Crow, a chief of the Six Nations responded:

*"It is true we all Suspected that you Intended to encroach upon our Lands but we are now Satisfied and believe you have no such Intention ... you must no doubt know what Lands we have heretofore Granted you and we Expect that you will not suffer any of your foolish young Men to settle or encroach upon our lands. The Boundaries you mentioned were Settled by our respective Chiefs and we hope you will Observe them and make no Encroachments upon us ...."*

At the conclusion of the treaty on October 21st it was agreed that a delegation composed of both whites and Indians should be designated to perform that portion of the treaty relating to the delivery of prisoners, Negroes, and horses. Those selected for this task were John Gibson and another man for Virginia, two Iroquois, three Delaware (including the chief, Wingenund), and two Shawnee, one of them Cornstalk's son, Elinipisco. In addition an Iroquois chief, the well-known Seneca, Guyashuta, and the Delaware chief Pipe were appointed to accompany these delegates to the Shawnee villages to "assist in the Execution of their purpose". With that out of the way the commissioners passed out to the Indians the typically liberal presents which always concluded every treaty, and their business was done.

Once more, as in the peace following Pontiac's War eleven years earlier, it was now hoped that the "Indian Problem" had been settled; in addition to the earlier treaties with the Iroquois, peace treaties had now been signed with both the Shawnee and with the Cherokee, agreeable to all parties; white settlement was prohibited north and west of the Ohio. To be sure, there were still malcontents among the Indians who would fight as long as they would breathe. The notorious Cherokee with the fascinating name of Dragging Canoe gathered a band of dissatisfied warriors around him and harried the southern frontier settlements for years.

But the Indian Problem would never be settled, of course; there was never anything more than a momentary lull, now and then, in a continuous war of extermination. The two races were so enormously different culturally that a boundary between the two was a vital necessity. That border between the white and red men was obvious enough; if you crossed the Ohio River going west, you were on Indian land; if you crossed it going east you were on white land. But the irreconcilable difference was that both sides claimed control of the other's land; the Indian's by previous settlement, the whites by right of the various treaties, such as Stanwix, Hard Labor, and Sycamore Shoals.

What might eventually have come to be known as *Dunmore's Peace*, however, would surely have lasted longer than it did, had it not been for the rebellious spirits in Massachusetts; there had been a *Massacre* by English Lobsterbacks of six Bostonians in 1770, and a Tea Party was held in that city in 1773, with the consequent Boston Port Act closing the town. Events in the far distant west along the Ohio River, or the little news they heard of them, were of slight concern to easterners, who had seldom ever so much as seen a wild Indian.

At a time when no one had thoughts of a Continental Congress or a Bunker Hill, Henderson, on March 17, 1775, had signed the Treaty of Sycamore Shoals with the Cherokee, purchasing from them the land which that nation had already decided to yield as a result of Stuart's influence five years earlier at the Treaty of Hard Labor. Henderson's purpose, however, was not to gain a treaty for the English government; he was the organizer of the Transylvania Company, and his goal was the establishment of a feudal empire in the west, with himself at its head.

It was on March 23rd, only six days after the signing of this treaty, that Patrick Henry thundered to the Virginia House of Burgesses:

*"Give me liberty, or give me death!"*

and three weeks later, on April 18th, 1775, Paul Revere may have said to his friend:

*"If the British march, by land or sea from the town tonight, Hang a lantern aloft in the belfry arch of the North Church tower as a signal light...."*

and he on the opposite shore would be ready to ride and spread the alarm .... Due to the bungling of their commanding officer, however, it was not until the early morning hours of the 19th before the British actually marched out from the town, "two if by sea", and onto the road to Lexington and Concord and Revolutionary War. In those two minor engagements they suffered nearly three hundred casualties, compared to eight of the minutemen, before they finally, barely, reached the safe haven of Boston. On June 15th George Washington was appointed commander-in-chief of the army by the Continental Congress, but without waiting for his arrival the militia fortified Breed's Hill, placing cannon on the eminence there which overlooked Boston. Lord Howe, commander of His Britannic Majesty's forces in North America could not ignore the gauntlet thrown in his face, and on the 17th a battle was fought on this hill which would come to be known as the Battle of Bunker Hill. Although the rebellious Americans were finally driven from the hill, after having inflicted on the British another incredible loss of a thousand men, it was an eventual victory for the militia, as Howe would be forced to evacuate the city the next year.

# Chapter VII

## Boone - II

After warning the surveyors and settlers in Kentucky in the summer of 1774, Boone had returned to North Carolina. During the remainder of the year, throughout Dunmore's War, he had been in charge of the defense of the Clinch River settlements. Then began the great land venture; Col. Henderson and his Transylvania Company had signed the treaty of Sycamore Shoals, on the Watauga River, with the Cherokee on March 17, 1775. But even before the final signatures were put in place, even before the Cherokee began receiving their goods, valued at £10,000 sterling, Boone was on his way, following Dr. Walker's trail, cutting a road through the Cumberland Gap, and so into Kentucky, a distance of two hundred miles. Thousands of immigrants would come west along Boone's famous Wilderness Road; it was a wagon-road only as far as Powell's Valley, from there on everything had to be hauled on pack-horses. Boone chose for himself a location that he had spied several years before on the Kentucky River, about ten miles south of present Lexington, and the little community was named in his honor, Boonesborough.

Everything must have seemed to be in their favor in that fall of 1775, after Daniel had returned with his family. It was time; Daniel would soon be forty-one, and he was to have no more children. Although they had lost James, Daniel and Becky still had seven children, ranging from sixteen-year-old Israel down to the newest Boone, little Jesse, not quite two and a half. The Delaware were friendly, and a treaty had been signed by the Iroquois seven years earlier. That spring the Cherokee had sold (for the second time) their Kentucky claims, this time to the Transylvania Company, and even now the Shawnee chiefs were on their way to Pittsburgh to sign another peace treaty, according to the Camp Charlotte agreement. It should have been a time of peace and prosperity.

It was not to be. On December 23rd Major Arthur Campbell and two boys, Sanders and McKinney, had crossed the river. Believing indeed in peace and prosperity, they had not even taken their rifles along. The two boys began climbing the hill opposite the settlement, while Campbell worked his way a few hundred yards upstream, where he began marking a claim. Major Campbell knew Indians, however; in 1758, when he was fifteen, he had been captured and spent three years living among them, learning their ways, and he took precautions. The two boys did not know Indians, nor would they now have time to learn.

Not only were these three out, but there were a dozen or more hunters from Boonesborough in the woods, as well. There was no other way to provide the settlement with the requisite amount of meat, and if Indians were about, then all of these men were in mortal danger. Only ten minutes had passed since Campbell had separated from the boys, when those in the fort heard a flurry of shots. Immediately the cry was raised that Indians had killed all three, but as a rescue party started out they met Campbell running toward them, yelling that he had been attacked only about a quarter mile away. Boone and a group of men headed for the spot where Campbell had been attacked, but nothing more than a few moccasin tracks could be found. Toward evening the hunters began to straggle in; they had seen no Indian sign, and they were each and every one totally unaware of their danger. But the boys

did not return, and search parties were sent out, day after day, looking for them. On the 27th, just two days after Christmas, the body of young McKinney was found, lying scalped in the midst of a cornfield about three miles away. Nothing was ever heard of Sanders again; he had undoubtedly met the same fate, at a somewhat further distance and, wherever he had fallen, his body had been left for the wild animals.

But perhaps this was just an isolated incident. When told of such occurrences the older Indian chiefs, as they signed treaty after treaty, routinely shrugged their shoulders, replying only that they had no power to control some of their "foolish young men", as they called them. At the Pittsburgh Conference the Indians told the Virginia commissioners that several of their foolish young men had burned a few "deserted and worthless cabins". But word came back that those few deserted cabins had actually been Fort Blair at the mouth of the Kanawha, and the surrounding settlement[19]. Again the chiefs, knowing from their own sources that the report was correct, merely shrugged, as if to say, "After all, what can we do?"

Which was indeed true; according to Indian custom, any young brave who wanted to go on a raid against an enemy tribe could not be restrained. He might be advised against such an action, but if he was determined to go there was nothing to stop him, and it was considered only normal if others wanted to join the fun. Indians had no sheriffs and no jails, they had neither bureaucrats nor tax collectors. The only constraints were societal pressure, and in Indian society the only two means by which a young Indian brave could gain status in his tribe was to become a highly-respected hunter, and to kill his enemies and take their property. Horses, slaves, and scalps were such property. The more horses you stole, the more slaves you brought home to take the place of your wife working in the fields, the more scalps you collected, the higher you rose in your society. Enough plunder of this type might even eventually lead to your being made a chief. On the balance sheet was the fact that you might be killed; such was life, or death, rather.

*   *   *

It was a Sunday in Boonesborough, July 7, 1776, and after church services were held Jemima Boone and her two best friends, Betsy and Fanny Callaway, decided to go on a pleasure jaunt. They would take a canoe and lazily paddle up and down the river. Only a day or two before Jemima had suffered an injury common to the frontier women who traditionally went barefoot in all but the coldest weather. She had stepped on a sharp piece of cane stubble, and she wanted to soak her foot in the cool water while the other girls paddled. Betsy was the oldest, at sixteen, and already engaged to Samuel Henderson. Fanny was two years younger, about the same age as Jemima, who would not reach her fourteenth birthday for another three months. Even at that tender age Jemima already had a serious suitor, Flanders Callaway, the older brother of her two friends. It was the rule rather than the exception for girls to marry young on the frontier.

The girls drifted downstream a quarter mile or so, but they were not skilled canoeists, and even in the fairly placid water of the river they ran into trouble when they tried to turn around to head back. Try as they would they could not manage to gain the "safe" shore with the stubborn craft, and soon they were in the shallows on the "dangerous" side. Dangerous enough, anyway; half a dozen Indians had spotted the girls, and were following along, hiding in the dense cane, hoping that the canoe might drift close enough to capture the young squaws. It did. When it had come within a few yards of shore the Indians grabbed them and silenced their screams by waving knife and tomahawk in the girls' faces. Then quickly up the hillside and away they went.

The Indians were five Shawnee and a Cherokee, an odd assortment, but easily enough explained. The Shawnee had come south to reconnoiter the fort, and they had run into the Cherokee chief, Hanging Maw, who was heading north in an attempt to incite the northern tribes to attack the Kentucky forts, peace treaties be damned. The Indians had not yet joined the British; indeed, word of the Declaration of Independence would not reach Boonesborough for another month. Fortune smiled on the girls, however, for Hanging Maw was rather lenient, as hostile Indians went, with young female prisoners, and he had been a visitor at Boone's cabin. Recognizing Jemima, and assuming the other two girls were also Boone's daughters, he chortled to himself as he led the girls toward the Shawnee towns. He had pulled a good one on old Boone this time.

Fortunately one of the boys of the community happened to notice the empty canoe on the opposite bank, and sensing that something was amiss, he hurried back to the fort and spread the word. Soon a crowd reached the shore, and a moment later the same boy was swimming the river to fetch the canoe. Their worst fears were soon confirmed when they found the trail of Indians and captives on the other side, but now there was a further delay in taking up the rescue. Having been at church earlier, the men were all dressed in their Sunday-go-to-meetin' clothes, and those were unsuitable for the job at hand. Once more the lad was given a task: run to the settlement and help bring back the standard forest apparel for all frontiersmen, breechclouts, moccasins, and rifles, while the men searched out the trail the Indians had taken. To his dismay, when he returned the boy was denied permission to go; they said he was too young.

The men quickly changed into their traveling gear and took up the trail. The girls hadn't been gone long, and the Indians could not have gotten far, they knew, but as always with Indian prisoners, it was not just a matter of overtaking them. If their captors had an inkling that rescuers were near and the prisoners might be recovered, rather than allow the captives to be liberated, they would unhesitatingly be tomahawked. Col. Richard Callaway and a group of men rode with all possible speed for the ford of the Licking River, which crossed the Warriors' Path about fifty miles from Boonesborough. There he would set up an ambush for the abductors of his daughters, if the other group of pursuers had not yet caught up with them from behind.

The Indians had pushed on with all possible speed, such as it was, for they had not reckoned with a Boone, even if it was a female Boone. Jemima had not been raised by Daniel Boone for nothing, and she showed her training well. Because of her sore foot she had been placed on the only available horse. She was an accomplished rider, but the Indians were unaware of that, and this was a peculiar horse that she could not ride. When one of the warriors placed her on its back she promptly fell off, and when he put her back on, she tumbled off again before they had gone more than a few yards. Peculiar indeed. At first this was amusing — the young white squaw who couldn't even remain seated on a slowly-walking horse without falling off; but quickly enough the situation lost its humor for the Indians. Deciding that they could make better time afoot, the girls were forced to walk. Even then they were the clumsiest of creatures, constantly tripping or stumbling over roots, or catching their clothes in the bushes, or accidentally breaking off protruding twigs, all as if they were on a Sunday stroll. Betsy, the only one with shoes, managed to dig her wooden heels into the soft ground at every opportunity, until she was caught at it, and the heels were knocked off.

They had covered only about ten miles when time came to make camp[20]. The girls were bound for the night, and at first light Hanging Maw started his troupe on the journey north. Boone, John Floyd, Flanders Callaway (Jemima's lover), and the rest of the pursuers were not far behind, but in spite of the girls, Indians could travel quickly enough when they wanted to. Expecting pursuit, they had divided up when they entered the cane brakes, and now the trail was hopelessly lost, although for the most part they were following the wide Warriors' Path.

Boone was certain that the Indians were Shawnee, and were heading for their villages on the Scioto. He had no intention of his oldest daughter living out her days in a smoke-filled Indian lodge, and knowing the country as he did, he left the trail and made a circuit. After he had covered another thirty miles, he made a sharp right turn, and it was not long before he found the trail he was searching for. There was even yet an occasional broken twig to mark the route, although fewer of them now; the Indians had grown more watchful, and sometimes they would leave the forest trail and turn aside for a while, but they might as well have spared themselves the trouble. By now Boone was too close to be shaken off, and the next day, about noon of this third day of pursuit, not far from the Blue Licks, the rescuers came across the carcass of a freshly-killed buffalo from which the hump had been cut. Within a few minutes Boone silently approached the Indian camp.

Believing themselves by now safe from pursuit, one of the Shawnee had just kindled a small fire, and was hanging strips of buffalo over it, while Hanging Maw had gone upstream for water. One guard had been posted, just as Boone had said he would be, but he had strolled back down to the fire, carelessly leaving his rifle behind.

Now came the most dangerous part. The plan had been to get as close as possible and then pour a volley into the camp. Instead the two sides spotted each other at almost the same instant, while they were still thirty yards apart. But the white men were armed and ready, and the Indians were not. Floyd's shot sent the one Indian sprawling into the fire, but he regained his feet and rushed for the safety of the woods, along with his companions. Jemima jumped up screaming, "There's Daddy", and the other two girls also jumped up, screeching at the top of their lungs. It can perhaps be pardoned in the sudden excitement, since the girls had by now given up hope of rescue, but it was not a wise thing to do. One of the Shawnee paused in his race for the woods to throw his tomahawk at Betsy Callaway, and another threw a knife, but both missed. Boone roared "Fall down!" to the girls, and they obeyed instantly, throwing themselves on the ground. The Indians had vanished like ghosts, although there was no lack of blood on the ground. Hanging Maw reached his southern home and lived to an advanced age, but two of the Shawnee never made it back to their village. Boone, after moving a few miles away, made camp for the night.

The next morning they resumed the course for home, which they reached uneventfully. Callaway and his men returned a day or two later; since the Indians had never reached the Licking River, it was a certainty that Boone had caught up with them. A month later Betsy Callaway married Sam Henderson, one of her rescuers; the next year, despite Daniel's misgivings about her age, fourteen-year-old Jemima married her rescuer, Flanders Callaway, and Fanny Callaway became the wife of John Holder.

This abduction of the girls during a supposed time of peace was a true Seven Days' Wonder. Far to the northeast, Capt. Matthew Arbuckle, commanding at Point Pleasant, heard of it and sent a message to the Shawnee demanding their immediate return. One of the chiefs assured Arbuckle that the girls had already been rescued unharmed. Half a century later the rescue would be immortalized, as James Fenimore Cooper fashioned the incident into an episode in *The Last of the Mohicans.*

# Chapter VIII

The Moravians: A Tale of Ultimate Sadness
Bright Hope

Perhaps what might have been the one truly bright spot in the twenty-five years of partisan warfare on the western border was the effort of the Moravian missionaries to convert the Indians to Christianity. At one time, just before the outbreak of the Revolution, it appeared quite feasible that a good portion of the Indian nations could be converted to an agricultural life style; were this be accomplished, the Indian Wars would be no more.

The Moravians were one of the older Protestant sects, dating back to the teachings of the English scholar John Wycliffe, and John Huss, a cleric in Prague in the early fifteenth century. Huss was excommunicated and eventually tried as a heretic for protesting the selling of indulgences. In 1415, 102 years before Martin Luther posted his 95 Theses at Wittenberg, Huss was convicted and burned at the stake (Erasmus wrote, "John Huss was burned, not convicted"), but not before his work had been adopted and carried on by others. But those followers, conscious of the savagery of the subsequent Hussite Wars, adopted a philosophy of non-violence; this became one of the basic tenants of the church, to the point that to engage in any act of violence, even in defense of one's own life, was considered a fall from grace which could never be absolved.

In North America the Moravian goal, that of transporting the "savage Indians" from their centuries-old hunter-gatherer culture of heathen worship into a more efficient (and less bloody) agricultural and totally pacifistic life style which was centered around the church, met with greater than anticipated success. In North America, beginning with the founding of Bethlehem in 1741 by the euphoniously-named Count von Zinzindorf, the Moravians settled in eastern Pennsylvania, in the present Allentown-Bethlehem region. Two early villages were established just east of Nazareth, *Friedensthal and Gnadenthal*, the names rolling off the German tongue — the Valley of Peace and the Valley of Grace. Moving westward, in 1746 the missionaries founded another village at present Lehighton. Originally called *Gnadenhutten*, Tents of Grace, but now known as *Gnadenhutten on the Mahoning*, it survived for less than ten years. At the outbreak of the French and Indian War this Indian village was destroyed, on November 24, 1755, but not by white men. Eleven Moravian mission workers died in that massacre at the hands of a war party of Muncee Indians. Among those killed was a young woman named Senseman, whose ten-year-old son, Gottlob, survived. Many years later the Reverend Gottlob Senseman would accompany his fellow Moravian missionaries to their new Christian villages in Ohio.

Following the end of that war, and Pontiac's Rebellion which immediately followed, the missionaries moved northwestward, founding the town of Friedenshutten (Tents of Grace) on the Susquehanna (Bradford County, Pennsylvania) in 1765. In April, 1770 the most famous of the Moravian teachers, David Zeisberger, led a large group of Moravian Indians down the Allegheny to Pittsburgh, thence down the Ohio about 30 miles to the Big Beaver, and up that river another twenty miles to the Falls of the Beaver (Beaver Falls, PA), where they halted and commenced making a settlement, calling it *Friedenstadt*, the Village of Peace[21]. But even here, separated from all the other white and red settlements, the enmity from both the red and the white man was still too great for Christian Indians to maintain a true village of peace. Despised by Indians for adopting Christianity, they were nevertheless persecuted by whites because they were Indians; an Indian was an Indian, and even though they were Christians, the Indian converts were looked upon with distrust. Not understanding the basic principles of that religion, their white neighbors could never rid themselves of the fear that at any moment these so-called "Christian Indians" might revert to their heathenish traditions and murder them all in their sleep.

And so once more Zeisberger, with twenty-eight followers, mostly Delaware, set out early in April of 1772; they crossed the Ohio, into "Indian Country" and, arriving on the eastern bank of the Tuscarawas River, two miles southeast of present New Philadelphia, Ohio (Tuscarawas County) on May 3rd, they gave their new home, the first Christian town in Ohio, the name of *Schoenbrunn*, or Beautiful Spring. Here they believed they could be left alone, isolated enough to be able to follow their religious beliefs without interference or fear from either hostile Indians or their fellow Christians.

Only five months later Joshua, a Mohican elder, followed the first group, leading a large group of Mohican Indians from Pennsylvania, and establishing *Gnadenhutten* (Tents of Grace[22]) on October 9th, 1772. This was primarily a Mohican village, located on the east bank of the Tuscarawas, and about nine miles south of Schoenbrunn. At last all seemed to be going well for the Indian missions. By the end of 1775 Zeisberger was able to report to the church leaders in Bethlehem that the combined total population of Schoenbrunn and Gnadenhutten numbered well over 400 residents, and all indications were that conditions would only continue to improve.

In April, 1776, a third Ohio village was founded, this time at the specific request of the Indians themselves. Netawatwees, known as Newcomer, and head chief of the Delaware, had been converted to Christianity; he confidently expected the entire Delaware nation to adopt Christianity as its official religion within the next five or six years. In order to make room for the Christian Indians the capital of the Delaware nation in Ohio had been moved west from Newcomerstown to the village of Goschachgunk, located at the confluence of the Tuscarawas and the Walhonding, and Netawatwees asked that a mission be established at that site. This was *Lichtenau*, the lovely Meadow of Light, on the eastern bank of the Muskingum; two miles below present Coshocton, Ohio.

But trouble was brewing in the east, and the good times were not to last. A rebellion had broken out between the North American colonists and the English ministers, and scarcely had the residents of Lichtenau begun to settle down to their peaceful employments when a declaration was announced in Philadelphia, in July — a Declaration of Independence. The skirmishes at Lexington and Concord, the battle between minutemen and redcoats on Breed's Hill, and the siege of Boston were already a year in the past; but Philadelphia and Boston were as distant from the Indians at Schoenbrunn and Gnadenhutten as if they had been on the moon.

In spite of these problems, and perhaps overly encouraged by their early results, the missionaries believed that their neutrality would enable the villages to continue, relatively undisturbed by the remote events going on to the east. Unfortunately their staunch supporter, Netawatwees, died that fall of 1776, and thus almost all control over the Delaware nation was lost.

By the next spring it was made abundantly apparent to the missionaries that neutrality was not possible, nor even peaceful coexistence. One obstacle lay in the way of success; and that obstacle was distrust, and it was insurmountable. It was the one factor which alone was to result in the downfall of the Moravian communities and the death of several hundred innocent Christian Indians. That distrust was surely understandable; in that year of the Bloody Sevens the Moravian villages on the Tuscarawas sat between the American colonists on one side, and their hostile brothers on the other. The Americans, to the east, were convinced that the Christian Indians were giving aid and comfort to raiding war parties on their way to attack the frontier settlements; as a result American men, women, and children were being killed. To the west the belligerent tribes were just as surely convinced that the Christians were sending messages to those settlements, warning them of approaching attacks and thus destroying the Indians' main tactical element — surprise; as a result Indian warriors were being killed.

And there was very good reason for these suspicions; on both sides they were well grounded in fact. It was in the nature of the Moravian Indians to welcome any visitors to their communities; many of their red guests were relatives and acquaintances, and there was always the possibility that some of these could be converted from their paganism. But when a band of hostile Indians appeared, heading east and painted for war, it was the barest minimum act of Christian charity for the missionaries to give warning to those whose lives were in danger.

Nor was it only the settlers in their cabins and villages eastward whose lives were in danger from the hostile Indians; so also were the lives of the missionaries, and so also the lives of their red converts. An absurd myth, developed and nourished by devious or unknowing writers, has grown up in recent years to the effect that the hostile Indians loved their red brothers who lived in the Christian villages. Nothing could be further from the truth; the hostile Indians despised the Christians and ridiculed their creed of absolute pacifism. The belligerent Indians needed every warrior available to fight the white man; it was traditional for Indian war parties purposely to abduct young white boys for adoption into the tribe; thus would be gained one more Indian warrior. But every Indian converted to Christianity was a warrior lost, no less than if he had been killed. The hostile Indians could never understand that no Christian Indian dared engage in acts of violence; to do so would be to endanger his immortal soul. Up to the very end of the Border Wars the hostiles persisted in their belief that if only they could succeed in getting the converts away from their missionaries (perhaps they should even kill the missionaries), then the Christian Indians would soon forget their white man's God, and they could then be enticed into accompanying the raiding parties against the whites.

But that was an impossible dream; the Christian Indians would never again take up the war hatchet. They would die first, and to prove it many of them did. For the hostile Indians to believe otherwise was to believe in miracles, and miracles, no matter how badly they were desired by the belligerent Indian nations, were not at hand.

About the middle of April, 1777 a rumor reached John Heckewelder, second in command of the western missions, then at Schoenbrunn, that several large parties of hostile Indians were on the way to murder the missionaries and destroy the villages of the Christians. The missionaries therefore left Schoenbrunn one night, under cover of darkness, but the next day Heckewelder returned, alone. There he found an Indian war party, headed by the Muncee [Delaware] chief Newalike, from Sandusky, pressing those former members of his tribe to leave the village and save themselves, since "all living there would soon be murdered, if they remained in the parts ...."

Heckewelder immediately informed Zeisberger, who was then at Lichtenau, of the situation. Zeisberger, not too alarmed, nevertheless came at once to Schoenbrunn, but finding matters worse than he had expected, he declared that the town should be abandoned[23]. The church was torn down by the converted Indians that it might not be made use of for heathenish purposes, and the congregation left the place the same day, April 19, 1777. Schoenbrunn, the Beautiful Spring, had been in existence for less than five years.

Heckewelder later wrote that the reason given by the hostile Indians for their intended destruction of the Moravian town was that they feared the Americans would harm them if they continued there, but Heckewelder was not such a fool. He knew better, and he concluded that the real reason was that they (the hostile Indians) wanted the Christian Indians to go over to the British side, joining them in their war against the Americans. Chief White Eyes, however, and the rest of the Delaware council were determined to remain neutral in this struggle, and they determined that it would be best for the Christian Indians to relocate to Lichtenau, the small village recently established on the east bank of the Muskingum, about two miles below Goschachgunk, which at that time served as the main residence of the Delaware nation. As they had recently signed a peace treaty with the Americans at Fort Pitt, the Americans had every reason to believe that the chances were quite good that this nation, at least, would be kept out of the Revolution. Lichtenau thus became the major Christian Indian village in Ohio, now surpassing Gnadenhutten in size, by far.

Not long afterwards Heckewelder, now at Lichtenau, decided to return to Bethlehem, hoping to marry Sara Ohneberg. When he arrived at Newcomerstown, seventeen miles distant, White Eyes immediately hurried up to him with another chief, Wingenund, and some of his young men. The Delaware chiefs insisted on accompanying Heckewelder at least as far as Pittsburgh, saying that they would not allow him to travel alone while the Sandusky warriors were out on war excursions, without a proper escort and they themselves at his side. While on the trail to

Pittsburgh one of the scouts discovered a suspicious track, and White Eyes asked Heckewelder if he were afraid. Heckewelder replied to the effect that he was not, as long as White Eyes was with him. White Eyes replied: "You are right, for until I am laid prostrate at your feet, no one shall hurt you." "And not even then," added Wingenund, who was riding behind Heckewelder, "before this happens I must be also overcome and lay by the side of our friend White Eyes."

But now things were going from bad to worse; the situation in that spring of 1777 must have seemed dismal indeed, for the war had given the British a chance to gain not only the continued support of their Indian allies, but also their subservience. In an effort to prevent the frontier people from heading east to join the Continental army opposing the redcoats, Henry Hamilton, Governor-General of Canada, offered the Indians not only war materiel, but also food and clothing for the non-combatants. Thus relieved of the necessity of hunting for their families, the warriors were free to take up the tomahawk against the hated white invaders. Valuable plunder was to be had; prisoners and scalps were worth money and rum, and scalps were easier to carry than prisoners. There were guns and iron knives and horses, and prisoners to delight their villages with torture. For the Indian warriors there were two roads to this good fortune. One led south, across the Ohio River into Kentucky, while the other led due east, with a pause as they passed through the Christians' town, on their way to western Virginia and Pennsylvania — and then back again, with their grisly trophies.

# Chapter IX

The Incredible Adventures of Simon Kenton

Simon Kenton was the second of the great triumvirate of bordermen-frontiersmen of Boone, Kenton, and Lewis Wetzel. Simon, fourth son and seventh of the nine children of Mark and Mary Miller Kenton, was born April 3, 1755, in Fauquier County, Virginia.

In the summer of 1771, after fighting an older rival for the affections of a young woman, and fearing that he had killed his opponent in the ensuing brawl, sixteen-year-old Simon headed west over the mountains, without even stopping at home to tell his parents he was leaving. Along the way he changed his name, and for the next nine years he would be known as Simon Butler. By autumn he had made his way nearly as far west as Fort Pitt, and there he met up with two men, John Yeager and George Strader. Like John Finley, Yeager had been in the Kentucky lands years before. Although Finley had been a trader for only a few weeks, Yeager had been taken captive by the Indians as a child and had lived with them for many years. But it didn't matter, both men had been there, and they had seen the land, and they would never forget it.

And just as Finley had done with Boone, so Yeager fired young Simon's imagination with tales of the land out west; all that was necessary was to float down the placid Ohio until you came to paradise. Building a canoe and filling it with traps and enough provisions to last them through the winter, the three men set off. Down the broad Ohio they floated, on what must have been a fantastic voyage, with precursors of the future for Kenton. They passed Logstown, where John Gibson had his trading post, and Yellow Creek, soon to have its name written in the blood of Logan's family. They passed Mingo Bottom and Wheeling Island, then Grave Creek with its imposing burial mound, and on down they floated, past the mouths of the Kanawha and the Muskingum, and then the Big Sandy, where Kentucky began. On past little Limestone Creek, which was to be home to Simon for many years. But Yeager was looking for the cane-lands which he had seen so many years before, and by now, with winter coming on and Yeager insisting that they must have floated by them unnoticed, they turned around and backtracked, all the way back to the Kanawha. Ascending that river to the Elk, there they established a base camp, and spent the winter of 1771-72 hunting, trapping, and exploring the land. They made a good harvest that winter, and in the spring headed back down the Kanawha to the Ohio, where they met a trader. Exchanging their furs for provisions for another year, the men returned to their camp on the Elk. Kenton and Strader were young men, Simon only seventeen that April, but Yeager was older and experienced; he should have known that such a situation could not endure when there were Indians about. It was the law of the forest.

They came in the night, in a dark night in March, 1773, as the three hunters stood around the campfire in front of their open-faced cabin. A sudden burst of gunfire, and Simon dove for the safety of the woods, along with Strader, both of whom were uninjured. Yeager, either wounded or dazed, started walking toward the Indians, probably with the intention of speaking to them. But the Indians, with upraised tomahawks, never gave him a chance. The two young men met up later on, but they were a sorry-looking pair. It was March, and they were barefoot, with no clothes except what they were wearing, no provisions, and worst of all, they were unarmed. For several days they struggled through the wilderness until finally, nearing the Kanawha, they came to a settler's cabin where they recovered.

Moving on to the mouth of the Kanawha, Simon joined another band of adventurers which included the Greathouse brothers. He soon left them and joined a party led by Dr. John Wood, and with them traveled all the way to the mouth of the Little Miami. But the Indians were becoming so troublesome that the entire group decided to abandon their canoes and return to Virginia, overland. It had never been done before from that point in the wilderness, and their guide for the entire journey was eighteen-year-old Simon Butler, who brought them all back safely to Greenbriar County.

But this was too close to home and the hangman's noose for Simon, so he went back out to Fort Pitt once more, where in the spring of 1774 occurred one of the most providential meetings of his young life, with Simon Girty. Ever since his return from Indian captivity more than a dozen years before, Girty had been earning his living at Pitt as a scout and interpreter. Girty was now in his early thirties, but he and young Simon became close friends. When Lord Dunmore arrived both Girty and Butler signed on as scouts, relaying messages back and forth between Dunmore and Lewis, although both men missed the battle on October 10th.

Receiving his discharge from the service Simon, like so many others, had not forgotten about Kentucky. In the fall of 1775 he set out once more, this time with Thomas Williams as his companion. While hunting at the Blue Licks they first heard of other white men in the country, and of the settlements made by Boone, Harrod, and Hinkston (afterwards becoming Ruddle's Station). They spent the remainder of the winter visiting from one fort to another, finally settling at Hinkston's. By the spring of 1776 Butler and Williams were back at an earlier camp which they had built on Lawrence Creek. With the Indian war now thought to be over, settlers were beginning to pour into Kentucky, and Simon was kept busy for the next year piloting them to choice locations, while making tomahawk claims of his own. But the Shawnee had become so aggressive that it was impossible for small isolated groups to remain in the wilderness, and it was necessary to return to Hinkston's, where Simon became a hunter for the settlement, on into the spring of that next terrible year of 1777.

There could hardly have been a more dangerous occupation. In order to avoid scaring the game it was necessary for the hunter to go alone. When the game was sighted and approached, it could easily enough be brought down with a ball from the hunter's rifle. But then it was necessary to remain in the vicinity long enough to gut the animal and pack it on the horse, and there may be other ears in the forest besides your own — Indian ears, which could tell the direction and distance from which your shot had been fired; and following the trail that you and your horse made, even had the warrior not known that you were heading back to the fort, was child's play for these men of the forest.

*   *   *

Major George Rogers Clark had been given command of the Kentucky colony, and Kenton was one of the first appointed scouts. One day in early spring he and five others were sent to the now-deserted Hinkston's to bring in some flax needed for clothing. But early in the year as it was, it wasn't early enough; they almost rode headlong into a portion of the two hundred Shawnee warriors which Blackfish himself had led southward to destroy the three Kentucky settlements. They managed to get away, but they saw so much Indian sign, obviously headed for Harrod's Station, that Simon sent the other five back with a warning to Clark, then at Harrod's. Clark could have used the warning; on the morning that the six had left for Hinkston's another party of four men, out making maple sugar, were fired on by a large force of Shawnee. Three of the men were killed, but the fourth managed to escape to give warning before the Indians arrived.

Meanwhile Kenton, all alone, went on to bring a warning to Boonesborough. Thus it was, by this courageous decision, that Simon Butler, *nee* Kenton, happened to be at Boonesborough when Blackfish and over a hundred Shawnee warriors attacked just at sunrise, April 24th, in what was to become almost a classic routine of Indian stratagem.

Kenton was standing guard at the gate with two others, watching two men who had just gone out into the field in front of the fort. Suddenly they were fired on by a small band of Indians. As the two men turned and fled back toward the fort, the Indians, surprisingly, pursued, charging straight for the open gate. So quickly did they advance that one of the men was caught and tomahawked from behind before he could reach the gate. Kenton, running out, watched in disbelief as the victor, pausing momentarily beside his victim, whipped out his knife. He was nonchalantly taking the scalp when Kenton's bullet brought him down.

Back inside, Boone, hearing the firing, rushed out with ten men and advanced toward the edge of the forest. This was what the main body of Shawnee were waiting for; as soon as Boone and his men reached a certain point, the warriors sprang from their ambush, cutting off the retreat of the now badly-outnumbered Kentuckians. Inside the fort were only eight riflemen, the rest were women and children. If Boone and his fourteen followers failed to return to the fort, the sun would set that evening over the ashes of Boonesborough.

Unhesitatingly, Boone gave the order to charge through the wall of Indians; it was to be every man for himself. Except Simon Kenton, of course. As he saw an Indian raising his musket and aiming at Boone, Kenton's snap shot brought him down. Then it was reverse your rifle and club your way through. Almost miraculously they were all making it back to the fort, even the six wounded men, then seven, as Boone fell, his leg broken by an Indian's bullet. A warrior reached Boone and, screaming, swung his tomahawk aloft, hesitating just a moment too long. Kenton had reloaded, and at near point-blank range his shot killed Boone's assailant. Yet another brave rushed up to take Boone's scalp; Kenton, reaching Boone at the same moment, knocked him spinning with the butt of his rifle. Not quite done with his heroic deeds for the day, and before the other Indians could react, Kenton heaved Daniel over his shoulder like a sack of meal and raced back to the fort, dodging and twisting this way and that as the Indians fired in vain.

The Indians continued around the fort for a few days, but growing disheartened, went back to Harrodsburg, in search of easier prospects. They were not completely gone, however; they returned on May 23rd and 24th, finally giving up for good after failing to set fire to the stockade wall. Easier prospects were not to be found at Harrod's, but it seemed they might be at Logan's Station. Although there were only some two dozen able-bodied men at Boone's, and between sixty and seventy at Harrod's, Benjamin Logan had only about fifteen defenders. Still, if the Indians were unable to gain entrance to a fort by surprise or by stratagem, and if they were unable to fire it, they rarely, almost never, succeeded in overwhelming a stout-hearted defense. Logan's was no exception to the rule. Logan himself slipped out under cover of darkness and made his way to the Holston settlements for reinforcements.

Finally the long-awaited relief began to come in; in July, William Bailey Smith arrived at Boonesborough with fifty mounted North Carolina riflemen, mostly Boone's old friends and neighbors from the Yadkin. In August Colonel John Bowman arrived with one hundred Virginia militiamen, and took over command of the Kentucky militia. With enough men now to protect the forts and to guard the workers in the fields, the Shawnee finally gave up and retreated back across the Ohio. Kentucky had barely survived its third year, but the Indians would be back.

## Second Interlude: The Girty Brothers

Of the Girty brothers, there were four. Beginning with the oldest, Thomas was born in 1739, followed every two years thereafter by Simon, James, and finally George in 1745. Their father was an Irish emigrant, who settled at Chamber's Mills, now Fort Hunter (Dauphin County), just north of present Harrisburg, Pennsylvania. There he married an English girl named Mary Newton, sired four sons by her, and carried on a trade with the Indians. In 1749 he decided to try his hand at farming, so he and his family joined a large number of settlers on Sherman's Creek, in present Perry County, but the Indians objected so strenuously to this invasion of their domain that the government evicted the squatters, burned their cabins, and returned the settlers to Chamber's Mills. The old man's chief claim to fame, aside from being the father of the three most infamous renegades on the border, was getting himself killed two years later in a drunken brawl with an Indian named the Fish. Whereupon the Widow Girty married a man named John Turner in 1753, and the next year the Girty boys had a new stepbrother, John, Jr. John Turner's chief claim to fame, aside from killing the Fish, the Indian who had killed his wife's late husband, was that, for a few moments in 1756, he was in command of Fort Granville during an Indian attack.

*    *    *

With the outbreak of the French and Indian War in 1755, a number of forts were built for the protection of the local inhabitants; among these was Fort Granville, on the banks of the Juniata, not far from present Lewistown, Mifflin County. In July, 1756, a large war party of Indians, made up mostly of Delaware, but including some Shawnee and a few Seneca, left the Kittanning[24] and headed east. As they passed the Blue Mountains to the south, Fort Granville lay directly in their path. On July 22nd they appeared briefly before the fort and demanded its surrender, which was of course refused, and the Indians, not attacking, soon disappeared into the forest. After more than a week had passed the commander, Captain Edward Ward, having seen the enemy disperse, assumed that they had left the vicinity, and on the morning of the 30th he led almost his entire force out, several miles distant, to guard the farmers who were then desperately trying to harvest their wheat. Left in command was Lt. Edward Armstrong and twenty-two men; second in command was John Turner, Sr.

The Indians had not left; they watched as Ward marched out, and that very afternoon they launched a furious attack against the now seriously-weakened fort. Unsuccessful in their attempts to storm the fort during the day, under cover of darkness they gained a deep ravine by which they were able to approach within a few yards of the fort, where they succeeded in setting the stockade wall ablaze. Shooting through the hole which had burned through the wall, the Indians killed Armstrong and another man who were trying to put out the fire, and wounded three others. The Indians now once more proposed a surrender, assuring the defenders that if they continued to resist, every one of them, men, women, and children, would be slaughtered, but if only they would give up, no one would be harmed. Turner, now in command, looked at the blackened hole in the stockade, then at the seventeen men left standing, then at the women and children, including his own family, huddled together inside the fort. Foolishly believing the Indians, he proceeded to talk the others into surrendering, then threw wide the fort's gates. One of the soldiers was immediately tomahawked; another, although wounded, managed to escape with the story of why Granville had fallen. All the rest were taken prisoner and marched westward toward Kittanning as the fort burned.

Upon his arrival at the Delaware villages John Turner did not have long to regret his decision. He was bound to a post, and after three hours of torture an Indian scalped him, still alive; another of the Indians then held up a small boy with a tomahawk in his hand to deliver the final stroke. All the while his wife and children had looked on in horror; Thomas was seventeen years old, Simon was fifteen, Jim thirteen, George was eleven, and John Turner, Jr. was a child of only two. The new Widow Turner and her son John were taken downriver by some of the Delaware to Fort Duquesne, thence westward into the wilderness.

With the loss of Fort Granville by Indians from the Kittanning, it was decided that Col. John Armstrong should lead an expedition against that location.

Destruction of the Delaware villages there would be a serious blow to the Indians, it would provide some measure of relief to the frontier, and there was always the possibility that some of the Granville prisoners might be rescued. Accordingly, at first light on the morning of September 8th, only about a month after the Girtys had been brought there, it was attacked by Armstrong at the head of three hundred Pennsylvanians. The Indians were taken by surprise, between thirty and forty of them were killed, and eleven white prisoners were rescued, among them Thomas Girty. But the remaining prisoners, including the three Girty boys, were hurried across the Allegheny; after Armstrong's force had left they were brought back to the burned town, where they again witnessed the spectacle of Indian torture, this time a man and woman who, attempting to escape with Armstrong, had been recaptured by the Indians.

Abandoning Kittanning, the Indians parceled out the three Girtys to the various Indian tribes; Simon was given to the Seneca, James to the Shawnee, and George to the Delaware. With these tribes the boys spent the next three years, their formative teen years, until George Croghan's treaty at Easton, Pennsylvania, in 1759. Mrs. Turner, with five-year-old John, was finally reunited with Thomas and her other three boys, now young men, at Pittsburgh. But it's an ill wind, and the boys had, if nothing more, learned the Indian tongue and the lay of the Indian land and the Indian ways; for better or for worse, depending on whose ox is being gored, each of the three had gained a definite advantage.

Thomas, after his return to Pittsburgh, where he continued to live throughout the Revolution, worked in the Indian trade. Although not fully trusted because of the activities of his brothers, Thomas was faithful to the Americans, sometimes serving as a scout for the military. After the Indian wars he moved to a stream about five miles north of Pittsburgh, named Girty's Run in his honor, where he died November 3, 1820.

Simon probably obtained the greatest advantage from the captivity, having been adopted into the Iroquois League at a time when it had reached its greatest power. After his return home he learned the Delaware language as well, and in 1774, with such a background to recommend him, he served as a scout and an interpreter for Lord Dunmore. In the early part of the Revolution he was instrumental in enlisting men for the patriot cause.

But then, early in 1778, seven men crept out from the shadow of the walls of Fort Pitt; Alexander McKee was deserting, and with him went Simon Girty, Matthew Elliott, Robert Surphlitt, John Higgins, and two of McKee's slaves. They headed north, for Detroit, where Girty joined the British. For the next sixteen years he lived among the Indians and led raids against the frontier settlements; he was at Battle Island in June, 1782, when Crawford was defeated, at St. Clair's Defeat in '91, and at the Fallen Timbers in 1794.

Upon reaching manhood Jim Girty was employed about Fort Pitt as a laborer and interpreter, until late March of 1778, when he was sent by the commissioners at Pittsburgh to deliver a message to the Shawnee, regarding the murder of

Cornstalk, and asking them to preserve the peace. He was found by McKee at Old Chillicothe and easily persuaded to join their cause. He arrived at Detroit in August, where he was hired as a Shawnee interpreter. He led his first expedition against the white settlements that fall, and accompanied Bird in 1780; later that summer he was at the Shawnee towns when they were raided by Clark. In 1782 he participated in Crawford's defeat, and at the Indian towns spoke in favor of John Slover being burned. That September, while his two brothers were with Caldwell on the Kentucky Expedition which culminated in the Battle of Blue Licks, he was at the Siege of Wheeling, September 11-13th. After the Revolution he established a trading post on the St. Mary's of the Maumee known as Girty's Town (Ohio). Upon the approach of Harmar's force in 1790 he was forced to move north to another post on the Auglaize River, where he remained but four years. In 1794 he was driven from there by Wayne's advance, to Detroit, and then after Fallen Timbers and Greenville he crossed over into Canada. There he lived in the township of Gosfield until his death on April 5, 1817.

George, youngest of the three, also became a trader and interpreter about Fort Pitt until 1778, when he became entangled in Willing's Mississippi Expedition. Capt. James Willing of Philadelphia had removed to Natchez in 1774, but in 1777, upon the outbreak of the Revolution, he returned home, where he received a commission as captain in the navy. His orders were to proceed to the Mississippi and secure the cooperation and neutrality of his former neighbors, and to obtain provisions which he would then bring back to the states. He departed Fort Pitt on January 10, 1778, aboard the armed boat *Rattletrap*, and succeeded in securing a pledge of neutrality from the inhabitants of the Natchez region. One of the officers of his command, picked up at Pittsburgh, was Lt. George Girty. However, once in Mississippi Willing became more interested in privateering, if not downright looting and piracy. At New Orleans he captured a small British vessel and, rather than returning with supplies for the United States, he sent his troops back north under the command of Lt. Robert George who, arriving at Kaskaskia, placed them under George Rogers Clark.

Upon returning to the Illinois country with Lt. George in the spring of 1779 George Girty learned, probably for the first time, of his brother's desertion from Pitt the year before and, accordingly, Girty deserted from Kaskaskia with a few other disaffected soldiers in May, 1779. From there he headed for Detroit, where he immediately found employment in the Indian Department. In June, 1780 he accompanied Bird's notorious Kentucky Expedition; he was at the Shawnee towns in 1780 when they were raided by Clark, and John Slover saw him at Pipe's Town in 1782, when Crawford was burned. Of the three brothers he was said to be the most brutal, and the closest to pure Indian in nature, but this is understandable, as he was the youngest, only eleven years old, at the time he was taken captive. After three years living as an Indian boy that life must have seemed preferable to him. When his brothers deserted the Americans, it was only natural that he should join them, despite his military rank. He later lived among the Delaware at Pipe's Town. The date of his death is uncertain, but it is believed that he died at his brother James' home circa 1810.

## SECOND INTERLUDE: THE GIRTY BROTHERS

*    *    *

The name of Simon Girty will often recur in these pages; sometimes as a villain, sometimes as a hero. He saved the life of his old friend Simon Kenton, still known to him as Simon Butler, from death at the stake, but was unable, if he tried at all, to save another friend from the old days at Fort Pitt, Will Crawford. In Girty's favor, in this instance there was really nothing he could have done.

But in the final analysis Simon Girty was a renegade who made unrelenting war on his former friends. He was not the foulest of monsters as often described by old-time writers, nor was he the noble-hearted man of the forest as often described by new-time writers; he later bragged of having killed Col. David Rogers, and he aided in the capture and resultant deaths of Col. Lochry and his men. The Border Wars continued year after year, with the resultant slaughter of innocent white women and children, in part due to his efforts, and for that he must bear a portion of the guilt and shame. To help control the usually intractable Indians he had been sent, along with his two brothers, on Bird's shameful 1780 expedition into Kentucky, which resulted in a massacre of women and children every bit as horrendous as the massacre of the peaceful Moravian Indians two years later.

*He is left to history's judgment*

# Chapter X

## The Adventures of Lewis Wetzel

On September 21, 1731, the Britannia, from Rotterdam by way of Cowes, England, arrived at Philadelphia. Among those on board were Hans Martin Wetzel, Sr., his wife, Maria Barbara Wetzel, and their children Hans Martin, Jr., Nicholaus, and Katherina. They had come among a company of nearly three hundred Germans led by Lutheran Pastor Rieger. Two years after their arrival a son was born, and given the name John. In 1741 the Wetzels settled in Frederick County, Maryland, on a farm adjoining that of Jacob and Anna Maria (Dereux) Bonnett, Huguenot emigrants from France, who had arrived in 1733 aboard the Elizabeth. They remained in Maryland until 1752, when the two neighboring families together moved to farms about fifteen miles southwest of Winchester, Shenandoah County, VA.

In 1756 John Wetzel married his neighbor, Mary Bonnett. John, like many another young man of his times, had a restless foot and an eye for land, and that meant frontier life for his family. Soon after they moved to Rockingham Co., Virginia, where their first child, a son named Martin, was born in 1757. In 1759 a daughter, Christiana, was born, and George, the second son, appeared on the scene two years later. It was about this time that John moved his family back to Pennsylvania, but this time a little further west, settling in Lancaster County about 1762. In August of 1763 the third son, Lewis Wetzel, was born, followed by Jacob in 1765 and Susannah in 1767. In 1770, after the opening up of the western Virginia lands following the Treaty of Fort Stanwix, John moved his family to the Monongahela country, probably somewhere in the vicinity of Dunkard Creek, a (West) Virginia tributary of the Monongahela which enters that river just inside the Pennsylvania line. It was there that his seventh and last child, the fifth of the Wetzel boys, John, Jr., was born in October, 1770. From there he traveled on to the Ohio and selected a homestead on Wheeling Creek, fourteen miles from its mouth on the Ohio, not, as is often stated, because of a wish for solitude, but simply because the land closer to the Ohio had already been claimed by the Zanes.

But Dunmore's War interrupted the peaceful farming life along the banks of Wheeling Creek, as elsewhere along the western Virginia border. When Crawford arrived at Wheeling with a call for militia, John and his son Martin, the only one of the boys old enough to serve, joined up and marched with him. To Martin, just past his sixteenth birthday, it must have been exciting times, perilous indeed, for any boy; the only consolation, if consolation was needed, was that there were others no older than he.

John and Martin Wetzel returned home from the war to their family, and it was expected that farming, hunting and raising a family would dominate the Wetzels' lives for the immediate future, as it was assumed that the coming peace treaty with the Shawnee would ensure peace. But less than six months after their return, an engagement between British redcoats and American militia took place at the towns of Lexington and Concord, in Massachusetts, and Boston was besieged. A year later independence was declared, and in an effort to put down the rebellion the English, from their occupied posts along the Great Lakes, began sending war parties of Indians into the western frontier settlements. To the majority of Indians, it was as if the Treaty of Pittsburgh had never been; they did not want it to be. For the English the logic was straightforward enough; if the settlers of the Upper Ohio were sufficiently harassed by Indians, they would be unable to send soldiers to fight in the eastern theater of the war. Thus, early in 1777 the *Border Wars* erupted again, this time officially sanctioned by England, and this time with a fury that was not to cease for nearly twenty long, bitter, slaughter-filled years.

The Indians could hardly wait for decent weather to begin. Early in the spring of that year, about the first week of April, a man was killed near Wheeling, just across the river, where the town of Bridgeport, Ohio, now stands. Thomas Ryan, a recently-appointed lieutenant of militia for the new Ohio County[25], was killed while working in his fields near Wheeling, and the slave working with him was abducted. And at about the same time another early settler, Roger McBride, was killed and scalped about ten miles up Wheeling Creek, only a few miles from the Wetzel farm. Because of the severity of the Indian depredations in the vicinity, the Wetzels had forted at Shepherd's, six miles upstream, but the father had come back with Lewis and Jacob to spend some time working their fields. It may have been one of these same small war parties who, early one morning, appeared at the Wetzel cabin. Lewis, then thirteen years old, and Jacob, two years younger, were the only two present. The evening before Captain John had decided to return to the fort for the night, planning to return on the following day.

Early the next morning Jacob began to prepare their breakfast, and Lewis, with a bridle on his arm, started out to fetch the horse from the meadow. But as Lewis opened the door and stepped out into the yard two of the Indians, hiding in ambush not far from the cabin, fired at him, probably believing that he was the man of the household; fortunately one ball only grazed his chest, while the other tore a hole through his shirt. Still, he ran toward the cornfield, hoping to be able shake off pursuit, but as he crossed the field and reached the steep edge of the creek bank his foot slipped; the two who had fired at him were close behind, and Lewis was captured. Jacob also ran, but out in the open no 11-year-old boy could outrun an Indian warrior in his prime. After securing the two boys, one of the Indians attended to Lewis' wound with chewed-up sassafras leaves, while the others searched the cabin for any plunder. Taking everything they considered of value, including most importantly Captain Wetzel's rifle, they quickly herded their prisoners, who knew better than to offer resistance, across the creek and toward the Ohio, which they crossed that evening.

The next night they encamped on McMechan's Creek; having covered about twenty miles more. Feeling reasonably secure from pursuit, and the boys seemingly resigned to their fate, the Indians failed to check closely the bonds of their captives, and were soon asleep. But not the two captives; Jacob, who had been bound a little less tightly than Lewis, began working the rawhide thongs until he was able to free himself, and then he helped Lewis slip out of his bonds. With the strictest adherence to absolute silence, the two boys crept stealthily out of the camp. Having reached a safe distance they paused, whereupon Lewis decided that they could not walk all the way home, nearly forty miles, barefoot, and so as Jacob waited in what must have been an agony of suspense, Lewis sneaked back into the Indians' camp, where he procured two pairs of moccasins from under the very noses of his sleeping would-be captors.

Jake's relief upon his older brother's return was short-lived, however, since, having done it once, Lewis was willing to try it again. The Indians had his father's rifle, and a rifle would be useful, perhaps necessary, on the journey home. So back went Lewis a second time, and again Jacob was forced to endure an anxiety which can only be imagined. If his brother did not return, would Jacob, with the Indians alerted, be able to continue his escape on his own and, all alone, find his way home? For if they were caught now there would be no adoption into an Indian tribe. Both boys would be tomahawked and scalped, and their bodies left in the forest to feed the wild animals.

He need not have worried, since even at that age Lewis Wetzel was beginning to show the daring, woodsmanship, and prowess which in future years would make him the most renowned scout on the border. His stalking ability, the ability to move through the woods without being seen or heard, was so incredibly prodigious that it seemed almost miraculous; indeed some people did not credit the stories they had heard until it had been demonstrated to them. But now, having returned with the rifle, there was no more hesitation. Lewis guided his brother on the same path along which they had been taken earlier that day. But they had not gone far when they suddenly picked up the sound of pursuit. The Indians had discovered the escape of their prisoners, and knowing that the boys had only the one chance of finding their way back to the river, were following after them in the dark. Quickly leaving the path the brothers waited until the Indians had passed, then reemerged and, with incredible nerve, began pursuing their pursuers. It was not long before the sounds of the returning warriors were heard, so once more they entered the forest and, waiting until their former captors had again passed them by, they now regained the path and continued their journey toward the river and home.

When they were able to travel no longer they sat down and awaited the light of morning. From there, cautiously making their way through the forest, they finally arrived at the Ohio, nearly opposite Wheeling. But the river was high, and they had no means of crossing, other than by swimming. When the Indians had brought them to the river they had all crossed in a canoe which the Indians had hidden in some willow bushes, but there was no canoe now. Swimming would be dangerous, not only because of the strong current, but because of the weakened condition of the boys after four days of captivity. They had eaten little; they had been offered some meat, but it was maggot-ridden and the boys refused it, although the Indians seemed to relish it. In addition to their fatigue and lack of nourishment, Lewis was further weakened by the loss of quite a bit of blood, and the exertions of swimming were certain to reopen his wound. But they were not safe yet, and they had to get across.

According to their cousin, Lewis Bonnett[26], they finally came to the conclusion that their best chance was for each to take the largest chunk of driftwood they could manage, tie their clothes to that, and then, using it as a float, push it ahead of them as they kicked and paddled their way across. The only alternative would be to wait on the Ohio shore until someone came along the river who could be induced to pick them up and ferry them across. Deeming it unwise to sit idly on the Indian shore, they pushed off into the river; Jacob made it safely across, but in his weakened condition Lewis had considerable difficulty, finally managing to land about a hundred yards below Jacob, but with his father's rifle still secured to his piece of wood.

But they had made it; they were close to Fort Henry, and they were safe. Arriving at the fort they were hailed as if they had arisen from the dead. Indeed, their escape and their ability to negotiate twenty miles of wilderness, while at the same time avoiding Indian pursuit, and then to come out finally on the river within near-shouting distance of their objective, was almost as marvelous as the tale of Lazarus. Captives escaped often enough, but with rare exceptions they were hunted down in the woods by the Indians, and there killed, or they became lost and eventually died of exposure. And it is because two mere boys, the older barely in his teens, had been able to accomplish a feat which would have taxed an experienced woodsman that we now have the story of their abduction, captivity and escape. The next day Col. Zane had the boys safely transported to their family at Shepherd's Fort.

# Chapter XI

$\mathcal{T}$he Zanes - II
The 1777 Siege of Fort Henry,
and McColloch's Leap

To the Honourable the Legislature
of Virginia

The petition of the inhabitants of Wheeling
Town — Humbly Sheweth

That whereas a Town has been laid out
on the Land of Ebenezer Zane & Lots & Streets
laid off in a convenient manner, and for the
good & prosperity of those who have become
purchasers of Lots & inhabitants of said Town
It appears necessary to your petitioners that an
Act may be pass'd by your Honourable body
Establishing said Town by a Law giving such
Privileges to the proprietor & purchasers as are
usual in such cases — We your petitioners
therefore Humbly pray that a Town may be
Established by the Above name on the Land of
Col Ebenezer Zane in Ohio County on the Ohio
River & that Trustees may be appointed.
According to Law & your petitioners as in
Duty Bound will ever pray &c

Ebenezer Zane          James Sprnox
John McIntire          William Depryest
Elijah woods           Thomas Shallu
Archi Woods            Stephen Carr
Andw Woods             Alexander Vanch
                       Wm McConnell
                       John McDarmad
                       Philip Dover
                       David Danley

Ebenezer Zane
Facsimile signature

In the spring of 1774 Andrew Zane had gone down to Kentucky with Jim Harrod, but like all the others that summer, he had been forced to return to the Wheeling settlement of his older brothers. Isaac, now twenty-one, was still living among the Wyandots on the Mad River, in his twelfth year of captivity, while Mr. Zane was at the family home on the South Fork of the Potomac, with daughter Elizabeth. Sometime in the first few years of the Revolution, probably about 1777, the mother of the Zane brothers, Mrs. William Zane, died. Betty, or Betsy, Zane was sent to live with an aunt in Philadelphia, while William went west to join his sons at their station on Wheeling Creek. He was there at least in the year 1777, when he wrote a letter in which he mentioned his Indian captivity.

1777 was well-named: the *Year of the Bloody Sevens* it would be called, and such stories as the killing of Ryan and McBride, and the abduction of the two Wetzel boys would become all too familiar along the Upper Ohio before winter finally put an end to the Indian raids. This was only the beginning, worse was yet to come, much worse. An article in the *Maryland Journal* in the spring of 1777 gives only an inkling; referring to incidents beginning in mid-April they reported:

*... an express came to Fort Pitt, with an account that the widow Muchmore and her three children, were found almost burned to cinders, and her late husband killed and scalped near where the house stood, opposite the mouth of Yellow Creek on the Ohio. The same day another express arrived who brought an account of a man being found murdered near Wheeling[27]; also one Ogden, a Jersey man, was found killed and scalped near the mouth of Raccoon Creek.*

*All the above murders were perpetrated on or near the Ohio.... Lieutenant Mason, at the head of ten militia, gallantly followed the murderers of the Muchmore family, and after a pursuit of twenty-five miles, came up with the savages, who fought for some time and then gave way. Mr. Mason and his little party followed them some miles further, but having no provisions, and being in danger of falling into an ambuscade, returned to the field of battle, where they found one dead Indian, whom they scalped, some horses and other booty which the savages had taken from some white people. Mr. Mason thinks that they either killed or desperately wounded more of the Indians, as much blood was seen on the ground. This brave young man was born near Winchester in Virginia, and will no doubt meet a reward adequate to his merit.*

But help for the beleaguered settlers was on the way; at about the same time as the Muchmore killings Brigadier General Edward Hand had been appointed to command of the Western Department. Hand was an Irish physician who had come to America with the army in 1767; he was immensely popular with both his superiors and his subordinates, and he was to prove to be equally popular with the frontier people. At the outbreak of the Revolution he had served with Washington in the eastern theater until his promotion to Fort Pitt; he arrived there on June 1, 1777, succeeding John Neville as commander of the fort.

By July this same Samuel Mason, as a result of his bravery and leadership abilities, had been promoted to captain. On the 17th he wrote to Gen. Hand of the raid on Tomlinson's Settlement at Grave Creek, and the ensuing pursuit, mentioned in the *Journal* article above. A band of Indians had raided the settlement and gotten away with a number of horses; Lt. Samuel Tomlinson, Joseph's brother, had followed them in canoes down the Ohio for several miles to the mouth of Sunfish Creek on the Ohio shore, where they landed and found the trail. This they followed inland until nightfall, when they came upon the Indians' campfires, but the accidental discharge of one of the men's rifles warned the Indians, who evaporated into the darkness. Having lost the advantage of surprise Tomlinson withdrew his men back to the Grave Creek fort, and sent a messenger to Col. Shepherd, then at Shepherd's Fort. Shepherd ordered now Captain Mason to take his company and pursue the Indians; on the 15th Mason and about fifty men proceeded downriver, and then followed the stream up to the Indians' former camp, but finding that it had been abandoned two days before, it was decided to return to Wheeling. As they slowly paddled back up the Ohio they were suddenly fired upon by a party of Indians concealed along the western shore. The men were eager for a fight; they had come down to kill Indians, and they were not going home empty handed. As soon as they landed a minor skirmish ensued, with as much conversation as shots being exchanged, but the outnumbered Indians soon disengaged. After lying on their arms all night to prevent surprise the men pushed on upriver the next morning, when they suddenly found a number of moccasin tracks heading straight toward Tomlinson's. These they followed, but when they arrived at Grave Creek they found that the tracks were those of Capt. Jesse Pigman and fifteen of his men, who were returning from a scout to the Little Kanawha. Upon his return Mason was appointed commander of Fort Henry, where he was stationed with a company of militia.

Only a month later, about the middle of August, White Eyes, a friendly Delaware chief, informed Gen. Hand that Fort Henry was soon to be attacked by an extremely large party of upwards of 200 Indians, a mixed lot of Wyandot, Shawnee, Delaware, and Mingo. Hand immediately sent warnings to all the county lieutenants, but most important was the message he sent to Col. David Shepherd[28], the county lieutenant of the newly-erected Ohio County. Along with the information concerning the proposed attack on Fort Henry was an order for him to leave Shepherd's fort, six miles from the Ohio, and remove to Fort Henry.

Capt. Samuel Mason was still the nominal commander at Fort Henry, with his company consisting of about thirty men. Shepherd, now running all of Ohio County defenses from Fort Henry, requested reinforcements from Fort Pitt, and Gen. Hand sent down three detachments. They consisted of the companies of Captains Shannon, Marchant, and Leach, but on Thursday, August 28th, Shepherd wrote to inform Hand that he had dismissed the three companies, as there has been no sign of Indians in the vicinity. Privately, Shepherd complained that the soldiers ate too much beef, for nothing.

Capt. Joseph Ogle had been out on a scout with his company of thirty-eight men[29], as far north as Beech Bottom, and they returned the night of August 31st. They reported to the commander that there was no sign of any Indian activity anywhere in the vicinity. But the Indians were more vigilant; they had undoubtedly watched the departure of the three militia companies, and knew that the fort had been weakened. During the night a band of about two hundred Indians set up an ambush in the curve of the creek to the southeast of Wheeling, within an area of cornfields and thick brush which bordered the creek.

About daybreak the next morning, Monday, September 1st, a dense fog from the river overhung the entire area as Andrew Zane, a lad named John Boyd, Sam Tomlinson, and a Negro named Loudon left the fort to look for Dr. James McMechen's horses. McMechen, from Delaware, had decided to leave the settlement and return east. The four men had not gone far when, approaching the crest of the hill (present U.S. 40), they were attacked by a small band of Indians, probably no more than a half dozen. Young Johnny Boyd was run down and tomahawked. Zane ran back toward the fort, and was nearly cut off by more Indians, but he escaped by jumping over the edge of the bluff and reached the fort, as did Tomlinson and Loudon. As they entered the fort yelling "Indians! Indians!" Col. Shepherd, not realizing the size of the war party, ordered Mason out to reconnoiter. Mason took twelve or fourteen volunteers and headed up the hill; there they found a plainly marked trail, purposely left by the Indians who had returned to the site of the ambush. The trail followed the hill down to the creek, then curved around to the right, back toward the mouth of the creek. As Mason and his men approached the cornfields which bordered the creek, one of the men marching next to Mason saw an Indian off to his left; giving a yell and firing, he saw the Indian fall. But Mason had blundered into a well-designed Indian ambush; the men were completely surrounded and cut off. Mason and his sergeant, a man named Steel, slightly separated from the others, encountered two Indians at point-blank range. All four fired at the same moment; both Indians fell, so did Steel, mortally wounded, while Mason received a wound in the hand. Providentially finding a downed tree nearby, along the banks of Wheeling Creek, Mason hid himself in the leafy branches of the top. After remaining in hiding during the remainder of the day, he escaped up the creek to Shepherd's fort after darkness had fallen. Another of Mason's men, John Caldwell, turned and headed back up the hill, chased by an Indian who threw a tomahawk, but missed. Caldwell also managed to reach Shepherd's fort, unharmed. Of the entire party who had gone out, all were killed except Mason and Caldwell.

Hearing the sudden burst of gunfire coming from the vicinity of the creek, the men in the fort now realized that there was more than just the handful of Indians that Zane and the others had seen. Because of the fog they were unable to see what was happening, but Capt. Ogle led out a relief party of another dozen or so men, including his brother Jacob, to the rescue of Mason. No sooner had they approached the scene of the action than they were enveloped by the Indians as well. Three of his men, together, made a dash back to the fort; William Shepherd, the oldest son of Col. Shepherd, Thomas Glenn, and Hugh McConnell. Shepherd was only nineteen, and as he raced toward the fort, his foot was caught by a grapevine. He stumbled, and before he could recover the Indians were upon him with their tomahawks. Tom Glenn was chased up the river a short distance before he too was overtaken and scalped. McConnell made it to the fort, where he then had the unpleasant task of telling his little sister Rebecca that she had been made a widow; her husband, Will Shepherd, had been cut down by the Indians, leaving her and her newborn child. A half dozen more of the militia reached the fort, although some were wounded, one of them so seriously that he died the next day.

After fierce fighting Ogle escaped to the cornfield with one of his wounded men, and together they managed to gain the fort that night, where he learned that three or four of his men had been killed, five were wounded, and four others had escaped. Altogether fifteen men had been killed[30], one lieutenant and fourteen men; five more, including Capt. Mason, had been wounded, and five privates had escaped, among them John Caldwell, the only other man of Mason's command who was not killed. Of the fifteen killed the loss was especially great for Col. Shepherd; he had lost both his oldest son and a son-in-law. The lieutenant mentioned here as the officer killed had only recently come up from the Grave Creek settlement; the morning of that very day he had gone out with Andrew Zane and tripped the Indian ambush. Never lacking in courage, Lt. Samuel Tomlinson, who six weeks earlier had preceded Mason in leading a party of men up Sunfish Creek in pursuit of Indian horse thieves, had ventured out again with Ogle's party, but his luck had run out.

Within minutes of the time that Ogle's men were reaching the safety of the fort, a small body of horsemen arrived on the scene. Francis Duke[31], deputy commissary for Ohio County, had arrived at the head of a relief party from Beech Bottom fort. But upon seeing the horde of Indians milling about, they realized that their chances of reaching the fort were infinitesimal. All but Duke, who was twenty-six years old and determined to help the defenders; the others were unable to dissuade him from making the attempt. Charging for the gate at full speed he made it to within 75 yards before he was shot from the saddle. There he lay, in the heat of the late summer sun and in the dust of the road, throughout the remainder of the day, in full sight of those within the fort; too far away for anyone to venture out to retrieve him, and too close to the fort for the Indians to molest him. Until after dark, when they dragged his body into one of the cabins, stripped him, and took his scalp.

At about the same time that Duke was killed another horseman appeared on the crest of the hill overlooking the settlement, on the Fort Pitt road[32]. Major Samuel McColloch, commander of Van Meter's fort on Short Creek, also attempted to reach the fort, but after descending a short distance and finding his way blocked he wheeled his horse and began to backtrack. Just as he reached the crest of the hill he ran into another party of Indians who had been out searching for survivors of the Mason-Ogle disaster. In back and in front were Indians, too many to force his way through; on his left rose a precipitous cliff, straight up. On his right was nothingness; the cliff dropped off almost vertically for nearly three hundred feet. Realizing he was bounded on all sides, the major made a split-second decision; his choices were to be captured by the Indians, or to go over the cliff. Better to die quickly in the plunge down to the creek than to die slowly at the hands of the Indians. Over the cliff he

finally received the reward adequate to his merit which the *Maryland Journal* had prophesied for him.

A large group of men gathered around to gawk at the infamous head with its one protruding tooth, like a wolf's fang, and to admire the returning heroes. Setton and May related how they had found Mason and, as he was sitting on a log, one of them stepped up behind him and sank a tomahawk in his brain. After hacking off the head they rolled it in clay to prevent its putrefaction before they could return and claim the reward. But as the affidavit for the reward was being filled out, one of the men in the crowd suddenly pointed to John Setton and blurted out: "Why, that man's **Wiley Harpe**!".

Although Setton vehemently denied it, the truth was soon proved by various marks and scars on his body. He and May were lodged in the Natchez jail, and almost immediately escaped. Soon thereafter they were recaptured and taken to Greenville, where on February 4th Wiley Harpe, a.k.a. Little Harpe, alias John Setton —

"... who has been found guilty of robbery at the present term was this day set to the bar and the sentence of the court pronounced upon him as follows, that on Wednesday the eighth day of the present month he be taken to the place of execution and there to be hung up by the neck, between the hours of ten o'clock in the forenoon and four in the afternoon, until he is dead, dead, dead!"

On January 8, 1804, at a little after noon, Harpe and May were taken to the Gallows Field, about a quarter-mile north of Greenville, and there they were executed as the court had directed. After the bodies were cut down both were beheaded and, as had been his brother's fate, Wiley's head was placed on the stub of a nearby tree limb, keeping company in death with the head of James May.

# Chapter XII

The Foreman Massacre,
and the Death of Cornstalk

Extract of a letter from David Zeisberger, Goschachgunk, to General Edward Hand, Fort Pitt:

*September 22, 1777*

*At present we know that 40 of the Wiondots are gone it is said to Weelunk of any more that are out we know not.*

\*     \*     \*

The double ambush at Fort Henry, with the loss of so many defenders of the frontier, had discouraged the settlers, many of whom decided to return to the relative safety of the east. There were others who would have left, but for the shortage of horses, many of them stolen by Indians. But the attack on Fort Henry was only the first of a double calamity, and bad as it was, worse was yet to come.

Three weeks later smoke was reported from Tomlinson's settlement on Grave Creek[36], and in spite of Zeisberger's warning, on the 27th another party from Fort Henry set out to investigate, under Captain William Foreman, who had recently arrived from Hampshire County. Col. Shepherd advised against the expedition, but after three weeks of inactivity the men were tired of being cooped up in the fort, and Shepherd finally consented. Foreman's command consisted of forty-six men in three companies: Foreman with twenty-four, Capt. Joseph Ogle with ten, and Capt. William Linn (Lynn) with nine. Foreman was an unfortunate choice to command. Not only was he totally inexperienced in Indian warfare, but he refused to take the advice of those who were.

The intention was that they would investigate at Tomlinson's, then cross the river, descend as far as Captina, Island and Creek, eight miles further down the river, while looking for Indian sign on the Ohio side. At Grave Creek they found that Tomlinson's settlement had been abandoned and the buildings burned, but unable to find any canoes, they decided to forego crossing the river, and to return to Wheeling the next morning. During the night Linn and his scouts, among them Martin Wetzel, heard noises coming from the river above, and suspecting that Indians were crossing above them, Linn hastily advised Foreman that an ambush was being prepared for them; the only safe route back to Wheeling, he advised, was to leave the river trail and return along the sides of the hills, away from the river. But instead of listening to the experienced frontiersman, Foreman became angry; he had no intention of taking orders from an illiterate backwoodsman. Scoffing at the idea that there might be Indians about, he ignored the advice and marched back along the same direct route down which he had come the day before, with Ogle's men following along. They had been at Fort Henry and they, at least, should have known better. Linn knew better, and so did the nine men of his command who accompanied him; they skirted the trail to the right, following along just below the crest of the hill.

About four miles north of the Creek, at a point known as the Narrows, or McMechen's Narrows, those *forty of the Wiondots* who *are gone it is said to*

*Weelunk,* led by their chief, Half King, lay in wait. They had taken up a position on the northern edge of a large sinkhole, on the hillside overlooking a small stream which formed the border of the northern edge of the depression. The militia would have to pass along and through this sinkhole if they remained on the trail, then cross that small stream before beginning to ascend the next hill, the hill containing the Indian ambush. Just as they reached the stream a volley of shots from the Indians on the hillside above downed those in the lead, including Foreman and his son, Hamilton, and Joseph Ogle's brother, Jacob[37]. But Linn's party, hearing the sound of gunfire ahead and off to their left, hurried on and approached the scene yelling loudly, as they fired a few shots in the general direction of the Wyandots. They managed only to disrupt the ambush and pull one man, who had been shot through the thigh, breaking the bone, to a safe hiding place.

The loss to Foreman's and Ogle's party was great enough, but it would have been much worse if Linn had not intervened. The Indians, believing themselves outflanked, began to withdraw from the Narrows although, not being pursued, they soon returned to scalp and mutilate the men who had fallen. Of the thirty-six men who were ambushed, only fifteen managed to escape[38]. Four days later, after reinforcements under Major James Chew had arrived at Wheeling from Pitt, he and Col. Shepherd led a relief party to bury the dead; they found the badly-mangled remains of twenty-one men, and Martin Wetzel later stated that this was one of the most disagreeable jobs he had ever undertaken.

On October 3rd Col. Shepherd wrote to General Hand that he had given permission for the scout downriver only after being convinced that:

*... their party was Sufficient for any Scouting party of Indians they might fall in with as it was hardly to be Supposed, that Forty Six of our best Riffle Men well Equipt Should be Over power by Numbers of Indians.*

On the same date Major Chew reported to Hand:

*Since my arrival Col. Shepherd and myself marched & Buried those Unfortunate Men, in the late Action a moving sight. Twenty One Brave fellows, cruelly Butcher'd, Even after Death.*

In 1835 a marker was placed along the river near the site of the action, which read:

*This humble stone is erected to the memory of Captain Foreman and twenty-one of his brave men, who were slain by a band of ruthless savages — the allies of a civilized nation of Europe — on the 26th of Sep. 1777.*

> *"So sleep the brave who sink to rest,*
> *By all their country's wishes blest."*

Due to erosion caused by river flooding, however, the men were re-interred in 1875 and, along with the marker, were moved to the Mt. Rose cemetery in Moundsville, where the marker may still be seen today, just inside the cemetery gates. The following inscription was added at that time:

*This monument was originally erected above the Narrows on the Ohio River,*

*four miles above Moundsville, on the grounds where the fatal action occurred, and
with the remains of Captain Foreman and his fallen, placed here June 1st, 1875.*

A new marker has been placed along the highway by the Daughters of the
American Revolution, just a short distance west of the actual site of the ambush.

*　　*　　*

## *The Murder of Cornstalk*

The last important event to occur in this bloody year was an act of pure
vengeance, and if it had not been clear to all parties before that this was to be a war
of extermination, it was made so now. The roots of this tragedy lay nearly twenty
years in the past, in Augusta (now Rockbridge) County Virginia. It was here, on
October 10, 1759, that the Gilmore family had been slain by Indians; John Gilmore,
his wife, his son Thomas, and the wife of William Gilmore. Thomas's wife and his
three children, one of them a boy named Robert, were abducted, but a rapid pursuit enabled the men to overtake the war party of Shawnees, who were led by none
other than Cornstalk. The widowed Mrs. Gilmore and her three children were rescued and returned safely to their home.

Fifteen years later this same Cornstalk had led his Shawnee warriors against
Andrew Lewis' force at Point Pleasant, and now, in this first week of November,
1777, Cornstalk had come with two companions to Fort Randolph, the newly built
fort which had replaced Fort Blair at Point Pleasant. He had come to inform the
commander, Capt. Matthew Arbuckle that, in spite of the Treaty of Pittsburgh two
years earlier, the Shawnee had declared for war on the side of the English. He himself, Cornstalk continued, was opposed to the war, but since it was a tribal decision
he could not now oppose it, and he would have to go with the tide. Still, he felt it
his duty to come to the commander and advise him of the Shawnee decision.

Upon hearing that, Arbuckle decided it would be best to detain the three
Indians as hostages. On November 7th he wrote to his superior, Gen. Hand at Fort
Pitt, to say that he had detained the Shawnee chief and the other two, a young warrior called Red Hawk and a one-eyed Indian familiarly known as Old Yie. Since
Cornstalk did not return within a reasonable amount of time his son, Elinipisco, who
had fought here alongside his father three years ago, came across the river to inquire
about his father[39]. He too was placed in custody along with the others.

On the following day, two of the young men stationed at Fort Randolph crossed
the Kanawha to hunt for deer, against orders, of course, and one of them would pay
for his disobedience. It was his misfortune that they chose to return along a path
already selected by a small band of Shawnee who had secreted themselves on a
nearby hillside to spy out the fort. As the two men passed along the path below
them, the Indians opened fire. One of them, named Hamilton, was unharmed; he
fled across the river, yelling that his companion had been killed. That unfortunate
was a member of Capt. John Hall's company which had only recently come west

from Augusta County to participate in Hand's proposed expedition. The firing attracted the attention of those in the fort, and at the sight of Hamilton, several of Hall's men jumped into a canoe to retrieve the scalped and bloody body of their companion-in-arms, Ensign Robert Gilmore; he would have no more unhappy experiences with Cornstalk's Shawnee warriors.

Immediately upon landing with his corpse, an armed mob of men approached the fort, screaming that the Shawnee who had killed Gilmore had been brought there by Elinipisco. Arbuckle and Capt. John Stuart met them at the gate and tried to dissuade them, but they were powerless to stop the infuriated men. As a number of men rushed into the room Cornstalk calmly arose, telling his son and comrades that if they were to die they should die as men. It was his last speech, immediately he received a half dozen or more rifle balls in his body. Elinipisco, Red Hawk, and Old Yie died in the next few seconds.

*   *   *

If the settlers had been disheartened by the events at Fort Henry, they were totally discouraged now. Following the dual tragedies at Fort Henry and the Narrows all the smaller settlements along the Ohio broke up; the constant threat of Indian attack, combined with the loss of so many men in the double massacre had been too much for those isolated families. David Shepherd left his fort at the forks of Wheeling and moved with his family the six miles to Fort Henry; John Wetzel and Lewis Bonnett took their families to the supposed safety of Dunkard Creek, where John Wetzel, Jr., had been born seven years before. Of those latter two families only Martin Wetzel remained behind, as part of the militia at Fort Henry.

But they were to find no safety there; if anything the Indians ravaged those settlements worse than they had Wheeling Creek. In late March, 1778, three major and separate attacks took place on the Dunkard Creek settlements; by the end of the month they had been wholly evacuated.

## *Fourth Interlude: The Will of the American Pioneer*

These are a few of the better-known events of that year of the bloody sevens, but they are only a few. The majority of such fearful happenings of this year, and of all the other years along the frontier, were unrecorded. Dead men tell no tales, nor do dead women or dead children, and as Dale Van Every wrote of that horrible year:

*The 1777 siege of Wheeling and its accompanying double massacre gained a place in contemporary records on account of the number of casualties at one place and time. Of the many lesser attacks then and later most escaped such notice. There remain passing references in the correspondence of Hand and the commanders who succeeded him to some of them. Private letters, family legends, occasional contemporary items in eastern newspapers offer scraps and bits of information about others. Reports and rumors circulated by word of mouth exaggerated some episodes while overlooking others. Their number and similarity often made accounts seem merely repetitive. John Hayward, the tireless compiler of border annals, was able later to assemble a list of more than 400 separate attacks on the southern frontier alone. The Draper Collection and evidence accumulated in many university and historical society libraries have served to recover traces and hints of many others in every region. But most of the raids from July to November of this year, as in every other year of the Revolution's border war, remained unrecorded, the identities of the men, women, and children who perished unknown. The confusion of the times, the extreme isolation of most habitations, the circumstance that many families had so recently arrived that they were still strangers in their neighborhoods, the fact that all too often there had been no survivors to tell the story, the very multiplicity of horrors which made no one instance worth wide comment left most such local tragedies a presently forgotten mystery. Sooner or later a militia patrol ranging an area for Indian sign came upon another burned cabin. If there were bodies these were buried. If not there was often little clear indication whether the family had been carried off as captives or had fled in time.*

*Yet it was the sum total of these unrecorded family-size disasters and the readiness of other families to continue to brave the constant threat of a similar fate that was to decide the issue of the revolution in the west. It was upon these bewildered and distraught families that ultimate victory or defeat entirely depended. The major Indian purpose was to make the settlers' existence unbearable in order to compel them to retreat back over the mountains. With this the English pupose coincided, chiefly on account of the added hope that the ensuing opportunity to spread the Indian terror east of the mountains might disrupt the main rebel war effort on the seaboard. Success for either objective depended upon breaking the will of the settlers and their families to stand their ground. In striving to achieve this result the primary weapon was the Indian raid.*[40]

Success depended upon breaking the will of the settlers and their families to stand their ground. In the final analysis the English and Indian purpose was a failure; the will of the settlers to stand their ground could not be broken, no matter how horrific the Indian raids might become. Many settlers did give up, some of them before they got so far even as the western border; others gave up almost immediately upon arrival, while yet others after only such a long and bitter struggle that they could stand it no more. But for every pioneer family who left there was always another to take its place.

Little wonder that they left. It was year after year of nearly unendurable anxiety. In one aspect of the war the Indians were eminently successful; they imposed a mental anguish for years which was more nearly unbearable than that faced by any other group of humans in history. Many an "Indian alarm" in a small settlement occurred in the nighttime hours. Without warning a sudden piercing scream awakens the community, followed by confused shouting and the call to arms, only to have it all end as suddenly as it had begun. It was nothing more than a young woman having a nightmare, her home attacked by savages, her babies being butchered. These nightmares were such a common occurrence that they were scarcely remarked upon, nor were the dreamers chastised. The terrible dreams seemed so real, because they were based on actual, almost everyday, events.

And sometimes the dream was real, but no one would listen. In the spring of 1781 many of the residents in the Crooked Run area of Monongalia County, (West) Virginia, had forted at Harrison's Fort. One of them, Tom Pindall, asked three young men, named Crawford, Harrison, and Wright, to accompany him, his wife, and his sister, Rachel, to his farm to spend the night. They had not been asleep long when the men were awakened by the two females, who claimed that they had heard strange noises outside, like the whistling of a stallion. The men had heard nothing and, calming the women by telling them that it was nothing more than the howling of the wind, they all went to sleep.

Early the next morning, reassured by the fact that nothing had happened in the nighttime, Pindall went into the woods to catch a horse, while the three young men went to the nearby spring to wash. As they were thus engaged three guns were fired at them by Indians from close range; Crawford and Wright were killed, but Harrison escaped to the fort. The two women, who were still inside the cabin when they heard the shots, ran toward the fort, but were pursued by Indians, who overtook and killed Mrs. Pindall, although Rachel also managed to reach the fort.

Little wonder, then, that men like the Wetzels, the Zanes, and the McCollochs, Crawford and Brady and Kenton and Boone, were esteemed by their compatriots. And these, their recorded exploits, are only the meager few of which we have an account, the thousands of other murders and abductions during those savage years will remain forever unknown, because *all too often there had been no survivors to tell the story. The very multiplicity of horrors ... made no one instance worth wide comment.*

# Chapter XIII

## Boone - III

One of the necessities of life on the frontier was salt; it was vital for curing meat, which would otherwise spoil, and it was also used for curing hides. Fortunately for the Kentucky stations there was salt in abundance, although it was underground, remnants of huge prehistoric seas; it was merely a matter of producing it. In early January, 1778, Boone loaded up the pack-horses with the station's enormous iron salt kettles which had been brought out by Col. Bowman the previous summer, a generous gift of the Virginia Legislature. Leading a party of about 30 men, he headed for one of the licks to make the year's supply of salt. They traveled about fifty miles to one of the best locations, this one called the *Blue Licks*, near Limestone (present Maysville, Kentucky). All the salt licks were well-known spots along the forest trails; they were favored hunting sites, as the animals would come from miles around to lick the salty earth. But salt-making was a laborious process; trees had to be felled and then cut into firewood to keep the fires going 'round the clock, and the kettles had to be kept filled as they boiled. Finally, after thousands of gallons of water had been boiled down, a few bushels of salt could be scraped from the inside of the kettles, placed in bags, loaded on horses, and a few men would transport it back to the station. For those who remained in camp the process continued unceasingly.

And while the men worked, someone had to provide them with food. This was Boone's job, as he was acknowledged as one of the best hunters. They always kept out three hunter-scouts, Boone going alone in one direction, while Flanders Callaway, his son-in-law, with a companion, Thomas Brooks, went the other. For salt making was not only hard work, it was also extremely dangerous work. The Indians knew quite as much about the salt licks as did the pioneers. Thus the reason for the journey to the licks in the dead of winter; it was hoped that no Indian war parties would be out this early in the season, as the warriors would be too busy trying to find enough food to keep their families from starving. The full moon of February is known as the *Hunger Moon*, for good reason; among the Indians it was as often referred to as the *Starving Moon*.

But with the outbreak of a rebellion in the North American colonies, and a declaration of their independence, the British government enlisted the Indians as allies, despite the best efforts of the new American government to keep them neutral, if nothing more. Supplies, mainly food, gunpowder, and lead, were furnished to the Indians by the British, and this enabled the Indians to carry on their war with the pioneers without spending every waking moment providing for their families. And carry on the war they did.

Boone's party had been at the licks nearly a month, and they had made several hundred bushels of salt, about half of it already sent back to Boonesborough. On the 8th of February Boone, Callaway, and Brooks left camp, Daniel heading southwest, and making a wide circuit to find enough meat to feed the men. It was a bad day, snow falling intermittently, sometimes blindingly, not a good day for hunting. Finally he succeeded in killing a buffalo, and after butchering it and loading a couple hundred pounds of meat on his horse, he turned and headed back to camp. But before proceeding far that strange sixth sense which all great woodsmen have impelled him to turn around; not thirty yards behind him were four Shawnee warriors, and most surprising of all was that they were painted for war. This was no hunting party.

Boone abandoned the horse and meat, and took to his heels. But the Shawnee were young warriors, and Boone, in excellent condition but in his mid-forties, was no match for them. After running half a mile or more, they were close enough to fire at him, and Boone surrendered. He was quickly led back to the Indian encampment, where to his absolute astonishment he beheld a war party of a hundred twenty warriors and two French-Canadian trappers, led by Blackfish himself. They had come down from their village on the Little Miami, and they were headed straight for Boonesborough. Their scouts had already found the salt-makers at the Blue Licks, and there was to be a slight diversion while the Indians surrounded the camp and killed all the men there. Then on to Boonesborough which, totally surprised and poorly defended, would fall easily, especially as the stockade wall had never been completed. Then a forced march of the captives, through winter weather, back to the Shawnee towns. The women and children would suffer most, and many of them would never make it. Hunting for food was hard enough in the winter; did Blackfish have enough food for all his warriors, and all his prisoners, too, on the way back to their town, Boone asked?

But, he then told Blackfish, the men at the Licks will surely resist, and some of your men may be killed. Besides, the people of Boonesborough have had enough; because of your destruction of their corn fields the previous summer they are near starving, and are ready to join the British. If you will promise not to harm them, he continued, I will talk the men here into surrendering, and we will willingly go with you back to your villages. Then, in the spring, after the weather improves, we can come back down to Boonesborough, where the people will be glad to give up without firing a shot.

It was a part of Indian strategy never to risk life if an advantage could be gained without hazard. And besides, the British had been telling the Indians for the past year that, sooner or later, the frontier people would have had enough and, in despair, would depart. Boone was persuasive; here were thirty white men who could be taken prisoner without firing a shot. Then, the next spring, if their own leader, the great Boone himself, advised his people to surrender, they would surely agree.

Thus it was a short time later that from the forest came the voice of Boone, calling out to his men that they were surrounded by a large war party, but if they would lay down their arms they would not be harmed. Fortunately the men had the good sense to trust their captain, and so on February 18th Blackfish led his warriors back into Old Chillicothe[41], with twenty-eight prisoners in tow, without having fired a shot, and without having any of his warriors as much as wounded.

But, all unseen and unsuspected, something else had accompanied those twenty-eight men who were taken captive. It was as invisible as a ghost, and the name of this ghost was Knowledge, and the Shawnee did not comprehend its power. It was the knowledge of the locations and strengths of the Shawnee villages. Prior to this time it was known in only the vaguest sense where the Indian towns lay, but once the Indians had decided to return home, these twenty-eight men were led in a bee-line to the most important of all the villages. Were any of these men, frontiersmen all, to escape and return to their homes in Kentucky, the next most obvious step would be for them to lead an army back across the river, heading straight as an arrow for the Indian towns.

It was the worst mistake the Indians ever made. Of course the Indians could easily retreat, and often they did, but they could not retreat their hundreds of acres of crops with them. Those had to remain, at the mercy of the men who knew well enough that if they destroyed the Indians' *Three Sisters*, maize and beans and squash, the Indians would be forced to spend the winter with their English masters.

A dozen or more of the captives were adopted into Indian families to replace fallen braves. Boone himself, his leadership qualities evident, was adopted into the family of Blackfish, and for the same reason. Ironically enough, it was Boone who had led the men who rescued Jemima, and one of those men, perhaps even Boone, had fired the shot that killed Blackfish's son. True to his word, Blackfish did not allow torture or death to befall any of the Boonesborough men.

A month later Blackfish and forty Shawnee started for Detroit, with Boone and a number of captives in tow, those whom they did not want to adopt. Boone was taken to be interrogated about the Kentucky defenses, the captives would be sold to the British; from Detroit they stood a good chance of eventually returning home. Better, at least, than if they had remained with the Indians.

Lieutenant-Governor Henry Hamilton interviewed Boone, and was as impressed with him as had been the Indians. His intention was to buy Boone, parole him, and allow him to return home, a fairly common policy regarding officers. He offered Blackfish a hundred pounds, sterling, for him, at that time the equivalent of five hundred dollars, indeed a princely sum. Blackfish instantly refused; the British could do what they wished with the other prisoners, but Boone was not for sale. Ten days later they left Detroit, with Boone the only white man, and returned home. They took a roundabout course, visiting various Shawnee, Wyandot, Delaware, and Mingo towns, Blackfish wanting to advise them of the proposed expedition to Boonesborough in the spring.

Apparently well contented with life as an Indian, Boone became a great favorite. In early June he was taken to one of the salt licks on the Scioto, and it was there, while helping the Indians make salt, that a defeated war party returned from Donnally's Fort on the Greenbriar and Fort Randolph at Point Pleasant. The move toward Kentucky could not be postponed any longer, and Blackfish probably intended to use Boone, now known as *Sheltowee*, Big Turtle, as negotiator and interpreter. If Boone was to escape, now was the best time. Out in a hunting camp, on the morning of June 16th, and while the men were gone hunting turkeys, Boone calmly mounted his horse and rode out of camp. When the hunters returned and looked around, Sheltowee was nowhere to be found. He had left for home.

His journey through the wilderness was a marvel of endurance and woodcraft, but when he arrived at Boonesborough it was only to face another disappointment. Becky, after no word had come for three months, had given up hope; she had packed up and returned to the Bryans in North Carolina. Daniel's first thought was to go after her, but Kentucky needed Boone, and he could not leave, not now. With Boone's defection, the Indians would arrive soon, perhaps in a few days, and the fort was in no condition to repel an attack. The difficulty was always in getting the men to build the fort, and then keeping their defenses in good repair, when it was far more important to them to spend their time staking claims to the best land they could find.

Boone got the men started repairing the fort, and not long after Simon Kenton arrived with the joyous news of the conquest of the Illinois country by George Rogers Clark. But all was quiet now; no Indians appeared, and the scouts who were sent out could find no sign. Had they given up? Then on July 17th William Hancock, another of the saltmakers, straggled into the clearing on the far side of the Kentucky River. He was a poor woodsman, and it had taken him nine days to make the journey that Daniel had made in five, and he was almost dead on his feet, but in spite of his appearance he brought important news. Boone's escape had caused the Shawnee to postpone their attack for three weeks, and although nine days of that were gone by, there was still time to prepare for the attack.

Still nothing happened. Six more weeks dragged by since Boone had arrived. Each day they expected to see a scout come running in with news that the Indians were close at hand. So it was time to take the offensive, and Boone was the man. He led out a band of thirty men on a reconnaissance in force to the Indian towns, although a third of the men soon developed cold feet and returned. Boone went forward, and with him were Kenton and Alexander Montgomery, great woodsmen in their own right. They found several small groups of Indians, fought a few skirmishes, gained the information they needed, and returned home, although at one point they had to carefully edge their way around Blackfish's warriors, heading for Kentucky. But they all arrived safely back at the fort, and about ten o'clock the next morning so did the Indians; it was September 7, 1778, and the Indians meant business, all four hundred fifty of them.

They were mostly Shawnee, led once more by Blackfish, and with French-Canadian Lieutenant De Quindre as aide, but there were also Wyandot and Ottawa. The other chiefs were Black Hoof, the aged and highly respected Moluntha, and Blackbird, a Chippewa. They did not even bother to hide their presence; after all, they had come only to escort the Kentuckians back across the Ohio, then home. The Negro interpreter Pompey, waving a flag of truce, hailed the fort and asked for Boone. Going out for a parley with Blackfish, Sheltowee sadly informed his foster-father that while he had been living with his friends on the Little Miami, the great Virginia father had sent out another man to replace him, and so Boone was, unfortunately, no longer in charge.

Returning to the fort, he had William Bailey Smith quickly don his full-dress major's uniform, then with the resplendent Smith strutting at his side, he returned to the conference. The Indians were duly impressed, as they always were, with a glittering uniform. Obviously this was the man with whom they would now have to deal, and it was obvious that Smith was by no means as eager to surrender as Boone had surely been.

For three days they negotiated; eight or ten men from the fort taking part, with twice that many Indians. Finally Squire Boone let it slip, accidentally on purpose, that they had bought this land from the Cherokee. Turning to one of the Cherokee warriors nearby, Blackfish demanded to know if that were true. Upon being assured that it was, Blackfish seemed to be taken aback. In that case, he said, it was only right that the white men should remain here. They would now proceed to draw up a treaty to which all parties would make their marks, and which would show the Ohio River to be the dividing line between white and red man, then the Indians would depart. It all sounded almost too good to be true. But paper and quill were obtained, the requisite articles were drawn up, and all signed.

Now, added Blackfish, there was but one small ceremony, the very smallest of details to attend to, before the Indians could go home. It was their custom, he explained, that whenever a treaty was signed, each participant should catch each other by the shoulders and bring their hearts together, to show that this was to be a true and lasting peace. However, since there were twice as many Indians as whites, the only proper way to do this would be for each white man to embrace two Indians, simultaneously. Understandably suspicious, the Kentuckians reluctantly agreed; after all, there was little else they could do. Blackfish calmly approached Boone and locked an arm in his, while another brave took Boone's other arm. A sudden shout from Blackfish, a shot fired by one of the Indians in hiding as a signal, and now began an unequal tug of war, two against one. Shots began to come from the walls of the fort, as the Indians attempted to drag the white men toward the woodline. But it was Daniel Boone, as always, who saved the day; pulling his arm free a mighty blow sent the Shawnee chief to the ground, stunned. The other Indians, thinking he had been killed, were dismayed, and this brief respite gave the former negotiators all the time they needed to pull free and race for the fort. They waved their hats wildly as they ran, the agreed-upon signal for treachery, and the walls blazed with rifle fire. Squire Boone took an Indian's bullet in the shoulder that knocked him down, but he was up again in an instant and made the fort, as did all the others, unharmed.

For the next few days the sniping went on, but the attackers had brought no cannon, and without artillery it was nigh impossible to reduce a fort, even a wooden fort made without nails. Once they tried the old trick of loudly packing up and withdrawing, making as much noise as possible as they filed away through the forest. Then silence, absolute. But these were Kentucky frontiersmen inside the fort, and not even the most gullible among them was fooled for the fraction of a moment. Silence prevailed for several hours, but then the Indians, seeing that the men inside the walls had no intention of coming out, suddenly began again their relentless shooting at the walls. On the seventh night the Indians scattered flax along a fence and set it afire, hoping it would connect to the fort and ignite the palisade wall. The

Kentuckians calmly tore down the fence where it touched the fort.

Now was the time come for siege warfare, introduced by the French commander, De Quindre. The Indians began digging a tunnel from the bank of the river to the wall of the fort. When it was completed the Indians would pour into the fort and slaughter the badly-outnumbered defenders. For two days they kept at it, coming closer and closer; then the rains came. When daylight of the tenth day dawned, it brought an unexpected sight. The Indians were gone. Not deceptively, but really and truly gone. No one could understand, until suddenly, in the growing light, one of the men yelled and pointed in the direction of the tunnel. Now they could all see, the heavy rains during the night had caved in the unsupported tunnel, and the attackers, discouraged at what they had initially thought would be an easy conquest, had decided to try elsewhere.

*   *   *

But Boone had played his role too well; he had surrendered the saltmakers, he had appeared to his fellow captives to be well content with Indian life, he had engaged in secret talks with the despised Hair-Buyer Hamilton, and he had talked of surrendering the fort to the Indians. Many of his own friends and neighbors in Boonesborough were openly suspicious, if not outright hostile. It was no help that Rebecca had returned to the Bryans, as many of her family were known Tories. Charges were filed against Boone by the ever-jealous Col. Callaway, Jemima's father-in-law, and Boone was court-martialed for treason. Most of the testimony directly affecting Boone came from two of the captured salt-makers who had escaped, little Andy Johnson and Will Hancock. Both had been dismayed at Boone's cheerfulness in the Indian village, while they themselves were so miserable, and Hancock had been with Boone at Detroit. There he had seen with his own eyes as Boone negotiated the surrender of Kentucky with Hamilton.

The charges were ridiculous, of course; treason is seldom plotted in so public a manner. Boone's concept of strategy was so far above the others that they were incapable of comprehending it, even when it was explained to them. As soon as the testimony was finished, the officers of the court withdrew to deliberate, but they were quickly back. Boone was not only acquitted of all charges, but he was at the same time rewarded by being promoted to major. It was not merely an exoneration, it was a vindication of every single action that Boone had performed.

As soon as the verdict was in Daniel was off to fetch Becky; he found her living near her brother, Will Bryan, who had married Daniel's sister, Mary. All the rest of that winter of 1778-1779, and on into the summer of 1779 they remained there. Daniel was eager to get back to Kentucky, but his former friends and neighbors at Boonesborough had suspected him of Toryism; some of his friends had been killed by Indians, allies of the British and the Torys, and he would not forget that he had been court-martialed for treason, nor would he return to Boonesborough.

# Chapter XIV

*F*urther Adventures of the Wetzels:
Martin Wetzel

This was life for the frontiersman on the western border throughout 1778 and 1779; you tried to raise your crops in order to feed your family, and you fought the Indians. If you were one of the lucky and/or accomplished ones, like Boone or Kenton, you managed to do both. If you were killed your widow would marry again, and perhaps again, if necessary. After Michael Cresap died in October of 1775, the Widow Cresap married Col. David Rogers. Four years later Rogers was killed by Simon Girty, and the Widow Rogers married the Reverend John Jacob.

If you avoided being killed by Indians, it was likely that you would be taken captive by them. If you were taken captive the best you could hope for was to be ransomed; escape from an Indian town was nearly impossible. If caught while attempting an escape your death was certain. In 1777 the third and fourth youngest of the five Wetzel boys had been abducted, but had, with daring and cleverness, escaped before their captors could convey them to their distant village. The next year it was the oldest brother's turn.

In April, 1778, Martin Wetzel and John Wolf were out on a scouting expedition when they suddenly ran into a Shawnee war party; Wolf was panic-stricken, and although Martin took to his heels, yelling at the same time for Wolf to do the same, the latter, obviously petrified, stood still and allowed himself to be taken. Martin was chased by five braves, who fired at him, one shot grazing his hip, another his shoulder, but this served only to spur him on. Coming to a small stream he leapt across, and landing on the other side was dismayed as two Indians lying in wait rose up from the underbrush bordering the creek and fired at almost point-blank range; both missed. Martin ran on, outdistancing his pursuers, and just as he was beginning to hope that he might escape, suddenly he came to a narrow but deep ravine; landing somewhat awkwardly on the other side, his foot slipped and he fell into the gorge, and, slightly stunned, he was also captured. The two young men were led to one of the Shawnee towns; Wolf unwisely continued to bemoan his fate, which behavior was certain to bring down upon him the worst that the Indians could offer. Over and over he said that if Martin should escape, he should tell Wolf's family what had become of him. Martin, on the other hand, acted in the opposite manner, as Boone had, as if nothing could please him more than becoming an Indian prisoner. The expected occurred, and after suffering the usual indignities, John Wolf was burned at the stake. Martin, however, was adopted into an Indian family, and for nearly three years he played the part of a happy Indian captive to perfection.

Finally, in January, 1781, a horse-stealing expedition was planned into Kentucky, and Martin, having allayed all the Indians' suspicions, was at last permitted to go along. His escape from captivity into Kentucky has been dramatized by numerous writers who have delighted in showing the vengeful spirit of the Wetzels, as Martin calmly and separately stalks his three victims, then shoots or tomahawks them from behind before escaping to one of the white settlements.

The tale of his marvelous exploit and his arrival in Kentucky with the scalps of the three Indians was first given wide circulation by Col. John McDonald, who wrote accounts of the Wetzels and Simon Kenton for a Cincinnati newspaper[42] in the mid-1830s. According to McDonald, the smile on Martin Wetzel's face contrasted starkly with the hatred that had burned in his heart ever since the day of his capture, but finally his golden opportunity arrived.

The story of his escape is so typical of McDonald's vivid imagination, including even Martin's thought processes and rationale, that the central portion of it is given here. Having been taken by the Indians —

*... by his cheerful disposition, and apparent satisfaction with their mode and manner of life, he disarmed their suspicion, and acquired their confidence, and was adopted into one of their families. How much his duplicity overreached the credulity of those sons of the forest, the sequel will show....*

Three Indians then take him, innocently enough, on a hunting trip.

*While hunting one evening some distance from the camp, he came across one of his Indian camp mates. The Indian not being apprised that revenge was corroding in Wetzel's heart, was not the least alarmed by the approach of his friend, the white man. Martin watched for a favorable moment, and as the Indian's attention was called in a different direction, he shot him down, scalped him, and threw his body in a deep hole .... He then hurried to camp to prepare, as usual, wood for the night. When night came, one of the Indians was missing, and Martin expressed great concern on account of the absence of their comrade. The other Indians did not appear to be the least concerned at the absence of their companion ... the subject was dismissed for the night; they eat their supper, and lay down to sleep. Martin's mind was so full of thoughts of home, and of taking signal vengeance on his enemies, that he could not sleep; he had gone too far to retreat, and whatever be done, must be done quickly. Being now determined to effect his escape at all hazards, the question he had to decide was, whether he should make an attack on the two sleeping Indians, or watch for a favorable opportunity of dispatching them one at a time. The latter plan appeared to him to be less subject to risk of failure. The next morning he prepared to put his determination into execution. When the two Indians set out on their hunt the next morning, he determined to follow one of them (like a true hunting dog on a slow trail), until a fair opportunity should present itself of dispatching him without alarming his fellow. He cautiously pursued him until near evening, when he openly walked to him, and commenced a conversation about their day's hunt. The Indian being completely off his guard, suspecting no danger, Martin watched for a favorable moment when the Indian's attention was drawn to a different direction, and with one sweep with his vengeful tomahawk laid him lifeless on the ground, scalped him, and tumbled his body into a sink-hole, and covered it with brush and logs, and then made his way for the camp, with a firm determination of closing the bloody tragedy by killing the third Indian. He went out, and composedly waited at the camp for the return of the Indian. About sunset he saw him coming, with a load of game he had killed swung on his back. Martin went forward under the pretense of aiding to disencumber him of his load. When the Indian stooped down to be detached of his load, Martin, with one fell swoop with his tomahawk, laid him in death's eternal sleep. Being now in no danger of pursuit, he leisurely packed up what plunder he could conveniently carry with him, and made his way for the white settlements, where he safely arrived with the three Indian scalps, after an absence of nearly a year.*

Treacherous, sly, deceitful, and most importantly, murderous; such was Martin Wetzel as seen through the eyes of John McDonald, although one wonders where he had hidden the scalp of his first victim during the night he spent in camp, while calmly sleeping beside his two prospective victims. But as a prime example of the attitude of the majority of the frontier people toward the Indian, this story was picked up by most of the later writers, who often expanded upon it. Martin Wetzel then began to figure in many other Indian killings, on many an expedition, each time with bloody tomahawk in hand, and at times and in places which Martin Wetzel never saw. In time the name of Lewis Wetzel began to be interchanged with his brother Martin's, so that sometimes it is Lewis, sometimes Martin, who wields the blood-stained tomahawk. Nor is this surprising, as McDonald wove some accounts of Lewis Wetzel's adventures that surpassed his narrative of Martin's escape. Like many of the legends of the Border Wars, it makes a thrilling story, but it contains only a grain of truth. Martin was an Indian captive, and he escaped while the Indians were on a horse-stealing expedition; the rest is pure fiction from McDonald's wild imagination.

But it is because of the ridiculous blood-and-thunder stories of this ilk that the name of Wetzel has been associated not only with reckless daring, but with daylight murder of innocent, defenseless, or unsuspecting Indians. One noted historian criticized Lewis Wetzel because once *"he detected an Indian lurking near Fort Henry ... and killed him without warning."* Wetzel's colleagues would have laughed at such a hare-brained remark.

Martin's actual escape was much less exciting. He was taken along on this horse-stealing expedition, and as the Indian party approached the Ohio, they split up into smaller bands, as was their customary practice. Revenge may have been corroding in Martin Wetzel's heart, but he simply waited until those few with him were out of sight, then he slipped into a hollow log and patiently waited until nightfall permitted him to cross the river unseen. From there to one of the white settlements was nothing more than avoiding any of the roving packs of Indians, a routine task for any Wetzel worthy of the name. Even had he been caught, he could easily have explained his situation as nothing more than having gotten separated and lost from his Indian companions, since he was in completely unfamiliar territory.

As it turned out, his greatest danger lay ahead of him, not behind. When he finally appeared at one of the Kentucky forts, probably Boonesborough, no one there believed that he was anything but a renegade, an Indian spy come to seek out information on the defenses of the fort. He was closer then to being killed on the spot than at any time since his capture by the Indians. After all, he had been gone nearly three years, and the English language was unfamiliar to him after so long a period of disuse. With his black scalplock and black eyes, breechclout and moccasins, he looked and acted (and smelled) like an Indian. No one in the settlement knew him, until finally Daniel Boone was summoned, who either knew Wetzel, or knew of his captivity, and Martin was freed of suspicion.

In 1868 Martin's son, John Wetzel (1797-1879), was interviewed by Draper, who wrote down the following account, as Martin himself had told it to his children:

*Martin was taken in the spring of the year, and was a captive some two years and nine months. In order to escape he joined a horse-stealing expedition into Kentucky with about a dozen other Indians. Near Boonesborough the Indians scattered to steal horses, and Martin hid in a log until it was safe for him to escape. But because of the length of his absence as well as his appearance, he was suspected of being an Indian spy. It was Boone himself who cleared him of any suspicion. About 1782 he returned east through the Cumberland Gap to Shenandoah County, Virginia, where he met and married Mary Coffield, and finally returned to Wheeling. After his return from captivity Martin Wetzel never went on another military campaign against the Indians, although he did sometimes serve as a local scout.*

A short and succinct account of four harrowing years of a man's life; captured by Indians, life among them, his escape, life in Kentucky, his marriage, and finally the return home, all in one short paragraph buried in the Draper manuscripts. No mention here of two days spent stalking his Indian comrades, cutting them down one after another with a tomahawk, and throwing their bodies into a convenient hole. In McDonald's stories the woods appear to be full of holes.

As he had escaped to the cane-lands of Kentucky, he returned east by the safest and most accessible route, the Wilderness Road through the Cumberland Gap, carved out by Boone in 1775. Visiting his relatives in Virginia, he met Mary Coffielt (now Coffield), and after their marriage Martin finally returned, with his bride, to his family on Wheeling Creek. Their first child, Sarah, was born the following year.

He had been held captive for two years and nine months; it had been more than three years since he and John Wolf had left their homes on Wheeling Creek, and for nearly that long their families had no inkling of whether they were alive or dead. Two young men had been taken captive, after several months with no word they were presumed dead. After the abduction of Lewis and Jake in 1777, and their escape, and now the captivity of Martin, and his return, the rejoicing must have been great in the Wetzel household, in that spring of 1781, when word came from Kentucky that Martin was alive and well and would eventually be returning home. It would be yet another year before Martin and his new bride finally showed up on the Wetzel doorstep; the joy would not last long.

*   *   *

It was this same John McDonald who told of Martin Wetzel on Brodhead's Campaign in the spring of 1781, when sixteen Indians had been taken prisoner and bound to trees, whereupon Martin Wetzel approached them, helping to kill each in turn with the same gory tomahawk he had used to kill his Indian friends. But Martin

Wetzel was not on Brodhead's Campaign; it was at just about that time that he was escaping from his enforced exile into Kentucky.

And it was this same John McDonald who had reported that the Wetzel cabin had been attacked by Indians, in 1777, and that Captain John Wetzel had been killed and scalped. This story, like Martin's escape, became the basis for an entire saga, eventually reaching proportions in which the entire family, save one or two or three, were killed: Lewis Wetzel returns from a hunting trip to find his home in ashes, the scalped and violated bodies of his mother and a sister lying near the scalped and mutilated bodies of his father and a baby brother. Over the ruins of his cabin and the graves of his family Lewis swears an oath of eternal vengeance against the red man; he will kill every Indian that comes within his power so long as he shall live. Sometimes one or two brothers are with him, and all swear the same oath. It takes little research to find that the entire story is a complete fabrication, but so pervasive has this myth become that many people can be found who still believe that Lewis Wetzel's hatred of the Indians was the result of the massacre of his family.

And it was McDonald who told the story of a famous Indian chief named George Washington; as that worthy rode innocently toward a peace conference with the whites, he was treacherously murdered, shot down from behind by Lewis Wetzel who had been lurking in the woods, hoping only for a chance to kill one of the peace delegates. Then, instead of being hanged for the assassin that he was, Wetzel was instead applauded by his friends and neighbors for the murder of this peace-loving Indian. But Lewis Wetzel did not kill the Indian George Washington, nor was that Indian a chief, nor was he going to a peace conference. An expose of this chimerical tale will be found in the Seventh Interlude.

*   *   *

The Wetzels had been living on the frontier for more than a decade now, and although three of the sons had been taken by Indians, all three had managed to return home safe and sound. The odds that this would continue indefinitely were against them. Every family on the border was affected by the Indian wars; nowhere was it safe, and those who thought differently were usually the first to suffer. In 1774 James Roberts had considered his family safe, hidden away in that little cabin on Reedy Creek, not far from Sycamore Shoals, in the extreme easternmost tip of Tennessee. There they were visited by Logan, and not one was left to tell what had happened that day. Almost every individual living on the western border could tell from first-hand experience, if not of one or more family members, then of a relative, a friend, or a neighbor, who had been killed by Indians. Soon it would be the Wetzels' turn.

# Chapter XV

$\mathcal{T}$he Most Adventuresome George Rogers Clark,
1778-1779
Kenton is Taken, and a Double Massacre

On March 5, 1777, George Rogers Clark had received his commission as major of Virginia militia, and the new Governor of Virginia, Patrick Henry, had placed Clark in charge of the defense of Kentucky. One of his first actions was to select scouts (*spies,* they were called in those days); men of the stature of Simon Kenton and Michael Stoner. At the same time he appointed four captains to serve under him; Daniel Boone, James Harrod, Benjamin Logan, and John Todd. These were all seasoned veterans, all with years of frontier experience behind them. Boone was forty-two years old, Harrod was thirty-four, Logan was thirty-three, and the youngest, Todd, was twenty-six. Youngest, that is, except for their commander, Clark, who at the time was only twenty-four.

But despite being younger than any of the men under him, Clark was in command because he was one of that rare breed, a true leader. It was said that his men would not be afraid to charge straight into hell, if George Rogers Clark would lead them. But not only did Kentucky gain a great leader, in Clark they had a man who understood, and the importance of that one single phrase, *Clark understood,* can never be over-emphasized. He understood that poor Kentucky was doomed to extinction unless the Illinois country could be brought under American control. He understood that the western settlements, and that included not only Kentucky but Wheeling and Pittsburgh as well, would never be free of Indian attack as long as the Indians received help from Detroit, and the Indians would continue to receive help from Detroit as long as that post was controlled by the English.

Ergo: (1) bring the Illinois country under American control, and (2) capture Detroit. The only way to accomplish this was by a direct invasion of both, and invasions required large numbers of men. But there were no such large numbers. Even had there been, they would not have gone, nor could they have been blamed for their refusal. The idea of even a few hundred men marching overland, leaving Kentucky all but defenseless, and taking the posts of Kaskaskia and Kahokia on the Mississippi, and Fort Sackville on the Wabash, and then actually trying to hold onto those posts, in the face of the English army, was a madman's dream. It was a good thing that Clark never told them about it, because it was as absurd an idea as anyone could imagine.

But Clark was the one who understood, when others did not, could not, or would not. If the English were able to persuade the western Indians to join their Ohio brothers, then Kentucky could not be held. The defense of Kentucky demanded that Clark remain throughout that summer and fall of 1777, but he could at least gather information. On April 3rd he sent out two of his spies to visit the Mississippi posts and determine their strength; when the two men, Benjamin Linn and Samuel Moore, returned on June 22nd, Clark's idea now became a certainty. The posts were virtually undefended, and they could be captured merely be walking in and, in a sufficiently loud voice, demanding their surrender. There were no British troops on the Mississippi, all of them having been withdrawn to Detroit. The only defense was at Kaskaskia, and that was provided by local French militia under the command of a former French officer named Rocheblave, now serving the British. Clark was sure that with as few as five hundred men the entire Illinois territory could become an American bastion in the west.

Finally, on October 1st, Clark left Harrodsburg and headed for Williamsburg. The people of Kentucky were genuinely sorry to see their young commander leave; they were certain he would never return. A man with such talents would be of much greater use to the Continental Army on the eastern front fighting large English armies, they thought, than whiling away the war in some insignificant frontier outpost. Clark had already sent a letter to Governor Henry containing a brief outline of his plan, and Henry was aghast at the difficulties and dangers involved. Then Major Clark arrived in Williamsburg, and called on the governor at his mansion. When he left, Lieutenant-Colonel Clark had been given authority to raise seven companies of militia, totaling three hundred fifty men, and had been granted over a thousand pounds for incidental expenses. It was not the five hundred men that Clark had hoped for, but with hard work and good judgment, and maybe a little luck, it just might be enough. In his sights was the British post on the Wabash known as Fort Sackville, a new installation which the British had built in 1770 on the site of the old French Post St. Vincent, now Vincennes. Publicly, his orders were to use the men and spend the money on the defense of Kentucky; his secret orders told him to head for the Illinois.

He arrived at Redstone on February 1, 1778, and immediately ran into problems raising men. The terrible injuries inflicted on the border settlers during 1777, which were certain only to increase, had made the frontiersmen unwilling to leave their families to join any militia project, no matter whither or whence. Then had come the murder of Cornstalk in November, and the Shawnee would not even wait for spring weather for revenge; they would be on their way to Boonesborough, via the salt licks, even before the Starving Moon had risen. In addition, the Pennsylvania-Virginia border dispute was still raging, and Pennsylvanians had no intention of helping defend Virginia's Kentucky County; no more were the Virginians willing to leave the area to the grasping Pennsylvanians.

Three months later, on May 12th, having managed to round up a scant one hundred fifty volunteers, Clark sailed from Redstone, heading for the Falls of the Ohio, present Louisville, Kentucky. Along the way downriver he picked up a few more adventurers, including a party of settlers headed for Kentucky, among them the formidable William Linn, who knew Indians better than had William Foreman. But by the time he left the Falls on June 26th desertion had cost him nearly as much as he had gained; his force totaled not the five hundred he had at first envisioned, not even the three hundred fifty authorized by Virginia, but only half that number, one hundred seventy-eight. It was not enough, but it would have to do.

Rowing night and day, his little flotilla reached the mouth of the Tennessee River in just four days, having averaged over a hundred miles a day. Even better time had been made by the man pursuing them. When Clark had left Kentucky, Linn had remained to help his family get settled; then an express arrived from Pittsburgh with news so momentous that Linn undertook the incredibly risky trip, alone, through four hundred fifty miles of wilderness, to overtake Clark. But to anyone headed for a showdown with French militia, as Clark was, the news was momentous indeed; France had declared war on England, and had signed an alliance with the Americans! If Clark could only surprise them now, they could capture Kaskaskia without firing a shot.

In order to avoid being seen by Indians posted along the Mississippi, the men left the Ohio and marched the last one hundred twenty-five miles overland. They arrived at Kaskaskia[43] just as darkness settled down on the close of a propitious day, the Fourth of July, and the surprise was complete. The Americans entered the town during the night, and the first Commandant Rocheblave knew of their arrival was when huge Simon Kenton awakened him by whacking him on the shoulder. Simon brusquely ordered him to get dressed quickly, so that he could get downstairs and properly surrender the fort. The French militia had been fearful of these uncouth, savage-looking barbarians roaming their streets, rifles cradled in their arms, but when informed of the treaty between France and the United States they flocked to take Clark's oath of allegiance.

Simon Kenton was next sent with two companions to spy out the more vital post at Vincennes; possession of the Mississippi posts was important, but Vincennes controlled the Wabash, and the Wabash was the connecting link between the St. Lawrence, the Great Lakes, Detroit, and the Mississippi. Kenton soon returned with the news that there was not a single redcoat there. The English had never even harbored a suspicion that, after such a year as 1777 had been, the Kentucky settlements could possibly consider a counterattack in the west. Leonard Helm, with but a single platoon of militia, was sent to take Vincennes, and soon Simon Kenton was on his way back to Kentucky with the staggering news of what Clark had accomplished.

But time had not been standing still while Clark was gone: in February Boone had been taken captive with his saltmakers, but had escaped and returned; the Kentuckians had withstood a siege, and now it was their turn. If Lieutenant-Colonel Clark could be a hero, then Colonel Bowman could be a greater hero, and upon receipt of Kenton's message, he decided to act. But John Bowman was a cautious man, to employ the most generous term. He wanted to know exactly what he was facing before he began a campaign into Indian country, and so he sent out three spies; what happened next is recorded in Kenton's own conversation with Judge John H. James, of Urbana, who visited the old pioneer for two days early in 1832:

*Bowman got me and two more to go to Chillicothe and make discovery — Alex. Montgomery got killed, I got taken, and George Clark escaped, who piloted Bowman there next spring, '79. I did not return anymore ... till the Summer of 1779.*

"Alex Montgomery got killed, I got taken, and George Clark[44] escaped. I did not return any more till 1779." It could be no more succinct than that, but there is much more to tell, especially concerning those simple three words: *I got taken.* No man faced more moments of total elation intermixed with absolute despair than did Simon Kenton during those next few months.

The three men crossed the Ohio on September 7th, 1778, and headed for the

Indian towns; it was the very same day that Blackfish and his warriors arrived outside the walls of Boonesborough. Kenton, Clark and Montgomery reached the Indian town of Chillicothe on the Little Miami, near present Xenia, Ohio, after two days of hard traveling. They were come to gather information, but what caught their eye was a superb compound of formerly Kentucky, now Indian, horseflesh. After gaining the intelligence Bowman wanted, they selected out of the herd seven of the finest, mounted up and started off during the night, but not unnoticed. Riding hard, they outdistanced their pursuers and reached the Ohio on the morning of the second day. But the weather had turned bad, the Ohio was boiling, and the horses would not attempt the crossing. Refusing to give up such fine animals, and feeling safe from pursuit, they decided to hobble the horses and wait out the storm.

By the next morning, September 13th, the weather had not cleared, it was as bad as the day before, and now they knew they could delay no longer. While Montgomery and Clark went to fetch the horses, Kenton started up the back trail for a last look-see. He did not like what he saw — five mounted Shawnee. Afoot he could probably have outrun them, but not even Lewis Wetzel could outrun a horse, and neither could Kenton. He was taken and bound, just as Montgomery arrived in search of Simon. Alex fired but missed, turned, and fled, but he was no match for a Shawnee runner. In only a few minutes the warriors returned with Montgomery's scalp, which was repeatedly dashed in Kenton's face. Clark, who could not swim, was not pursued. At the first sign of Indians he had thrown a piece of driftwood into the river and, clinging fast to it, had eventually managed to reach the other side, more than half-drowned.

Daniel Boone had escaped them, but now the Shawnee had Kenton, and he was doomed to the stake. After surviving the gauntlet a vote was taken, and Kenton was told that he was to die by fire, but not here, and not yet. He was to be taken north to Wapatomica, on the Mad River, where his agonies could be enjoyed by a much larger audience. Arriving at Mac-a-chack, eight miles from where he was to be burned, he was again forced to run the gauntlet, but this time he was determined to escape. As he neared the end of the line he suddenly crashed through the wall of Indians at top speed and broke for the forest. So amazed were the spectators at this display of poor sportsmanship on Kenton's part that he gained a decided advantage. But he had no more than entered the seclusion of the woods when his bad luck returned; he ran straight into a band of Indians, led by Blue Jacket, headed for this village. One of the warriors struck Kenton with the pipe end of his tomahawk, laying him flat and leaving an indentation in Simon's skull the size of a dollar that could be felt to the day he died. He was hauled back to the village, and after a few days it was on to Wapatomica and another ordeal of the gauntlet, then nothing but waiting until the day of his burning.

But now fate smiled on him; Simon Girty arrived, and although not at first recognizing his old friend, Simon Butler of the Fort Pitt days, it seemed to be just one more white captive painted black, as soon as Kenton made himself known Girty delivered an impassioned speech which resulted in another vote which reversed the previous one. Kenton was taken in by a squaw to replace a lost son, and for three weeks Girty and Kenton roamed the forest, visiting the nearby Indian towns. Then the bad luck returned, this time in the form of an angry and defeated war party just back from western Virginia. When they saw this white man walking around like one of their own, while their comrades had been slain, they demanded he be burned at the stake. Another vote was taken, and in spite of all Girty could say in his behalf, the vote was unanimous for his death by fire; so much for Indian "adoption". Girty, playing for time, was able to talk them into taking Kenton to the Sandusky towns, fifty miles to the north, and accordingly a party of five guards set out to escort him there. Along the way they stopped to drink from a creek, and Simon, finishing first, stepped across the creek and sat down. Angered at this movement without first receiving permission, one of the guards struck Simon across the arm with his war club, breaking the bone. Nor was this all; they had not gone much further when they passed an old man sitting at the side of the trail, as his wife was cutting wood. On learning of the reason for the journey, the man grabbed his squaw's ax and swung a blow at Kenton's head. Although he swerved to avoid the blow, the ax struck his collar-bone, breaking it. Paying no attention to the two wounds, his guards pushed him on. For the next eleven days he was marched along the trail, stretched out and tied to the ground at night, forced to run the gauntlet once more, and then tied to the stake, all the while enduring the most extreme pain at every movement from the two broken bones.

Finally they reached the camp of Logan, the Mingo chief, and there Kenton's wounds were finally treated, and Logan appeared to take an interest in Kenton's case. But then it was on to Sandusky, and the great event. Kenton was tied to the stake, but no sooner had the wood been lighted than a sudden torrential downpour, out of a clear-blue sky, doused the flames. The next day he was on his way back to the stake when a resplendent figure, dressed all in scarlet and gold, came riding into the village. It was Pierre Druillard, nothing more than a trader from Detroit, but this was the man who handed out the British presents to the Indians, and the rum. He had come to escort this valuable prisoner back to Detroit, for interrogation, he said. Druillard startled the Indians with the news that General McIntosh was coming from Fort Pitt with an army to invade the Indian country; the information this white man held about that campaign, combined with his knowledge of the defenses of Kentucky and of the Illinois country, was much too important to be lost. Logan, friend to the white man, had sent out messages to Detroit, and they had been received. Kenton had been saved again.

\*   \*   \*

At Fort Pitt Gen. Hand had been replaced by Brigadier General Lachlin McIntosh, and in June Congress ordered him to make an attack on Detroit and Henry Hamilton, if to do nothing more than contain Hamilton. But on the last day of that month the Tory leader, Col. John Butler, camped for the night on a hill overlooking the beautiful Wyoming Valley in eastern Pennsylvania. With him were about a hundred of his Rangers and nearly five hundred Indians. Thus giving up the element of surprise, his intent seems to have been to frighten the settlers, rather than forcing an engagement; but the Wyoming settlers were not so easily frightened. They gathered in their stockades and prepared to fight, although the first two small forts approached by Butler surrendered on demand. That was too much for the veterans in Forty Fort. Out they marched, four hundred fifty in all, on the third day of July, breathing fire and destruction for the damned Tories. Butler set fire to the two captured forts and withdrew a mile or more; the Americans assumed he was retreating and pressed on, heedless. Today a large, impressive monument marks the site where they ran straight into Butler's trap, and where they lie. As they approached the Tories in a breastwork of trees and logs, hundreds of screaming Iroquois suddenly appeared on their left flank, cutting them to pieces as they fled in panic. Col. Butler later reported a total of two hundred twenty-seven scalps, and five prisoners. On the other side, one Indian had been killed, and two Rangers. The Iroquois had reason to celebrate, and they needed to celebrate while they could, although they were to have one last major fling.

John Butler was nearing sixty now, and his health was failing. His son, Walter, recently escaped from American imprisonment, hurried to take his father' place. In November, with the aid of the Mohawk chief Joseph Brant, Walter led his first independent command, a large force of four hundred Iroquois, two hundred rangers, and fifty regulars from the King's Eighth Regiment. They were headed for Fort Alden, in Cherry Valley, on the New York frontier, under the command of Col. Ichabod Alden, with three hundred continentals and half that number of local militia. On November 8th Gen. Hand, who had been transferred from the danger zone of Pittsburgh to the danger zone of Albany, received a warning from Fort Stanwix that the Indians were on the move. He immediately ordered Col. Jacob Klock to reinforce Fort Alden with his Tryon County militia, but Klock moved so slowly that he did not arrive the next day, as scheduled, nor the next. Then came word of the attack, and Klock, although only twenty miles away, made sure he did not arrive until the day after the Indians had left.

The attack, beginning at noon on November 11th, was at first marked by incompetence on both sides; before they even came in sight of the fort the Indians gave up the element of surprise, on which their success depended, by foolishly shooting two woodcutters, thus alerting the garrison. But Alden, the American commander, was so inept that he had refused to take seriously the repeated warnings that an attack was imminent. Some of the residents of the valley had requested permission to take refuge in the fort, but they were denied. Indeed, Alden himself was not even in the fort, but was enjoying more comfortable living quarters in a private home a quarter mile distant. When the alarm was sounded he raced for the fort, but was killed before ever reaching it; twelve other soldiers were killed outside the fort, and another dozen captured, along with Alden's second-in-command. Butler's objective had been to overwhelm the fort with a sudden onslaught, but now even Brant could not restrain his Indians; sensing the chance for slaughter they scattered like a flock of pigeons, bypassing the fort entirely as they headed for the defenseless houses in the settlement.

The best known abuse occurred at the home of Robert Wells, a well-known pioneer, and a long-time and valued friend of Sir William Johnson, John Butler, and Joseph Brant. Their friendship meant nothing to those Indians who burst through the door of the Wells' home, however. In a few moments Robert Wells, his mother, his wife, a brother and a sister, three sons, a daughter, and three servants, a dozen in all, were cut down in a bloodbath. In a poignant letter from Niagra John Butler later wrote of his old friend:

*I would have crawled miles on my hands and knees to have saved that family, and why my son did not do so God only knows.*

With only his own Rangers and the detachment of regulars remaining to him, Butler was now outnumbered by the men in the fort that he had come to besiege. He assembled his force on a hillside nearby and awaited the counterattack from the fort which he expected at any moment, but no attack came. Evidently the continentals in the fort were so demoralized by the loss of their officers in the first few minutes of the assault that they never even considered leaving the safety of the fort.

When the day was done Brant's Indians had totaled over thirty scalps, many of them women and children, and over seventy prisoners. Butler spent most of the next day in the valley, but with the weather turning bad again, and two feet of fresh snow, he began his march back to Niagra. Col. Klock arrived the next day, but after spending a few hours at the scene, and without even helping to relieve the sufferings of the survivors, he turned around and headed for home.

\*     \*     \*

The double massacre at Wyoming and Cherry Valley was too much for Congress; their previous orders to McIntosh to proceed against Detroit and the western tribes were revoked, and Clark was forgotten, as they pondered a counterstroke against the wicked Iroquois. It would not take place until late the next summer, but it was coming, and it would destroy the mighty Confederation of the Iroquois.

Perhaps the most important single aspect of Clark's campaign had been his subjugation of the western Indians. These tribes had always been more closely aligned with the French anyway, and with Clark's impressive victories they were now further removed from British influence than ever before. During the fall months Clark established a supply line with New Orleans; his latest dispatches had told him of McIntosh's proposed assault on Detroit, and as Christmas approached he waited to hear that Detroit had fallen. But the only news he received was that a massacre had taken place in Pennsylvania, and as a result the campaign against Detroit had been canceled. Hamilton had not been contained in his nest.

But that was not the worst news; just before Christmas a runner arrived at Kaskaskia and informed Clark that Lieutenant-Governor Henry Hamilton had left Detroit on October 7th, and had sailed down the Wabash with a mixed force of six hundred men, militia, regulars, and Indians. On December 17th he had retaken Vincennes, and Helm and his squad of men were now prisoners. It was the worst blow of all. Hamilton would spend the next three months in winter quarters at Vincennes, but as soon as the spring weather cleared he would march his army west against Clark's insignificant rag-tag army; that is, if Clark was so foolish as to remain at Kaskaskia that long. The most bitter pill of all was the certain knowledge that the Indians would be forced into an admission of what they already knew, that might was right, and that the English would eventually prevail. Kentucky was doomed, for certain-sure; no one could deny that it had been a gallant effort on the part of Clark and his fewer than two hundred men, but it was obvious to all that the end was now in sight.

# Chapter XVI

Retaliation, Followed by Two More Massacres:
1779-1780

Well, it wasn't so damned obvious to Clark. The Wabash was in flood, and as far as one could see there was nothing but a broad expanse of water, stretching on and on for miles to the north, south, and most importantly, to the west of Vincennes. Hamilton and his soldiers, safe inside the walls of Fort Sackville, were as secure from the danger of a land-based assault as if they had been on the Isle of Capri. But if Hamilton was going to wait, and then attack, Clark would attack without waiting.

But how to cross the great flood plain? Clark himself was probably able to walk on water, by a sheer act of will power, but not one of his men could, no matter how hard they might try. The answer to the problem was simple enough; if you cannot walk on the water, then you must walk through the water. Forget that it is the dead of winter, and the water is freezing, bitterly cold. Forget that there are chunks of ice bumping into you as you wade through it. Sometimes the water is only knee-deep, sometimes it is chest-deep. Forget that at the end of the day you must look around for a high spot of ground on which you can spend the night. By morning your clothes will have frozen to you, because there will be no fires. A campfire reflecting off the water in the midst of a flood plain at night would be a beacon of light for miles around. Forget that when you finally reach the Wabash you won't know it, for all the land will be indistinguishable from the river, and when you reach the river how will you get across, anyway, and if you do get across how will you be able to convince those inside the fort that it might be in their best interests to surrender?

Insurmountable difficulties. No normal person would harbor a suspicion that an attack could be made against him. Only a madman would even consider such a foolhardy plan. Only madmen would follow such a madman. But, always remember this: Clark understood, and he was a leader. If you cannot stand still, if you cannot go back, then you must go forward. Clark would announce the day of his departure for Vincennes as February 5, 1779, and Clark's men would follow, every single one. And they would survive one of the most grueling marches ever made by any group of men, and the astounded Hamilton, outwitted at every turn, would surrender Fort Sackville on February 25th. Walking on water would have seemed easy after this. The Illinois country was once again in American hands, while Hamilton was on his way to Williamsburg, in irons. And under guard, to prevent his being lynched along the way by the friends and relatives of the many victims of his Indian allies.

With the failure of McIntosh's anticipated campaign on Detroit the previous fall, Clark now contemplated a direct attack on the British bastion. But he had received word that Col. John Montgomery was on his way to join Clark at Vincennes with a regiment of five hundred Virginians, and there was the prospect of Bowman joining up with Clark, bringing along his three hundred Kentuckians. If Clark could only wait until those men arrived, with a thousand men under his command, and the new French alliance, while the French residents of Detroit were becoming increasingly dissatisfied with the English, success against the Indians' major supply depot was certain. Against his better judgment, Clark waited. When Montgomery finally arrived, he had only a hundred fifty men.

Bowman did not arrive at all. Instead, in late May, looking to his chance for glory, Bowman led his men against Chillicothe, the Shawnee town on the Little Miami River. He had no trouble getting volunteers; Chillicothe was the town from which so many of the raids against Kentucky had been launched, and this was the first large-scale assault into the enemy's territory. Even a group of men from Redstone, who had been at the Big Bone Lick collecting specimens for shipment back east, heard of the expedition when they reached the mouth of the Licking River (Covington, Kentucky). Two companies were organized at Harrodsburg under the command of Benjamin Logan and Silas Harlan[45]; marching to Lexington they joined with the Boonesborough men under Levi Todd and John Holder. The general rendezvous was to be at the mouth of the Licking, and there a company from the Falls of the Ohio joined them under William Harrod, and the Redstone men who were heading back to Pennsylvania with a boatload of relics came aboard. Altogether Bowman crossed the Ohio, May 28th, with nearly three hundred men. But of all the famous Kentuckians, Daniel Boone and Simon Kenton were conspicuous by their absence; Boone was still in North Carolina with Becky, and Kenton was still a prisoner in Detroit. Leaving thirty-two men to guard the boats, Bowman moved toward the Shawnee towns, led by Will Whitley and Kenton's former companion George Clark, who still may not have known how to swim, but who surely knew where Old Chillicothe was.

It was Bowman's good luck that the Shawnee were very weak at the moment; the great schism of the Shawnee nation had finally occurred, and Louis Lorimer had taken four hundred warriors to settle across the Mississippi. Bowman reached the Shawnee town late in the evening of the 29th, without having seen a single Indian, and it was decided to postpone the attack until first light. In the town itself there remained only about a hundred warriors, under the principal chief Blackfish, and perhaps twice that number of women and children. As the plan was developed, the army would attack and envelop the town, upon a prearranged signal, in three wings; Logan was to be in charge of the left, Holder in the center, and Todd on the right, with Bowman. Just after Logan had reached his position they were spotted by the village watchdogs, who began barking furiously, thereby alerting the Indians to their danger. Then someone on the right foolishly fired his rifle, and the whole town was immediately in an uproar. The warriors quickly herded the women and children into the forest and along a path not yet occupied by the Kentuckians, and then returned to occupy the central council house.

Logan, certainly wondering what had happened to the rest of the army, bravely ordered his men to take cover in the remaining deserted cabins; then, tearing off the doors and holding them in front of them as shields, and with the Shawnee trapped in their principal cabin, he was moving forward to attack the council house, unaided, when word finally reached him from Bowman. That word was to begin an immediate retreat. Dumbfounded, Logan could not believe it, but it was true; someone had started a rumor that Simon Girty, at the head of a hundred warriors, was marching to the relief of Blackfish from the Piqua towns, only twelve miles distant. Still in disbelief, but with the rest of the army beginning to withdraw, Logan had no choice but to obey.

134

They fired the cabins and rounded up a large herd of horses, while others quickly worked to destroy the crops surrounding the village, then the retreat commenced.

But militia did not know how to retreat; Bowman, county lieutenant of all of Kentucky, should have known that, if anyone did. The Indians, seeing their attackers falling back, charged out of the council house and counterattacked. The retreat became the typical rout. Order was finally restored and, fourteen miles out, when Indians were again discovered on their back trail, they were attacked by Logan and Harrod, and driven off. The retreat was then resumed without further incident.

They reached the Ohio early on the morning of June 1st, and recrossed in their boats, swimming the horses across. They had lost seven men, but the Indians, outnumbered three to one and taken by surprise, had lost only five. The Indians would have counted it a victory if not for the fact that one of the many wounded in the battle had been Blackfish, who had taken a rifle ball in the thigh, breaking the bone. He lingered on for several weeks before he died, and his death was a severe blow to the Shawnee. Only a year and a half ago they had lost Cornstalk, and now Blackfish was gone.

Two days after Bowman had completed his journey by crossing the Ohio, another even more remarkable journey began. On the night of June 3rd Simon Kenton, having been aided by one of the traders, slipped out of Detroit with two others, Coffer and Bullock, and began his trek back to Kentucky. As a matter of course Indians were routinely posted around the outskirts of the town to intercept any escapees, but they never caught a glimpse of Kenton or his companions. Other Indians were sent out to recapture him, but they followed the usual course of escaping prisoners, straight south; Kenton knew better, and his route was straight west, toward the Wabash country. After thirty days, and having covered some four hundred miles, the three men crossed the Ohio back into Kentucky, feeling good at being home again.

When Kenton arrived at the Falls of the Ohio in early July he learned that Clark was still at Vincennes. Bearing news of great import regarding the defenses of Detroit, and the chances of success if an expedition could be launched against it without delay, Kenton, hardly pausing to take breath, headed out for Vincennes, all alone, and reached it without incident, of course. Clark was anxious to go, but with only Montgomery's small force, and with Bowman just returned to Kentucky from his somewhat less than auspicious "first great campaign into the Indian ground", there was no possibility of finding enough men to attack Detroit, and the best trump card for ending the Border Wars at a single stroke was reluctantly discarded.

*      *      *

In the meantime efforts were underway elsewhere to provide for the common defense, and to combat the Indian problem. In April, 1779, Col. Daniel Brodhead[46] had replaced the ineffectual McIntosh as commander of the Western Department. As a result of the Iroquois involvement with John Butler in the Wyoming Valley

Massacre in July, which had then been followed by son Walter Butler and Joseph Brant leading the Iroquois to Cherry Valley in November, General Washington decided that the first priority in the Indian War was to break the power of the Iroquois League. He summoned General John Sullivan and placed him in charge of an expedition to move up Pennsylvania's Susquehanna River and into New York, and to defeat the Iroquois wherever he found them. He was also to take prisoner as many hostages as he possibly could, to help ensure the future good behavior of the Iroquois.

To cooperate with Sullivan, Brodhead was ordered to make a simultaneous advance up the Allegheny from Fort Pitt, thereby cutting off any possible retreat of the Iroquois. After sending out the orders, however, Washington contemplated the difficulties involved, and came to the conclusion that, since Sullivan's army already consisted of two separate divisions, too great a distance separated the eastern from the western segment of the army. Sullivan would start out from Easton, Pennsylvania, and move northwest through the Wyoming Valley to a rendezvous at Tioga on the New York-Pennsylvania line with his second division, which was under the command of Brigadier General James Clinton, who would be advancing southward from the Mohawk Valley. Three hundred miles west of Sullivan, on the other side of Pennsylvania, was Gen. Brodhead at Fort Pitt, with most of the intervening distance still a wilderness.

Believing that there was too great a possibility of communications going awry, which would result in a lack of the necessary coordination, Washington then sent orders to Brodhead advising him that he was free to demonstrate in any direction he thought most favorable to the accomplishment of Sullivan's mission. But by the time the messages were received at Pitt, Brodhead's preparations for an advance up the Allegheny were already in such a state of preparedness that he concluded it was best to proceed with the original plan, and sent letters to Sullivan so informing him.

It was not until June 18th that Sullivan finally started out from Easton; like Braddock and Forbes before him, his progress through the mountains was agonizingly slow. It took nearly two months to cut a road and haul the materials necessary to supply an army[47]. He arrived at Tioga on August 10th, and settled down there to await Clinton, who arrived on the 22nd.

Well aware of Sullivan's anticipated advance, Col. John Butler, his son Walter, and three hundred fifty Rangers left Niagra in May, advancing to Seneca Lake, and then cautiously towards Tioga, Sullivan's destination. The Indians were slow to come to Butler, but toward the end of June Joseph Brant arrived with three hundred warriors. Still, when he neared Tioga, Butler had only his Rangers and some four hundred unenthusiastic Indians. Good reason to be unenthusiastic, they thought; when Clinton joined up with Sullivan, the Rangers and warriors combined would be outnumbered by more than five to one. Clinton's army might have been slow, but it was no Braddock in command this time. It was a juggernaut with extreme protection from surprise. The lessons learned at the Battle of the Monongahela on that hot July day in 1755 had not been forgotten.

Butler's only remaining hope was to select a defensive position from which to ambush the lead elements of the army as they rolled forward across the New York line, thus neutralizing the disparity in numbers. On August 29th, five miles east of present Elmira, New York, in front of the Indian village of Newtown, Butler selected a steep wooded ridge along a narrow stretch of the trail that Sullivan would have to pass. He posted his Indians on the wooded heights to his left; they would descend on Sullivan's strung-out vanguard as soon as Butler's Rangers attacked from the front. It was the same strategy he had employed at Wyoming, but there he had enjoyed the element of surprise, and the militia had stumbled unwarily into the trap.

But John Sullivan was not militia; when his scouts brought word of the ambush on the hillside ahead, Sullivan, rather than rushing blindly forward with numbers in his favor, calmly sat down to wait, while his ace-in-the-hole was brought forward. After Brant and Butler, Rangers and Indians, had stewed for three hours, wondering what was causing the holdup, they were suddenly treated to an ear-shattering blast of artillery. Sullivan had brought along field howitzers, and now the shells exploded in front of the Indians, to each side of them, in back of them, and on top of them. Those which landed in back of them were probably the most discomfiting; the Indians, totally unused to such a cannonade[48], assumed that the explosions in their rear meant that they had been surrounded on their hill, and now they must fight their way out of their own trap. One of Sullivan's brigades charged up the hill and, after a brief skirmish, the Indians turned and fled. Butler later reported five Rangers and twelve Indians killed; Sullivan had lost only five men, one of them the officer who had led that initial assault up the hill.

The numbers may suggest that this was a battle of minimal importance, but here the numbers do not tell the story. This short engagement, of only a few hours total elapsed time, was one of the most critical conflicts of the Indian Wars. Although Butler tried valiantly, the demoralized Indians could not be stopped. They were headed for home, to protect their families and possessions, and they would kill the man who got in their way.

\*   \*   \*

Excerpt from a letter of Col. John Butler to Col. Mason Bolton, September 8, 1779:

*I endeavored, but to no purpose, to prevail upon the Indians to make a stand at Canadasego[49]; the Rebels took possession of that Village the 7th instant in the evening. Joseph Brant ... says that to all appearance they cannot be less than 3000.*

\*   \*   \*

For generations hordes of America's fiercest warriors had come out of this Iroquois heartland to destroy their enemies; now that heartland lay open and defenseless, and Sullivan wasted no time. Leaving behind the artillery, now no longer needed, within a matter of hours he was moving against the Iroquois villages.

Town after abandoned town he entered, unopposed, and his army had all they could do to destroy the hundreds of acres of crops and burn the village before Sullivan moved them on to the next town, to repeat the process. More than a century of almost uninterrupted victory had brought the Iroquois nation to an incredibly high level of prosperity. Most of their homes were solid log structures, they owned large herds of horses and cattle, even hogs and poultry. Each town was surrounded by acres of gardens, cornfields, and orchards. What Sullivan's army left behind was nothing but smoking ruins. So rapidly did the Iroquois flee before him that Sullivan was unable to fulfill one of the objectives of his campaign, that of taking prisoners to be used as future hostages. The Indians did not loiter about, waiting to be taken captive. Finally, on September 15th, Sullivan entered and systematically destroyed the inner sanctum of the Iroquois kingdom, Seneca Castle on the Genesee. Within a matter of hours he had turned his back on the ruins of the town and headed his army toward home, his assignment completed. Those field howitzers had sounded the death knell of the Iroquois League.

\*     \*     \*

Excerpt from Col. John Butler's letter, September 8th, 1779 (continued):
*The 7th instant in the evening a runner came in from the Ohio, informing that the Rebels were come up the Allegheny, and had penetrated as far as Canawaga[50] ....*

\*     \*     \*

Brodhead, meanwhile, having assembled his army, had left Fort Pitt on August 11th, and begun his move northward. With him were over six hundred regulars and militia, including Col. John Gibson and Major Sam McColloch, and led by John Montour. Their goal was the Iroquois villages on the upper reaches of the Allegheny. About a week after their departure the advance, led by Joseph Nicholson, had a skirmish with a war party of about thirty Seneca who were heading south, but for the remainder of the trip they scarcely saw an Indian, too dispirited were they by Sullivan's unstoppable advance. It was a totally uneventful campaign for most of the men. Before Brodhead could reach their villages the Seneca and Mingo had departed; he destroyed a dozen deserted towns along the Allegheny, then returned to Pittsburgh on September 15th, without having suffered a single casualty.

Extract of a letter from Gen. George Washington to Col. Daniel Brodhead, October 18th, 1779:

*I am exceedingly happy in your success in the expedition up the Allegheny.... With respect to an Expedition against Detroit——- I cannot at this time direct it to be made, as the state of the force at present with you is not sufficient to authorise the clearest hopes of success....*

\*   \*   \*

But there had been disaster as well; in June of 1778 Col. David Rogers had set out from Fort Pitt to descend the Ohio and Mississippi to New Orleans, and bring a badly-needed shipment of food and gunpowder back to Pitt. After an exhausting journey of more than a year, Rogers finally passed St. Louis and began the final leg up the Ohio. For this most difficult leg of the journey he had been joined by twenty-three men under Lt. Abraham Chapline, sent by Clark as a reinforcement.

On October 4th, 1779, as Sullivan was following his back trail across Pennsylvania, and perhaps because of the extra security these new men provided, Rogers allowed himself to be lured into an ambush at the mouth of the Licking River. More than forty of the men were killed, including Rogers himself, and many more taken captive, including Chapline. Only thirteen escaped. The loss of the men was bad enough, but the loss of supplies, especially the badly-needed gunpowder, only made it worse.

And at just about the same time that Washington was writing to congratulate Brodhead, and to advise him against any move toward Detroit, Daniel Boone and Rebecca were arriving back in Kentucky. As usual he was leading a large party of emigrants, including two of his brothers, but they were not going to Boonesborough. Daniel had had enough of the short-sighted and distrustful people there, so this group of pioneers moved about ten miles north, founding a settlement there known as Boone's Station. He had missed all the excitement of 1779, but unhappily, there was more to come.

\*   \*   \*

If the Americans could mount a wilderness offensive, so could the British. And if Americans could haul artillery through the wilderness, then so could the British. With Hamilton in confinement in Williamsburg, Major Arent De Peyster was now in command at Detroit. He ordered Captain Henry Bird of the Regular Army to lead a force against Clark in Kentucky, at his fort at the Falls of the Ohio. Along with the Indians he was to take two cannon, a light field gun and a six-pounder. No more sieges, no more polite but drawn-out discussions of surrender, now it was either surrender or die.

But their plans were known to the Americans; Abraham Chapline had been one of those captured when Simon Girty attacked Col. Rogers' supply boats. He had been taken to Sandusky, and there he saw the preparations and heard the stories. On April 28, 1780, Chapline escaped and made his way to the Falls of the Ohio, reaching there on May 19th. He reported not only the news of the proposed advance against Kentucky, but also the alarming fact that the British were bringing cannon. It was hard to believe, but Chapline had a high reputation; then George Hendricks[51], one of the saltmakers captured with Boone more than two years before, arrived with verification of Chapline's information.

Bird had already left Detroit on April 12th, but he was moving slowly. It was difficult to carry cannon in a canoe, then over a portage by packhorse, then back in the canoe again. And there were problems with the recalcitrant Indians. They did not want to attack Clark, the one man they would avoid at all costs, but with the aid of Alex McKee, Matthew Elliot, and the three Girty brothers, all of whom were expert at handling Indians, several bands of warriors joined Bird. On June 5th there was to be a rendezvous at the mouth of the Miami River, but a week later Bird was still waiting for the Chillicothe Shawnee to arrive, although his Indian force had by now swelled to seven hundred. After they crossed the Ohio there was more trouble. The Indians flatly refused to attack Clark. Instead of moving west toward Clark, they insisted on moving in the other direction, then up the Licking River to some of the smaller stations. They reasoned that these settlements were so much closer to the Indian villages that they were a greater danger to them; privately, they were eager to see the cannon in action, blasting holes in the walls of the white man's hated forts.

Bird had little choice but to agree, and on June 20th, they arrived at Ruddle's Station on the Licking, where Bird tried to keep the Indians hidden until the artillery arrived. Controlling the Indians when fresh scalps were in sight was an impossible task, as Bird was soon to learn. The Indians fired at several men outside the walls, giving the alarm, and the men in the fort defended themselves bravely until about noon, when the lighter field piece was brought up. Two shots were all that were required, and Isaac Ruddle, after receiving Bird's personal guarantee that no one would be harmed, surrendered his station. Ruddle's was one of the newer and larger settlements in Kentucky, and it was to gain two distinctions this day. It was the first fort in Kentucky's long and violent history to surrender, and it was to become the scene of an infamous massacre.

No sooner had the gates been opened than the Indians swarmed in, knives and tomahawks ready, each one eager to get as many scalps as possible, and the slaughter began. Bird made heroic efforts to control the Indians, but he was rudely shoved aside whenever another unarmed victim came into view. Some three hundred men, women, and children were in Ruddle's, another fifty were at Martin's, the next station on the list. But when the Indians finally straggled into Detroit with their prisoners for ransom, there were only about a hundred left alive. A few of the potential captives may have been adopted into one of the tribes, and a few may even have escaped, but the majority of those other two hundred inmates of Ruddle's were hacked to pieces before the sun went down that day.

From Ruddle's they moved on to Martin's Station, but now Bird demanded a pledge from the Indians of safe conduct for the prisoners. Then the cannon was brought into play, again there was no choice but to surrender, and again the prisoners, after having been assured of safe conduct, were butchered. With his artillery Bird could have taken every station in Kentucky, there would have been neither stick nor stone left standing, but Bird had had enough, and now they were running low on food. There had been enough cattle at Ruddle's to feed the army for the rest of the summer, if they had been kept alive and on the hoof, but the Indians had wantonly killed the livestock as viciously as they had the prisoners, and now the meat was rapidly spoiling in the hot summer sun. Then two Tories, deserters from Harrodsburg, arrived. They brought the astonishing news that Clark, far from being several hundred miles distant in the Illinois country, as everyone believed, was instead back in Kentucky, marshaling forces for an immediate attack on the Indians.

It was the last straw, the hungry Indians were ready to retreat back across the Ohio, with the scalps, prisoners, and plunder in their hands, and again, Bird had no choice but to agree. Without his Indians for protection, he was not willing, with a pair of cannon on his hands, to be caught red-handed by a mob of enraged frontiersmen, who would accept no explanations from a Britisher that the massacres were all the Indians' fault. With the Indians going north, the disgruntled and frustrated Captain Henry Bird, the alleged victor, had to stir his stumps to get out of Kentucky as fast as he could. It was a mighty poor substitute for victory.

# Chapter XVII

## Retribution: 1780-1781

Martin's Station had fallen on June 28th, 1780. Now it was the settlers' turn, and they had the man they needed. Although there were in fact a number of Tories now in Kentucky, having fled from the wrath of their neighbors in the east, this was one time that a Kentucky Colonel had no difficulty in raising volunteers. Within a month of Bird's retreat George Rogers Clark had rendezvoused nearly a thousand men at the mouth of the Licking, on August 1st, and they were headed for the Shawnee. The list of captains in this campaign reads like a "Who's Who" of Kentucky's greatest pioneers, among them Daniel Boone, William Linn, Simon Kenton, Jim Harrod, and Benjamin Logan.

Nor was it only Clark who was moving to punish the Indians. Field artillery had finally arrived at Fort Pitt, and Col. Brodhead ordered a rendezvous of troops for August, in a stroke against the Wyandot towns which would coordinate with Clark's campaign against the Shawnee. In early July a mixed party of seven Wyandot and Delaware had attacked the cabin of James Stoops, in the dead of night, which was a rather unusual circumstance for Indians. Stoops escaped, but his wife and three-year-old son, Willie, were taken captive. Only two weeks before Brodhead had sent out the renowned scout, Captain Samuel Brady, with a group of seven men to gather information. Brady was, as always, successful, capturing two Wyandot squaws as well, although one of them made her escape a few days later. While heading back to Pitt three of Brady's men became so overcome with exhaustion that they left the group, heading home by a different route.

As they neared Beaver Creek Brady and the three remaining men saw an Indian war party returning with two captives, a white woman and a small boy. The chief was riding a horse with the boy behind him, then the white woman, followed by the remaining warriors, all on foot. Brady waited until the chief was within a dozen paces, then brought him down with a rifle ball through his body. But the boy, little Willie Stoops, had been tied onto the horse, and he was carried off by the Indians. During the short ensuing battle the second of the squaws escaped, but in return the woman captive, Jane Stoops, was rescued. Brady returned to Fort Pitt, not only with the intelligence that Brodhead desired, but also with Jane Stoops and a Wyandot chief's scalp. Willie Stoops was taken to one of the Wyandot villages, where the little boy narrowly avoided being killed in anger over the death of the chief and the loss of the woman prisoner; he would remain an Indian captive for another three long years before he was eventually taken to Detroit, ransomed, and the family was reunited.

At almost the same time another party of Wyandots was defeated near Fort McIntosh; about the middle of July the Moravians had sent word that a large party of Wyandots were headed for Wheeling. These, about thirty in number, had crossed the Ohio in thirteen canoes, about five miles below Fort McIntosh. Beginning their descent, they attacked a party of five men working in a field, killing four and capturing the fifth. But their canoes had been discovered on the very day they had crossed, and an ambush was prepared for them by Captain Thomas McIntyre, on the opposite shore. Quickly the Indians returned to the river, planning on recrossing the river to avoid pursuit, then continuing these lightning-strokes as they proceeded south, downriver. Upon reaching the canoes they tied their prisoner to the lead canoe, and moved out onto the river. When they came within about fifty yards of the ambush several of McIntyre's militia, seeing such a large party advancing directly toward them, became rather "timid", as the saying was, and began to withdraw. The Indians saw this movement, gave a frightful yell, and began paddling downstream furiously, trying to avoid the fusillade of bullets which came from the river bank. Four or five of the Indians were killed, and probably as many more wounded. The captive, Will Bailey, nearly drowned before one of McIntyre's men swam out to the canoe with a knife between his teeth and cut Bailey free from the bullet-riddled canoe.

But it was the success of these encounters that doomed Brodhead's chances for a campaign against the Indians; a bountiful crop of wheat was ripening, the best ever, and men were busily getting in their crops. With Indians raiding this far east, and with work in the fields, they refused to join, so on the last day of July a frustrated Col. Brodhead sent a circular letter to all the county lieutenants stating that his expedition was postponed until later in the fall, when the men would be available.

Not so with Clark. Not only did he have enough men, he had brought artillery from Louisville, a six-pounder which he had captured in Illinois and transported to Louisville. A taste of their own medicine was in store for some soon-to-be surprised Shawnee. On the second of August the men began moving up the Miami, with the cannon and the heavier stores in canoes. Clark, guided by Kenton, moved his men so rapidly that the Shawnee would have suffered a terrible defeat, but for one man. As they approached the Indian town of Chillicothe, one of the Kentuckians, a Tory sympathizer, sneaked off into the night and gave the Shawnee their first notice of Clark's approaching army. The Indians hastily pulled out, firing the town, so that when Clark arrived there was nothing but smoking ruins.

Leaving some men to destroy the hundreds of acres of corn which surrounded the village, the others moved on to the next town, Piqua, and here the Shawnee, although outnumbered three to one, made a desperate stand. Clark had sent Benjamin Logan with a column to attack the town from the flank, but Logan's men had been delayed trying to work their way around a swamp, and were unable to get into position before Clark brought up his cannon. When splinters of the long house began flying about their ears, the Shawnee beat a hasty retreat into the woods. But they had not given up; as they had the year before they soon launched a counterattack against the despised "militia", expecting to cut them down, just as they had Bowman's men the year before.

To their regret, however; for what they thought were militia were by now battle-hardened veterans who were as good at bush-fighting as the Indians, and they were led by George Rogers Clark, not John Bowman. The fight did not last long; when it was over the number of Indian scalps totaled seventy-three, while Clark had lost twenty men. Clark especially mourned two of the fallen men; Sam Moore, one of the two scouts he had sent to Kaskaskia in 1777, had been killed. The second was

Joseph Rogers, who had been an Indian captive for six years. When the battle was at it highest pitch, and his Indian guard's attention was momentarily diverted, Joe Rogers made a dash for the American lines, but his body was riddled with bullets, front and back, and he died in the arms of his cousin, George Rogers Clark.

Piqua was burned, the fields of corn destroyed, and the army recrossed the Ohio without further incident. They had not destroyed the Shawnee, but they had taught them and all the other Indian tribes that the Kentuckians could and would retaliate. It was Clark who had led them, and he would lead them again.

It was also at about this time that Simon Kenton received what must have been joyous news. William Leachman, his old rival whom he thought he had killed in 1771, had been only stunned, and there were no murder warrants outstanding for Simon. It was surely with a sense of relief that he was able to drop the alias of *Butler* and revert to the name of Kenton.

But there was sadness as well. In October, Daniel Boone had gone on a hunt to the Blue Licks with his beloved younger brother, Edward. On their way back home Daniel had shot a bear, which had not fallen, but lumbered off downstream. Daniel pursued, while Ned remained with the horses. Just as Daniel reached the fallen bear he heard a number of shots in back of him, then silence. Knowing that his brother was either dead or a prisoner, Daniel returned to his station. The men who went out the next day found Ned's body lying in the forest; it had been decapitated by the Shawnee.

*   *   *

One way or another, 1781 was to be the turning point in both the eastern phase of the Revolution and the Indian wars on the western border. Cornwallis' surrender at Yorktown in October would signal independence for the newly-formed United States, and although great was the elation in the east, affairs in the west by that time were taking an opposite turn.

With Clark's victory over the Shawnee in August of 1780, the time was now ripe for an all-out assault on Detroit. Clark was commissioned brigadier general; during the winter he was to assemble all the necessary supplies, including artillery, at Pittsburgh, then sail down the Ohio picking up the assembled companies as he went, to a staggering total of 2,000 men. He was to reach the Falls of the Ohio by March 15th, and from there strike northward, through the heart of the Indian country, destroying everything in his path, crushing all Indian resistance before him, and finally reducing Detroit.

Clark reached Williamsburg in December, 1780, and began conferring with Governor Thomas Jefferson on the campaign. General Washington had given hearty approval to the plan, and in December he wrote to Brodhead, directing him to begin assembling the necessary supplies, and to give Clark every assistance in his power, as well as provide him with the largest possible detachment of regulars from Pitt that Brodhead could spare.

But then things began to go wrong. On January 4th Benedict Arnold, now a brigadier general in the English army, attacked and captured Richmond. Suddenly Virginia was facing danger from the east instead of from the west. Clark took part in some of the fighting, but was back in Pittsburgh in time to learn of the death of an old and valued comrade.

William Linn, nearly fifty years old, had traveled the roads and finally gone the way of most frontiersmen. He had been in Forbes' Campaign against Fort Duquesne in 1758, and had been wounded while serving under Angus McDonald in the summer of 1774. In 1776-1777 he was a first lieutenant in George Gibson's New Orleans expedition, which succeeded in bringing the much-needed supply of gunpowder to the western outposts. He had been with Col. Foreman at the ambush at the Narrows in September, 1777. Having rejoined Clark on the Ohio in 1778, he accompanied the expedition to Kaskaskia, finally returning to Kentucky to settle a station not far from where he had left his family at Louisville. In August, 1780, he had served as a colonel of militia in Clark's retaliatory campaign following Bird's invasion. But then, on March 5th, not far from his new home, he had been shot and mortally wounded by Indians.

More bad news was in store for Clark, terrible news. Despite the best efforts of the American commissioners, and even with the aid of French officers sent to Fort Pitt expressly for the purpose of maintaining the neutrality of the Delaware tribe, the final disaster of American Indian diplomacy occurred in early April of 1781. Several leaders of the Coshocton Delaware had gone to Detroit to pledge allegiance to the British cause. This was especially serious to the American frontier since the Delaware, better than any other tribe, knew the location and condition of the frontier settlements. Throughout the Revolution the majority of the Delaware had remained loyal to the American cause, but now, with Arnold and Cornwallis ravaging the eastern seaboard, with mutinies and desertions from the Continental army, and with Washington forced to send troops from his dwindling army to support Greene in the Carolinas and Lafayette in Virginia, they considered it time to join the side of what they perceived to be the ultimate victors. When Brodhead received certain news of this from the Moravians he acted quickly, deciding to strike them before they could cause serious trouble.

Disregarding Washington's orders to assist Clark, Brodhead sent a message to Col. David Shepherd, Lieutenant of Ohio County, to gather all available men for an expedition into the Indian country. He quickly assembled over 150 of his regulars at Pitt and sailed down to Fort Henry, where Shepherd had collected 134 militiamen, mostly from that county. These consisted of four companies under the command of Captains Joseph Ogle, Benjamin Royse, Jacob Leffler, and William Crawford[52]. Brodhead's army started overland on April 10th, in a surprise march toward the Delaware villages on the Muskingum. Under Brodhead were a number of well-known frontiersmen; other than Shepherd, a former commander of Fort Henry, there was Maj. Sam McColloch of Van Meter's Fort on Short Creek, and his younger brother John, three of the Wetzels (John, Sr., George, and Lewis), Hamilton Kerr, with Jonathan Zane as scout. A few of the Delaware who had remained friendly to the Americans helped guide the expedition; these were led by Pekillon, a minor chief.

Upon approaching Coshocton Brodhead ordered a final rapid march and succeeded in surprising the Indian town. In his 1824 *Notes on the... Indian Wars* the Rev. Joseph Doddridge detailed the plan of attack:

"The army reached the place in three divisions. The right and left wings approached the river a little above and below the town, while the center marched directly upon it. The whole number of the Indians in the village on the east side of the river, together with ten or twelve from a little village some distance above, were made prisoners without firing a single shot."

Due to high water the army was unable to cross the river to attack the Indian towns on the west side of the river, and those villages escaped destruction. Doddridge explains the fate of a number of the captives:

"Among the prisoners were sixteen warriors. A little after dark a council of war was held, to determine on the fate of the warriors in custody. They were doomed to death, and by the order of the commander were bound, taken a little distance below the town, and dispatched with tomahawks and spears, and then scalped."

The sixteen warriors who were thus *dispatched* had been pointed out to the American commander by none other than Pekillon, as having been especially active in raids against the frontier settlements. Several other warriors, still loyal to the Americans, were released; a number of the Indian women and children were taken back to Fort Pitt as hostages, although they were also soon released.

Brodhead naturally wished to continue the campaign against the remaining villages in the vicinity. The militiamen, however, having done so much with no loss to themselves (none killed and only one man wounded), and giving the difficulty of crossing the river as their reason, voted to return home. Faced with the potential loss of half his fighting force, the commander had no choice but to consent.

The danger to Virginia was considered so extreme that on June 21st the assembly voted to abandon Clark's expedition against Detroit altogether. Still, Clark did not give up. Most of the inhabitants of the Upper Ohio knew, as well as Clark, that the only solution to the Indian problem lay in driving the English out of that city. Brodhead had been recalled to the east, to face charges of malfeasance, and sturdy John Gibson had been placed in command of the western Department. He was, however, still forced to follow Brodhead's dictum that no continental troops be furnished Clark, and in this Gen. Washington acquiesced. So instead of two thousand men for a major assault on Detroit, Clark was reduced to depending on what militia and volunteers he could persuade to join him. Whatever was done, with Clark they knew it would be a desperate venture. From Pittsburgh to the Falls of the Ohio was over eight hundred miles by river, then another four hundred miles overland to Detroit, or six hundred if Clark chose to go by way of the Wabash. Distances such as these meant that the men would be away from home for a minimum of six months, perhaps as long as a year.

Brodhead's obvious jealousy of Clark's fame, and his inconclusive campaign against the Delaware, had done nothing more than stiffen Indian resistance to the Americans, and delay Clark. And although Virginia had by now relinquished its claims to the Pennsylvania counties, many of the Pennsylvanians yet considered the expedition to be nothing more than another land-grabbing scheme by Virginia. But in spite of this Clark had rounded up enough supplies and volunteers by early August to begin his campaign, although he was now five long months behind schedule. Courageous Col. Archibald Lochry[53], of Westmoreland County, had offered to lead a detachment of his own militia in Clark's expedition.

Experiencing the usual difficulties, it was not until July 24th that Lochry was able to set out with his hundred six men from near Hannastown. Moving down the Ohio, he had expected to meet up with Clark at Wheeling, but he reached Wheeling only scant hours behind; on the afternoon of the day that he arrived he found that Clark had gone on ahead at daybreak that very morning. Lochry sent a boat downriver with a message that he was only a day behind, and was hurrying on.

The Indians were assembling their own army at Sandusky, preparing to resist the coming invasion, when on August 8th Clark began moving down the Ohio. It was already late in the season for such a protracted campaign, and he could not wait for Lochry to arrive. He stopped overnight at Wheeling to pick up more men, and there he left a message for Lochry to hurry on, then moved out from Fort Henry.

Lochry and his men hurried downriver, hoping to catch up with Clark; they had reached the mouth of a creek about ten miles below the mouth of the Miami when they were hailed from shore. Pulling in to the bank Lochry and his men were quickly overwhelmed by a force led by Simon Girty and the great Mohawk leader Joseph Brant. Lochry and thirty-five others of his command were killed in the initial engagement; the remainder of the men who were not killed were taken captive, and those who survived did not reach their homes until nearly two years later, following the peace of 1783, when they were exchanged at Montreal and finally arrived home in May, 1783.

## Fifth Interlude:
## A Man of the Name of Wetzel

### The Developmental Account of an Alleged Incident during Brodhead's Coshocton Expedition, April 10-28, 1781

A particularly notorious incident, first mentioned by Dr. Doddridge, occurred during the retreat of Brodhead's army from Coshocton to Pitt. He stated that an Indian chief who had been granted safe conduct by Brodhead was brutally killed by one of the militiamen, while in the very act of negotiating with the colonel himself. The episode is described in this manner:

"Early the next morning an Indian presented himself on the opposite bank of the river and asked for the big captain. Broadhead (sic) presented himself and asked the Indian what he wanted, to which he replied:

'I want peace.'

'Send over some of your chiefs,' said Broadhead.

'May be you kill,' said the Indian.

He was answered, 'They shall not be killed.'

One of the chiefs, a well looking man, came over the river and entered into conversation with the commander in the street; but while engaged in conversation a man of the name of Wetzel came up behind him with a tomahawk concealed in the bosom of his hunting shirt and struck him on the back of his head. He fell and instantly expired."

Seven years later, in 1831, Alexander Scott Withers repeated the story:

"... an Indian, making his appearance on the opposite bank of the river, called out for the 'Big Captain'. Col. Broadhead demanded what he wished. I want peace replied the savage. Then send over some of your chiefs, said the Colonel. May be you kill, responded the Indian. No, said Broadhead, they shall not be killed. One of their chiefs, a fine looking fellow, then came over; and while he and Col. Broadhead were engaged in conversation, a militia-man came up, and with a tomahawk which he had concealed in the bosom of his hunting shirt, struck him a severe blow on the hinder part of his head. The poor Indian fell, and immediately expired."

Although the wording is nearly identical to Doddridge, even to the misspelling of *Broadhead*, the name *Wetzel* has been omitted, stating only that, while they were engaged in conversation, a militia-man came up. Withers obtained most of the materials for his book from two earlier amateur historians: Hugh Paul Taylor's newspaper articles and Judge Edwin Duncan's unpublished collections. Evidently neither of these gentlemen had included any information on the tomahawked-from-behind Indian story, as Withers has quite obviously copied the entire episode, word for word, from Doddridge.

Eight years later the *Western Christian Advocate* of Cincinnati began publishing a five-part series[54] on the Wetzels, written by Col. John McDonald, of Kentucky. But McDonald was not a Wheeling native. Born in 1776 he had lived some distance north of Wheeling when a child, but had been raised in Kentucky. He may have seen Lewis Wetzel at some time, on one of Wetzel's later trips to Kentucky, and he undoubtedly knew Jacob Wetzel at the time when Jacob and Simon Kenton were protecting the Kentucky frontier.

But even though he was associated with Kenton on some of his later exploits (post-1791), McDonald's knowledge of events which had occurred earlier in the vicinity of Pittsburgh and Wheeling could have come only from stories told him as a boy, which he then described for the *Advocate* some fifty years later. He acknowledges Doddridge as his primary source as he recounts the event:

"In the year 1780, an expedition was set on foot, to proceed against and destroy the Indian towns situated on the Coshocton, a branch of the Muskingum river.[55] The place of rendezvous for the troops was Wheeling. The command of the expedition was conferred on Col. Broadhead, a soldier of some distinction in those days. Martin Whetzel was a volunteer in this campaign. The officers of the frontier armies were only nominally such; every soldier acted as seemed right in his own judgment. This little army, of four hundred men, went forward rapidly, in order to fall upon the Indian towns by surprise. They were secretly and actively pushed forward, til they surrounded one of their towns before the enemy was apprised of their danger. 'Every man, woman, and child were made prisoners, without the firing of a gun.'"

[McDonald uses the quotation marks - ' ', here and below, to indicate that this sentence was taken from Doddridge's *Notes*.]

"Among the prisoners were sixteen warriors. 'A little after dark a council of warwas held to determine the fate of the warriors in custody. They were doomed to death, and by the order of the commander were bound, taken a little distance below the town, and despatched with tomahawks and spears, and then scalped.'"

McDonald adds, gratuitously:

"In this work of death, Martin Whetzel, with a kind of fiendish pleasure, sunk his tomahawk into the heads of the unresisting Indians."

Then, continuing from Doddridge:

"'Early the next morning an Indian presented himself on the opposite bank of the river, and asked for the 'Big captain'. Col. Broadhead presented himself and asked the Indian what he wanted? To which he replied, 'I want peace.' 'Send over some of your chiefs,' said Broadhead. 'May be you kill,' said the Indian. He was answered, 'They shall not be killed.'"

"One of the chiefs, a well-looking man, came over the river and entered into conversation with the commander in the street; but while engaged in conversation Martin Whetzel came up behind him with a tomahawk concealed in the bosom ofhis hunting-shirt, and struck him on the back of his head. The poor Indian fell and immediately expired.'"

Says McDonald:

"This act of perfidy and reckless revenge, the commander had no power, if he had the disposition, to punish, as probably two-thirds of the army approved the vindictive deed."

The militia man has now become *Martin* Wetzel, but this is an impossibility, since Martin was not on this expedition against the Indians, for the very good reason that at the time it took place he was a captive of the Shawnees, from 1778 into 1781. After his escape he made his way to the Kentucky settlements, and then eventually returned to his Virginia home. Brodhead's expedition to Coshocton took place in April, 1781, before Martin had returned to Wheeling.

In that same year of 1839 Joseph Pritts published his *Incidents of Border Warfare*. His version of the Coshocton Expedition is an exact duplication of McDonald's newspaper articles, even to copying the mistake of the year of the expedition as 1780, and the misspelling of *Broadhead*.

"... an Indian presented himself on the opposite bank of the river .... but while engaged in conversation Martin Whetzel came up behind him with a tomahawk concealed in the bosom of his hunting-shirt, and struck him on the back of his head. The poor Indian fell and immediately expired."

In the 1840's Dr. Lyman C. Draper, in an effort to determine the facts of this episode, wrote a letter [December 22, 1848] to Major Lewis Bonnett, Jr., a cousin of the Wetzels[56], and with whom Lewis Wetzel had lived in the 1780's. In his reply to Draper Bonnett denied that the man involved in this incident was a Wetzel, writing:

"But of Brodhead calling over the river requesting some of the chiefs to come over, the Indian reply was, 'may be you kill.' Brodhead answered, 'Not.' The chief then came over, and whilst talking with Brodhead, a Militia man stepped up, and having a tomahawk concealed under his hunting shirt, drew it unobserved and sunk it in the back part of the chief's head, so that he expired in a few minutes — I never understood that it was a Wetzel that done the deed; all that was ever said, it was a Militia man that done the act."

The connection between Doddridge/Withers and Bonnett is obvious; at the time of this correspondence Bonnett had read Withers and had been strongly influenced by it in his subsequent "recollections". But as to the heart of the story he specifically told Draper: "I never understood that it was a Wetzel."

The problem lies in determining who first gave this story to Doddridge, who was then residing at Wellsburg, about 20 miles north of Wheeling. Since he got much of his material from the old pioneers who were still living in the early 1820's in the vicinity of Wheeling, it may have come from one of them. It is much more likely, however, to have been a confused rendition of several other stories, picked up by Doddridge, which had been passed on by oral tradition.

Only two years later, in 1851, Wills De Hass, copying the description given by Doddridge, relates:

"... an Indian presented himself on the opposite bank of the river." Then follows the standard:

Brodhead:	"What he wanted?"
Indian:	"I want peace!"
Brodhead:	"Send over chiefs."
Indian:	"May be you kill?"
Brodhead:	"Shall not."

De Hass then continues with his version:

"One of the chiefs, a well looking man, came over the river and entered into conversation with Col. Brodhead in the street; but while engaged in conversation, a man belonging to the army, by the name of John Wetzel, came up behind him, with a tomahawk concealed in the bosom of his hunting shirt, and struck him a blow on the back of his head. He fell, and instantly expired."

De Hass was a resident of Moundsville, south of Wheeling, while working on his *Indian Wars*; even though he interviewed many of the descendants of those early pioneers, there is no doubt that he lifted this particular incident bodily from Doddridge, while adding the name of *John* to Doddridge's plain *Wetzel*. Of course this would have to be Capt. John Wetzel, the father of Martin, George, Lewis, Jacob, and John, Jr. The muster rolls of Brodhead's Expedition, however, list only John, George, and Lewis Wetzel as being members, serving in Capt. Ogle's company. Jacob was not along, as he was not yet 16 years of age, and John, Jr. was only ten The eldest son, Martin, was not on this expedition, as it was at just about this time that he was managing his escape from Indian captivity in southwestern Ohio and, heading south to the Kentucky settlements, had not yet returned to Virginia.

By De Hass's time the tomahawking of the well-looking Indian chief had been accepted as fact, and all the details had become well established except for some lingering doubt as to exactly which of the Wetzels it was who had committed the dastardly deed. Doddridge, born in 1770, was only eleven years old at the time of the expedition and, like all the other writers [including McDonald, b. 1776, five years old in 1781; Bonnett, b. 1778, three years old; Withers, b. in 1792, eleven years after the event], he had no firsthand knowledge of the Indian-Tomahawked-From-Behind story. His version must have come from someone else, probably many years later, as he was preparing his manuscript for publication. And every other person who has told this story (while many, at the same time, have taken great delight in accusing Doddridge of being quite unreliable) has done nothing more than parrot Doddridge's own words.

Even though he used Doddridge as one of his references, the meticulous historian C.W. Butterfield did not mention this particular incident while describing Brodhead's campaign in his account of Crawford's 1782 Expedition. Butterfield probably had reservations about its verity, since he was unable to find any independent recitation of the episode outside of Doddridge.

The first hint that the perpetrator might have been Lewis Wetzel did not appear until nearly a century had passed. In their 1879 *History of the Pan-Handle*, Newton, Nichols, and Sprankle described the incident, again in Doddridge's words: after an Indian had appeared on the opposite side of the river and asked for the 'big captain' —

"Brodhead sent him for his chief, who came over under a promise that he should not be killed. After he got over it is said that the notorious Indian fighter, Lewis Wetzel, tomahawked him."

In 1884 the incredibly prolific Edward S. Ellis published his *Life of Boone*, which contained two chapters on Simon Kenton, and one on the Wetzels. The two paragraphs below, which describe that *"wild beast Martin Wetzel"*, come from the Wetzel chapter, and were manifestly copied from McDonald-Pritts. While he did not include the killing of the sixteen warriors, there is no doubt that Ellis had read either/or McDonald-Pritts, giving the year as 1780, and even describing Martin Wetzel's behavior by using the same term, *perfidy*.

"Martin Wetzel acted the part of a wild beast and committed acts for which no law human or divine can find justification. No red Indian ever showed greater perfidy than did he. During Colonel Brodhead's expedition in 1780, Martin Wetzel was a volunteer. An Indian messenger, under promise of protection, came into camp and held an interview with Brodhead. While they were talking in the most friendly manner, Martin Wetzel stole up behind the unsuspecting red man, and quickly drawing a tomahawk, which he had hidden in his hunting-shirt, struck the Indian in the back of the head a blow which stretched him lifeless on the ground."

"Colonel Brodhead was exasperated at the atrocious act, yet he dared not punish Wetzel, for three-fourths of the army would have rallied in his defence."

\*    \*    \*

## Lewis Wetzel: Miscreant and Wretch!

But sometime within the next eight years Ellis changed his mind; when his *Indian Wars of the United States* appeared in 1892 it contained the standard "big Captain" story, with one alteration:

"While Colonel Brodhead was returning to Pittsburgh from his expedition into the Indian country, a warrior approached the side of the river opposite to the encampment, and called out that he wished to see the 'big Captain.' Colonel Brodhead came forward and asked what he wanted. 'To make peace,' was the reply. Colonel Brodhead told him to send over some of his chiefs. The Indian asked whether they would be harmed. The colonel assured him they should not suffer the least injury."

"Under this guarantee, one of the finest looking chiefs ever seen by Colonel Brodhead crossed the river, and began conversation with the officer. While thus engaged, a militia man sneaked up behind the chief, whipped out a tomahawk he had concealed under his clothing, and clove the skull of the guest in twain. The name of this wretch was *Wetzel*, and he was never punished for his crime. The attempts to do so almost caused a revolution in a portion of the west, where the people regarded him as a hero. Since that day the miscreant has figured in unnumbered histories and romances as the ideal frontiersman, worthy only of admiration for his exploits."

The victim, first described by Doddridge as a well looking man, has now become one of the finest looking chiefs ever seen by Colonel Brodhead. And although Ellis does not give us the first name of the *miscreant*, it is obvious from his reference to a near-revolution caused by attempts to punish a militia man for killing an Indian, as well as from his remark concerning the unnumbered histories and romances of an ideal frontiersman, that the "wretch" to whom he refers could only be Lewis Wetzel. Since Ellis had identified the villain as Martin Wetzel in his earlier book, it is understandable that he did not now want to contradict himself by actually writing the name *Lewis Wetzel*, but there is no doubt as to which of the Wetzels he means. The final portion of his description: "attempts to punish the militiaman for this almost caused a revolution in a portion of the West ..." is nothing more than Ellis confusing the shooting of *Indian George Washington*[57] by Wetzel near Fort Harmar (Marietta, Ohio) in 1789, eight years after this incident.

There is a moral to this story somewhere, as well, which has more than a little to do with the quality of truth vs. the injection of venom. Is it any wonder that, only a dozen years later, Zane Grey, in writing a novel about Lewis Wetzel, would try to "soften a little the ruthless name history accords him". Grey's novel, *The Spirit of the Border*, turned out to be as factual as Ellis' history.

But by 1917, when *Frontier Retreat on the Upper Ohio* was published by the Wisconsin Historical Society (using the Draper Manuscripts), *Lewis* had become the accepted *Wetzel*, and the not-unexpected villain:

"An Indian presented himself on the opposite bank of the river and asked for the 'Big Captain'. Brodhead responded with the question as to what he wanted. To which he replied in substance that his desire was for peace. "Send over some of your chiefs," said the American commander. "May be you will kill them," was the response. He was answered that they should not be killed. One came across, a fine looking man, and entered into conversation with Brodhead. But while thus engaged, Lewis Wetzel, one of the militiamen, came up behind the chief with a tomahawk concealed in the bosom of his hunting shirt and struck him on the back of his head with the weapon, causing instant death."

It is unnecessary to compare this to the version published nearly a hundred years earlier to see that it is nothing more than "stylized Doddridge". It was not taken from the Draper Manuscripts, as is implied, and it was the second time that the editor of *Frontier Retreat*, Louise Phelps Kellogg, had inserted this unsubstantiated "story" in what was supposed to be a work of historic merit. In her *Introduction* she went to considerable pains to include Doddridge's account of this "murder of the Indian chieftain". As she summarized it there:

"A characteristic episode of the expedition reveals the vindictive temper of the frontier militia. During the stay during the Moravian villages a chief of the hostiles was invited into camp under the strictest promises of safe-conduct from the commandant. As they were conferring together a noted hater of Indians (sic!) among the soldiers silently crept forward, and without excuse or warning buried his tomahawk in the envoy's forehead. By such savage deeds as this must the frontier spirit be judged."

Lewis Bonnett, who stated he ... "never understood that it was a Wetzel that done the deed", was one of the rare individuals with whom Draper corresponded who had actually known Lewis Wetzel. Kellogg's version is just one more copying of the original 1824 account, but this time with the addition of the name Lewis to "a man of the name of Wetzel".

By this time Capt. John Wetzel and both sons Martin and Lewis had been specifically identified as the perpetrator, but Kellogg was historian enough to know that Martin had not been a member of that expedition, and besides, she had the complete roster of the names of the participants. Checking that roster Kellogg knew that if it had been a Wetzel, then the only possible candidates were John, Sr., George, or Lewis; but no writer had ever claimed that it was Lewis until a century after the actual incident.

Kellogg inserted here a brief sketch of the life of Lewis Wetzel; in a gross over-simplification she stated that he was bitterly hostile to all the Indian race as a result of his capture by Indians when he was about fourteen. Although neglecting to mention the death of his father, Captain John Wetzel, at the hands of the Indians in 1786, she did mention several incidents in Lewis' life. But Kellogg, who was supposed to be writing history, editorialized instead, and in doing so let slip her own personal prejudice against Wetzel. In the conclusion of her biographical sketch she sneered that, although Wetzel was considered a border hero by his peers, *"his attitude towards Indians was that of many of the lower class upon the frontier."*

But Kellogg also had access to the papers concerning Lewis Wetzel's arrest following his wounding an Indian near Marietta, Ohio, in 1789. She knew that Wetzel had been arrested and, for want of a jail at Marietta, had been lodged in Fort Harmar, from which he soon escaped. Upon being (illegally) recaptured by the military at Limestone (Maysville), Kentucky, he was turned over to one of the judges of the Federal Territory at Fort Washington (Cincinnati), John Cleves Symmes, who immediately ordered his release, as the Indian had by then recovered, and the only witness against Wetzel had left the country. At that time Wetzel was described by Judge Foster, another of the judges of the territory, and from him we have the best description of not only his physical appearance, but also of Wetzel's moral character. Following the physical description Judge Foster stated that:

"His morals and habits, compared with those of his general associates and the tone of society in the West of that day, were quite exemplary."

Judge Foster could hardly have been described as being a member of the lower class upon the frontier, and knowing this, as she must have, and with no other evidence, it seems rather disingenuous of Kellogg to disparage Lewis Wetzel in such a manner.

\*　　\*　　\*

But this is becoming rather tedious. In 1824 it started out as *a man of the name of Wetzel*. Then it becomes simply a militia-man, then John Wetzel, then Martin Wetzel, and finally Lewis Wetzel. But at least, for nearly two centuries, there has never been a question but that the assassin had a *tomahawk concealed in the bosom of his hunting shirt*. Everyone could be in agreement on the weapon and the place of concealment.

The point which must be stressed is this: *every single account of this episode is nothing more than a barely altered reiteration of Doddridge's original 1824 version, which he had picked up from some unknown source. There is not one other independent version of this incident.*

No other writer has ever given any details of this "murder", except those which they copied from Doddridge. There is no mention of this in any of the official correspondence, and other than Ellis, who mistakenly attributed efforts by Harmar to punish Wetzel for shooting an Indian in 1789, nothing is said about any punishment for a militiaman who would so brazenly kill an Indian, one who had just been given safe conduct by an officer. In 1846 another of the old pioneers stated that just before the expedition set out, her brother (William Boggs) and Lewis Wetzel, having broken into the guardhouse at Wheeling, tomahawked an Indian chief who had been placed there by Brodhead for safekeeping. It is hardly credible that 17-year-old Lewis Wetzel would then be allowed to accompany the expedition and tomahawk another Indian, who had been given safe conduct, while Brodhead was standing there "in the street" negotiating with him, *and nothing be done to him.* Could not Brodhead see who the "miscreant-wretch" was? Wetzel had had smallpox while in his teens, and his face was badly scarred; his appearance was so striking that had Brodhead not known him, he could hardly have failed to recognize him from among the one hundred-plus militia.

*   *   *

## *Fiction Stranger Than Truth*

But even more important than the question regarding Kellogg's rationale is another: Did this incident even occur? Was there ever any Indian who was tomahawked from behind while talking to Brodhead? There are so many similarities of this story with certain others that it seems hard to believe that all of them took place, exactly as described. The basic elements of this Tomahawked Indian Chief story sound suspiciously like a mish-mash concoction of five different incidents which occurred in the 1770s and 1780s, and which, 40 years later, could all have been rolled up into one single thrilling and exciting adventure story for Doddridge, viz:
1)   The killing of the Shawnee chief Cornstalk in 1777.
2)   Lewis Wetzel and Billy Boggs tomahawking an Indian chief named Killbuck in the guardhouse at Wheeling, just prior to the commencement of Brodhead's Expedition.
3)   The account of Martin Wetzel's escape from captivity.
4)   Brodhead's militia killing the sixteen Indian warriors at Coshocton, and
5)   Certainly not to be forgotten, Hugh McGary's tomahawking the Indian chief Moluntha at the Indian village of Wapatomica, five years later, during Benjamin Logan's 1786 campaign.

**The Deaths of Cornstalk and Killbuck:** The Cornstalk murder has already been covered in Chapter XII. It was almost certainly the death of Cornstalk, who had been placed in the guardhouse at Fort Randolph (Point Pleasant) for safe-keeping, that Lydia (Boggs) Cruger, sixty-five years later, confused with the guardhouse at Wheeling. The Delaware chief known as Killbuck lived for many years after 1781, being baptized by the Moravians in 1788, and dying peacefully in bed in 1811. No other source describes this "Killbuck" story, and it seems reasonable to assume that it did not happen.

**Martin Wetzel:** The story of his captivity and escape is described fully in Chapter XIV. The alleged tomahawking of his Indian captors was another of John McDonald's fabrications.

**The Sixteen Indian Captives:** As described earlier, they were tied to trees before being killed; this has been authenticated by the Indians themselves; after their failed assault on Wheeling in September of that year, they attacked and captured another small blockhouse. Several of the prisoners taken were tied to trees and then toma-hawked, the Indians saying to the other captives who witnessed this: "Now we be militia."

**Hugh McGary:** Following the disastrous *Battle of Blue Licks* in August, 1782 (Chapter XXII), Major McGary was condemned by many of his fellow Kentuckians as being chiefly responsible for leading them into the ambush. Four years later, at Wapatomica (present Zanesfield, Ohio), during Benjamin Logan's campaign, the aged Shawnee chief Moluntha was placed under the protection of Logan. In spite of this, and in revenge for his own humiliation and for the loss of so many men (including one of Daniel Boone's sons), McGary, who was one of the militia officers, approached Moluntha, as he was "standing in the street talking to several officers", and asked whether he had been at the Blue Licks. Probably not understanding, Moluntha smiled and nodded his head, whereupon McGary pulled his tomahawk and, before any of the officers there could stop him, killed Moluntha with a savage blow to the head. Moluntha "fell and expired instantly." McGary was court-martialed for this violation of orders, but his punishment was so slight, a temporary loss of command, that it was no more than a slap on the wrist.

\*     \*     \*

Since Dr. Doddridge is the original and only author of this Coshocton episode, it is now necessary to return to his *Notes* to solve this "puzzle wrapped in an enig-ma". As he described it, during the course of a military excursion into the Indian country, but after the fighting has ended, a peaceful Indian who has been given safe-conduct by the commanding officer is struck down by a militiaman, name unknown, who is wielding a tomahawk, while the chief engages in conversation with an officer. The details are so amazingly similar to the *McGary-Moluntha* inci-dent of 1786 that one wonders how Doddridge treated that particular episode.

Doddridge didn't. There is nothing in the *Notes* pertaining to the Wapatomica Campaign. The conclusion is inescapable that Dr. Doddridge, who had no person-al knowledge of the event, was told a story of an Indian having been given safe con-duct, speaking with an officer, and then being struck down by a militia man's tom-ahawk. The narrator of the story could recall the name of neither the Indian nor the militia man, nor even the year during which the campaign took place. Doddridge may have been told that it "happened in the 1780s, perhaps during Brodhead's expedition."

Lewis Bonnett had heard the story of Moluntha, but there was no association of that chief with any of the Wetzels, nor was Bonnett, who was still a child at the time, and more than sixty years later he was unable to distinguish between the campaigns of Brodhead and Logan. This is the reason for his telling Draper that he "... never understood that it was a Wetzel that done the deed; all that was ever said, it was a Militia man that done the act."

*     *     *

It is truly unfortunate that this cobbled-up story has been fastened onto Lewis Wetzel, but even more unfortunate is the continuation of this Wetzel-Brodhead myth. Even the novelists have taken their shots at the Wetzels for this "atrocity". In 1928 Thomas P. Boyd published his *Simon Girty*, in which Brodhead's Campaign is described. In this version the chief who is invited to confer with Brodhead is "an agreeable looking man," who crosses over in a canoe. Then:

"While the two men stood there one of the Wetzels (either Jacob or Lewis was capable of what followed) stepped noiselessly up behind the chieftain. Wetzel had a tomahawk lying against his breast beneath his hunting jacket. Suddenly the tomahawk flashed outward and up, then down. The blade went into the back of the chieftain's skull and he fell dead. That ended the peace parley."

Poor Jacob was only fifteen years old at the time, and for him to have committed, at that age, such an act as the one imputed to him, in the face of his commanding officer, would certainly have marked him as a rather precocious youth, disregarding of course the fact that Jacob was not even along on that expedition. The presumption of guilt is the same for John, Martin, Lewis or Jake — any of the Wetzels were capable of such an act of perfidy.

But this was fiction, so perhaps the writer can be excused on the basis of literary license, just as Zane Grey, following McDonald's lead, later wrote of the massacre of the Wetzel family, and then placed Lewis Wetzel at the 1782 Siege of Fort Henry. More literary license. But while that may excuse novelists, the same is not true for modern historians. In the past decade alone two historical works have appeared which continue the myth, Timothy Truman's *Straight Up to See the Sky,* and Allan W. Eckert's *That Dark and Bloody River.*

Eckert's version of the incident is not only rather unique, but it also adds a new twist to the Killbuck legend. After the Indian chief is offered safe conduct Lewis Wetzel, rather than calmly walking up behind the chief, suddenly leaps out from behind the shrubbery, tomahawk in hand. Col. Brodhead, unable to find the culprit, returns to Wheeling, where he then lodges Killbuck (and Son-of-Killbuck, as well) in the guard-house. Wetzel and Billy Boggs break in, tomahawk the father but not the son, and escape, leaving the tomahawk protruding from the chief's head.

\*    \*    \*

And so the story is perpetuated. Most unfortunate of all, however, is that Lewis Wetzel, who was truly a savior to the frontier people, has been condemned by historians, quasi-historians, and the general public for murdering in cold blood two peace-loving Indians. One of them was the "well looking chief" at Coshocton in 1781, the other a "peace emissary" at Marietta in 1789. And he has been castigated not only for killing these two, but despised even more because he then escaped a just and deserved punishment. *But Lewis Wetzel killed neither of these Indians!* The stories are true only in basics, not in detail. No Indian chief was killed while talking to Brodhead; this was almost certainly a confusion of Hugh McGary killing the Shawnee chief Moluntha. The alleged murder of an Indian delegate to a peace treaty at Marietta, just one more of John McDonald's *Fanciful Tales*, will be covered in the Seventh Interlude, *Lewis Wetzel vs. George Washington*.

Or, as someone once said, *"Never let the truth get in the way of a good story!"*

# Chapter XVIII

The Moravians - II
Hope Dims

1777 had been a disastrous year for the pioneers and the Moravians alike, and by the end of that terrible year the future of the Christian Indians must have appeared bleak. Even though Schoenbrunn had been abandoned in April because of the danger to both the converted Indians and to the missionaries, war parties were constantly traversing the road through Gnadenhutten, heading east to raid the frontier, or returning back west toward their homes. Soon Gnadenhutten succumbed to Schoenbrunn's fate; by the summer of 1778 Gnadenhutten contained between 50 and 60 cabins, but the danger was now considered so great that it too must be abandoned, and Lichtenau once again absorbed the refugees. After six years of struggle and hardship in the Ohio wilderness, only this one Christian Indian village remained, this Meadow of Light. True, it was an enormous village, with over four hundred converts, but it was too large. While the economy was basically agricultural, the men still hunted occasionally for game, and the size of the community drove away the game for both Christian and non-Christian Indian alike.

For this reason an attempt was made in 1779 to re-establish the two former towns of Schoenbrunn and Gnadenhutten, using segments of the Lichtenau population. Joshua, the Mohican elder who had founded Gnadenhutten, had died on August 1, 1775, and been buried in the cemetery at Gnadenhutten[58]. His son, also named Joshua, was one of the Licthenau emigrants who helped re-establish his father's old village. By trade young Joshua was a cooper, a barrelmaker, and the cooper's shop in which Joshua lived and worked would play a tragic role in the lives of the inhabitants.

The old location of Schoenbrunn was soon deemed unsatisfactory, and the inhabitants moved across the river, to the west bank of the Tuscarawas, almost opposite Schoenbrunn, and founded the village of New Schoenbrunn. During the next twelve months the situation seemed to be progressing relatively smoothly, so much so that it was decided to abandon Lichtenau altogether and establish a new community, which was given the name of Salem. Founded by Heckewelder, it was located on the Tuscarawas River, between Gnadenhutten and Newcomerstown, six miles below Gnadenhutten, and a mile and a half southwest of present Port Washington, Ohio.

Even so, prospects for the Moravian Indians and, by extension, their Delaware allies were growing dim in 1779. Early the next year, in February, 1780, Col. Brodhead had sent a letter to Zeisberger, in which he proposed to the friendly Delaware Indians that they remove to a new location on the Beaver River, a few miles north of Pitt, and at the same time Brodhead invited the Moravians to accompany them. Not only were they in danger from the hostile Indians, but it would be far easier to furnish them with supplies. Nevertheless the Moravians remained; in spite of the constant danger, in spite of all the warnings, for it was apparently impossible for the missionaries to believe that anyone would actively wish to harm either them or their Christian converts. They were hurting no one, they engaged in no wars, and they were doing good.

1780 was not to be a year of diminished warfare on the western border, even though the concentration of the British war effort against Washington and his Continentals was taking place in the east; it had not been as easy to put down the rebellion in the American colonies as the British ministers had at first believed. In the fall of 1777 Gentleman Johnny Burgoyne had been forced to surrender his army at Saratoga, and the next year England's old enemy, France, had entered the war against England, allying themselves with the Americans; as a consequence of the arrival of a French fleet in American waters the British had been forced to evacuate Philadelphia.

In late March, 1780, the Joseph Mallott family, including fourteen-year-old Catherine, started out from Maryland for Kentucky; they were descending the Ohio in two boats, with Joseph in the rear boat with the stock, and his family in the lead boat. The lead boat was the one that Simon Girty and the Indians struck. They killed two men and a child, and took twenty-one prisoners. Joseph's wife, two daughters, Catherine and Keziah, and two sons, Peter and Theodore, were all captured. Catherine eventually married her captor, Simon Girty, and remained in Canada when her husband fled there[59], as did the two sons. Keziah married a Chicago-Peoria trader, but Joseph, husband and father, had escaped; supposing the rest of his family to be dead, he returned to Maryland and remarried.

To the south, in Tennessee, Col. Patrick Ferguson had been killed at King's Mountain in October, 1780, and his highly touted riflemen were defeated by even better riflemen from Tennessee, led by Colonels William Campbell, Isaac Shelby, and John Sevier. The next year, as Lord Cornwallis was heading for Yorktown and ultimate defeat, with American victory and independence appearing more and more a reality of the near future, disaster was looming for the Moravian missions. In mid-August of 1781 a large body of hostile Indians, Shawnee, Wyandot, and Delaware, about three hundred fifty in all, suddenly appeared on the outskirts of Gnadenhutten and began setting up a semi-permanent camp. They were led by Matthew Elliott, and he was there to ensure that this was not to be a sporadic, hit-or-miss raid against an isolated settler's cabin. This was the eastern wing of a major two-pronged assault; this half was aimed at destroying the principal settlements along the Ohio, principally the fort at Wheeling, and from there on into eastern Pennsylvania. Elliott had deserted from Fort Pitt with McKee and Simon Girty in March, 1778, and together they had made their way to Detroit, where Elliott was made a captain in the Indian Department. His influence with the Shawnee, among whom he married, was especially great.

The Indians had come from the Shawnee capital of Wapatomica, and they had come, said the leaders, Half King and Elliott, to escort the Christian Indians back to the Sandusky villages. The Christian Indians, as Elliott explained it to them, were in great danger from the Americans, who were even then plotting to murder all the Moravians and steal their land. It was the typical lie, and it fooled no one, the missionaries least of all; they had heard all this before, and they knew that trouble was afoot. The hostiles had not traveled all that distance, from the Sandusky River to Gnadenhutten, merely to provide escort service for the despised Christian Indians.

As soon as they had arrived, Zeisberger fired off a message to his superiors at Bethlehem, and another to General Brodhead at Pitt, to the effect that an immense force of hostiles had appeared, and were most certainly plotting some mischief.

He was wrong, the mischief had already been plotted. Even as Zeisberger wrote, a second large war party was moving south to invade Kentucky. Elliott, Alexander McKee, and the Girtys had been in the process of assembling the largest possible force of Indians at the Sandusky towns, in order to resist George Rogers Clark's planned invasion and assault on Detroit. Clark was the one military leader whom they feared most of all, and if Detroit fell to the Americans, the only remaining route open to the Indians would be to the west, across the Mississippi, which meant giving up all hope of ever retaining the Ohio Territory. The danger was so great that the greatest Indian strategist then living, the Mohawk chief Joseph Brant, had even come to Sandusky from New York to take charge of the Indian resistance to Clark. But when word reached them that Clark was not leading his army across country from Pittsburgh, as they had expected, but rather was proceeding down the Ohio, their plans were quickly, drastically, altered.

The visitors at Gnadenhutten settled down to a comfortable routine of eating, sleeping, and visiting with relatives. The occasional Moravian cow was killed to provide a meal; it was certainly easier than hunting deer, and besides, most of the game had already been driven away from the Christian villages. Zeisberger had sent out his warnings immediately, but the newly-arrived Indians seemed to be in no hurry to depart; two weeks passed, and still they lingered, casual, yet suspicious. The messengers Zeisberger had sent out returned, but before they had reached the village they were detained by several warriors, who had been posted to watch for anyone entering or leaving the town. Brodhead had kept Zeisberger's letter, and fortunately he had sent none in return, so although they were closely searched, no incriminating documents were found on the messengers, and they were released.

For more than two weeks the discussions between the two sides continued, peacefully enough, although Elliott was especially insistent. The Indians endeavored to persuade the missionaries to abandon their towns on the Tuscarawas and lead their converts to the Indian towns on the Sandusky. There they would be cared for by their English brothers, there they would be allowed to worship in peace, there they would escape the danger hovering over their heads from the evil Long Knives.

While Brant, Alexander McKee, and Simon Girty raced southward to intercept Clark on the Ohio, Elliott and the Wyandot Half King had taken charge of the other large force and headed east, intent on destroying the Upper Ohio frontier stations; these were the warriors that had encamped at Gnadenhutten. But word of Clark's movement downriver had reached Wapatomica too late, by a matter of hours. Brant, with an advance force of thirty warriors, reached the mouth of the Miami River just as Clark's flotilla passed by. With too small a force to engage, and in agony over missing his great opportunity, Brant was forced to watch as his enemy moved on, unmolested and unsuspecting.

But as he waited for the remainder of his forces to come up he saw a small craft coming down the river, too close to the north shore; it was the dispatch boat which Lochry had sent on ahead asking Clark to wait. Clark had been too strong to assault, and had slipped past, but not so the boat with the messages; after taking it Brant became aware of Lochry's detachment yet to arrive. In the meantime Simon Girty and sixty more Indians had joined him, and as Lochry's party came into sight of the high bluff overlooking the river, one of Lochry's captured couriers was forced out into the water as a decoy.

As he followed his prospective commander downriver in an effort to catch up, Lochry had reached the mouth of a creek (now called Laughery Creek, Dearborn County, Indiana) about ten miles below the mouth of the Miami. Upon approaching this creek Lochry was hailed from the shore by someone he recognized. It was an old trick, and it worked time after time. The iron will necessary to resist the plaintive cries for help was almost always lacking, even in men hardened to border warfare. The thought was ever present that this person had escaped from Indian captivity, and could not a few moments be spared to save the poor unfortunate from recapture and agonizing torture?

Lochry and his men could not resist the temptation to pick up one of their own comrades; not only for humanitarian reasons — it was vital that they find out what had happened to their messages to Clark. But as they drew near they were attacked with a suddenness and a viciousness which they, experienced backwoodsmen though they were, could not withstand; all were captured or killed, every single one.

A few minutes after the fighting ended, as Lochry sat on a fallen log waiting to be interrogated by Brant and Girty, one of the warriors walked up behind him and calmly sank his tomahawk into the back of Lochry's head. Thirty-five others were also killed, and sixty-four had been captured. By this one stroke of good fortune Brant had accomplished all that could have been wished for in the western theater. With the loss of a hundred men and his sorely-needed supplies, George Rogers Clark would lead no assault on Detroit this year.

The mischief had already been plotted. The Indians at Gnadenhutten were waiting, giving Brant enough time to reach Kentucky before launching the second phase of the assault against the Upper Ohio. On the first day of September they were gone as suddenly as they had appeared, dividing up into several smaller groups, heading east, and each with a specific objective. Two days later, about an hour after daybreak and just as the fog was lifting, the Delaware chief Pekillon, he of Brodhead's expedition less than five months before, appeared on an island in the Ohio. He had brought eighty warriors, and it was Monday, September 3rd, 1781. The island on which he now stood lay just opposite Wheeling, and Fort Henry was to be assaulted once more.

# Chapter XIX

$\mathcal{T}$he Moravians - Part III
Forlorn Hope

Despite being poised between the crushing jaws of two angry gods, the Moravian missionaries, principally David Zeisberger and John Heckewelder, had managed to hold together their struggling communities in the Ohio wilderness for nearly a decade. With true Christian charity they welcomed red war parties with one hand, while sending secret warnings to the white settlements with the other. As of 1781 the three Moravian villages were under the general control of David Zeisberger, who traveled constantly from one to another. John Heckewelder was in charge of Salem, with William Edwards at Gnadenhutten, and at New Schoenbrunn, Gottlob Senseman, he who would never forget that November day in 1755 when his mother and ten other mission workers had been killed by Indians at the Tents of Grace, Gnadenhutten on the Mahoning. Gnadenhutten was an ill-fated, never-to-be-forgotten name.

It is impossible, of course, to know how much longer this delicate balance might have been maintained, but it could not have continued, and it had ended abruptly on that mid-August day of 1781, with the arrival of the Indians. Two weeks later, when a few of those same Indians suddenly appeared on the island opposite Wheeling, they did not hesitate to begin crossing, the river being typically low at this time of year. Inside the fort was the usual excitement and yelling when the Indians were first sighted, but thanks to Zeisberger's warning Col. Brodhead, now back at Fort Pitt, had sent the following message to Capt. John Boggs, whom he had just a month before ordered to the command of Fort Henry:

Fort Pitt, August 24, 1781

Sir -

I have this moment received certain intelligence that the enemy are coming in great force against us, and particularly against Wheeling. You will immediately put your garrison in the best posture of defence, and lay in as great a quantity of water as circumstances will admit, and receive them cooly. They intend to decoy your garrison, but you are to guard against stratagem, and defend the post to the last extremity.

You may rely on every aid in my power to frustrate the designs of the enemy; but you must not fail to give the alarm to the inhabitants within your reach, and make it as general as possible, in order that every man may be prepared at this crisis.

Daniel Brodhead, Col.,
Commanding Western Department

Thus the enemy was expected, and everyone was safe inside the fort.

\*   \*   \*

But not quite everyone. As the inhabitants of the fort peeped over the palisade walls at the warriors on the island, they suddenly heard screams coming from the opposite direction, from the foot of Wheeling Hill, two hundred yards to the east. Two young boys, 10-year-old Billy Ryan[60] and 12-year old Davy Glenn had slipped outside the fort that morning while the others were busy preparing for the upcoming attack. They had not strayed far; they were playing in the marshy area along the base of the hill, where the water oozed out of the face of the rocks. They had not gone far, but too far for their own safety. With a rush several Indians, of the majority who had maneuvered around to gain entrance to the front gate of the fort, were nearly upon them. As those in the fort watched in horror, the boys ran for their lives toward the fort, across a downed log, but the log was still wet with the early morning dew, and young Ryan, panic-stricken, slipped and fell. The first Indian to reach him split little Billy's skull open with a tomahawk. Glenn was grabbed by two or three warriors and overpowered; he was hurriedly forced back away from the fort and onto the island, out of sight of those inside. Then a volley of shots was fired, and at almost the same instant a third boy named George Reagen (sometimes *Rigger*) who had been outside the walls of the fort with the other two boys arrived at the gate; he had been shot through the wrist but was otherwise unharmed.

In command of the fort was Capt. John Boggs, formerly of Catfish Camp, but who had been more recently living on Buffalo Creek with his family. There they had been attacked by a war party on July 30th, and a few days later Boggs was ordered to take command of the post at Wheeling. With him he had brought his wife and fifteen-year-old daughter, Lydia. His son, William, eighteen years old, had not come with them, for he had been taken prisoner when the Indians had attacked the Boggs's cabin, and was now an Indian prisoner on his way to Detroit.

Col. Zane was not in the fort. When the Indians had burned all the buildings in 1777 he had vowed that he would rebuild his house in the form of a blockhouse, two stories, with the upper floor projecting a foot or more over the lower, with portholes in the floor through which shots could be fired at any enemy foolish enough to come under the walls. In case of another attack Zane had resolved to remain in his home, providing a cross-fire for the fort. Since Fort Henry stood on a steep bluff overlooking the river[61], with another bluff falling off sharply to the south, just opposite the Zane blockhouse, the fort could be approached only from the north and the east. Since the defended Zane cabin stood some sixty or seventy yards from the southeast corner of the fort, the only feasible point of attacking Fort Henry was from the north and northeast points. As long as only a few defenders could control that zone of fire, the Indians had no chance to storm the fort.

Inside the blockhouse Zane had a picked band of four or five men, among them his brother, Jonathan, one of the deadliest shots on the border. Others were George Green, the Colonel's elderly slave, Sam, and a young man named Andrew Scott [62]. Andy's wife, Molly, had insisted that she remain with her husband; someone might be needed who could help load the rifles, or cast bullets or prepare food or dress wounds, and the men might be too occupied in the defense of their sanctuary.

Deeply chagrined at being unable to take the fort by surprise, the Indians clustered about the hillside, discussing the possibility of attack. But now, finally, everyone was safe inside the fort, and without cannon the Indians had no chance of success. Their leader was the Delaware chief Pekillon; the same chief who, with Col. Brodhead only a few months before, had pointed out those sixteen Indian warriors, raiders of the settlements, and marked them for death. But Pekillon's assault on Fort Henry was poorly planned and worse coordinated; those on the island were supposed to stay out of sight until the others had had a chance to gain the base of Wheeling Hill, whence they could rush straight into the open gate of the fort, while those in the fort were being distracted by the Indians remaining a safe distance away on the island.

But as always with Indians, the sight of those three boys was an irresistible attraction. While some of the Indians appeared on the island, in full view of the fort, most of the others had crossed the river and approached it from the east, from near the base of massive Wheeling Hill, which began its ascent only a couple hundred yards east of the fort's double-hung front gate. It was here, near the spring at the base of the hill, that the boys had been playing, and foolishly gathering walnuts, when they were as foolishly fired upon, alerting the inmates of the fort to the principal danger from the east. The settlers had been warned a week before that the Indians were coming, of course, and the attack was unsuccessful.

Not more than a few moments after Reagen's entrance the warriors on the hillside saw a most unusual sight; a young woman had come out of Zane's cabin and run quickly up the slight slope to the sallyport gate at the southeastern corner of the fort, where she instantly disappeared. Before the remaining Indians had had time to assemble at the base of the hill, the gate swung in and the same woman reappeared, carrying a bundle in her arms. The Indians were too far away to waste powder firing at a squaw, Andrew Scott's courageous wife, Molly. Never quite certain of how long an Indian war party would stay outside the walls, Col. Zane had decided that, before the Indians got any closer, someone should run over to the fort for a few pounds of powder from the magazine. Molly volunteered, and with the help of Capt. Boggs's daughter, Lydia, returned after only a few minutes.

As it turned out, it had been an unnecessary risk, however slight. After milling around for a few hours, engaging in their usual destructive looting and plundering, and killing the cattle and hogs, the attackers set fire to all the buildings within reach, and sullenly withdrew in search of easier pickings. But they had not obtained their one primary objective, their one major goal, the reduction of Fort Henry.

From Wheeling the war party broke up into several smaller groups; one group began the return trek to Gnadenhutten with their prisoner, while another fifteen or twenty moved up Wheeling Creek to Shepherd's abandoned fort, and from there quietly approached the blockhouse of Jacob Link[63] on Middle Wheeling Creek, a dozen miles east of Fort Henry. In spite of the warnings, the men at the blockhouse were engaging in one of their favorite pastimes, a shooting match. Here was something the Indians could handle; they attacked with success, surprising the men and quickly entering the blockhouse. Link and at least one other man named Miller were killed, possibly another as well, and several prisoners were taken. Link's wife and child, fortunately, had gone to visit Moses Shepherd, along with one of the Wetzels, probably Jacob.

The next day the same band attacked the home of one Peek, on the Dutch Fork of Buffalo Creek, killing at least one, and taking more prisoners. Among those taken were a man named Blackburn, seventeen-year-old Presley Peek[64], and William Hawkins. The Indians then approached the Hawkins' house, but Hawkins spoke so loudly as they came near that his wife and three of the children had time to remove themselves before the Indians entered, all except one daughter, Elizabeth, who was also taken prisoner. Hawkins may have been recognized by these Indians; in April he had been a private in Ogle's company during Brodhead's Expedition. Recognized or not, the prisoners were all marched a mile or so from Hawkins' house, where Hawkins and Blackburn were first tied to trees, then tomahawked and scalped, their bodies left standing where they died. There was a good reason for this unusual method of execution; as one of the warriors said to the captives:

*"Now we be militia!"*

\*     \*     \*

In all this activity little Davy Glenn had not been forgotten; he had been captured on the morning of the 3rd, and sometime in the evening of the next day he was brought into Gnadenhutten by some of his captors. Early the next morning he was brought before McKee and the Indian chiefs, and interrogated. He admitted that the missionaries had sent messages to Fort Pitt and elsewhere, advising them of the arrival of the hostiles at Gnadenhutten, and that the settlements had thus been warned of their imminent danger. The Indians were infuriated; the missionaries had assured them that they had never sent out information regarding the activities of the belligerent Indians, and as a result they had been unsuccessful in taking Fort Henry. Not only had they warned the settlements of approaching danger, but they had lied. Now friendly persuasion was out and ultimatum was in: abandon your villages, accompany us back to the Sandusky towns, or you will be slaughtered on the spot[65]. The missionaries, completely unaware of what information had been divulged, were suddenly seized, stripped and searched. When the Indians had first arrived at Gnadenhutten, the missionaries, knowing hostile Indians as they did, had sent their wives to Schoenbrunn, out of the sight of the warriors. Now another group of Indians was sent to take the missionaries' wives into custody; these could always be used as bargaining chips if Zeisberger and Heckewelder still proved reluctant.

But the missionaries had no choice. As Heckewelder later wrote, they were only too glad to get off with their lives, and the lives of their converts. Indeed, at one point it seemed to him as if they would all be killed before the day was over. On two separate occasions infuriated warriors struck at one or another of the missionaries, but both times another Indian turned the weapon aside. Preparations were made for an immediate evacuation of all three villages. On the 7th another war party came in; they, however, had been unsuccessful, and were in an even fouler mood than before, when they learned how the missionaries had betrayed them. On the 8th Heckewelder traveled to Salem to organize the evacuation there. On the 9th, a Sunday, Zeisberger, accompanied by the other missionaries and all the wives, arrived to take charge at Gnadenhutten. The converts were allowed to hold one final church service that day, and the next morning, September 10th, one week to the day that Davy Glenn had been taken at Wheeling, the village was plundered by the warriors of anything that might be of value, then the Christians began the long march toward the Sandusky, and the village that would come to be known as *Captives' Town*.

The missionaries asked that some of their clothes be returned to them; Pipe, the Delaware chief, spoke to his people for that purpose, and some articles of clothing were produced, but very few. As Heckewelder later described the animosity of the hostiles toward the Christian Indians:

"... but as the most as also the best of our Things were in the hands of the Wyandotts; we were told that they would by no means return any thing, & threatened; that if we would say any thing more about it, they would know what to do with Us — meaning they would dispatch us."

A number of the warriors had gone to Schoenbrunn, looking for plunder; when they had finished they fired the town. The last act of wanton destruction, passive though it was, was designed to teach the Christian Indians a lesson they would never forget. Around the village of Gnadenhutten were the fields, now ready for harvest; Heckewelder estimated it as between four and five thousand bushels of corn, plus that which had already been gathered. After all the hard work, after the long wait for the anticipated harvest, the last thing many of the Christians saw of their home was the warriors driving all the cattle into the still-standing cornfields. Along with everything else, it must have broken their hearts.

A few days after their departure a group of militia under Col. David Williamson entered Gnadenhutten, now strangely deserted except for a few stray Christian Indians who were trying to harvest what little corn had been left standing. The militia had been following the return trail of the war parties who had just attacked the western Pennsylvania settlements. The retreating Indians had too big a head start on them, but here at Gnadenhutten the militia found proof of what many had been preaching all along. Anyone could see the signs of a large Indian encampment which had been in existence over an extended period of time, proof indeed that this village of so-called "Christian" Indians had been the staging ground for the assaults on the frontier settlements. In just this last attack twenty of their friends and neighbors had been killed in a week's time, more had been taken captive. Williamson returned to Fort Pitt with his Indian captives, but Gen. Daniel Brodhead, well aware of the services which the Moravians had faithfully provided, immediately ordered their release.

*   *   *

Perhaps if the Christian Indians had gone to the Sandusky villages when the hostiles first arrived at Gnadenhutten, they might have been better treated. As it was, they could hardly have been treated worse. Their cattle had been left to fend for themselves in the woods, or slaughtered, their fields trampled and destroyed, and they had been given no time to harvest their crops. The hostiles knew that avenging frontiersmen would soon be on their trail, and they had no desire to await them. Before daybreak on the morning of the 7th one of the young women of the village, grief-stricken over the threatened destruction of her beloved teachers, had sneaked out into the nearby woods, mounted one of the Indian ponies, and sped off to the east, pursued but not caught, and bearing the news of what had happened.

When the last of the Christians finally arrived at the Sandusky, Zeisberger, Heckewelder, Edwards, and Sensemen were hurried on to Detroit to be interrogated by De Peyster, and the Moravians were left to shift for themselves. It was early October, 1781, and winter was fast approaching. When a few of the converts tried to build a church, it was immediately torn down by the warriors, and they were told that anyone who tried to build a place of worship for the white man's God would be killed. There was no housing, there was little food, and even less help from the British, who had no concern for a few hundred more Indian dependents. Their eyes were all turned eastward — Cornwallis was trapped at Yorktown, the French fleet to seaward, the Americans, with the French under Lafayette, to landward.

The winter was worse than expected. Christian Indians starved by the score that winter in Captives' Town. What Hunger did not kill, Pestilence and Exposure did. They asked to be allowed to return to their villages to scavenge for food, they were refused. And as they died, the hostiles mocked them, asking, where was their white God now?

*   *   *

Finally, late in February of 1782, permission was granted for about a hundred fifty of the starving Christians to return to the Tuscarawas, for the purpose of gathering and bringing back to their families any grain they could find. February had been a relatively mild month, but after the fields had stood abandoned all winter there could surely have been little hope of finding much, but even a few handfuls were that much more to feed their starving children. It was a bad time to return.

Because at almost the same time that they were searching the fields on hands and knees, picking up each kernel found in the frozen fields, other war parties were striking the frontier. Two men, a father and his son, were fired upon; the son was

176

killed but the father escaped. A man named Carpenter was taken captive, but by great daring he also managed to escape, bringing back word that his abductors had been Moravians. William White, Timothy Dorman and his wife were attacked as they headed for one of the frontier forts; White was shot, then tomahawked and mutilated, the Dormans were taken prisoner. On February 17th a party of Delaware attacked the cabin of Robert Wallace on Raccoon Creek, in the northern part of Washington County. Wallace was absent, but upon his return he found his cattle lying dead in the yard, his home ransacked, and his wife and three children taken captive; an infant daughter only a few months old, a son, two and a half, and another son of ten years[66]. Wallace immediately raised the alarm, but a snowfall during the night covered the trail and prevented pursuit.

In early March Col. Williamson once again led a squad of about a hundred militia toward the deserted Moravian villages, this time on the trail of the marauders. It was assumed that those villages were being used as the base for the attacks, and they hoped that if a sudden surprise raid were made against the towns, some of the Indians lingering there might be caught, perhaps even a few prisoners might be rescued. If they could not catch up with the warriors, at the least they would destroy the towns and prevent their future use by the hostiles. Williamson had reached the Ohio with a hundred sixty mounted horsemen, but only about a hundred managed to cross; the others could not force their horses to swim the icy flood-waters of the Ohio. The trail led straight for the Tuscarawas towns, and those across the river, pressing on, soon came across a grisly discovery. As those in the lead followed the trail they saw, a short distance ahead, what appeared to be someone sitting by the side of the road. It was the naked and mutilated body of Mrs. Wallace. The Indians, safe from pursuit, had stopped to have a little sport with their victim. When they had finished they cut off a sapling about two feet above the ground, and sharpened the point. Two or three of them then lifted up the screaming woman and forced her down on the sharpened point, leaving her there to suffer a drawn-out, agonizing death, sure to be found, impaled on the stake, by the next traveler who happened by. There would be no rescue of Mrs. Wallace, nor of the infant daughter. Nearby the militia found its bloody and scalped corpse. It, too, had been impaled on a stake in the same manner, but in a savage sense of humor the baby's neck had been broken; she had been placed with her body towards the Indian country, but her little head had been bent and twisted around to face the Ohio, as if looking in vain for her rescuers.

The militia reached the site of supposedly abandoned Gnadenhutten on the evening of the 6th of March, and secreted themselves along the riverbank. At daylight of the 7th they were amazed to find a large party of Indians there; by the mode of wearing their hair these were obviously not warriors, but just as surely they must be accomplices. Before they reached the village several Indians who had approached the river were killed, but one, escaping southward, reached Salem with the news of an attack upon Gnadenhutten. Stealthily approaching the village, uncertain of what they would find there, the militia encountered the Moravians. Acting in their most sincere manner, they assured the Indians that their intention was to take them to Pittsburgh, where they would be fed and housed until the war was over. It was far better than returning to the Sandusky villages, and the Indians were readily disarmed. Runners were sent to bring in the Indians at Schoenbrunn and Salem; those at Schoenbrunn, unsuspecting, came at once, but Salem was found to be deserted, and no one could account for their disappearance.

After the Schoenbrunn residents had arrived, and once the men were disarmed, they and the older boys were taken to the mission house, segregated from the women and younger children who were lodged in the cooper's house of Joshua, son of the town's founder. Several of the men were found to have their heads plucked and shaven; while not in itself proof of their guilt, it raised serious doubt as to the innocence of all those in the village. Then someone noticed that some of the horses were animals which had belonged to white families, and a search of the village was begun.

What they found, among other things, was the torn and blood-stained dress of Mrs. Wallace; it was all the proof they needed, and it was the death knell of the Christian Indians. Their fate was now debated, and a vote was taken, with only eighteen of the men voting to return with the Indians to Pittsburgh, as had originally been planned. All the others voted for death. No man who had seen Mrs. Wallace's naked body, sitting in that frozen, upright position alongside the road, would ever vote in favor of any Indian, Christian or heathen, man, woman, or child.

The next morning, March 8th, in back of the cooper's house was found a mallet, and deeming that this instrument had been found for the very purpose, the slaughter began. Each one, man, woman, and child, was systematically knocked in the head and scalped. After every one of them, ninety in all, had been dispatched, the buildings, the cabins, corn cribs, even the church itself, were then put to the torch, as had been those in Salem. The Indians would never again use these buildings as their jumping-off point for attacks on the pioneers. Then the militia, gathering up their scalps and the rest of the plunder, including nearly a hundred horses, headed for home with a satisfying sense of achievement.

Ninety Indians, twenty-nine men, most of them Christians, along with twenty-seven women and thirty-four children, all of those Christians, were systematically butchered by white men. The light had finally gone out on Moravian Hope [67].

# Chapter XX

The First Major Disaster:
The Crawford Expedition, June, 1782

After the Indian raids in the early spring of 1782, with the generally approved massacre at Gnadenhutten[68], and the universally approved surrender of Cornwallis at Yorktown, the frontier people were moved to attempt another major assault on the Indian tribes, such as Clark's expedition against the Shawnee in 1780. It was obvious that even the best defensive posture was incapable of stopping the guerrilla tactics of the Indians; a small party could cross the Ohio unobserved and, at will, strike a defenseless cabin or two, kill and take captive the inhabitants, then recross the river before anyone was aware of their attack. If Detroit was unassailable, then it would only be by mounting an offensive campaign at the heart of the Indian territory that relief from their constant incursions could be brought to a halt.

Conditions at Fort Pitt were in a terrible state; the men were poorly clothed and worse fed, they had not been paid for months, and desertions, even mutinies, were commonplace. Gen. William Irvine, who had taken command of the Western Department upon Brodhead's recall the previous November, supported the contemplated project against the Sandusky Indians[69], principally the Mingo, Wyandot, and now-hostile Delaware, although he was unable to furnish any regular troops, and could provide no more than minimal material support. He did, however, lend his own personal aide-de-camp, a young Russian nobleman called "Major Rose", and the fort's surgeon, Dr. John Knight.

Irvine had been granted broad authority by Congress, including the power to call out the local militia for such an expedition, if he felt the defense of the country warranted it. However, he preferred not to use this authority except as a last resort. Still, Irvine insisted on three elements before he would give official sanction to such an expedition. The number of men involved should be great enough to insure a victory, but not so large as to impede progress; Irvine declared that the minimum number would be three hundred, more would be preferable. Secondly, all the men must *volunteer* for this campaign, and they must agree to place themselves under his orders, subject to the same military laws and regulations, exactly as if they had been lawfully called out. Since the regular establishment had not the means to provide for them, each man would have to supply his own weapons and ammunition, provisions for the entire trip, and a horse, else he would have to walk. Most importantly, the army must move swiftly so as to utilize the element of surprise, while keeping out flankers to prevent riding into an ambush.

In the latter part of May men began to assemble at Mingo Bottom[70], on the Virginia shore about twenty miles above Fort Henry, and just opposite the trail leading to the Muskingum and beyond. As usual, the first order of business for the militia was electing their commander. David Williamson was one of the most popular officers, especially as a result of his involvement in the "Moravian affair", but although he had led two expeditions in the past half-year, neither had progressed beyond the towns on the Tuscarawas. More popular even than Williamson, however, was Col. William Crawford, the veteran of so many campaigns, and Irvine had let it be known that he preferred Crawford. So it was that he was chosen to lead the four hundred eighty-eight men assembled there, but by the narrowest of margins, a mere five votes, with Williamson then becoming second-in-command.

William Crawford was born in Orange County (now Berkeley Co.), Virginia in 1732. He had served in Braddock's Expedition against Duquesne, and participated in the Battle of the Monongahela, and then throughout the remainder of the French and Indian War, and Pontiac's Rebellion. In 1770 he accompanied Washington on his tour down the Ohio. As already noted he served in Dunmore's War, and was colonel of the 7th Virginia Regiment during the Revolution, being one of those brave few who crossed the Delaware with Washington on Christmas Day, 1776, and participated in the victory at Trenton the next day, and at Princeton on January 3rd, 1777. Because of Crawford's knowledge of the frontier, a Virginia regiment was raised and marched to Fort Pitt in the spring of 1778. In May Crawford arrived to take charge of the regiment, under the command of General McIntosh, who had replaced Gen. Hand.

\*    \*    \*

On the 25th of May the army finally set out from Mingo Bottom, guided by three of the best scouts on the border, John Slover, Jonathan Zane, and Tom Nicholson[71]. Most of the men were mounted, and they should have advanced swiftly toward the Sandusky towns, but the usual lack of discipline among the militia led to their downfall. Knowing they had a long campaign ahead of them, and as long a return trip, yet they were prodigally wasteful of their provisions, reasoning that they could always hunt for more. They were slow to get moving in the morning, and once started they were equally as difficult to keep on the trail, often wandering away from the army, in little groups of two or three, to hunt. Quite often they would simply stop where they were, to debate what course they should next follow. On May 29th they finally reached the Tuscarawas, less than fifty miles from the Ohio, having spent four days for an objective which they should have reached on the second day. Then six more days passed before they came in sight of the Sandusky.

Their sluggishness was their downfall; Irvine's most important dictum had been neglected and, far from being surprised, the Indians could hardly have been better informed of the army's progress. Runners had observed the army since the day following its crossing of the Ohio, and an Indian army equal in size to the militia was already collecting to repel the invaders. In addition, De Peyster sent Col. William Caldwell, a Tory and former resident of Wyoming, now second in command of Butler's Rangers, to bring up a force of Rangers and Lake Indians from Detroit, and to reinforce the threatened towns.

About one o'clock on the afternoon of June 4th Crawford's army reached the Sandusky, but where they had expected to find a large Wyandot village, they found only an obviously deserted area, overgrown with weeds and brush. The men now began discussing a return; they had only a few days' provisions left, barely enough to last until they reached home. The army halted while a council was held. John Slover remembered the area from years before, when he had been brought here as an Indian captive, and he felt that the Indian settlements could soon be reached[72]. But, argued some of the officers, would they not also be deserted? Jonathan Zane advised an immediate retreat, giving as his opinion that the Indians had withdrawn only to gain time to bring together an overwhelming force. Crawford, knowing Zane to be exceptionally well-versed in Indian strategy, accepted his judgment, but in spite of this it was finally agreed to continue the march the rest of that day and, if no Indians were found, the army would commence its retreat the next morning.

And just as with Custer a century later, the Indians were found soon enough. Crawford sent out a small force of mounted scouts to reconnoiter; the area was now mostly open plain, dotted here and there with groves of trees. The scouts had not gone far when they passed a large and especially beautiful grove of trees, at a spot about three miles northeast of the present town of Upper Sandusky, Ohio. About a mile beyond they suddenly ran into that overwhelming force of Indians that Zane had predicted. While one of the scouts raced back with word for Crawford, the others returned to the large grove, dismounted, and prepared to hold back the warriors until Crawford could arrive. Most of the Indians were Delaware, about two hundred of them, under their war chief Pipe, but they were also accompanied by Wingenund and Simon Girty. Zhaus-sho-tah, war chief of the Wyandot, had brought in more than three hundred warriors from that tribe, but for the moment they were being held back by Matthew Elliott. Pipe had been hurrying his Delaware forward to take possession of that grove, since known as Battle Island[73], but Crawford reached it first, and the Indians spread out to begin an encirclement. Crawford's militia, with the advantage of position on their side, stood their ground and fought well, protected by the trees. Several of the men climbed up into the leafy branches of those trees, where they took deadly aim on any of the Indians who tried to crawl forward through the tall prairie grass. But Elliott, now present and in command of the entire force, was in no hurry to press the attack, as he was being constantly reinforced by greater and greater numbers of Indians.

The battle continued the remainder of that day, June 4th. So far the Americans had been fairly successful, even if they had been unable to obtain their initial objective, destroying the Indian towns. Another council was now called, with arguments raging on the proper course to take; the scouts insisted on an immediate withdrawal before they were completely surrounded, while the majority of the officers wanted to stay and fight their way out, some even thinking that they could break the Indians' line with a mounted charge.

On the morning of the 5th there was nothing more than some long-range sniping back and forth. Then, in the early afternoon, one of the sentinels in the northeast corner of the island caught sight of a body of mounted men riding toward them; to their dismay it turned out to be Caldwell and his Rangers, finally arrived. Soon Alex McKee arrived with a hundred fifty Shawnee, and the encirclement of Battle Island was completed. So far Crawford had lost only five men killed and about two dozen wounded, but now there was no longer a choice; the American force was surrounded, outnumbered, and running low on supplies, those supplies which they had been wasting since starting out from Mingo Bottom. One of the scouts found a break in the Indians' line, and Crawford, belatedly supported by all the officers, gave the order to begin the retirement through the gap as soon as it was well dark. The dead were buried, and fires burned over their graves to prevent the Indians from digging up the corpses for their scalps. Litters were prepared for the wounded who were unable to walk, and then the men began slowly filing out, westward, in the direction of the Sandusky towns, the only option available to them.

All would have gone well; the army had almost escaped, but suddenly a burst of Indian gunfire was heard nearby, completely innocuous as it turned out, but as usual a militia retreat threatened to turn into a militia rout. In the darkness the men stumbled into a large marshy area, and the army bogged down, quickly turning into individual groups of disorganized units, becoming more and more separated. Now it was every man for himself, and it took hours for them to disentangle themselves from the swamp. Many of the horses became so mired down that they could not be extricated, turning mounted cavalry into foot soldiers, certainly not a healthy situation when it was necessary to retreat from an ambitious and energetic enemy. Even though the men had managed to slip past the Indian line, and in that sense their withdrawal was successful, in the confusion some of the wounded had been left behind. By daylight the main body of the army had reached the deserted Indian village, Old Town, which they had passed two days before, and here they halted in order to give the remainder of the scattered forces time to catch up. Men continued to troop in, and soon they had collected into a sizeable force of about three hundred.

Now it was discovered that Col. Crawford was no longer with them. Crawford had done his best to lead his men out of their predicament, but suddenly he realized that his son, a son-in-law, and a nephew were not with the main body. He allowed the entire army, such as it was, to pass him by, as he looked in vain for his relatives[74]. Finally, after the last man had passed, Dr. Knight, the surgeon, who had remained by Crawford's side, persuaded him to give up his search, and hurry on, in an effort to catch up with the rear guard. They eventually joined four other men, but they had now become no more than stragglers themselves.

Col. Williamson assumed command and headed the men east, but as soon as there was sufficient daylight the Indian force began their pursuit. By early afternoon they had caught up, near Olentangy Creek, an affluent of the Sandusky, in present Crawford County, and here they brought the army to a standstill. The Indians charged, but once again, under the steadying influence of Williamson and Rose, both of whom were highly respected by the men, the militia stood its ground. Within an hour the attackers became dispirited and withdrew from the assault. Suddenly a tremendous thunderstorm drenched the area, and with most of the firearms now useless, the retreat was resumed. The Indians refused to break off the engagement entirely, following along and taking shots at the rear guard when possible, but always from a safe distance. Due to this continuous fire upon them, those men in back began pressing forward, breaking up the line of march and threatening to cause a panic. Near the front were nine men, all that was left of Captain John Biggs's company, all of its officers dead or missing. Recognizing a potential disaster, Williamson called for the lead company to file to the left, and after the army had passed to take up its position in the rear; this strategy was successfully repeated at intervals throughout the day, so that no one company suffered greatly.

By nightfall they had reached the vicinity of Wingenund's Town[75], having covered about thirty miles from Battle Island, straight line distance, but the men had actually traveled closer to forty. Many of them were now afoot; those horses that had not been abandoned in the swamp close by the battlefield had finally given out. In addition the army was encumbered with a steadily-increasing number of wounded and disabled. At daybreak, just as the lines were formed to continue the retreat, the Indians once again appeared in their rear and opened fire. To the relief of the militia, however, it was nothing more than an attempt to induce a rout; when the militia once more stood firm and volleyed back, the Indians gave up the pursuit.[76]

On the evening of June 13th the survivors of the expedition went into camp at the old Mingo Town, opposite Mingo Bottom, whence they had departed twenty weary days ago. The campaign which had begun with such high hopes a mere three weeks before had ended in the worst disaster to date. With so many of the officers killed, or missing and then killed, there has never been an accurate account of the exact number killed. As commonly happens, the victors overestimated the number of enemy casualties, while the vanquished understated it. For the victors: Caldwell had been wounded during the battle, and his second-in-command, John Turney, reported to De Peyster that he had personally counted one hundred dead militia on the battlefield of Battle Island itself, but this was an absurd exaggeration. Alexander McKee said that the total number killed, during the battle and including the subsequent pursuit, when the majority of the casualties occurred, numbered between two hundred and two hundred fifty. This included all the prisoners taken by the Indians, whether they were tomahawked or tortured to death. The Indians, however, did not concern themselves with giving estimates; they were interested in scalps and prisoners, not numbers.

On the other hand, Maj. William Croghan, at Fort Pitt, wrote that the total number killed, captured, and missing was not more than fifty, while Major Rose reported to Gen. Irvine that it was less than thirty, as absurd a number as Turney's figure. Since no official returns were ever given, the number of men killed, which of necessity must also include those who were captured by the Indians, as well as those who were "missing", was probably in the neighborhood of one hundred to one hundred fifty, between one-third and one-fifth of the entire army.

Roving bands of Indians, those who had not joined the pursuit of the main army, continued to track down the stragglers, many of whom, as usual, could not even agree on whether to remain together as a group, or break up into small parties. Knowing Indians as they did, there should have been no question; a few warriors would not attack the main body of the army, there being so much less risk in chasing down two or three panic-stricken fugitives.

\*   \*   \*

Col. Crawford and Dr. Knight, unable to catch up with the army, had overtaken two other officers on the day following the retreat from Battle Island, Captain John Biggs[77] and Lt. Ashley, and two other men. Crawford's horse had already given out, and he and Knight were taking turns riding Knight's. Ashley and Biggs had both been wounded, Ashley so seriously that he was barely able to move, and with only one horse between them they had not managed to get far. Knight placed Ashley on his horse; Crawford and Knight then took the lead, on foot, with the two mounted officers a hundred yards or so to the rear, and the other two men some distance behind.

The next afternoon they finally regained the trail by which they had come out. They were now about a mile and a half down the Sandusky River from present Leesville, at the point where the army had left the river and bore away toward the Indian towns. Knight and Biggs felt it was unsafe to remain on the open road, but Crawford assured them that the Indians would not pursue them past the open plains, which they had by now left far behind. Suddenly they walked straight into a small band of Delaware from Wingenund's camp, only a couple miles distant; Biggs and Ashley wheeled their horses about and escaped, as did the two men bringing up the rear, but Crawford and Knight were taken easily.

Within the hour they had been brought into Wingenund's Town; it was now Friday, June 7th. In the evening of Sunday, the 9th, five Delaware warriors who had posted themselves to the east brought in the scalps of Lt. Ashley and Capt. Biggs. There was no mistaking them, two of the Indians were riding Knight's and Biggs's horses, but the two men who had accompanied the four officers had escaped once more. In the camp were nine other prisoners, all closely guarded, and one of whom was an officer well known to both Knight and Crawford; John McKinley had been an officer in the 13th Virginia Regiment.

A few of the Delaware Indians in the camp were former Christian Indians who had been at Salem and thus had escaped the massacre at Gnadenhutten three months earlier. Reverting to heathenism, they now informed Dr. Knight, in quite good English, that in revenge for the murders of their friends and relatives at Gnadenhutten, they personally would insure that no captive ever again escaped the most hideous torture. Knight, after his return to Fort Pitt, passed this on to Gen. Irvine, but Irvine, misunderstanding, assumed that this was the attitude of all the hostile Indians, and he so informed Gen. Washington. It was for this reason that Washington advised all his commanders that no soldier should ever allow himself to fall into the hands of the hostiles, as they were now all determined upon revenge for the massacre of their Moravian brothers.

It is entirely due to this misconception that later apologists have attempted to excuse the horrific agonies inflicted upon Crawford, by claiming that the Indians were only satisfying a blood-lust engendered by the slaying of "their beloved Moravian brothers at the hands of the evil Williamson". Indeed, some have even tried to assert that the Indians were confused, that they believed they had captured "the hated Williamson" rather than Crawford. Such a perversion of the truth is ridiculous on the very face of it, if not by Knight's testimony alone, then by the fact that Crawford was very well known to both Wingenund and Pipe, as well as to many others of the Delaware tribe. There was no doubt who it was that was in their grasp, and it was Wingenund and Pipe themselves who were now determined that Crawford should suffer death by long drawn-out torture. Wingenund, until the disaffection of the Delaware, had been on good terms with the whites, and was quite friendly with the Moravians. He had been a friend not only of Crawford, but of the missionary Heckewelder, as well. Pipe, however, had always been an implacable foe until finally, with the approach of Wayne's army in 1794, he realized the futility of the cause, and counseled negotiation. Pipe and Crawford had both been present at the 1778 treaty held at Fort Pitt, both had been involved in the negotiations, and both had signed the treaty. But the attitude of Pipe toward the Christian Indians in 1782 was too well documented to believe that he was now feeling any desire for vengeance for their deaths; exactly the same can be said for the other hostile Indians. However, since the Wyandots usually killed prisoners simply by a blow of the tomahawk to the head, it now became necessary for Pipe and Wingenund to deceive their host, the Half King, as to their true intentions, if they were to achieve their goal of Crawford's torture.

Upon their withdrawal from the Allegheny two years before, the majority of the hostile Delaware had become neighbors of the Half King, along the Upper Sandusky; their two principal villages were Wingenund's Town, twenty-eight miles to the east, and Pipe's Town, along Tymochtee Creek, the principal western branch of the Sandusky. The next day, Monday, the 10th, the thirteen captives were led out of Wingenund's camp and headed west. Crawford had learned that Simon Girty was at Half King's Town, and at Crawford's request he was taken there, where he had an interview with Girty. Crawford later told Knight that Girty had promised to do all in his power to save them, but knowing the intentions of the two Delaware chiefs, he probably did nothing. Even had he made any effort to save Crawford, it is unlikely that any means in his power would have been successful. Knight was taken to Upper Sandusky, the former site of Half King's Town, now called Old Town. Early the next morning, the 11th[78], he was paid a visit there by Pipe, who painted Knight black, and informed him that he was soon to go to one of the Shawnee towns, "to visit his friends." The deaths of both Knight and Crawford had already been determined upon.

About an hour later Crawford was brought in from Half King's Town, and Pipe greeted him in the same manner as he had Dr. Knight. The deceitful chief told Crawford that he was to be returned to Half King's Town, where he would be adopted into one of the Wyandot families, saying this while he stood before Crawford and painted him black! That done the thirteen prisoners were once more rounded up and started on the trail northward, with Crawford and Knight being held back a short distance from the others, thus having the "honor" of being guarded by the two

Delaware war chiefs themselves. They had not traveled far when they passed the bodies of four of their former comrades, lying tomahawked and scalped alongside the road where they had fallen.

Just past this point they reached the spot where the trail forked. Northeast, to the right, lay the path to the Wyandot town, eight miles distant; on their left, northwest, the same distance away, was the road to Pipe's Delaware village. Hope must surely have died in the breasts of the two men as Pipe and Wingenund turned them to the left. Soon they overtook the five remaining captives, among them John McKinley, surrounded by a number of squaws and boys; all seven men were then ordered to sit on the ground, with Knight and Crawford, having been brought here for a purpose, being kept a little distance from the rest. At a signal from one or the other of the chiefs the women and boys fell on the five prisoners and tomahawked and scalped them, then began the mutilation. An old squaw hacked off the head of McKinley with her tomahawk and delightedly began kicking it around on the ground, while the scalps were repeatedly flung in the faces of the two survivors. Knight was then given into the custody of a Delaware warrior named Tutelu, to be taken to one of the Shawnee villages the next day, and the march was resumed, but with Knight a hundred yards behind Crawford. Now, as they neared the Tymochtee, nearly every Indian they met beat them with their fists or with sticks. Finally they were greeted by about thirty to forty warriors, and twice that many squaws and children. It was here, about three-quarters of a mile from the actual site of Pipe's Town, to a small bend of Tymochtee Creek, that the squaws and children had been brought for safe-keeping during the advance of the American army.

A large post, some twelve feet or more in height, had been firmly planted in the ground, and both men knew what was in store for them; the same fate was intended for John Slover, the only one of the three chief scouts to be captured. Knight was taken a little distance from Crawford, and both were ordered to sit on the ground. A mob of Indians then beat Crawford with clubs, sticks, and thorn-covered blackberry canes, until the blood poured freely from his wounds. Dr. Knight was then given the same brutal treatment, as Crawford was led to the post, around the bottom of which a rope had been tied. The free end of this was fastened to the bonds which held Crawford's wrists, being long enough to allow the victim to sit down, or to walk once or twice around the stake, and return. As soon as he was secured the warriors loaded their guns, with powder and wadding only, and from a distance of only a few feet began firing these into Crawford's body, the genitals being the preferred target. The stinging, burning particles of coarse black powder penetrated the skin, while the still smoldering pieces of wadding were forced into the burnt skin by the closeness of the explosion. In only a few minutes every inch of Crawford's skin was charred and burned and smoking; Knight estimated that not less than seventy rounds had been fired at him. Several Indians then surrounded him, cutting off his ears and genitals; when they backed away Knight saw the blood pouring down his commander's face and legs.

Now the real torture began. The fire had been built some fifteen to twenty feet from the stake; the purpose of fire being not to burn the prisoner, but to provide the means of torture. Hickory poles, each about a dozen feet in length, had been placed on the fire so that they were by now burned in two. Four or five of the Indians then, taking turns, would pick up one of the blazing sticks, and stab Crawford with the blazing, sharpened point as he tried to walk around the stake, but no matter which way he turned, there was no escape from at least two or three of his tormentors. In the meantime several squaws, not to be outdone in fiendishness, scooped up some of the burning coals onto boards, and began throwing them on Crawford's naked body, so that in a few minutes the unfortunate man had nothing to walk on but red-hot coals.

Crawford had by now endured the torture for nearly two hours, but he was fortunately nearing the end of strength. When his legs could no longer support him, he slowly sank to the ground, lying on his stomach, on the smoldering coals. Now one of the Indians rushed in and tore the scalp off the insensible but still-living man, and one of the squaws, an old harridan, scooped up more coals on a board and, walking over, dumped them on Crawford's naked skull.

Incredibly, the charred remains of what had once been a human being gave a low groan, and as all watched in amazement, slowly regained its feet and once more commenced its slow shuffle around the stake. The delighted Indians, who had a few moments ago supposed their entertainment to be at an end, once more began jabbing the burning sticks into his body, but now, mercifully, at last, the thing tied to the stake appeared to be totally insensible to pain. Exactly how many more minutes Crawford's life lasted is not known, for at this point Dr. Knight's Shawnee captor, after slapping Crawford's scalp in Knight's face and assuring him that the same end awaited him, pulled the doctor to his feet and marched him off to Pipe's house.[79] Here he was securely bound, and spent the remainder of the night.

The next morning his guard, Tutelu, started Knight for the Shawnee villages, forty miles away and to the southwest. Tutelu was on horseback, and drove Knight before him, covering, as Knight estimated, about twenty-five miles the first day. The next morning Tutelu informed his captive that they would reach the Shawnee village around noon, and having untied Knight, he turned his back as he began to stir up the fire. Knowing that he would never have another opportunity to escape, Knight picked up the largest stick he could lay his hands on, small though it was, and with all his might struck Tutelu on the back of his head. The Indian was only momentarily stunned, but he fell with his face in the fire. He recovered quickly, but instead of facing the doctor he ran off howling into the woods. Knight grabbed the rifle and tried to shoot, but he pulled the cock back so violently that he broke the mainspring. Quickly he grabbed Tutelu's blanket, a pair of moccasins, and carrying the now useless gun, began his journey home, through two hundred miles of a wilderness entirely unknown to him, which was populated by a savage enemy who were still out diligently searching for fugitives from Crawford's army.

For the first two days he traveled mainly north and east, then turned and headed almost due east, avoiding, however, the road by which the army had come out, and on which he and his late commander had been captured. He had eaten practically nothing during the six days that he had been a prisoner, and was unable to eat anything now, due to a blow from one of the tomahawks that had swollen his jaw to the point that he could not chew. He could not make a fire, of course, and after a few days he left the gun in the woods; now the swelling began to subside, and he was able to survive on what little he could find, unripe gooseberries, nettles, some herbs which he recognized, a few service-berries, and best of all, two young black-birds and a turtle, all of which he ate raw. On the morning of July 4th, 1782, an aus-picious day of independence for John Knight, being the twenty-first day since his escape, he appeared at the gates of Fort Pitt, very much bedraggled, very weary, and very much glad to be home.

Excerpt of a letter from Gen. William Irvine to Gov. William Moore of Pennsylvania:

*"This moment Doctor Knight has arrived, the surgeon I sent with the volunteers to Sandusky. He was several days in the hands of the Indians, but fortunately made his escape from his keeper, who was conducting him to another settlement to be burnt."*

*   *   *

John Slover, meanwhile, the only one of the three scouts to be captured, had been taken with two other prisoners to the Shawnee village of Wapatomica, where Zanesfield, Ohio, now stands. Slover knew the Indians well; he had spent twelve years as their captive in western and south-central Ohio[80]. After running the gaunt-let one of the men was beaten to death, and the second was sent to another town for burning. That evening a council was held, and at first Slover was treated with rel-ative kindness; he shocked them by informing them that Cornwallis had surrendered the October before, this being the first any of the Indians had heard of it.

News of Yorktown had not reached De Peyster at Detroit until April 3rd, 1782, and he had successfully concealed it from the Indians for over two months, when the word finally got out. De Peyster then tried to downplay its implications for them, but the Indians understood well enough what it meant for them; if the British now withdrew from the conflict the Indians would have to face the vengeance of the bor-dermen alone. After eight years of waging relentless border warfare, without the aid of their English allies the Indians could not hope to stand against the American forces, once those were freed of the strain of fighting the English military.

But the next day Matthew Elliott and Jim Girty attended the conference. Girty, an adopted Shawnee with considerable influence, told the Indians that Slover had lied, that Cornwallis had not been taken. Moreover Girty maintained that he had interrogated Slover, who had confessed to Girty that he intended to take a Shawnee scalp and escape at the first opportunity. Girty's first statement might have been believable, but the second was patently a lie; no one would have been so foolish as to state such an intention to a known renegade, an adopted Shawnee to boot, while a captive in a Shawnee village! Strangely enough, however, the Indians seemed to accept his word, gradually altering their attitude toward Slover.

The council at Wapatomica continued for fifteen days, the assembled Indians waiting for word from De Peyster, to whom a message had been sent. The "speech" finally arrived on the next-to-last day of the council, which stated nothing more assertive than that provisions at Detroit were low, and they could no longer afford to feed prisoners, thus advising the Indians that no more prisoners would be accepted. The hostiles then declared that they would take no more prisoners, and understanding what else had been left unspoken, planned three major assaults against the Americans, aimed at the settlements in the interior of Kentucky, at the Falls of the Ohio, and at Wheeling. For, if British aid were to be withheld from them, they must attack the frontier without delay, and they must ensure that these strikes be so violent as to compel the settlers to flee across the mountains.

The next day George Girty arrived at the head of about forty Delaware warriors. Girty and some of the Indians came to the house where Slover was staying. After Slover's arms had been tied behind his back, Girty stepped up to him, cursing and striking the bound man. He then painted Slover black and told him he was going to get the treatment he deserved. Slover was led to a town about seven miles away, known as Mac-a-chack, where he was to be burned. During the night he managed to loosen his bonds; stepping quietly over his snoring guards he made his way to the horse pen, and with the rope which had until recently bound him now serving as a halter, he mounted one of the Indian ponies and slipped away. The horse was a good one, but safety lay across the Scioto, fifty long miles to the east. He crossed that river before noon, but before they had gone much further the horse began to falter. When it was finally unable to continue Slover jumped from its back and raced ahead at his top speed. Hearing shouts behind him sped him on, and he did not stop until an hour or two before midnight. Finally pausing to rest he waited until the moon rose and then continued on until daylight. By the next night he had reached Coshocton, where he swam the Muskingum, then moved on a few miles before resting again. On the third day he came to Newcomerstown, and by that night he was within five miles of Wheeling. The next morning he reached the island just opposite Fort Henry, and John Slover's famous *Race for Life* was at an end.

Excerpt of a letter from Gen. Irvine, Fort Pitt, to Gen. Washington, July 11th, 1782:

*"A certain Mr. Slover came in yesterday, who was under sentence of death at the Shawanese towns."*

Slover was the last to come in, and he brought word that the Indians were on the way; the Sandusky campaign was over, the Indian Campaigns now began.

## *Sixth Interlude: Vengeance and Torture*

### *The Indian Concept of Vengeance*

Logan gained vengeance, not only for the murder of three of his family members, but also for the murder of nine other members of his tribe. He sought that vengeance not upon Michael Cresap, whom he incorrectly believed to be the instigator at Yellow Creek, nor upon Josh Baker, nor yet upon the Greathouse party. Instead, with a small band of warriors, he journeyed several hundred miles south, to present-day Tennessee, and there he had found the cabin of John Roberts.

One of the lesser-discussed aspects of the American Indian is that they lived in a truly tribal system, with all that that implies. Since the individual is the same as the tribe, any harm done to any individual is harm done to the tribe as a whole, and vice-versa. Or, as expressed by John Donne, "No man is an island". To the Indian warrior, if someone killed a member of his tribe, it was the same as if a member of his own family had been killed. To the redman, therefore, revenge was completely impersonal; or perhaps *apersonal* would be a better term. His role as a warrior was to seek vengeance for that death; whom he killed was totally irrelevant, as long as he was not a member of his own tribe. The guilty person would almost certainly go unpunished, but that was of no importance whatsoever.

If a raiding party from his tribe went from Wapatomica, for instance, to Wheeling/Fort Henry, and one of the warriors were killed, then the surviving warriors must seek revenge. If there are white captives in the village, whether they had been "adopted" into the tribe or not, the demand may be made that they be burned at the stake, thus giving the satisfaction of having avenged their brother's death, while at the same time gaining the enjoyment of watching a helpless person suffer unspeakable agonies. Witness Simon Kenton. If no captives are available, then the warriors may go on a raid and kill a settler, along with his entire family, perhaps in Kentucky, or western Virginia, or Pennsylvania.

"But," some would say, "that settler in Kentucky, his wife, his children, they had done that Indian no harm!" But to the Indian, that was entirely beside the point. It is a tribal society in which he lives, and anyone outside the tribe is an enemy, and they are all the same. A white man in Kentucky, or a white woman in Pennsylvania, or a white child in Tennessee, what is the difference? A distinction such as that meant absolutely nothing to an Indian, and he would not have been able to grasp the concept if someone had tried to explain. *White man kill me — I kill white man* would have summed up the entire philosophy of justice. Only under one particular circumstance would one warrior try to kill one other specific Indian; that would occur only if a member of your own tribe killed a member of your family, or in some way caused harm to your tribe. Then he was *persona non grata*, and his life was forfeit. If you could catch him, that is.

For us, in modern society, the concept of being satisfied with punishing *any* person, while allowing the one guilty of the crime to go unpunished, is so alien that we are not really capable of comprehending it. But that is no more alien to us than our system of punishing only the guilty was to the red man. Were those warriors alive today they would chide us for our temerity in often allowing an obviously guilty person to go free, as a result of our fear that we might sometime mistakenly punish an innocent person. This was the primary reason that the Iroquois League became so powerful; if you killed a Mohawk or an Oneida or a Seneca, no matter which, the entire Iroquois Confederation would come down, not on you, but on your entire tribe, and destroy it. And they did. You, as an individual, might be absent at the time, and thus escape punishment, and individuals often did, but vengeance was gained, nonetheless. Your tribe would not, could not, escape. It was for this reason that the other tribes fled before the mighty Iroquois.

### *Torture*

It is also exceedingly difficult, perhaps impossible, for modern people to understand why the pioneers hated the red man with such an intensity. The usual drivel about the white man *stealing the poor Indians' land* does not suffice to explain this hatred, nor does the fact that the pioneers considered the Indians to be "heathen savages" and "less than human". While it is true that the American aborigines were heathens in both the religious sense, being neither Christian, Jew, nor Moslem, as well as in the popular sense, unenlightened or uncivilized[81], they were nevertheless competing against a society that was profoundly Christian. Being heathens, the Indians raised captive white children as heathens, and the intensely religious parents would almost rather have seen them killed than to know that they were being raised away from the church, with no chance of eternal salvation.

It is also true that the Indians killed women and children, and they delighted in doing so, but neither does this explain the intensity of feeling. Eventually the settlers began to retaliate, and some few of them did not hesitate to kill any Indian who came within their power, old men, women or children; to them it was a war of extermination, no quarter asked, none given. But that such men were few and such occurrences among white men were rare is obvious from the reports we have of them; it was uncommon enough that the killing of a single Indian woman or child was remarked upon. One of the more unnoteworthy campaigns of the Border Wars started out from Fort Pitt in early March of 1778, under the leadership of General Edward Hand. After proceeding about forty miles up Beaver Creek they discovered an Indian village, but upon attacking it they found it contained only one man, some women, and several children. The man was killed, one of the squaws was taken captive, but before Hand could interfere another of the squaws was killed, while the rest escaped. Ten miles further up a supposed camp of salt makers was found to be nothing more than another woman and an Indian boy; the boy was killed and the squaw taken prisoner. Because of high water from the melting snows the expedition returned to Fort Pitt; since that day the campaign has been derisively stigmatized as Hand's *Squaw Campaign*, because an Indian woman was killed and two others taken captive, all in a single day.

But even during the massacre of Logan's family in 1774, at the commencement of the Border Wars, the one child who was with the Indian party at Baker's Station was spared and sent to its father. After eight years of Indian atrocities, however, three out of every four of Williamson's men voted not to spare a single man, woman, or child among the ninety Indians at Gnadenhutten, Christian and otherwise, in 1782, although the feelings of horror and disgust at this cowardly deed were widespread throughout the country. Outside the border, that is; outside the one specific area of the country which had borne the daily brunt of Indian depredations for the last decade.

In spite of widespread belief to the contrary, Indian warriors raped and sodomized almost all the white women who fell into their power, before killing them. Historians of the nineteenth century could not describe such acts on the written page, and as a result of their hesitancy to describe those gruesome details the myth has grown up of the noble red man who kept himself "pure" while on the warpath. Myth indeed! One of the first writers even to mention this fact, Theodore Roosevelt, in his 1890's *Winning of the West*, stated without any elaboration that the Eastern Woodland Indians were not quite as bad in this "one respect" as the Plains Indians:

"Their female captives were not invariably ravished by every member of the band capturing them, as has ever been the custom of the horse Indians."

Not invariably.

*     *     *

But still, even their paganism, their killing of women and children, and their incessant raping of captive women does not explain the pioneers' deep-seated hatred. For that there must be a deeper, stronger reason, stronger than religious beliefs, a reason stronger even than the loathsome murder or abhorrent rape, something even worse than the killing of innocent women and helpless children. It was not the Indian method of warfare, nor yet their worship of heathen gods, that so determined the American frontiersman on a war of utter extermination. It was something else, and one does not have to search far to find it. In a word, it was torture; in two words, it was a satanic ritual.

The Indian killed women and children, and delighted in doing so; but even greater was their delight in torturing helpless victims. No one has ever described it better than Vardis Fisher; although in this instance he was referring to the Indians of the Rocky Mountain fur trade, the description is just as apt for their Eastern Woodland brothers of half a century earlier:

*Torture for the redmen was as normal as beating their wives. The wolf ate his victim alive, but he was not aware of that. But the red people tortured for the pure hellish joy of seeing a helpless thing suffer unspeakable agonies. It was chiefly for this reason that mountain men loathed them, and killed them with as little emotion as they killed mosquitoes.* (Vardis Fisher, *Mountain Man*, p. 237.)

Loathing may be too mild a term for the feeling which the frontier people had for the American Indian. The emotion was much, much stronger than that. It is only necessary to read some of the accounts of the early settlement of western Virginia and Kentucky to find example after revolting example of torture. It was perhaps not so much the practice of torture itself as it was the red man's enjoyment of inflicting pain, and his custom of taking captives solely for the purpose of this enjoyment. An excellent illustrative example may be found in one of the earliest histories of border warfare, McClung's *Sketches of Western Adventure*, published when people still knew why Indians tortured their victims. The story is the familiar one of Simon Kenton being marched from one Indian village to another, where he was to be burned at the stake. Along the trail they passed an Indian and his squaw cutting wood with an axe. The man seized his woman's axe and swung a vicious blow at Kenton, but the other warriors shielded him from the force of the blow. Then, speaking of the Indian's fury, McClung writes:

"He would instantly have repeated the blow, had not Kenton's conductors interfered and protected him, severely reprimanding the Indian *for attempting to rob them of the amusement of torturing the prisoner.*"

As Kenton himself later told a friend, speaking of the Indian character:

"The General observed ... that an education obtained in the school of Indian warfare was well calculated to teach white men the native disposition and character of the aboriginal, and that he was a regular graduate from the school of torture, which was a fair picture of the disposition and true character of the Indian race, and that the lessons which his cruel preceptors had taught him were engraven upon his memory, his mind, and in particular his body."

At that point Kenton called upon his listener to feel the indentation in his skull, which had been the permanent result of the tomahawk blow given him a half century before.

The standard rationalization often heard now is that the American Indian learned of burning people at the stake from the white men who had come here from Europe; somehow this is meant as a defense of the agony inflicted upon the Indians' victims. These apologists, however, do not explain that the Europeans burned people at the stake in order to save their souls, the only method known to them to drive out demons[82]. The purpose was not to make the victim suffer, but to prevent eternal suffering. They well knew what would happen to the immortal soul if the person died while he was in the power of the devil; they knew of the "hellfires of eternal damnation", because they had been taught that this was Truth. That people enjoyed watching this spectacle is true, because this was visible proof of the ultimate power of God; here they were given visible proof of Satan being defeated by the church; the devil was losing one of his victim's souls. It was not necessary to live in constant fear that you would be eternally damned, for the church would save you.

These same apologists who try to expiate the Indians' torture shake their heads in disbelief upon hearing that in the fourteenth and fifteenth centuries people willingly confessed to being possessed by the devil, or to being witches and warlocks, knowing that they would be burned. Why, it is asked, would anyone be so stupid as to confess, when they knew what awaited them? But they fail to understand that those people confessed exactly because they wanted to be burned. They wanted to be saved from damnation, and they knew that the pain would be insignificant, because they had seen others burned; they had seen the person at the stake lose consciousness from smoke inhalation after only a few moments, and they did not suffer the agony of hours of pain. *The cause of death for a person who was burned at the stake was asphyxiation, while unconscious, not from a burning of the flesh.*

But not so with the Indians. They did not burn their victims as a religious ritual, and to imply that their practice was nothing more than what they had learned from white men is not only to preach false history, it is a grotesque absurdity. Everything possible was done to draw out the torture as long as possible, to ensure that the victim would not die too soon, depriving them of their enjoyment and robbing them of their entertainment! According to Dr. Knight, Crawford pleaded with Simon Girty to shoot him, and so end his agony, but Girty refused. The common reason given is that had Girty shot Crawford to end his torment, the Indians, cheated of their entertainment, would have been so infuriated that they would probably have replaced Crawford's corpse with the live body of their "brother" Simon Girty.

It is beyond the scope of this *Sketchbook* to detail the many methods of Indian torture; some few are briefly described in these pages, such as those relating to Col. Crawford and to Jacob Greathouse, but even in those many of the gory and obscene details have been omitted, in the name of decency. But for those who are interested, and who have a strong enough stomach, it is not difficult to find many more graphic descriptions of this form of Indian entertainment in any number of volumes dealing with the Indian wars.

# Chapter XXI

## Lewis Wetzel - II

One of the survivors of Crawford's unfortunate campaign, Thomas Mills[83], had managed, alone, to get within a few miles of the Ohio before his horse gave out. Leaving the animal to graze and recover Mills reached the Ohio at Short Creek, a few miles above Wheeling. There he crossed the river and ascended the creek to Van Meter's Fort, where he found 18-year-old Lewis Wetzel, and after some effort finally persuaded Wetzel to accompany him in an effort to retrieve his horse. Wetzel tried to dissuade him, explaining that the danger was certain to be extreme. Although the Indians which had been engaged in the victory over Crawford had returned to Wapatomica, and were no longer in pursuit of the stragglers from that expedition, there were without doubt many other bands of warriors roaming the area about the Ohio shore, searching for anyone who had not yet managed to cross the river.

But Mills persisted, and horses were valuable, and finally Wetzel agreed. Also at Van Meter's was Joshua Davis, Mills' fifteen-year-old cousin, and he wanted to go along. He was big for his age, he had argued, he was old enough to serve in the militia, the distance was not great, and if they did chance to run into Indians, then three guns would be better than two. Mills, contradictorily, now tried to argue that the danger was too great, but Wetzel agreed with Josh's reasoning, and together the three crossed the river at Wheeling, at daybreak the next morning, and started out on the Indian trail leading west.

*     *     *

Although he was not yet twenty years of age, Wetzel was by now establishing himself as the pre-eminent Indian fighter on the frontier; his daring, woodscraft, and athleticism were considered first rate by men who knew, and one of his most remarkable feats was the ability to reload his rifle while being chased through the woods by an enemy. Those who have loaded a flintlock rifle know the complexity of the process; a charge of powder must be poured carefully down the muzzle of the barrel, then the ball is centered in the muzzle and forced down on top of the powder with the ramrod, or wiping stick. The final step is to prime the pan with powder, and close the frizzen on the pan; all this while not spilling the powder. Yet how difficult was it to perform that task while trying to run at full speed, and how much more difficult when running through the forest, being chased by foes with murderous intent, who are determined on your speedy demise, but who are not encumbered by trying to load a rifle, nor even by carrying one? When loading on the run it was not possible for Wetzel to move at his top speed. When being chased by Indians he took extremely long strides, like a lengthened-out dog trot, yet even at that rate he could still outdistance all but the swiftest runners. And at the same time he must still maintain a sharp lookout on the trail ahead; it would do his escape effort little good if he ran into the arms of an approaching enemy, or if he brained himself on a low, overhanging tree limb whilst trying to outdistance his pursuers.

\*     \*     \*

After traveling about ten miles Wetzel, Mills, and Davis reached a spring[84], where they saw the horse some distance ahead, tied to a tree. Wetzel urged caution, but Mills recklessly approached the animal, whereupon a volley of shots was fired at him by a party of Indians in ambush. Mills fell with a ball through his leg, and as the Indians charged out of their hiding place, Wetzel fired a snap shot at them and had the satisfaction of seeing one fall. Unable to provide any assistance to his fallen companion without the sacrifice of his own life, Wetzel turned and fled. Josh, following along a short distance behind, heard the crack of rifles, the scream of Mills, Wetzel's customary roar, the *Deathwind*, announcing the demise of an Indian, and the confused shouting of the Indians. Suddenly Wetzel burst into view, followed by several warriors; having fired and missed, but also knowing the white man's gun to be empty as well, they had dropped their rifles and started out in pursuit, tomahawks in hand. No doubt they had expectations of soon running him down, but they did not yet know Wetzel as Indians would later come to know Wetzel.

As soon as the warriors appeared Josh fired a hurried shot at them, apparently somehow managing to miss them all, and then took to his heels. Fast as he was, Wetzel overtook him almost immediately, reloading his rifle as he raced by. After about a mile of pursuit, Wetzel yelled to Josh that there were only four Indians following; with his rifle now reloaded Wetzel spun and fired, killing the foremost. Nearly exhausted by his first all-out burst of speed, Josh told Wetzel that he could no longer keep up Wetzel's pace, whereupon Lewis advised him to trot, as they were some distance ahead, while he reloaded. Soon another Indian, who had cut across through the woods, came out of the brush almost on top of them; Wetzel swung about to fire, but the Indian grabbed the barrel of the rifle. Wetzel, twisting his body quickly, forced the muzzle against the warrior's chest, pulled the trigger, and the Indian fell.

Another mile was covered at nearly top speed, and Josh had been exerting himself just to keep Wetzel in sight, but now he had reached the end of his rope. No white man could keep up with Lewis Wetzel in a foot race, even when Wetzel was reloading as he ran, as was later to be proven conclusively in a public exhibition. As Wetzel himself said, "God never created a man who could run me down." He was not boasting, it was merely a statement of fact.

When Josh gasped out that he would have to give himself up to the Indians, Wetzel yelled out:

"Josh, at the next turn of the hill there's a high bank and a clump of bushes right below it. You jump down and lay there until the Injuns pass — they'll follow me. I'll meet you at the creek."

When they reached the bank Josh jumped; one of the Indians, obviously also exhausted, paused there while the other doggedly continued his pursuit of Wetzel. Only a few moments later the report of Wetzel's rifle was heard; the last remaining Indian turned and headed back toward his comrades, and Josh and Lewis met up at the creek, returning home safely. A few days later a party under John McColloch went out to bury Mills; they found him scalped and, typically, mutilated, and with his ankle broken by an Indian bullet.

*   *   *

At this time Lewis Wetzel's hatred of the Indian was probably no greater than that of any other typical frontiersman; he and little brother Jake had been abducted by Indians, as had his older brother Martin, but all three had escaped relatively unharmed. He had seen his share of Indian atrocities, but then, so had everyone else on the border. At the outset of 1782 neither the Wetzels nor the Bonnetts, his mother's family, had suffered a personal tragedy at the hands of the Indians. But sometime during the course of 1782, probably in the fall of the year, his older brother George, twenty-one years of age, set out on a hunting and trapping trip, and was shot by Indians while in a canoe on the Ohio. The actual details are confused and debatable; whether George was alone, or accompanied. If there were others present, who were they? For many years it was even debated whether the year was 1782 or 1786, and whether the father and one or more of the brothers had accompanied him. The Wetzels' most recent biographer, C.B. Allman, stated that George had been killed in 1786, while on the Ohio in a canoe with his father, that Captain John had been killed as well, and that the two Wetzels, father and son, were buried together in a common grave at Baker' Station, close by Graveyard Run[85], Marshall Co., WV.

Allman based his conclusion on two premises; that John Wetzel, Sr., had indeed been killed in 1786, by Indians, while with companions in a canoe on the Ohio, and on the statement in a letter written by Wetzel's nephew, Lewis Bonnett, Jr., to Dr. Draper:

"I remember the day that we received the word my Uncle John Wetzel and my cousin George had been killed by the Indians. My father was raising a horse stable at the time the news came. Jacob and John, Jr., were at the raising."

But what Bonnett had actually written to Draper was that he remembered when the news came that his **Uncle John had been killed.** In order to prove his own version of the incident, i.e., that George had been killed along with his father, Allman had inserted the words **and my cousin George.** Lewis Bonnett was only four years old at the time of cousin George's death, and at that age it is unlikely that he would have been impressed with such a detail. He had been eight when word came that Captain John had been killed, and that was the event he recalled for Draper.

In 1803 a petition to the Virginia Legislature was filed on behalf of the four remaining brothers, "... **Martin, Jacob, Lewis and John Whitzel.**" This petition asked that a pension be granted to these four men on behalf of their services to the country during the Indian wars, and gave details substantiating their claim. In order to lend weight to their petition it was signed by such notables as Col. Ebenezer Zane, his brother Jonathan, Moses Chapline, Isaac Williams, and Joseph Tomlinson, all of whom had lived through the border wars, and who were not only well acquainted with the contributions of the Wetzels to the defense of the Upper Ohio, but who knew the history of the family itself. Specific details, such as the years that George and Capt. John Wetzel had been killed, came directly from these four brothers and their mother, who was still living on Wheeling Creek.

Among the reasons stated for the granting of a pension to the Wetzels of Ohio County:

"... in the year 1770 their father came to said county and settled on Wheeling Creek, where he resided till his death in 1786, when he was killed by the Indians; that from the said year 1771 till the conclusion of peace with the Indians, their father, together with their brother George, who was killed by the Indians in 1782, lived in a state of warfare on the Frontier, continuously, spending the greater part of every season in hunting and destroying the enemy without paying any attention to their own private affairs, but the greater part of the time their efforts being merely volunteer and not in any regular service, they could neither receive pay or pensions from their country."

"Your petitioners further state, that it is well-known to the whole country where they live, that their father and his sons during the period of Indian warfare aforesaid, rendered more service and protection to the frontier than any family that ever lived on it, and more to their private detriment...."

Capt. John Wetzel, along with Martin, Lewis, Jacob, and John, Jr., *during the period of Indian warfare aforesaid, rendered more service and protection to the frontier than any family that ever lived on it.* But in spite of this glowing testimonial of their services to the country, by those who were in a position to know, the petition was denied. It was as great an injustice as ever Boone, Kenton, or Clark suffered at the hands of their government. While others who had done little or nothing routinely received pensions, while a scoundrel such as Wilkinson was promoted to command of the U.S. Army, as he raked in money from both the Americans and the Spanish; and then, that not one of the Wetzels should receive a penny in compensation for the hardships and dangers while performing their public duty ....

But injustice aside, the facts remain: George Wetzel was killed by Indians in 1782, Captain John Wetzel was killed by Indians in 1786. When Draper traveled to Wheeling in 1845 to interview Lewis Bonnett, Jr., personally, he had written down Bonnet's version of the death of George Wetzel, as follows:

"George Wetzel, Old John Wetzel, Martin and Lewis, and Miller most likely, went down the Ohio on a hunt. While paddling along near shore, they were fired on by Indians in ambush, and George Wetzel mortally wounded; and he said, *'All lie down — I'll paddle the canoe around the point of yonder island — I'm a dead man anyway.'* The others did as he ordered. The Indians kept firing into the boat as long as it was within their reach, killing a dog in the boat, and one bullet barely grazed Martin on the shoulder. Martin and Lewis loaded as they lay, and shot at the Indians, and most likely with good effect. George soon got the canoe beyond reach — and soon died; was buried at the head of Captina Island; died that night. A very handsome young man, very clever and beloved."[86]

Following this interview a correspondence developed between Bonnett and Draper, but in his later years, his failing health, of which he complained in almost every letter, caused his memory to become clouded. In addition he had by this time been influenced, as had many others, by the work of Alexander Scott Withers, and, in an effort to be as precise as possible, the letters contain a mixture of Bonnett's recollections and stories that he had been told, with some of Withers' statements stirred in.

The death of "Old John" Wetzel will be presented in *Chapter XXIV*, following the abduction and rescue of yet another of the Wetzel boys, John Wetzel, Jr. Still, it is not difficult to understand how the stories of the deaths of George and John, Sr., became intertwined; the circumstances of their deaths at two separate sites were yet so uncannily similar that it would be surprising had they not been blended into one story.

# Chapter XXII

$\mathcal{T}$he Second Calamity:
Blue Licks, 1782

Over a thousand warriors from the Ohio, the Wabash, the nearer Lake Indians, and even some distant Cherokee had assembled during and following the great Indian Council at Wapatomica. Soon Caldwell had recovered from his wounds, and was ready to lead the first element of the massive three-pronged expedition. But since Slover had attended several of the councils before his denunciation, and had then escaped with word of the three planned expeditions, a major change was proposed. As soon as they could be made ready, provisions assembled, and ammunition from Detroit distributed, the largest force would now proceed against the Pennsylvania frontier. When those were destroyed, with the deceitful Moravian missionaries now removed from the scene, with Indians blocking any relief from Virginia, and without the continuous support from Fort Pitt, it was believed all the other settlements would collapse.

At the head of one hundred fifty Rangers, and supported by Alex McKee and eleven hundred Indians, the massive Indian force had begun their march eastward and had already crossed the Scioto, when runners caught up with them, bringing distressful news: George Rogers Clark had assembled an army of four thousand men; he had crossed the Ohio, and was now in their rear, headed for the defenseless Indian villages which had been stripped of all their warriors for this blow against the frontier. It was Clark, they insisted, Clark the Nemesis, Clark who could move like lightning, and it meant their total destruction. The Indian army about-faced and hurried back to the villages, keeping a sharp lookout for signs of the mighty Clark colossus, but seeing nothing. Upon their return Blue Jacket, the new Shawnee war chief, lead a reconnaissance patrol toward Kentucky; he returned a week later saying that Clark was holed up in Fort Nelson, at Louisville, with not more than three hundred militia, and he was going nowhere fast.

But the Indians were losing interest fast; they had devoured their rations, but still had the ammunition which they could use for hunting; the English were always good for more. Many of them had been absent from their villages since May, when the first word of Crawford's intended campaign reached them. Now it was mid-August, and they were ready to go home. Many of them did. With only about half of the Indians remaining to him, and less than a hundred Rangers, McKee divided them into two fairly equal companies. Three hundred Indians would head south for Louisville, supported by Caldwell and fifty of his Rangers; McKee would be in overall charge, with Caldwell in military command, and Matthew Elliott, aided by Simon and George Girty, in charge of the Indians. At the same time Capt. Andrew Bradt and forty Rangers from Detroit would retrace their steps to the east, with Jim Girty in command of the remaining two hundred fifty Indians, where they would strike Wheeling's Fort Henry.

The Kentucky Expedition began first, leaving Wapatomica in early July. They crossed the Ohio at the mouth of the Limestone and turned southwest, along the great buffalo trail leading to the salt licks. Their goal was Bryan's Station, the first, largest, and most-exposed station on the route since the destruction of Ruddle's and Martin's two years earlier. After crossing the Ohio, about a hundred of the Indians were sent out in small groups to raid the settlements; the others halted to give those time to terrorize, before they attacked Bryan's Station.

This was the home of Boone's relatives, a clan of Bryan's, all closely interrelated with the Boones. In 1753 sixteen-year-old Rebecca Boone, Daniel's younger sister, had married William Bryan, one of the neighbor boys on the Yadkin, and later Daniel's cousin, John Boone married William's sister. Daniel, of course, had married Rebecca Bryan in 1756, and his younger brother, Edward, or Ned, had married Becky's sister, Martha. Will Bryan had been killed by Indians in 1781, but the men of Bryan's Station, less than fifty altogether, and outnumbered as they were by better than five to one, would never surrender to a pack of howling savages! The Indians surrounded the fort during the night of August 15th, and had they only waited a few hours, they might have been successful. The men inside the walls were preparing to depart that very morning, leaving the station defenseless; riding out to the relief of another fort which was supposedly under attack; such was the result of those small Indian parties which had been attacking the settlements for the past month. But as soon as someone appeared at the gate the warriors began firing, and thus the inhabitants were warned of their danger. Without the cannon which had proved so effective under Bird, the only possible way to reduce the station was by stratagem. This was tried, but the attempts were notable only by their failure.

A hundred warriors began an assault on the south-east corner, while the other two hundred lay concealed in the woodline at the opposite angle, ready to attack as soon as they felt that all the defenders had left that corner unprotected. But these were Kentuckians, veterans of the Indian Wars, and they knew a little strategy of their own. Except for a dozen men, all the defenders moved across to the northwest corner, the quiet side, while those dozen left the gate and hesitatingly approached the Indians who had noisily begun the attack. Instantly the two hundred warriors charged from the woods for what they believed was the unprotected side of the fort; before they were well within range they were met by a hailstorm of bullets, and as instantly did the warriors retreat. During the assault five warriors had been killed and two wounded. The Indians then withdrew below the cover of the creek bank and awaited the relief parties which were certain to arrive. Seventeen mounted men from Boonesborough approached the fort with not an Indian in sight and, although fired upon, they broke through the Indian lines to gain the fort, the first of the relief forces to arrive. The thirty or so men who were on foot were less fortunate; two were killed and four wounded before they were able to withdraw through a providentially nearby field of corn.

Now the Indians were reduced to rounding up the horses that had not been brought inside the stockade, slaughtering the livestock, nearly five hundred head of cattle and hogs, and destroying the fields, now in mid-August nearly ready for harvest. Inside the fort four defenders had been killed and three wounded. About 10:00 a.m. on the 17th Caldwell withdrew, with another plan in view; no mean strategist was he. With the consternation already having been spread by the Indian raiders, and knowing there would be other relief parties coming to the aid of Bryan's Station, Caldwell retreated back up the great buffalo trace, crossed the Licking River, and deliberately set up an ambush at the Blue Licks, waiting for the inevitable pursuit which he knew would shortly arrive. The day after the siege was lifted a mounted column of nearly two hundred men arrived at Bryan's, led by some of the leading pioneers of Kentucky; Col. Boone, of course, along with Stephen Trigg, John Todd, Robert Patterson, and Hugh McGary. Benjamin Logan was assembling another even larger force, and it was McGary who suggested that they wait for their arrival. But several of the men sneeringly implied that perhaps McGary was afraid of facing an Indian, and as always, there was the fear that the enemy would get away if not immediately followed. Off they raced, toward the Blue Licks and disaster.

On the morning of August 19th they reached the salt licks. Boone, with his experienced eye, had already pointed out to them that the Indians were leaving a broad trail, inviting pursuit. At the same time they were taking great pains to conceal their numbers, but they had not fooled woodscrafty Boone. Some of the Indians had indeed left for home, but Boone knew well enough that the Kentuckians were still outnumbered. Across the shallow Licking River, on the wooded hillside opposite and in the ravine leading up the hill, a few Indians could be seen, aimlessly milling about, seemingly unaware of or oblivious to the one hundred eighty-two horsemen who had just come pounding up. It was the surest of signs that these were decoys, tolling the Kentuckians on. It was obvious to all, and the only intelligent plan was proposed by Boone; spies should be sent out to determine the exact number of the enemy. Then, if it seemed feasible, the men should move back somewhat from the river. Half the men would take up a position here, on this side of the river, while the other half withdrew to move upstream, where they would cross unobserved, and then come down on the Indians from in back and above. The trappers would be trapped and forced to fight their way out, caught between two fires. The only sensible alternative to this was to await Logan's arrival.

But Hugh McGary, still smarting from the implication of cowardice, shouted that he, by God, was going after those damned redskins, and anybody that wasn't a coward would go with him. It was a totally irresponsible thing to say to a group of frontiersmen, and crossing the river was as foolhardy an act as could be imagined, but cross the river they did, every single one of them, even old Boone, who could not stay behind when others went forward. Dismounting, they formed their lines, and then up the ravine they all went, straight into the ambush cleverly prepared for them.

Had Caldwell and his Rangers not been along, the results might not have been so tragic. After the first volley the Kentuckians would have treed and then, firing back to hold the Indians at bay, they could gradually have gained their horses, on which they would quickly recross the river and retreat. The Indians, meanwhile, skulking from tree to tree, would have contented themselves with trying to pick off the odd straggler. Almost never would Indians charge an opponent, witness Battle Island, even if they held a distinct advantage in numbers. But Caldwell was a military man; he had chosen the ambush site carefully, and he had his well-disciplined Rangers with him. The forces were approximately even, he held the higher ground, and in back of the Kentuckians, their only escape route, was a river. And rivers were notorious for two martial elements: knee-deep water slowed down anyone trying to cross, and knee-deep water provided precious little cover. The Rangers and the Indians charged downhill and broke the lines of the frontiersmen.

Seasoned veterans though they were, it was too much for them; without discipline the militia once more became confused and disorganized. Among the seventy who were killed within the next few minutes, before they were able to get across the river, was Israel Boone, who died in Daniel's arms; his second son, and his second son to fall to Indians. Both Colonels Trigg and Todd were killed, and seven other men were captured, later killed. On Caldwell's side one of his Rangers had been killed, the only one who was lost during the entire campaign, and ten Indians were victims of the Kentucky longrifles, fourteen more were wounded. Hugh McGary, by the bye, had come through the battle unscratched.

The next day, the 20th, Col. Logan met the survivors staggering back to Bryan's Station. After providing what relief he could, he moved on to the site of the battle, arriving there on the 22nd, and disturbing the buzzards at their feast. They found the bodies so badly mangled by man and animal alike that they were scarcely able to identify any of the corpses. Logan ordered that all be buried in a common grave, and a long trench was dug on the hillside, just below the crest of the hill up which they had struggled. After the scattered remains had been gathered together and placed in it, they were decently covered, 23-year-old Israel Boone among them.

# Chapter XXIII

$\mathcal{T}$he Zanes - III

The Siege of Fort Henry

It was almost more than the frontier people could bear. The terrible massacre at Ruddle's Station two years before, then last summer the loss of Lochry and the thirty-five men killed with him, sixty-four others captured. Only two months ago came the loss of so many of the men under Crawford, and now nearly eighty more dead, or on their way to death, at the Blue Licks; it had been agreed that no more prisoners would be brought back to Detroit.

The question now had to be faced: was a sixteen-by-sixteen foot one-room log cabin with a dirt floor, surrounded by an acre or two of scraggly corn, really worth the cost? Many said no, and departed. Many others would have gone if only they had been able to find a single horse on which to carry the food necessary for the long journey back.

The Virginians were granted a slight breathing spell; the expedition against Wheeling had been delayed by dissension among the various chiefs as to their primary target. Without the steadying influence of McKee, Elliott, and Simon Girty to keep the Indians in line, the east-bound expedition almost ended before it had well begun. They had not gone far, having spent as much time arguing as traveling, and several of the chiefs were on the verge of turning back with their warriors, when word came of the great victory at Blue Licks. Thus encouraged, Capt. Bradt and Jim Girty continued on with their mixed force of Rangers and Indians.

This time there was no warning from the Moravian missionaries, who were still being held in Detroit. But ever since word had reached Wheeling of the disaster at the Blue Licks, scouts had been out constantly searching for Indian sign on both sides of the river. The earliest warning came about three o'clock in the afternoon of September 11th, a Wednesday, when scout John Linn (or Lynn) crossed the river and came racing up to the fort with word that a large party of Indians, more than two hundred as best he could determine, was headed their way, and not far off at that. The nominal commander in the fort was Capt. John Boggs, but upon Linn's arrival with the news he was sent for aid. The cannon was fired as the alarm, and Capt. Silas Zane, having returned from the east after Cornwallis' surrender, now took command of the fort, with his brother, Col. Ebenezer Zane remaining in his blockhouse, as he had the year before. Again Andy and Molly Scott stayed with him, along with George Green and the Colonel's slave, Old Daddy Sam[87]. Boggs had not gone much more than a mile when he suddenly was spurred on by the sound of the fort's cannon being fired the second time, and rifle fire as well. He had not gotten much further when he was overtaken by Ebenezer McColloch, who was coming down to Fort Henry from Van Meter's Fort on Short Creek; McColloch had approached within a half mile of the fort when he heard a heavy and constant firing about the fort. Boggs arrived at Catfish Camp the next morning, the 12th, and immediately word was sent out for the militia to assemble for the relief of the fort.

The Indians soon appeared on the island and, crossing, arrayed themselves north and east of the fort. There was no hurry; they had not really expected to surprise the fort, and they could not expect to overwhelm it as long as the Zane Blockhouse was stoutly defended. The fort was vulnerable only from the north and northeast sides, and in the final analysis it all came down to a question of either the use of fire, or a long-drawn-out siege. The Indians preferred the former, the Rangers the latter.

At almost the same time that the Indians reached the river so did a boat from Fort Pitt, in the charge of Daniel Copeland (Cope) Sullivan, who was transporting a boatload of cannonballs for George Rogers Clark and Fort Nelson at the Falls of the Ohio. With Sullivan were two men, and as the first shots were fired at them from the island all three quickly abandoned the boat at the wharf and hurried to the fort, the Indians so close behind as to wound Sullivan in the foot.

Capt. Bradt immediately demanded a surrender, which was rejected out of hand by Silas Zane; without uttering a word, he simply fired the little "French" cannon[88], as much of an answer as he cared to give. The year before the settlement had attempted to trick the Indians by placing a wooden gun, made from a hollowed-out log, over the wall of the fort. It had not been fired that day, and in the evening, after the Indians had departed, it was thrown over the wall. But when he had been taken captive Davy Glenn had told the Indians that the cannon had been only a wooden one, and now they jeeringly yelled at the fort to fire their cannon. Zane obliged, putting an end to any surrender negotiations and at the same time informing the Indians that they were facing real artillery. Capt. Bradt was heard to yell, "Stand back! Stand back! By God, there's no wood about *that* gun!"

The threat of the cannon, the difficulty of approaching the fort/blockhouse combination, with the bluff on the south and the steep river bank on the west, along with the open nature of the area surrounding the fort, all contrived to keep the Indians at a distance. Sporadic firing at the fort was maintained for the rest of the afternoon, until darkness fell, but the only damage was bullet holes in the palisade wall. The greatest chance of success was by burning the fort. If only the wall could be set afire the Indians stood a good chance of breaking through; outnumbering the men in the fort by a ratio of six or eight to one[89], the resistance inside would not last long. But it was nearly impossible to fire the fort as long as the Zane Blockhouse held the enemy at bay; thus the necessity of first reducing that abode to ashes.

As soon as darkness provided sufficient cover one of the warriors began creeping stealthily toward the Blockhouse, carrying a smoldering firebrand under him. As he approached the rear, or kitchen area, in which Daddy Sam was watching, he waved the brand to rekindle the fire before heaving it against the cabin wall. But before he had time to throw it a shot rang out from the old man's musket, and both Indian and firebrand fell to the ground. Twice more before morning light the Indians tried fire against the walls of the fort, both times unsuccessfully. Since the area around the fort had been kept clear, and given the difficulty of approaching the fort from any other direction, there was little hope that the fort could be burned.

With the arrival of daylight next morning, September 12th, the Indians were seen busily occupying themselves with another project. If they could not burn the walls of the fort, perhaps they could level them with cannon fire. The idea evidently having been spawned by the "wooden cannon" of the year before, and provided with an adequate supply of cannonballs from Sullivan's boat, the Indians now proceeded to fashion their own artillery piece. They found a log with a hollow cavity close to the size of the cannonballs, two inches in diameter, and bound it about with chains taken from the blacksmith's shop. A vent was crudely hacked near the enclosed end, a heavy charge of powder was followed by one of the cannonballs, the improvised field piece was pointed in the general direction of the fort, and all was ready. While the Rangers cautiously kept their distance, many of the Indians gathered around closely as the match was applied to the vent; a tremendous roar echoed though the valley, and the entire scene was enveloped by a dense white fog. As the cloud of smoke began to clear the inhabitants of the fort, peering over the walls, could see Indians writhing on the ground. Their marvelous cannon had disintegrated, blasting large chunks of wood and the pieces of chain binding it in all directions. Several Indians had been killed and numerous others wounded.

Throughout the remainder of that morning the firing was kept up on the fort, but inflicting no more damage than the day before. A little after noon the sallyport gate on the south wall suddenly opened and a young woman ran out; quickly she covered the distance between the fort and the blockhouse, and disappeared inside. The Indians were so startled by this totally unexpected apparition that they did not even have time to raise their muskets and fire at her in the few seconds it took to cross the open ground, being content instead merely to yell, "Squaw! Squaw!" But only a few minutes later and the door of the blockhouse was flung open, and the same woman appeared, racing back up the slight incline toward the fort, but this time carrying a large, bulky bundle before her. It could be nothing other than gunpowder, and now the Indians poured a volley at the slender figure sprinting up the slight incline to the fort.

That summer Col. Zane had requested gunpowder from General Irvine, and Irvine had, in July, issued a supply of powder from the stores in Fort Pitt to Col. James Marshel, county lieutenant of Washington County, to be distributed to all the forts. But by the time Col. Zane's request had been received Marshel had already issued all the powder to the other county lieutenants, and Zane was once again obliged to request a supply for Fort Henry. However, other than being the founder of Wheeling, Zane himself had no official government standing; he was not a county lieutenant (David Shepherd still held that post for Ohio County), and at the time there was no garrison of regulars at Fort Henry. Irvine nevertheless sent a supply of powder to Zane immediately, but with the understanding that Zane would keep the powder in his blockhouse, where it could not be pilfered by militia, nor used by the settlers for hunting for their families, nor burned up in one of the frontiersmen's favorite pastimes, target shooting, or "diverting at marks".

When Linn had arrived with the warning of the approach of the Indians there had not been time to accomplish everything. Boggs was sent out, the cannon was fired as a signal gun, and everyone within hearing rushed for the shelter of the fort, the women carrying what food and blankets they could lay hands on in a few minutes, and dragging the children behind them, while the men rounded up the horses and herded them into the fort. The cattle, hogs, and poultry were then chased into the woods to fend for themselves, where the survivors, if any, could be rounded up later. Once inside the fort everything was a-bustle; men prepared their rifles and checked powderhorns and bullet pouches, while the women got the children out of danger, much to the disgust of some of the more adventurous boys. Then the women stuck hatchets along the top of the wall; any Indian who tried to climb the palisade would find his fingers in serious jeopardy. Then began the task of preparing buckets of water to fight the ever-present danger of fire, and of casting bullets for the weapons. In addition, some of the molten lead was dribbled out along the ground, producing irregular-shaped bits of lead for emergency short-range use in the smooth-bore muskets, turning them into murderous shotguns, and for use as cannon fodder.

In all this rush and hurry Irvine's store of gunpowder was not transferred from Zane's to the fort; it was presumed that the Indians would, as usual, depart after a few hours of frustration, and there was more than sufficient powder in the fort to last throughout that day and into the next. There was not enough for a protracted siege, but that was such an unlikely event that it was hardly considered.

But the defenders of Fort Henry had not counted on Rangers; although they not uncommonly operated in Kentucky it was the first time they had appeared at Wheeling, and it was primarily because of the Ranger presence that the Indians continued to besiege the fort. By noon of the second day the supply of powder was beginning to run low; by one count the cannon had been fired sixteen times since the first appearance of the Indians the afternoon before, and the cannon had a voracious appetite. There was plenty of Irvine's powder still in Zane's Blockhouse, but the only means of getting it was to have someone run over to the fort and carry back a keg. Several men volunteered, but finally Col. Zane's sixteen-year-old sister, Elizabeth Zane, Betty, or Betsy as she was called, said that she was best qualified, as she was one of the swiftest runners, and perhaps the Indians might not bother to fire at a woman. Just as importantly, she pointed out, if she fell the fort would not have lost one of its defenders. What no one spoke aloud, but what was in everyone's minds, was that were she to be killed in the attempt, at least it would be a less painful death then being butchered by Indians if the fort were taken.

The distance from Zane's to the fort was not great, about two hundred feet, but only one shot would have been necessary to bring the girl down. But if ever the gods lent wings ... once again the south gate opened and the fort's savior entered with her precious burden of powder. The infuriated warriors now charged the fort, but the defenders poured a hail of bullets at them, and as the little French "Bulldog" was quickly swiveled around by Tate's skillful hands and discharged, a double-handful of those irregular-shaped bits of lead flew into the faces of the Indians, and they recoiled from the force of the blow.

The rest of the firing that day was long-range, although constant, with no damage being inflicted upon either side[90]. Once more during the night a final, now-desperate attempt was made to fire the fort, but it was no more successful than the other three had been. By the morning of the third day, September 13th, it was expected that reinforcements would soon begin arriving, and the Indians were ready to call it quits, nor could the Rangers see any means which offered any hope of success. It had been their first look at Fort Henry, and they departed with the impression that, if well defended, the fort was nearly impregnable, except to cannon. With the assault on Fort Henry a failure, about half the Indians and all the Rangers recrossed the river and headed for home, while the remaining warriors broke up into small parties to engage in their usual raids against smaller stations and individual cabins.

Inside the fort no one had been killed, nor had anyone received so much as a serious wound. The closely fitted-together walls of seasoned white oak were impenetrable by standard musket fire, and the only wound of the entire 44-hour siege was Cope Sullivan's, which he received as he and his two men raced for the fort upon their arrival at the beginning of the attack. By noon the Indians were gone, and shortly afterward the first relief force of Capt. Boggs at the head of about forty men came riding up from Catfish Camp. The Siege of Fort Henry was over, and so was the Revolutionary War. Never again in this century would British soldiers engage in armed conflict with citizens of the United States of America, thus characterizing the *Siege of Fort Henry, September 11-13, 1782*, as the last battle of the American Revolution. Preliminary articles of peace were signed in Paris two months later, on November 30, 1782, agreeable to their approval by the governments of both countries[91].

One of the parties of Indians moved on to Rice's Fort the next day, about fourteen miles from the Ohio on Buffalo Creek. They surrounded the blockhouse and demanded its surrender; upon the expected refusal they began an attack which was rather short-lived. The Indians then withdrew to consider matters, and after dark they fired a nearby barn in hopes that the flames would spread to the blockhouse, and of the light providing them with marks inside the fort, but in both of these they were disappointed as well, and they departed sometime shortly after midnight. The amazing circumstance about the assault on Rice's Fort is that it was so weakly defended, only six men being present at the time: Jacob Miller, Peter Fullenwieder, Daniel Rice, George Felebaum, George Leffler, and Jacob Leffler, Jr. During the first assault by the Indians Felebaum was shot through the head and died instantly, and then there were five. No better illustration of the security provided by a simple blockhouse could be given than this.

*     *     *

Once again it was George Rogers Clark who led the retaliatory raid against the Indian villages. Assembling over a thousand men (they would always follow Clark, especially when men like Kenton and Boone were the guides), he crossed the Ohio at the mouth of the Great Miami on November 5th. They followed the old trace, which moved northeast along the east side of the river, until it crossed the Mad River (present Dayton), then bent north-northwest until it crossed the Miami. Clark quite naturally assumed that the Indians knew he was coming, but that was not the case. On the morning of the 10th he sent John Floyd with three hundred men as an

217

advance; they reached the first village only scant minutes after the alarm had been given, but it was all the time the inhabitants needed to gain the safety of the surrounding woods. The army rode into the Shawnee towns that afternoon, destroying the villages and the crops, but the Indians fled before them, and Clark was unable to force them to make a stand against him.

While his men were put to work destroying the crops, Clark sent a mounted force of a hundred fifty men under Ben Logan northwest to destroy Loramie's Store, a British trading post, at the portage to the Great Lakes, about fifteen miles north of the Pickaway villages (present Fort Loramie, Ohio). At the same time another strong force was sent northeast, to destroy the villages along the Mad River. But after four days Clark was forced to begin his withdrawal, as bad weather was approaching; it was, after all, mid-November, and the Indians could not be forced into an engagement. Clark's men had killed ten warriors and taken another seven prisoner, but they had also recovered three white prisoners who had been captives of the Indians. Of Clark's army only one man had been killed and one wounded; Capt. Victor McCracken had received a slight wound in the arm during the first attack, but it had gangrened, and McCracken died just as the army reached the Ohio.

*　　*　　*

Word of the peace treaty signed in November, 1782, did not reach Fort Pitt until the following May, and in July, 1783, De Peyster gathered together the chiefs of eleven Indian nations to inform them of the official end of British involvement. The key word in his speech was "official". The English would secretly continue to encourage Indian raids against the settlements for more than thirty years into the future, until the conclusion of the War of 1812. In the meantime they provided the Indians with the supplies needed for such raids, as they continued to deceive them with hints of promised official support, sometime in the hazy future. It was to be yet another dozen years, no less bloody than ever, before the Indians were finally, sadly, undeceived on a hot summer day in August, 1794.

# *A Postscript:*

*In the summer of 1785 one of the founding fathers of the western country, Silas Zane, went on a trading expedition into the Indian country with George Green, who had so bravely defended the Zane cabin in 1781 and again during the 1782 Siege of Fort Henry. While on that trip, somewhere along the Scioto River, they encountered a roving band of Indians, and both men were killed.*

Chapter XXIV

$\mathcal{P}$art I - War and Peace Treaties

With the failure of the assault upon Fort Henry the Border Wars began shifting slowly westward; by 1782, after nearly thirty years, it was no longer the Upper Ohio Valley which claimed prominence, but rather the Middle Ohio, as the frontier moved westward. Within four years the center of military command had moved from Pittsburgh, at the Forks of the Ohio, downriver to Fort Harmar at Marietta, Ohio, and then only three years later it jumped westward all the way to Cincinnati's Fort Washington.

At Sandusky in September, 1783, and again at Niagra in the summer of 1784, the Indians had met under the leadership of Joseph Brant, determined to perfect a more closely-knit confederation in order to present a united front to the victorious Americans. Basing their claim on the outdated Treaty of Fort Stanwix of 1768, they insisted that the Ohio River remain the boundary between the white and red man. But the Congress of the United States had not fought this war for nothing; for years they had been forced to listen to the plaintive cries for help from the frontier people, who were being slaughtered daily by the Indians, and there had been hardly a penny to spare for their protection. Now Congress looked upon the Indian tribes in the same manner as they did the English, as a defeated nation. Congress wanted to deal with the Indian problem in the west, but they still had no money, the price of deflated Continental currency being what it was, and even worse, they had no military power. The Continental Army would be disbanded before the end of 1783, in accordance with the general public fear of a standing peacetime army, and except for the state militias there was no other military force in the country. Congress began what was to become a familiar pattern, as all congresses have always done; they talked interminably, they passed acts, and they waited for the problems to go away, or for others to solve the problems.

On October 15, 1783, only six weeks after the American and British commissioners had signed the Treaty of Paris, by an Act of Congress the Ohio River boundary was repudiated, and the western Indians living in now-American Ohio Territory were charged to begin preparations to remove themselves west of the Miami River, in western Ohio, which was by congressional fiat the new boundary. But there was no military power to enforce this declaration, and although some of the tribes seemed willing to negotiate, others were as defiant as ever.

Congress responded by passing another act. On June 3, 1784, they formed a semi-federal army, to be called the *First American Regiment,* and they did it by asking four states to supply the soldiers for their army; 110 from New Jersey, 165 each from Connecticut and New York, and 260 from Pennsylvania. The United States Army now theoretically consisted of seven hundred men; at least this was the "authorized" strength, but not until six years later would there be even that many. The commander of this army was Lieutenant Colonel Josiah Harmar, commonly referred to as General Harmar, who was named commander because he was from Pennsylvania and Pennsylvania had provided the largest contingent of men.

The first company of this miniature army straggled into Pittsburgh that December, but by the time the last company had arrived nearly an entire year had passed, and the one-year enlistments of those first-comers had expired. Instead of seven hundred men, the army was usually hard put to muster half that many. The next year, 1786, Harmar reported only three hundred men available for duty, and they were divided up at three widely-scattered posts: Fort McIntosh at the northern-most bend of the Ohio above Pittsburgh, Fort Harmar at the mouth of the Muskingum, and Fort Finney, a temporary post at the mouth of the Great Miami.

But Congress did more than enact, they also selected commissioners, then instructed them to negotiate peace treaties with the Indian nations. The Iroquois had been the first Indian nation to recognize the fact that without British support they had no choice but to seek an accommodation with the Americans. At the Treaty of Fort Stanwix in 1768 they had ceded to England their claim to all lands south of the Ohio River; on October 22, 1784, they signed the Second Treaty of Fort Stanwix, relinquishing all claims to lands north of the Ohio. The congressional commission-ers, George Rogers Clark, Richard Butler, and Arthur Lee, now moved west to Fort McIntosh, at the mouth of the Beaver River, some thirty miles below Fort Pitt, where they met with peace factions from the Delaware, Wyandot, Chippewa, and Ottawa tribes, and three months later, on January 21, 1785, they concluded a treaty with these tribes. Nor had the Shawnee been forgotten; a year later the commissioners, with Samuel Parsons replacing Lee, concluded a treaty with that nation on January 31, 1786, at Fort Finney, near the mouth of the Great Miami. As a result of these three negotiations, that which Congress had originally intended had been accom-plished, at least on paper. Basically the southern two-thirds of the present state of Ohio, all the way west to the Miami River, had been handed over to the United States by these peace treaties. At least on paper.

Peace treaties be damned, said many of the Indians; to the still belligerent fac-tions of Delaware, Shawnee, and Wyandot had now been added the Miami Indians, who had remained neutral during most of the Revolution. According to the Treaty of Paris the British were required to give up their lake posts, but this they refused to do, citing as the reason that the United States Congress refused to reimburse the dis-placed Tories for the loss of their property, as was also required by that treaty. It was a Mexican standoff; Congress could not reimburse the Tories because it was finan-cially embarrassed, it could not even keep its pitifully weak but grand-sounding *First American Regiment* paid, fed, and clothed. The British would continue to hold those posts *quid pro quo*, and as long as they remained in British hands, more important-ly as long as men like Alexander McKee, Matthew Elliott, and Simon Girty lived among the Indians, the peace treaties signed by those Indian nations were worth-less. The raids against the settlements decreased not a whit. The younger warriors were eager to gain renown, other warriors wanted plunder, especially horses. Slaves, particularly in the form of young women, were well worth the trouble of bringing home, although scalps were of little intrinsic value now. Because of their societal structure it was impossible for the tribal chiefs to prohibit these raids, even had they wanted to, and few of them did. The Indians had neither police, judges nor juries, nor jails nor penitentiaries to hold law-breakers.

The raids throughout that year of 1786 continued undiminished, it was as if there had been no peace treaties. One party of immigrants to Kentucky had just encamped for the night when they were attacked by Indians. In only a few minutes twenty-one of them were killed and five women were taken captive at what has since been known as the Defeated Camp Ground. But there was nothing remarkable about this, other than the larger than usual number of victims. It has been conservatively estimated that in the seven years between the Treaty of Paris in 1783, and Harmar's Campaign in 1790, over one thousand men, women, and children were killed by Indians — *and that was in Kentucky alone!*

While these American citizens were being killed by Indians, a portion of Harmar's army was busily engaged in driving out squatters who had moved north of the Ohio, onto land that Congress had decreed belonged to the land agents. Retaliation against the Indians was forbidden; Kentuckians could protect their own property, but they were strictly prohibited from crossing the Ohio to punish the Indian raiders, or even to rescue prisoners from fleeing bands of Indians, because of the "treaties" which had been signed. The Kentuckians were so infuriated by their own government protecting the Indians, at the same time by the inability of the government to protect its own citizens, that they decided to act on their own, however illegal it might be. On September 14, 1786, Ben Logan received orders from Clark to assemble a body of militia to march against the Shawnee towns, while Clark would march west to the Wabash.

Nearly eight hundred men assembled at Limestone; it took two days for them to cross the Ohio on September 29th and 30th, then the march began, guided by Kenton and Boone, passing by the very spot where Kenton had been captured and Montgomery killed eight years before. On the night of October 4th they encamped two days' march from the Indian towns, but just before daylight the next morning one of the Tory sympathizers, who had undoubtedly accompanied the army for the very purpose, deserted. He reached the outskirts of the Indian village of Wapatomica on the Mad River that day with the warning of the approach of Logan's army two days hence. As he spoke one of the other warriors silently walked up behind him, and when the man had finished speaking, he rewarded the traitor by sinking a tomahawk into his skull. Logan's men found his body the next day, lying where it had fallen.

One of the main objectives of Logan's campaign was to take as many hostages as possible, to help insure the future good behavior of the Shawnee, but to accomplish that surprise would be needed. As soon as he was advised of the deserter, Logan pushed the army on rapidly, no need to preserve the element of surprise now. On the morning of the 6th Logan divided his army in two; he would lead one force against Mac-a-chack, while Boone, with Kenton, who surely remembered the way, would take the three hundred others to attack Moluntha's Town (present West Liberty, Ohio), half a mile distant, where Kenton had suffered so as a prisoner. Four hundred Shawnee warriors had gone west to help defend the Wabash towns from Clark, and with the approach of Logan there was no choice for those remaining but to flee.

Even with the warning the Kentuckians had appeared sooner than expected; at about noon on October 6th both villages were attacked, and although there was some slight resistance, most of the Indians fled. Colonel Thomas Kennedy rode into a group of terrified women, hacking at them with his great broadsword, and wounding several; unfortunately one of those he wounded was a young captive white woman. The aged Moluntha raised the American flag above his house, and Boone and Kenton placed him under their protection, with orders that neither Moluntha nor any of his family were to be harmed. But some time later Major Hugh McGary[92], of Blue Licks notoriety, came striding up to the group of officers as they stood talking to the old Indian chief and, pushing away the guards, buried his tomahawk in Moluntha's skull. Kenton, when he found out about the death of the chief, said that had he been there he would have killed McGary on the spot. One of the young guards tried to, but was restrained.

Among the Indians in the village was a huge Cherokee warrior who had only recently arrived with a Cherokee war party, bringing with him two white women, captives from Kentucky, and he had personally assisted the other Indians in torturing them to death. As Boone and Kenton raced into the village this Cherokee as quickly raced out, but he halted at the edge of town, where he turned and fired, killing one of his pursuers. But when he had turned he was recognized. "Mind that fellow!" Boone roared, "I know him. That's Big Jim!". At almost the same moment a ball brought down the notorious Cherokee; Kenton, rushing forward, sank his knife to the hilt in the big Indian's chest. As Boone silently watched the others scalped the Indian who had slowly tortured and then killed James Boone, Daniel's first-born son, in that lonely camp on the Wilderness Road, thirteen long years before.

From Mac-a-chack the army moved eight miles north, where they destroyed Blue Jacket's Town (Bellefontaine, Ohio), then two miles east to McKee's Town, and two miles further to the village of Wapatomica (Zanesfield). All were destroyed, everything was destroyed; altogether more than two hundred cabins were burned, roughly fifteen thousand bushels of corn were destroyed, the army took all the horses and cattle they could round up, and killed the hogs. Ten Indians had been killed and thirty-two others, mostly women and children, were taken as hostages. The Shawnee would never return to the Mad River Valley; they abandoned the area and moved north, resettling on the Maumee and Auglaize Rivers in the northwestern corner of Ohio, where only a few years later Harmar, then St. Clair, then "Mad Anthony" Wayne would come looking for them.

## Part II - Further Adventures of the Wetzels: John Wetzel, Jr.

In the spring of 1786 John Wetzel, Jr., then in his sixteenth year, along with a neighbor boy a year or two younger named Fred Earliwine, went out in search of a mare and her foal, which had strayed. Four Indians lay in ambush beside the horse, tolling its bell, one of the simplest and at the same time one of the more effective of the Indian ruses, knowing that anyone searching for a horse would be lead straight to the sound of the bell. As the boys approached, the Indians rushed out from their place of concealment. While attempting to escape Wetzel was shot through the wrist, while young Earliwine was run down and tomahawked. The Indians had several horses, stolen of course, and they were able to move quickly, without discovery. Early the next morning they reached the Ohio at the mouth of Grave Creek, just below the abandoned Tomlinson settlement, where they had hidden the canoe in which they had previously crossed the river. One of the Indians spied a large hog nearby and, having shot it, placed it in the canoe, forcing John, Jr. to lie in the bottom of the canoe beside the dead hog. Three of the warriors got into the canoe, while the fourth began swimming the stolen horses across the river.

Fortunately for John Wetzel three men, the redoubtable Hamilton Kerr, Isaac Williams[93], and a German who is now remembered only by the name of Jacob, had come down from Wheeling to the Grave Creek Flats in order to look after the livestock which had been left at Joseph Tomlinson's now-deserted settlement. Hearing the shot, they hurried to the river, thinking that perhaps a party of *movers* to Kentucky had landed there and killed one of the hogs, which had been turned loose to forage. They arrived at the mouth of Grave Creek just as the Indians were entering the Ohio. All three Indians were still standing in the canoe, the one in the stern in the act of pushing out into the river with his paddle. Kerr fired, killing the Indian in the stern, and at the same moment Williams shot the Indian in the bow, both falling into the water. Kerr grabbed Jacob's rifle and shot the third warrior, knocking him out of the boat as well; although he was seriously, probably mortally wounded, he still managed to cling to the side of the canoe.

Seeing the head of yet another man peering out from the bottom of the canoe, Kerr quickly reloaded and leveled his rifle at young John Wetzel, who managed to yell out just in time that he was a white man. By now the canoe had floated some little distance down the river, but there it snagged on an outcropping of rock and Wetzel was able to crawl out and flounder ashore. Kerr in the meantime had fired at the fourth Indian, who had turned and was heading back for the canoe. No fool he; there were four rifles in the bottom of that canoe, along with the powder horns and balls, and he was unarmed and a long way from home. Slipping off his horse he gained the canoe and quickly turned it into the river, following the horses who were by now swimming across. In spite of several shots being fired at him he managed to escape and, turning the canoe adrift, mounted one of the horses and disappeared into the forest. A few days later some surprised residents of Limestone, Kentucky, having noticed a particularly strong and fetid odor coming from the river bank, stood wondering at the canoe they had found at the water's edge, its only occupant the foul and rotting carcass of a large hog.

## Part III - The Death of Captain John Wetzel

Little wonder that the name of Wetzel was known throughout the frontier. They were one of the first families to emigrate to the western border, and in 1777 sons

Lewis and Jacob were abducted by Indians, but managed to get away. Two years later their brother Martin was taken, and although he spent two years as a captive, he also escaped. The year following his escape his brother George was killed by Indians in 1782; in 1786 the fifth and last son, John, Jr., was also captured, then rescued the next day. And after all the peace treaties had been signed, in that same year of 1786 came the death of John Wetzel, Sr., at the hands of Indians. A father and his five sons: four of the sons were captured by Indians, but all eventually escaped, the fifth son was killed by Indians, and four years later the father was killed.

As with the death of the son George, so the death of the father, John, Sr., is shrouded in confusion. For many years it was believed that he had been killed in 1787, but that was an error; according to the records of the Ohio County courthouse his will was probated on August 19, 1786. The correct date of Captain John Wetzel's death is June 11, 1786. It has also commonly, mistakenly, been reported that his sons Martin, George, and Lewis were with him, and that both the father and son George were killed at the same time and buried in a common grave.

Little can be stated for certain, but the basic facts appear to be as follows: John Wetzel, Sr. was in a canoe near the mouth of Graveyard Run, seven or eight miles below Tomlinson's (present Moundsville, West Virginia), and about a mile below Baker's Station[94]. With him was his son Lewis; it is at least a possibility that Martin was also along, and perhaps another. However, the most reliable source appears to be the narrative of Captain Henry Jolly, written to the early historian Samuel P. Hildreth. Jolly says that the day after Capt. Wetzel was killed, he (Jolly) was one of nine or ten men who went with Lewis Wetzel to track down the Indians who had killed the elder Wetzel. According to Jolly, Capt. Wetzel had been accompanied in the canoe by two other men, named Andrews and Moore [perhaps *Miller*]; Lewis had also been in the canoe, but becoming ill he had asked to be landed so that he might lie down before continuing to the fort by land. It was after Lewis had disembarked that the three men in the canoe were suddenly hailed by Indians on the Virginia shore and ordered to land. Refusing to do so they bent into their paddles as the Indians fired at them, mortally wounding both Wetzel and Moore. Andrews left the canoe and swam to the opposite shore, and the Indians, after securing the canoe and the three rifles in it, paddled to the opposite shore as well and decamped. The following day Lewis Wetzel, Jolly and the others crossed the river at Baker's, and followed the trail for some miles, but were unable to come up with the Indians. The men at the fort buried Capt. Wetzel along the shore of the Ohio, on the south bank of Graveyard Run, about a hundred feet north of the location of the Baker blockhouse.

*     *     *

Logan's Raid had accomplished three things; it had forced the Indians to move farther away, making it more difficult for raiders to attack the Kentucky settlements. It had brought back a number of women and children to serve as hostages. Most importantly, however, it hardened Indian resistance to the Americans. Following

Logan's return to Kentucky, Joseph Brant, still acknowledged as the foremost Indian diplomat and strategist, called a conference of all Indian nations, to meet at Hurontown on the Detroit River. Delegates from eleven nations, Iroquois of course, along with Shawnee, Delaware, Miami, Wyandot, and others, assembled there in December to listen to Brant tell them what they already knew: the Americans and English had signed a treaty, but the war was not over; hundreds of successful Indian raiding parties had returned with scalps, horses, plunder, and prisoners; the American government, with an army more shadow than substance, had made no effort to protect its own citizens, nor was it even capable of protecting them; most importantly, it was the American pioneer who was the Indians' enemy.

On December 18, 1786, the new Indian confederation sent a declaration to the U.S. Congress, in which they repudiated the treaties of Stanwix, McIntosh, and Finney. As their basis they claimed the standard reasons: that these treaties had been signed by individual tribes, not by the Indian confederation as a whole (the fact that there had been no Indian confederation bothered them not at all), that those who had signed away the land had no authority to do so, and that they had signed under duress. No matter which individual Indian tribe signed a treaty (and then received the liberal presents for doing so), there was always another faction who claimed that the treaty was invalid because *they* had not signed. Signing a treaty with an Indian tribe was like counting the grains of sand on the beach, you could never finish, there was always another.

The war was not over. It would not be over until thirty more years of bloodshed had passed away.

# Chapter XXV

Lewis Wetzel - III
The Adventures Continue

Lewis Wetzel seldom took part in any organized military expeditions. During the near-debacle of Brodhead's Expedition in 1781, when Wetzel was only seventeen, he soon learned that the clumsy, slow-moving army, comprised of undisciplined and inexperienced militia, far from home and engulfed by a bewildering forest, was no match for the natives of that forest who were fighting in their own domain. But five years later, in 1786, he happened to be in Kentucky when Logan received the order from Clark to punish the Shawnee, and his father, shot by Indians on the Ohio, was only three months in his grave. Besides, these were Kentuckians, some of them veterans of ten long years of constant war, and Boone was one of the commanders, and Simon Kenton was the guide. It surely must have been difficult for him to resist the opportunity to avenge his father's death.

As with any great figure of this Heroic Age, stories of Lewis Wetzel abound. A few of them are factual (although dates and places may be confused), some are nothing more than garbled versions of stories regarding other individuals, most are fictitious. Sometimes historians have presented one story or another in the hopes of glamorizing Lewis Wetzel, others have done so in an attempt to tarnish his image. The first major writings about the Wetzels were historical works, such as those by Doddridge in 1824, followed by Withers and De Hass, which were accompanied by and often drawn from an enormous body of notoriously unreliable oral tradition. A series of biographical newspaper articles appeared in Cincinnati's *Western Christian Advocate* in 1839, written by Col. John McDonald, but he had appeared rather late on the western border scene. It was here that the notorious "Massacre of the Whetzel Family" first saw the light of day.

The most factual biography of Lewis Wetzel appeared in 1860, Cecil B. Hartley's *Life and Times of Lewis Wetzel, the Virginia Ranger*. Ten years earlier, in 1850, the novelist Emerson Bennett had written a story of Lewis Wetzel rescuing a lovely young damsel in distress from the midst of an Indian village; the tale was entitled *The Forest Rose*, and it was a true story, but only after a fashion. Nevertheless the theme became legion for any number of always beautiful, ever helpless young women being rescued from the foul clutches of villainous Indians, sometimes by Lewis Wetzel, sometimes by one or another hero. In 1883 Edward S. Ellis, writing as R.C.V. Meyers, produced a boys' book, *Wetzel the Scout*, which is classified as biographical but like the Boys' *Robin Hood*, or the *Boys' King Arthur*, would be better described by the modern term "historical fiction". Some of the tales are out-and-out fantasies, others follow the basic outline of known events quite closely. Wetzel's most recent biographer, C.B. Allman, in *The Life and Times of Lewis Wetzel* (later revised and reprinted as *Lewis Wetzel, Indian Fighter*), unfortunately intermixed the same, as well as occasionally quoting numerous of Meyers' fictions as fact.

Thus, when we read of Lewis Wetzel, we are oftentimes not quite certain whether the story has any basis in fact or whether it is merely the product of someone's overactive imagination. A "Wetzel Adventure" may be based on an actual incident, but with events misplaced as a result of the passage of time or confused memory. If a story contains dialogue, we can be relatively certain that it is contrived, except in those few rare instances where Wetzel's actual statements have been passed on. But in many cases we are not sure whether the episode described even deals with Wetzel himself.

The following selection of six of Lewis Wetzel's adventures are all considered to be factual in the main, although details of date or place may be disarranged. They were either publicly witnessed (as in *Lewis Wetzel vs. Michael Forshay* or *Lewis Wetzel vs. the Men of Gibson's Company*), or else the episode was so well known to so many people that it can be accepted as fact (*the Injun Gobbler* or the *Rescue of the Forest Rose*).

One indisputable fact stands out above all others; to the people of the border, to those people who knew him best, Lewis Wetzel was a hero. It may be that we moderns are no longer capable of understanding Lewis Wetzel as he was in his own time, and as he appeared to others, be they friend or enemy. It is probably true, as the noted artist Lee Teter has pointed out, that the American Indian, Wetzel's inveterate enemy, understood him far better than we.

### I - A Rifleman's Contest:
### Lewis Wetzel vs. the Men of Gibson's Company[95]

Although the year of the next episode is not known, it must have occurred during the early 1780s. Col. John Gibson had been on a scout with his company of regulars, and they have just come into Wheeling. You are about to observe a contest between Lewis Wetzel and two men from that company. One of those is the man who is acknowledged as the fastest runner in all of Gibson's company; he is standing under a large tree some hundred fifty yards distant. Next to him you see Lewis Wetzel, holding his rifle aloft in his right hand. Another man from Gibson's company is standing here beside you; he has proven himself in numerous competitions as the one who can load and fire his rifle faster than any other man in that company.

You see the puff of smoke from Wetzel's rifle as he fires, the signal for both men to begin running, and a fraction of a second later comes the report of the rifle. At the sight of the puff of smoke the man standing beside you begins loading his rifle. As the two men race toward you Wetzel, now slightly ahead of his opponent, can be seen loading his rifle. Just before he reaches you Wetzel fires his rifle again — the second time! A moment later the man standing beside you raises his rifle and fires, just as Wetzel crosses the finish line, ahead of his opponent! This is athletic prowess in the truest sense!

Extract of a letter from Isaac Leffler to Dr. Lyman C. Draper:

*Alexander Mitchell and Wetsel had been out spying, came into Wheeling Fort where they met Capt. Gibson and his company of regulars. Mitchell made a bet with Gibson for a gallon of whiskey that Wetsel could outrun any man in the company, and whilst running could load and shoot his gun oftener than any other man in the company could load and shoot standing still. Wetsel won the whiskey. [Draper Mss. 6E82.1 - 82.3.]*

In his letter Isaac Leffler also stated that he had:

*"lived in Wheeling and the neighborhood 47 years [i.e. from his birth in 1788 until 1835] and knew nearly all the first settlers. The four most prominent men in that region of country according to tradition was Lewis Wetsel, Capt. Samuel Brady, Major Samuel McColloch, and Major McMeachan; to these I would add Col. David Williamson."*

The company of regulars was probably a part of the 7th Virginia Regiment. Isaac Leffler was the son of Jacob Leffler, Jr., who had commanded a company of militia in Brodhead's Coshocton Expedition against the Delaware of 1781. Jacob, Jr.'s. son, Isaac, was born six years after the attack on Rice's Fort. According to Lydia (Boggs) Cruger, Isaac's grandfather, Jacob, Sr., was killed at Wheeling during the Siege of 1782, but no other account mentions this, and Isaac Leffler makes no reference to his grandfather's death at that time. Col. Ebenezer Zane would surely have mentioned Leffler's death in his official report (September 14, 1782) of that siege; he wrote to Gen. Irvine, at Fort Pitt:

*Sir: On the evening of the 11th instant a body of the enemy appeared in sight of our garrison .... The enemy kept a continual fire the whole day .... [and] continued around the garrison till the morning of the 13th instant, when they disappeared. Our loss is none.*

According to Mrs. Cruger, Leffler and another man named Neisinger had been on a scouting expedition in early August, 1782, and were some miles south of Wheeling when they pulled their canoe in to shore and lay down in it to sleep. During the night they were attacked by Indians, who killed Neisinger; Leffler fought off the warriors with the paddle until one of the Indians struck his hand, cutting off two fingers. Leffler then jumped into the water and escaped by swimming some distance; the next morning being quite foggy he managed to elude the Indians by wading in the river a mile or more, and finally reached Fort Henry. His hand was so badly mangled, however, that it was necessary for him to go to Fort Pitt for medical treatment. According to Mrs. Cruger, he was returning to Fort Henry from Pittsburgh, but not being aware that the fort was besieged he had approached within about two miles of the fort when he was captured and killed by the Indians, who then shouted to those in the fort that they had just killed the messenger who had been sent out for relief.

As with many of the oral traditions of the early frontier, this one is correct in almost all, but not quite all, of the details. Considering the lapse of nearly seventy years between the event itself and its telling, the only major error is rather slight; the year was 1783, not 1782, and Fort Henry was not under siege. De Hass, in his *History* (p. 283), describes a remarkably similar account, but he gives the names of the participants as *Joseph Heffler* and *John Nieswanger*. It is the same story of course, Joseph Heffler being the unfortunate Jacob Leffler.

## II - The Injun Gobbler

One of the more successful ruses of the Indian was to approach a settlement and, after carefully concealing himself, to imitate the call of a turkey. The settler thus decoyed out would as a matter of course head straight for the Indian, and when others heard a shot from the vicinity, there would be no alarm, assuming the hunter had fired at the turkey. One such instance occurred about 1790, when William McIntosh, of Grave Creek, early one morning heard a turkey gobbling across the river. In spite of being warned of the possibility that it might be an ambush, McIntosh, with his dog, crossed the river in his canoe. Shortly thereafter a shot was heard, but McIntosh failed to return. A party was assembled the next day; crossing over, they found the scalped corpse of McIntosh, not more than a dozen yards from the bank which he had started to ascend in pursuit of the fatal turkey, his faithful dog nearby.

An even better known instance of an Injun Gobbler, with the tables turned, involved Lewis Wetzel, a year or two previous to the McIntosh incident. Both Jacob Wetzel's son, Cyrus, and Martin Wetzel's son, John, described the incident to Dr. Draper, who wrote it as follows:

From Cyrus Wetzel: *Turkey Incident — A mysterious turkey had called at Wheeling, & some were decoyed out by it & killed. When Lewis Wetzel came home from some scout, & went & killed the Indian who imitated the turkey's call. Cyrus Wetzel has heard his father & others speak something of it. [Draper Mss. 3S:82.]*

From John Wetzel: *Heard Martin Wetzel tell of the turkey gobbler at Wheeling — decoyed & killed two or three — & Lewis went & killed the gobbling Indian. Draper Mss. E:21.]*

This is the original version of the *Injun Gobbler*, as told independently by two of Lewis Wetzel's brothers to their sons, and by each of them to Dr. Lyman C. Draper. This appears to be all the factual details concerning the incident. The location of the *Injun Gobbler Cave* has traditionally been placed along Wheeling Creek, about a mile east of Wheeling, where it may still be visited today. It is about a hundred yards south of the entrance to the railroad tunnel, known as Tunnel Green, and about half that distance from the mouth of another cave, known as *Wetzel's Cave*. According to tradition Wetzel was not deceived by the call, but instead crossed over the hill and, approaching the cave from the top, waited until the Indian showed himself, when a shot from Wetzel's fatal rifle ended the decoy.

Although some have attempted to denigrate Wetzel for this killing, by claiming that the Indian was a solitary (peaceable) hunter, merely seeking food for his family, or by characterizing the story as legend, there is no doubt that it actually occurred, and basically as it is described here[96]. Aside from the fact that it was a not uncommon practice of the Indian, it is absurd to maintain that an Indian hunter would travel perhaps a hundred miles or more from his home in order have the opportunity to hunt a turkey in the vicinity of one of the frontier settlements.

Even such a renowned historian of the Border Wars as Louise Phelps Kellogg, in her biographical paragraph of Lewis Wetzel, remarked:

*That autumn [incorrectly given as 1782] he detected an Indian lurking near Fort Henry imitating a turkey's call, and killed him without warning.*

That statement must surely rank as one of the most incredible in the entire catalogue of material relating to the Indian Wars. Surely no one actually believes that it was a common practice for one side or the other to shout out a warning that they intended to shoot? The biographical sketch continues in the same vein:

*Wetzel's vindictiveness towards the red race increased with the years: in 1784 in a time of peace he killed an Indian known as "Old Crossfire" and rescued a captive girl.*

Yet one wonders why an Indian, despite his colorful name, would have abducted a girl if this were indeed a time of peace. How was Wetzel to rescue the captive girl otherwise?

### III - The Rescue of The Forest Rose

The rescue of the renowned Forest Rose, after her abduction by Old Crossfire, is a much more complicated issue, and here one gets involved in the elements of oral tradition, confused recollection, hearsay, and romantic novels, all mixed together into a single episode. And again, the most reliable account comes from Jacob Wetzel's son, Cyrus, as Draper recorded it:

Girl Rescued — A young man came from old Virginia to Wheeling, named Frazier, & was taken sick there, & Rose Forrest nursed & took care of him. Frazier fell in love with this girl; & when sufficiently recovered to ride out, he accompanied her on horseback up to Short Creek, a few miles above Wheeling, on a visit to some of her friends in that settlement. On the way, a deer crossed their trail, & he shot & wounded it; & leaving his horse, he started in pursuit of his wounded deer — & Indians hearing the report of the gun, stole up, capturing the girl & horses, & made off. Frazier discovering the march stolen on him, hastened back to Wheeling with the melancholy tidings; & some one proposed to select a party & pursue the Indians, & Lewis Wetzel, who was then there, was the first selected. He promptly said he would not go — that if so many went the Indians would be sure to kill the prisoner, Rose Forrest, or the Forrest Rose, as Lewis called her; but he was willing to go alone. The young man Frazier begged hard to go, & Lewis finally consented if he would promise strictly to be under his orders, which he readily consented to do.

Lewis had just come in from a scout, & had discovered where a canoe was sunk at or near the mouth of Virginia Short Creek[97] — & thence he and Frazier steered their course. They waylaid the spot — Indians soon came, & after they got their canoe raised, & two Indians and the captive girl were in the canoe, Wetzel & Frazier shot & killed the two Indians. Frazier very naturally made for the canoe to rescue his sweetheart, while Lewis had to contend with two other Indians, who were on the bank with the horses, entirely unprepared for such an unexpected onset, having set down their guns, & Wetzel had his quickly reloaded, & shot one of these Indians before he had recovered himself from his bewilderment; & then Lewis pitched on the remaining & largest one — the left-handed one, Old Crossfire — & had a severe tussle, & finally knifed & killed him. Frazier & Rose were soon married, & went to Kentucky, whither Frazier was bound when take sick & detained at Wheeling. — Mr. C. Wetzel has heard his father so relate this incident, in substance.

*Old Crossfire* is the appellation given to an Indian who would shoot a flintlock rifle left-handed; that is, from the "wrong" side. Doing so puts the lock and pan (with its subsequent flash of powder) directly in front of the shooter's eye, which is certainly not recommended to anyone concerned with his eyesight.

These are the basics of the story of the rescue of Rose Forrest; but those who have read C.B. Allman's description of this rescue (pp. 153-162) may be confused, as Cyrus Wetzel's account sounds amazingly similar to Allman's *"Rescue of Rose Kennedy"* (pp. 162-165), rather than the other Allman story of the rescue of Rose Forrester. Allman took the tale of the Forest Rose from Emerson Bennett's 1850 novel of that name, but Bennett's story was a fictionalized version of the actual rescue of a different young lady, Washburn by name, and the two men involved in her rescue were the well-known scout Robert McClelland and one White, the fiancé of Miss Washburn. In his preface to the revised edition Bennett noted:

*"... with the exception of changing the names of the principal characters* [i.e., McClelland-White-Washburn to Wetzel-Maywood-Forrest] *to suit our convenience, we have followed tradition to the very letter, and introduced nothing but what really took place...."*

The story of Rose Kennedy's rescue was adapted by Allman from one of Lewis Bonnett, Jr.'s, letters (January 24, 1849) to Dr. Draper. In an earlier (1847) letter to Draper Bonnett had written that Lewis Wetzel and another man rescued a girl at the mouth of Short Creek [as described by Cyrus Wetzel, above], probably in the year 1784, but Bonnett confessed that he could not recall the name of either the young man or woman. In response to a second inquiry from Draper, he then wrote as follows:

*"The young man's name I have forgot, also the young lady's, but to the best of my recollection the young man's name was Reynolds .... a young woman lived in Wheeling Fort by the name of Rode Kennedy ... some will have her name as Rose but when I saw it in print [98] it was Rode.*

The details of the rescue which follow are the same as those given by Allman. Bonnett (b.1778) was Wetzel's cousin, his father being a brother of Lewis Wetzel's mother, Mary Bonnett Wetzel. Since he was only about six years old at the time of this abduction and rescue, his knowledge of the episode had to be based entirely on what he was later told. He informed Draper that he was unable to recall the names, so it is understandable that he could confuse Reynolds-Frazier. It would be indeed be interesting to know where Bonnett had seen the name *Rode Kennedy* in print.

Another Wetzel rescue is entitled *The Search for Tilly*, and it is described in Allman's book (pp. 146-153), but that story is suspiciously similar to the rescue of

Rose Forrest, as given in the Cyrus Wetzel letter. When it is noted that this particular story was taken from R.C.V. Meyers's fictionalized biography of Wetzel, *Wetzel the Scout*, it becomes readily apparent that this is nothing more than just another rewrite of the Rose Forrest/Forest Rose theme, but with the locale moved to Kentucky, and the names changed to Simon Bonnett and Miss Tilly.

There are, then, what appear to be four quite different stories of a young woman abducted and then rescued by a frontiersman and her fiancé, as:

*1) McClelland-White rescue Washburn,*
*2) Wetzel-Frazier rescue Rose Forrest, a.k.a. the Forest Rose,*
*3) Wetzel-Reynolds rescue Rode/Rose Kennedy, and*
*4) Wetzel-Bonnett rescue Tilly.*

However, the C.B. Allman-Emerson Bennett story of Wetzel and Maywood rescuing Rose Forrest near (present) Lancaster, Ohio, is actually the McClelland-White-Washburn affair. The incident given by Allman and Lewis Bonnett, Jr. (Wetzel-Reynolds-Rose Kennedy) is the Wetzel and Frazier rescue of Rose Forrest, as described in Cyrus Wetzel's letter. The Wetzel-Simon Bonnett rescue of Miss Tilly is that very same story, as improved upon by R.C.V. Meyers, and there was no Rose Kennedy abduction-rescue! That leaves Lewis Wetzel involved only in the Frazier-Rose Forrest episode, and the most accurate version of that incident is probably to be found in the Cyrus Wetzel letter, as told to him by his father, Jacob, Lewis Wetzel's brother.

### IV - Lewis Wetzel Kills Two Indians

The following story was related to Dr. Draper by Lewis Wetzel's cousin, Lewis Bonnett, Jr., who said that it occurred during the time when Wetzel was living in the Bonnett house on Britts Run, i.e., about 1787-1788, and in the spring of one of those two years. Wetzel, on one of his lonely hunts across the Ohio, came upon an Indian camp, which was untenanted, but the fire was still burning. Wetzel concealed himself nearby and waited; eventually he was rewarded for his patience by the appearance of the camp's inhabitants, an older Indian and two younger warriors, presumably the older man's sons. The two younger men were armed with bows and arrows, while the older was the only one with a gun, which he soon placed out of the way at the back of the camp, and all three settled down around the fire. Feeling that nothing would be gained by delay, Wetzel quickly raised his rifle and shot the older Indian, then charged into the camp with a roar, as Wetzel said, "as was my way". The two other warriors fled precipitately, Wetzel in pursuit of the larger of the pair; soon his rifle was reloaded and the race was ended.

It was not Wetzel's practice to talk about his solitary hunts, and for this reason many of his remarkable exploits will never be known, but on this occasion, upon returning to the settlement, one of the pioneers, knowing that Wetzel had been "across river", asked him point-blank: "Well, Lew, what luck?" "Not much." replied Wetzel, pulling the two scalps from his hunting bag. "I treed three Injuns, but one got away."

## V - McMahon's Reward Expedition

The year of the following incident is generally given as 1786, which, given the Indian depredations despite the peace treaties, is quite reasonable, and the time was probably in the summer of that year. Following a raid by several small parties of Indians in the neighborhood of Wheeling, a bounty was offered to the man who would first bring in an Indian's scalp. The amount is said to have been one hundred dollars, and so many men expressed an interest that Major William McMahon declared that he would lead a punitive campaign, following the route of one of the Indian war parties. Some fifty men, among them Lewis Wetzel, crossed the Ohio with McMahon and started on the trail. Since Wetzel so rarely accompanied an expedition of this type, it is then reasonable to assume that this episode occurred sometime in July or August, 1786, not long after the death of Capt. John Wetzel, and that Lewis went along in order to satisfy his thirst for vengeance.

Their route lead nearly straight west, but no Indian was seen until the men had nearly reached the Muskingum, when the presence of a large body of warriors was detected. Evidently a large war party had left one of the Indian towns and, upon nearing the Ohio, had split up into a number of smaller groups with the intention of later rendezvousing at this point. When the scouts brought back word of the size of the enemy it was obvious that a direct assault was not feasible, and prudence dictated a hasty retreat. While the men quickly began assembling to withdraw, Lewis Wetzel was observed sitting calmly on a log, watching the preparations, and as the men started on the back trail, some one of them asked Wetzel if he were not coming along. "I reckon not," he responded. "I come out here to fight Injuns, and now that I've found 'em I ain't running back to the fort without I kill at least one."

And so they left him, sitting there alone on his log, no doubt contemplating the ways of men who said that they wanted to fight Indians, but then passed up the present golden opportunity. But not for long did he worry about them; it was now necessary to determine how best to attack the enemy. Obviously he could not assault such a large group, but if there were other parties still out, they might be heading back in this direction. The strategy then should be to head back toward the Ohio, and waylay one of the war parties as they headed for home. He then backtracked some distance along the Tuscarawas, and late in the afternoon was finally rewarded by the smell of smoke. Following the scent he approached an Indian camp which seemed to contain only two Indians.

Wetzel settled down to wait until nightfall, but one of the Indians took up a firebrand and his rifle and headed off into the woods, while the other settled himself for sleep. The departed warrior had evidently gone to watch for deer at one of the salt licks, and Wetzel assumed he would presently come back. All night he waited for the hunter to return, but finally, near daylight, it was obvious he could delay no longer, and that he would have to satisfy himself with only one when he wanted two. Leaving his rifle, Wetzel silently crept into the camp and as silently dispatched the Indian with his knife. After taking the Indian's scalp[99], he retrieved his rifle and headed back for the Ohio, which he crossed only hours after the men of the "reward expedition" had done so, and claimed the bounty.

### VI - Michael Forshay

At about this same time occurred another of the few witnessed episodes in the exploits of Lewis Wetzel, which helps to explain why he was so successful in his pursuit of Indians. A relative newcomer to the Wheeling area was one Michael Forshay; since before his arrival on the border Wetzel had been in Kentucky, for the past year or two, visiting his brother Jacob, and the two men had never met. Shortly after Wetzel's return Forshay and a group of the locals were passing the time in one of Wheeling's taverns, probably Sam Mason's, where Mike had been bragging incessantly about his ability as a hunter, regaling his listeners particularly with tales of his prowess, but especially of his superiority as a hunter of Indians. He had heard of this Lewis Wetzel, he explained, but personally thought him much overrated. When Wetzel happened to appear, Forshay asked who he was, but was told by his comrades that he was some fellow just come in from the mountains. Yes, Forshay continued, there had never been a man, white or red, who could catch him napping when in the woods; there was no one better in woodcraft than he.

Wetzel, who never bragged himself, was unable to tolerate it in others. Finally he spoke up: "See here, mister," he said, "I ain't much on a hunt, but I'll bet you the liquor for this crowd that I can come in on you, in spite of you, and you won't see me nor hear me 'til I hit you on the shoulder, an' you kin pick yore ground — an' you kin say which shoulder I'm to hit, in the bargain."

Forshay could not back down in the face of the crowd, and the next morning preparations were made to settle the wager. The two judges were to be Josh Davis, the late Tom Mills' cousin, and Dan Carpenter. To his credit, Forshay chose an excellent location; for all his braggadocio Mike was no tenderfoot. In back of him was a steep bank, which left only the three sides to watch. There was no undergrowth in any direction for more than a hundred feet, with only a few trees, scattered here and there, and a thicket around the area. Upon reaching the chosen site, Wetzel told the other three to take their positions, while he disappeared on the hillside to their front. Forshay took his place, with Davis and Carpenter sitting beside a large tree about a dozen feet distant. "All ready," sang out Davis, and a moment later Wetzel's response came drifting toward them: "Keep a bright lookout, Forshay, or I'll take your scalp for you. Ready!"

Then not a sound was to be heard, not the shaking of a leaf nor the rustle of a bush. Forshay kept a sharp lookout indeed, as did the two judges. Minutes dragged by; it seemed impossible that anything could approach their position without being seen or heard. A snake perhaps, but no human, they were sure, could cover that ground without shaking a branch or brushing the dry leaves, while three experienced hunters were watching carefully. Forshay was turning his head back and forth, constantly covering the area all around him, when suddenly, without warning, Wetzel arose from the ground and, dashing toward Forshay, struck him on the shoulder. Forshay was so astonished by the sudden appearance of this apparition that he lost his balance and fell over backward. Recovering himself quickly, however, he claimed that it was a fluke: "Well, you beat me this time, Wetzel," he said, "but you can't do it again!"

Without answering Wetzel walked off toward the hillside, and a few moments later came his "Ready!" No man ever kept a sharper watch than did Forshay this second time; but for all the good it did him he might as well have tried to catch a glimpse of Wetzel while he was asleep. Before any of the three thought it possible for anyone to cross that great a distance Wetzel sprang out of cover and again struck Forshay's shoulder. Admitting himself beaten, Forshay paid off his wager, but like many an Indian warrior in the Happy Hunting Ground, he was never able to understand how Lewis Wetzel had made himself as silent and as invisible as a ghost.

\*     \*     \*

### Six More Years

The failure of the so-called peace treaties, the refusal of the British to give up their lake posts, and a sudden massive reinforcement of Detroit in June, 1787— all these combined to force Congress into taking two more actions. *An Ordinance for the Government of the Territory Northwest of the Ohio River* was passed into law on July 13, 1787; this notable document, the famed *Northwest Ordinance of 1787*, provided the basis for the formation of five future states, while it promoted public education and prohibited slavery in that territory. Most notably, however, for the first time a body of American citizens came under the laws, not of an individual state, but of a union of states. The territory extended from the western border of Pennsylvania (now resolved with Virginia) all the way to the Mississippi; settlers would soon be moving in, and the Indians would have to cooperate, or fight, or withdraw. In October General Arthur St. Clair was appointed governor, with Samuel H. Parsons, James M. Varnum, and John Cleves Symmes as the three federal judges. Within a year of the opening of this territory an estimated twenty thousand men, women, and children traveled down the Ohio to settle in the Ohio Valley basin.

In that same July of 1787 that the *Ordinance* was made law, Congress also directed General Harmar "to proceed to the most convenient place and make treaty both with the Aborigines of the Wabash River country and with the Shawnees of the central western part of Ohio, and to grant them all assurances consistent with the honor and dignity of the United States." But besides the Indian problem Congress had other matters to attend to in that momentous July, most importantly a new-fangled federal *Constitution*, which was finally signed on September 17th and sent to the various state legislatures for debate and ratification.

But it was not until the next summer, on July 9th, 1788, that St. Clair finally arrived at Fort Harmar at the mouth of the Muskingum, which was to be the seat of government of the Northwest Territory, and formally began his duties as Governor. One of the first matters of business was to call a council of the Indian nations, urging them to accept the now-disputed boundaries agreed to at Forts McIntosh, Finney, and Second Stanwix. He had received instructions from Congress the previous October that he was to remain firm on the boundary line westward to the Miami River, but there was now a greatly increased resistance on the part of the Indians. Brant had done his work well at the Hurontown Conference a year and a half previously, and the British were continuing to woo the Indians with vague promises of military aid. But even beyond that, the Indians could see for themselves how truly ineffectual was the American government's ability to protect its citizens from Indian incursions into the frontier settlements. Harmar's command was an army in name only.

By mid-December St. Clair had succeeded in assembling delegations from the Seneca, Chippewa, Ottawa, Sauk, Wyandot, Potawatomi, and Delaware nations. But in spite of his persistence the two most important tribes, the Shawnee and Miami, refused to attend. St. Clair and Cornplanter, the famed Seneca chief, dominated the conference; at one point Cornplanter arrogantly reminded the other Indian chiefs that it had been the mighty Iroquois, of which there was no other, who had ceded this land to the Americans at Fort Stanwix, and it was not for the likes of the western tribes to question the boundaries of that treaty. On January 9, 1789, the Treaty of Fort Harmar was signed by the chiefs of all the nations, the usual payments and presents were distributed, and everyone went home. Gov. St. Clair felt that he had followed his instructions to the letter, and that the Indians were now more divided than ever. What he had actually accomplished with his treaty of peace was six more years of war.

### Seventh Interlude
### Lewis Wetzel vs. George Washington, or
### Josiah Harmar's Revenge

The George Washington referred to here was not the first President of the United States, but rather a Delaware Indian named Que-shaw-sey. Anyone who has read the standard histories of Lewis Wetzel knows that one of the most important episodes of his eventful life occurred in 1789 when, in the company of one Veach (Vachel) Dickerson, Wetzel shot and killed the Indian "George Washington" at Marietta, Ohio, in the vicinity of Fort Harmar. As the story goes Gen. Josiah Harmar, then commander of the Western Department, had invited the Indians to a peace conference, and was so outraged by this wanton murder of one of the chiefs that he swore he would hang Wetzel for this outrage. He had Wetzel arrested and placed in irons at Fort Harmar, but Wetzel escaped, swam the Ohio to the Virginia shore, and returned to Wheeling. Harmar then sent Capt. Kingsbury with a detachment of federal troops to arrest Wetzel, dead or alive; finding him at Mingo Bottom, some twenty miles north of Wheeling, Kingsbury was prevented from apprehending Wetzel by a large body of frontiersmen, who swore that they would annihilate the entire body of soldiers if they attempted to take Wetzel, who had done nothing more serious than kill an Indian. Fortunately Major William McMahon was there, and through his timely intervention the proposed massacre of Kingsbury's soldiers was narrowly averted. Returning to Marietta, Kingsbury reported to Harmar, who, biding his time, sent out word that Lewis Wetzel was to be taken whenever an opportunity presented. Eventually, during a lapse in his customary watchfulness, Wetzel was arrested while frolicking in a tavern — so the story goes — in Limestone (Maysville), Kentucky, by a Lt. Lollor and a body of soldiers under his command. He was taken downriver to Fort Washington (Cincinnati), Harmar's new headquarters, where he was once more placed in irons and confined, there to await his now certain execution. But once again Wetzel's friends came to the fore, threatening to march on Cincinnati, destroy Harmar's army, and burn Fort Washington to the ground. Harmar at first ignored the demands for Wetzel's release, but seeing the tide of public opinion rising against him, however, he finally gave in and freed Wetzel, who, instead of being hanged for murder, was instead treated like a conquering hero by his friends.

So the story goes — but the story is mostly fictitious. Wetzel did indeed shoot the Indian George Washington, but the Indian suffered only a minor wound and soon recovered. The Indian was not an important chief, nor had he been invited to a peace conference. He was an Indian runner sometimes employed by Harmar, and the peace conference had taken place the winter before. Two treaties were signed at Marietta by Governor St. Clair and delegates from the various Indian tribes, as recounted in *Six More Years*, on January 9, 1789, some six months before Wetzel's assault on George Washington.

Wetzel was arrested for shooting a "friendly" Indian, and turned over to Harmer by civilian authorities [the only ones who had jurisdiction over a civilian]; he was turned over to the military and placed in the guardhouse at Fort Harmar for no other reason than that there was no jail in Marietta at that time.

Wetzel did escape, but Harmar did not send out bodies of soldiers and Indians to apprehend him; for him to imprison Wetzel without civilian authority would have been a serious violation of his powers.

Wetzel was taken prisoner again, and in Limestone, by a Sgt. Lollor, but this did not take place in a tavern. Wetzel was spending the night at the home of a friend, John Young. Lollor's men illegally broke into the house in the early morning hours, illegally seized Wetzel, and conveyed him to Cincinnati, illegally.

Wetzel was not turned over to Harmar for execution. Harmar was not even there, he was still in Marietta. Wetzel was instead delivered to one of the newly-appointed federal judges there, John Cleves Symmes, who immediately released

Wetzel on a writ of habeas corpus, as there were no witnesses against Wetzel, and the Indian had by that time fully recovered.

The settlers were in an uproar, but this was because of the illegal seizure of a private citizen from a private home, not because there was any danger of Wetzel being hanged for shooting an Indian. The soldiers were also alleged to have looted the town and stolen goods while at Limestone.

What "*the story*" does not tell is that Captain McCurdy, Sgt. Lollor's superior officer, was court-martialed for the behavior of the men under him; for their disorderly behavior, and for violating the rights of private citizens Young and Wetzel.

Of the early historians, neither Doddridge nor Withers commented on this *Wetzel/Harmar* episode, rather surprising in light of the supposed importance of the affair. The first historian to publish a description of this *murder of George Washington*, as it is outlined above, was Wills De Hass, who claimed this incident was of such significance that it "changed the whole current of Wetzel's life". In the 20-page chapter on the Wetzels (pp. 344-365) in his 1851 *History*, De Hass devoted nearly five pages to this episode, drawing mainly on the recollections of an "eye-witness", who for nearly a century and a half has unfortunately never been named — until now. De Hass begins:

When about twenty-five years of age, Lewis entered the service of Gen. Harmar, commanding at Marietta. His new duties growing distasteful, he took leave of absence, and visited his friends in the neighborhood of Wheeling. Shortly afterwards, however, he returned to duty, and was chiefly employed in the capacity of scout. It was whilst thus engaged that an affair occurred, which changed the whole current of his life. Of the Indians who visited Marietta, was one of some celebrity, known by the name of George Washington. He was a large, fine-looking savage, and of much influence in his tribe. The tine we write of was one of comparative peace, and Gen. Harmar was particularly anxious to preserve the good feeling then subsisting. Wetzel, during one of his scouts, met the Indian and shot him. The act was justly regarded as an outrage, and he was accordingly arrested and placed in close confinement at the fort.

From this point on De Hass begins quoting his "eye-witness" — occasionally interspersing it with his own commentary. The *eye-witness* statements are given below in quotation marks, and in italics.

"*Wetzel admitted without hesitation, 'that he had shot the Indian'. As he did not wish to be hung like a dog he requested the general to give him up to the Indians, as there were a large number of them present. 'He might place them all in a circle, with their scalping knives and tomahawks — and give him a tomahawk, and place him in the midst of the circle, and then let him and the Indians fight it out in the best way they could'. The general told him, 'That he was an officer appointed by the law, by which he must be governed. As the law did not authorize him to make such a compromise, he could not grant his request'. After a few days longer confinement, he again sent for the general to come and see him; and he did so.*

243

*Wetzel said 'he had never been confined, and could not live much longer if he was not permitted some room to walk about'. The general ordered the officer on guard to knock off his iron fetters, but to leave on his handcuffs, and permit him to walk about on the point at the mouth of the Muskingum; but to be sure to keep a close watch upon him. As soon as they were outside of the fort gate, Lewis began to scamper about like a wild colt broken loose from the stall. He would start and run a few yards, as if he were about making an escape, then turn round and join the guard. The next start he would run further, and then stop. In this way he amused the guard for some time, at every start running a little further. At length he called forth all his strength, resolution, and activity, and determined on freedom or an early grave. He gave a sudden spring forward, and bounded off at the top of his speed for the shelter of his beloved woods. His movement was so quick, and so unexpected, that the guards were taken by surprise, and he got nearly a hundred yards before they recovered from their astonishment. They fired, but all missed; they followed in pursuit, but he soon left them out of sight. As he was well acquainted with the country, he made for a dense thicket, about two or three miles from the fort. In the midst of this thicket he found a tree which had fallen against a log, where the brush were very close. Under this tree he squeezed his body. The brush were so thick, that he could not be discovered unless his pursuers examined very closely. As soon as his escape was announced, General Harmar started the soldiers and Indians in pursuit. After he had lain about two hours in his place of concealment, two Indians came into the thicket, and stood on the same log under which he lay concealed; his heart beat so violently he was afraid they would hear it thumping. He could hear them hallooing in every direction, as they hunted through the brush. At length, as the day wore away, Lewis found himself alone in the friendly thicket. But what should he do? His hands were fastened with iron cuffs and bolts, and he knew of no friend on the same side of the Ohio to whom he could apply for assistance. He had a friend who had recently put up a cabin on the Virginia side of the Ohio, who, he had no doubt, would lend him any assistance in his power. With the most gloomy foreboding of the future, a little after night-fall, he left the thicket and made his way to the Ohio. He came to the river about three or four miles below the fort. He took this circuit, as he expected guards would be set at every point where he could find a canoe. How to get across the river was the all-important question. He could not make a raft with his hands bound. He was an excellent swimmer, but was fearful he could not swim the Ohio with his heavy handcuffs. After pausing some time, he determined to make the attempt. Nothing worse than death could happen, and he would prefer drowning than again falling into the hands of Harmar and his Indians. Like the illustrious Caesar in the storm, he would trust the event to fortune; and he plunged into the river. He swam the greater part of the distance on his back, and reached the Virginia shore in safety; but so much exhausted that he had to lay on the beach some time before he was able to rise. He went to the cabin of his friend, where he was received with rapture. A file and hammer soon released him from his iron handcuffs.*

De Hass then describes Wetzel's defiance, Harmar's determination to punish him, and the proposed massacre of federal troops:

Information having reached General Harmar of Wetzel's whereabouts, he sent a party of men in a canoe to take him. As the boat neared the Virginia shore, Wetzel, with his friend, and several other men posted themselves on the bank and threatened to shoot the first man who landed. Unwilling to venture further, the party returned and Lewis made his way homeward, having been furnished by his kind friend with gun, ammunition, tomahawk, blanket, &c.

Exasperated at the escape of Wetzel, General Harmar offered a large reward for his apprehension, and at the same time despatched a file of men to the neighborhood of Wheeling, with orders to take him dead or alive. The detachment was under the command of a Captain Kingsbury, who, hearing that Wetzel was to be at Mingo Bottom on a certain day, marched thither to execute his orders. We will let an eyewitness finish the story:

*"A company of men could as easily have drawn old Horny out of the bottomless pit, as take Lewis Wetzel by force from the neighborhood of the Mingo Bottom. On the day that Captain Kingsbury arrived, there was a shooting match at my father's, and Lewis was there. As soon as the object of Captain Kingsbury was ascertained, it was resolved to ambush the captain's barge, and kill him and his company. Happily, Major McMahon was present, to prevent this catastrophe, and prevailed on Wetzel and his friends to suspend the attack till he would pay Captain Kingsbury a visit, and perhaps he would prevail with him to return without making an attempt to take Wetzel. With a great deal of reluctance they agreed to suspend the attack till Major McMahon should return. The resentment and fury of Wetzel and his friends were boiling and blowing, like the steam from the scapepipe[100] of a steamboat. 'A pretty affair, this,' said they, 'to hang a man for killing an Indian, when they are killing some of our people almost every day.' Major McMahon informed Captain Kingsbury of the force and fury of the people, and assured him that if he persisted in the attempt to seize Wetzel, he would have all the settlers in the country upon him; that nothing could save him and his company from a massacre, but a speedy return. The captain took his advice, and forthwith returned to Fort Harmar. Wetzel considered the affair now as finally adjusted."*

In this, however, he was mistaken. His roving disposition never permitted him to remain long in one place. Soon after the transactions just recorded, he descended the river to Limestone (Maysville); and while there, engaged in his harmless frolicking, an avaricious fellow, named Lollor, a lieutenant in the army, going down the river with a company of soldiers for Fort Washington, landed at Maysville, and found Wetzel sitting in a tavern. Lollor returned to his boat, procured some soldiers, seized Wetzel, and dragged him aboard of the boat, and without a moment's delay pushed off, and that night delivered him to General Harmar at Fort Washington, where he again had to undergo the ignominy of having his hands and feet bound with irons.

De Hass' eyewitness then concludes:

*"The noise of Wetzel's capture — and captured, too, for only killing an Indian — spread through the country like wild-fire. The passions of the frontiersmen were roused up to the highest pitch of fury. Petitions for his release were sent from the most*

*influential men to the general, from every quarter where the story had been heard. The general at first paid but little attention to these; at length, however, the settlements along the Ohio, and some of the back counties, were preparing to embody in military array, to release him by force of arms. General Harmar, seeing the storm that was approaching, had Wetzel's irons knocked off, and set him at liberty.*

*Wetzel was once more a free man. He returned to his friends, and was caressed by young and old, with undiminished respect. The vast number of scalps which he had taken, proved his invincible courage, as well as his prowess in war; the sufferings and persecutions by which be had been pursued by General Harmar, secured for him the sympathy of the frontiersmen. The higher he was esteemed, the lower sank the character of General Harmar with the fiery spirits on the frontier."*

Had Harmar possessed a tithe of the courage, skill, and indomitable energy of Wetzel, the gallant soldiers under his command, in the memorable and disastrous campaign against the Miamis, might have shared a very different fate. (Wills De Hass, *History of the Early Settlement and Indian Wars of Western Virginia,* Wheeling, H. Hoblitzell, 1851. Rep. Parsons, WV, McClain Printing Co., 1960, pp. 354-359.)

*   *   *

Under what circumstances, then, should a frontiersman, regardless at his motivation, be permitted to kill an Indian, a peace emissary who had been invited to a conference, and yet escape unpunished? It is to a great extent because of this specific episode that many historians have condemned Wetzel as a cold-blooded murderer who had no qualms about shooting a peaceable Indian in the back, a ruthless assassin who should have been hanged rather than being regarded as a hero. Even such a reputable historian as the imminently authoritative Dale Van Every (in his *Ark of Empire*) was mislead by the "established facts" of the case. He repeated the basic McDonald version, even going so far as to say that, after Wetzel was brought to Fort Harmar, "The irate commander [Harmar] ordered him confined in irons in the fort to await hanging...." and concludes with this analysis of Wetzel: "He might not appear outside his environment an altogether admirable figure, but any attempt to assess the behavior standards of his times must take into account the inescapable fact that he was considered by his neighbors and contemporaries an outstanding public servant." And if he is condemned by prominent historians, then how can the general reader be blamed for adopting the attitude that he was little more than a murderer?

But all those historians have accepted De Hass's eyewitness as an infallible source, without as much as even knowing his name. They have dutifully repeated the story, often word for word; but as historians they have all failed their basic responsibility, to research primary sources in order to substantiate the claims made in any secondary source. Too many details of the story are patently false, or made-up. How could this eyewitness have known the precise dialogue which took place between Harmar and Wetzel in the guardhouse that day at Fort Harmar? That Harmar should:

"give him a tomahawk, and place him in the midst of the circle (of Indians) and then let him and the Indians fight it out in the best way they could."

The general told him that —

"he was an officer appointed by the law, and by which he must be governed. As the law did not authorize him to make such a compromise, he could not grant his request."

The conversation is not only fictitious, it is *self-evidently* fictitious. Harmar was military — Wetzel was civilian. Harmar had no power to punish Wetzel, and both men were well aware of that. Why would Wetzel have asked for a combat which he knew he could not survive, to be "allowed" to fight to the death, to be killed by his enemies, when he knew that his own life was in no danger? It is incomprehensible that Wetzel could possibly have been executed for the crime of wounding an Indian, or of wounding anyone.

But who was this important eyewitness to the entire episode, beginning with Wetzel's shooting of the Indian near Marietta, on up to his final release at Cincinnati? He was a thirteen-year-old boy named Johnny McDonald, who was living at that time near Maysville, Kentucky, and who was no eye-witness. Fifty years after the events described here Col. John McDonald, of Poplar Ridge, began writing a series of reminiscences of the early border heroes, such as Wetzel and Simon Kenton (whom he had personally known), and which were published in the *Western Christian Advocate*, of Cincinnati, Ohio, in 1839. Here is the reason that neither Doddridge (1824) nor Withers (1831) had commented on the *Wetzel-Harmar* incident which was alleged to have had such an influence on Wetzel's life. Both would certainly have known of a large body of enraged frontiersmen who were prepared to massacre a squad of federal troops at Mingo Bottom, a mere 20 miles north of Wheeling in 1789, but both failed to mention it, because there had been no such attempt to take Wetzel at Mingo Bottom. The furor aroused over the illegal abduction of a civilian by military authorities, while not confined to the area around Mason Co., Kentucky (in which county was the town of Limestone, now Maysville), was still not great enough to cause an army of bordermen to travel to the very southwestern corner of Ohio to protest at the gates of Fort Washington. Nor would they have even had time to arrive there before Wetzel was released. The uproar apropos of Wetzel died down quickly, since Wetzel was released from custody by a federal judge as soon as he was brought to Cincinnati.

But what about that shooting match in —

"the neighborhood of the Mingo Bottom. On the day that Captain Kingsbury arrived, there was a shooting match at my father's, and Lewis was there."

This certainly sounds credible enough. In other words, "My father and I were then living at Mingo Bottom. There was a shooting match to be held at our home. I was there. Lew Wetzel was there. Then Captain Kingsbury arrived."

But we know from his own account that McDonald was living in Mason County, Kentucky as early as 1791. In November of that year, at the age of fifteen, he accompanied Simon Kenton on one of his expeditions after an Indian raiding party. Not long after St. Clair's Defeat (November 4th) four of "Kenton's boys" had been out hunting, only about ten miles from Kenton's Station (present Washington, Kentucky), when they were fired upon by Indians. Only one of the men, the euphoniously-named Fielding Figgans, escaped and managed to reach the settlement. Disobeying both his father and Kenton, young McDonald took his father's rifle, mounted his father's horse, and followed, surely feeling as much one of the "boys" as any of the others. To his dismay he joined them only just in time to help bury the dead that had been scalped and brutally mutilated by the Indians. McDonald's father must have moved his family from Mingo Bottom to Limestone (Mason County), Kentucky, probably sometime between 1786 and 1789; before the Wetzel-Harmar episode of 1789, not after. Johnny would have been, respectively, nine to twelve years old. The shooting match at which he saw Lewis Wetzel probably took place while the family still lived at Mingo Bottom, but McDonald did correctly recall his neighbors being in an uproar about Wetzel's having been forcibly taken by military troops in 1789 — but his neighbors were almost certainly the citizens of Mason County, Kentucky, not of Mingo Bottom, Virginia. Fifty years later it was easy for him to mix up memories of what had occurred at the Mingo Bottom with events in Mason County a year or two later.

McDonald said that the first time he saw Lewis Wetzel at Mingo Bottom was in 1787, or at the time of the "McMahon Reward Expedition". But it was certainly a year or two earlier than that, i.e., probably in 1786, just after Capt. John Wetzel had been killed by Indians in June. Lewis Wetzel joined the group, contrary to his usual practice, in a desire to avenge his father's death. De Hass places the incident in the summer of 1786; Charles McKnight, in his 1875 *Our Western Border*, and Allman agree, and these three say that only one man, not an entire family, was killed by the Indians who had crossed at Mingo Bottom, as McDonald related:

"The first I recollect of seeing this distinguished warrior, was when he attached himself to a scouting party, about the year 1787 or 1788. My father then lived on the bank of the Ohio, in Virginia, at a place known as the Mingo Bottom, three miles below Steubenville. A party of Indians had crossed the Ohio, not far from where we lived, and killed a family, and then made their escape with impunity. As the Indians had not crossed the Ohio in that neighborhood for a year or two previous, the settlers began to think they could live with safety in their cabins. This unexpected murder spread great alarm through the settlements, and revenge was determined upon."

And if Johnny McDonald were living at Mingo Bottom in the summer of 1789, then how could he possibly have been an eyewitness to either the Harmar-Wetzel confrontation at Marietta, or to the crowd of enraged frontiersmen who were planning on marching to Cincinnati? Kenton had established his Lawrence Creek station at present Washington, Kentucky, four miles south of Limestone, in the summer of 1784, complete with a fortified blockhouse and several cabins. For the next ten years, until the end of the Border Wars, it was one of the most popular and best-known areas in all of Kentucky, and the preferred "jumping-off place" for many of the settlers heading for the interior. In the latter part of the 1780s it would have been a natural for those men, like Johnny McDonald's father, who were constantly on the move westward from one location to another. Fifty years after the Harmar incident McDonald published his Wetzel Series in the *Western Christian Advocate*. He was then in his early sixties, and he described in detail several incidents, one in particular, which had occurred when he was an infant — the *Massacre of the Wetzel Family in 1777*, which appeared in his first "Whetzel" article, March 29, 1839. He admitted that —

"At which station or fort he (Capt. John Wetzel) located himself I cannot now *recollect, although I often heard the story in my youth* .... One day, in the midst of summer (Martin, his eldest son, being out hunting, and John having been sent on some errand to the fort), a numerous party of Indians surrounded the house, rushed in, and killed, tomahawked, and scalped old Mr. Whetzel, his wife, and all his small children."

In this version Lewis and Jacob were the only family members spared. John had been sent to some fort, Martin was away hunting, and McDonald was unaware of the existence of a fifth brother, George, who was later killed by Indians when McDonald was only six. But at the time of the abduction of Lewis and Jacob, John, Jr., was only a seven-year-old child, and he would not have been sent miles away, alone through the wilderness, on any errand, to any fort. The nearest fort was Shepherd's, six miles distant. Of course this massacre has absolutely no basis in fact, and along with a number of his other "eyewitness accounts", many of McDonald's *personal recollections* were based on what he had been told when he was a boy. He told the story of Martin Wetzel's escape from Indian captivity by tomahawking his three companions, but Lewis Bonnet, Jr., a cousin, a close neighbor, and a close friend of Martin's, who had surely spent many hours with Martin, during which Wetzel must have recounted the story of his Indian captivity, wrote to Draper as follows:

"Colonel McDonald says, when Martin Wetzel made his escape from the Indians that he killed all three of his Indian Companions. I never understood it in that way. Martin made his escape, and went to the fort, and told them that the Indians would steal their horses that night."

\*     \*     \*

It is not so difficult to determine what actually happened during that summer and fall of 1789. The records and correspondence relating to the shooting of "George Washington" still exist, giving the names and places, and there is no reason to depend wholly on oral tradition when official records tell the story. Much of the correspondence between Harmar and the others involved has been extracted by Gayle Thornbrough, and published in her *Outpost on the Wabash* (Indianapolis, Indiana Historical Society, 1957). De Hass' statement that —

"The time we write of was one of comparative peace, and Gen. Harmar was particularly anxious to preserve the good feeling then subsisting...."

— is nowhere near the truth, quite the opposite, in fact. Despite the treaties which the Indians had signed with St. Clair, not only had there been no decrease in the number of attacks upon the isolated settlers' cabins, there had actually been a sharp increase. By the 1783 peace which granted the Americans their independence, the English (in an effort to thwart their enemies, Spain and France), had signed away the Ohio Country, from the Great Lakes south to Spanish Florida, and as far west as the Mississippi, at the same time abandoning their allies, the Indians, to the Americans. But they were by now regretting that rashness; Joseph Brant, the "King of the Mohawks", had visited London in the winter of 1785-86, and had received vague assurances that Great Britain still supported them. The British continued to refuse to relinquish their lake posts (Niagra, Oswego, Detroit, and Mackinac) to the Americans, and from those they continued to supply the Indians with food, while the English traders provided powder and lead in return for stolen horses. During 1788 and 1789 conditions on the border had grown steadily worse rather than better; indeed in June of 1789, only mere days before Wetzel shot Que-shaw-sey, Sir Guy Carleton, Governor-General of Canada, was writing to London that the Indians —

"...seem now to be determined to remove and prevent all American settlements northwest of the Ohio. They have dispatched war pipes to the different nations, and sent a large deputation from the Wabash and Miamis to Detroit to announce their determination for war, and demand a supply of ammunition."

The next month, in retaliation for the unrelenting Indian depredations, Major John Hardin led a force of two hundred twenty Kentuckians toward the Wea towns of the Wabash region; on August 9th they discovered and attacked a Shawnee hunting party, killing not only men, but women and children as well. The frustration of the settlers on the western border, especially in Kentucky, was reaching the breaking point; they had been told that Governor St. Clair had made peace with the Indians the winter before, but those peaceful Indians were attacking the settlements with increased fury. Harmar's pitifully small army could not begin to cope with protecting the settlers, and Congress had no money to send more men. It is beyond credibility to believe that Harmar had so many troops to spare that he could send a detachment to Mingo Bottom in order to catch a man who had shot and wounded an Indian.

At this time Harmar himself was beginning preparations for a punitive expedition of his own against those Indian tribes. There is no question that he was "anxious to preserve the good feeling then subsisting". There was no good feeling. The primary reason for Congress having sent an army to the western border in the first place was to protect the settlers from the never-ending outrages of the Indians, but Congress had so little money that they could not even afford to keep their western army supplied with powder. And at this same time Harmar was writing to the Secretary of War, to Governor St. Clair, and to his subordinates, that the only solution to the Indian problem was to carry the war to the Indian towns. That program was carried into effect the next year, but to Harmar's regret.

Nor is De Hass' remark that the Indian was "of some celebrity .... and of much influence in his tribe...." any closer to the truth. McDonald had referred to him only as "an Indian", not even giving him a name. Que-shaw-sey was known to be a "friendly" Indian who was sometimes employed at Fort Harmar as a runner; a chief he was not.

### The Official Correspondence:

On July 9, 1789, Harmar wrote to Secretary of War Henry Knox concerning the shooting of the Indian known as George Washington:

"This George Washington is a trusty confidential Indian and was wounded by some vagabond whites from the neighborhood of Wheeling. He is well known to Governor St. Clair, and I believe there is not a better Indian to be found. The villain who wounded him I am informed is one Lewis Whitzell. I am in hopes to be able to apprehend him and deliver him to Judge Parsons to be dealt with; but would much rather have it in my power to order such vagabonds hanged up immediately without trial."

Harmar added that he had invited the Indian to come to the fort to have the post surgeon attend his wound, and had sent him some flour. The crux of the entire matter is Harmar's comment:

"I am in hopes to be able to apprehend [Wetzel] and deliver him to Judge Parsons; but would much rather have it in my power to order such vagabonds hanged up immediately without trial."

Harmar knew that he had no power over civilians, but would have much preferred to hang such "vagabonds" summarily. Unfortunately, based on this one statement alone, there has been no end of historians who have Harmar continually sending out not only parties of soldiers, but Indians as well, with orders to bring in this "villain Whitzell" dead or alive. If alive, Harmar would without hesitation hang him from the nearest tree; if dead, so much the better.

Less than seven weeks later, on August 26, 1789 Federal Judge John Cleves Symmes deposed:

### Federal Territory Northwest of the Ohio River

"Whereas Lewis Weitsel[,] charged with an assault upon and wounding and maiming of George Washington[,] an Indian in Alliance and friendship with the United States, lately made his escape from the custody of the United States Guard at Fort Harmar, and being retaken into custody at Limestone in the District of Kentucky by Serg't John Lalor and Patrick Delaney of the United States troops under the command of Capt. McCurdy[;] this day rendered in custody to the subscriber[,] one of the judges of the Feoderal (sic) Territory. These are therefore to certify that the said Lewis Weitsel, charged as aforesaid at the suit of the United States, has been in due form of law and agreeable to the proclamation and process issued for his apprehension by the Honorable Judge Parsons [in July, at Marietta] of the said Feoderal Territory delivered to the custody of the civil authority by Capt. McCurdy.

Given under my hand at Northbend this 26th day of August, 1789.
*John Cleves Symmes*

Thus the entire episode — Wetzel's "wounding and maiming" the Indian George Washington, his arrest, imprisonment, escape, abduction, travel time, and release; all this took place in no more than two months, from early July through late August, 1789. During all this time Harmar was still at Marietta, not arriving at Fort Washington until later on in the fall; the commanding officer at Fort Washington, still under construction when Wetzel was brought there, was Major John Doughty. Henry Jolly later reported that Wetzel told him that "Major Doty" had treated him with particular kindness.

*       *       *

The following commentary by Thornbrough succinctly explains the storm of protest in Kentucky caused by Wetzel's seizure:

"Wetzel's arrest by McCurdy's men [Lollor and Delaney] — the arrest of a civilian by the military — caused a storm of protest in Kentucky. In the September 26, 1789, issue of The Kentucky Gazette published at Lexington, was printed a letter to the editor dated September 10, which read in part:

*'Then know, Kentuckians, that a free citizen of our country, in the house of his friend, in the peaceable pursuit of his business, is seized by a military officer at the head of his soldiers, taken into custody, confined, and hurried, where? — to a magistrate — to a court of justice — or to any tribunal qualified to examine him ....? No; but out of your country — out of the reach of your laws — away from his friends, into a military garrison.'*

"In the *Gazette* of October 24, there appeared a letter from Henry Lee, county lieutenant of Mason County who, too, apparently felt that military authority had defied the civil. By his account the seventy men under McCurdy were given permission to visit Limestone when their boats reached that point. They behaved quite boisterously, stealing baked goods, plundering gardens, etc., and carried off considerable loot. From the *Gazette*:

*'About day light a sergeant and six men entered the house of one John Young, and forcibly seized a certain Lewis Witzel (who in attempting to defend himself from their Violence, wounded one of them in the hand,) and dragging him by the hair down to the bank, to one of their boats, they confined him therein and finally carried him away....'*

"Lee then went down to Fort Washington where Major Doughty was commanding. Doughty explained to Lee that Wetzel had been accused of the murder of an Indian, but that the Indian had recovered and the only witness against Wetzel had left the country. Doughty added that Wetzel had originally been arrested by Judge Parsons [[101]] and for want of a jail had been confined at the garrison from which he escaped. Doughty had instructed McMurdy to deliver Wetzel to Judge Symmes which he had done, and subsequently Wetzel had been released. McCurdy, who had proceeded on to Vincennes, had told Judge Symmes, that he, McCurdy, had in his possession $22.50 belonging to Wetzel for which he declared himself answerable. He disclaimed knowledge of the twenty-eight guineas which Wetzel said he also had had when arrested. Lee felt that McCurdy and his men had exceeded their authority and demanded McCurdy's arrest and trial."

Since McCurdy had continued on to his post at Fort Knox (Vincennes, Indiana), Gen. Harmar wrote to the commanding officer there, Major John F. Hamtramck, on October 25th, 1789:

"... By the enclosed copy of a letter from the County Lieutenant of Mason County in Kentucky to me, you will observe how he complains of the disorderly proceedings of Captain McCurdy's company in plundering the inhabitants at Limestone, on their passage down the Ohio River; I have answered him, if the representation is just, the offenders shall certainly be severely punished. You will please to make the necessary inquiry into this matter, and report to me accordingly."

This certainly does not sound as if Harmar was still thirsting for Wetzel's blood. There is not even a mention here of Wetzel's name, as he had been released two months earlier at Cincinnati by Judge Symnes, and by now that matter was considered settled. The problem now to be resolved was that of the *disorderly proceedings of Captain McCurdy's company*. Maj. Hamtramk responded on December 3, 1789:

".... Agreably to your request I have had an enquiry made about Capt. McCurdy. The Proceedings are enclosed."

These "Proceedings" were to the effect that the alleged plundering of Limestone by McCurdy's men was categorically denied. Period. Receipt of this denial was unsatisfactory to Harmar, now at Fort Washington, who had by this time received yet another letter (dated January 1, 1790) from the most persistent Lee, and on January 13, 1790, Harmar so advised Hamtramck:

".... In my letter of the 25th October I enclosed you a copy of a letter received from Colonel Henry Lee[,] the County Lieutenant of Mason County, relative to the riotous & disorderly proceedings of Captain McCurdy, and his company. All Kentucky is in an uproar about it. I am informed that they have advertized McCurdy in the Public Gazette upon the occasion. I have since received another letter from the County Lieutenant, who seems determined to prosecute the matter. Certain it is the regiment has been considerably disgraced by such conduct in the eyes of the people. You will therefore order Captain McCurdy under arrest, & to repair to headquarters in the spring with his evidences, for to receive his trial."

Further attempting to pour oil on troubled waters, Harmar answered Lee's letter on January 23, 1790, explaining that McCurdy was to be returned to Fort Washington for court-martial:

"I have received your letter dated the first instant from Limestone, and have to inform you that I have already ordered Captain McCurdy in arrest, & to repair hither for his trial. I expect he will be here about the latter end of April or sometime in the month of May next, but shall let you know the precise day of his arrival. The representation you have made me is of a very serious nature, and if the charges are supported, he ought to be dismissed the service. You wish to know what kind of evidence is necessary upon this occasion — deposition is entirely inadmissible unless by consent of both parties. The evidence must therefore be by <u>Viva Voce</u> as you term it, or face to face."

In April Hamtramck duly notified Harmar that McCurdy was on his way to Fort Washington. McCurdy arrived and a court-martial was convened; four months later, on August 27, 1790, Harmar sent McCurdy back to his post at Vincennes, with a message which advised Hamtramck of the final resolution of the charges: "The bearer, Captain McCurdy, is acquitted by the Court Martial. The 19 dollars and some 90/100 taken from Whitzell were received, and delivered to the court."

\*　　\*　　\*

## *One for the Road — A Final Commentary on Harmar, Wetzel, and Historians*

It is unfortunately true that any historian, including this one, may sometimes get so caught up in the details of what is happening under his very nose that he may forget all else that is going on around his ears. All those who repeat the Harmer-Wetzel story seem to have forgotten, or ignored, the fact that in 1789 the United States of America was still there. It had not gone away, and Gen. Harmar was certainly not operating in a vacuum. These authors have written as if they are unaware that at the time of these particular events the new Federal Constitution had just gone into effect, we had a new thing called a "President" (as of April 30, 1789), and people were still vitally concerned about their basic freedoms. Twelve amendments to the new Constitution had just been approved by the Congress and sent to the various states, where they were even then being vigorously debated and voted upon by the state legislatures. Although the Bill of Rights as we know it would not go into effect until 1791, several states had already ratified several of those amendments, and everyone knew it would not be much longer before all citizens would be guaranteed certain due process and justice rights — which had been specifically designed to protect private citizens (such as Wetzel) from the government (in this case, Harmar):

an indictment must be presented by a grand jury (where was Harmar's grand jury?), the accused must have access to legal counsel, he must be allowed to face his accusers, he has the right of habeas corpus (which eventually freed Wetzel), and all the rest.

The Ohio Country was operating under the Northwest Ordinance, not under martial law, and Harmar himself would have been court-martialed had he as much as arrested a civilian. [Fourth Amendment, protection against illegal search and seizure]. Given circumstances such as these, would any military officer have dared arrest, much less hang, a private citizen without first giving him benefit of "a speedy, public trial by a jury of his peers"?

As with so many other incidents in *The Wetzel Saga*, every subsequent writer has taken the details of this event — five pages from De Hass (via McDonald) — and enlarged, altered, expounded upon them to the point that the entire episode is now accepted as fact. It is not so! Harmar was undoubtedly embarrassed by Wetzel's escape from his garrison, but he had far more important matters to concern him than whether someone who had wounded an Indian would be tried by civilian authorities, as he prepared his own campaign against the Indians. At the (1786) Treaty of Fort Finney the Shawnee had agreed to give up their claim to all lands east of the Miami River, in western Ohio; from that time on the Ohio Indians were primarily confined to the area south and west of Lake Erie, but as is commonly the case, a treaty signed under duress is worse than no treaty at all. The Shawnee had signed under extreme pressure, said pressure being in the form of George Rogers Clark, as Van Every explained, "the one white commander before whose threats Indians learned invariably to quail."

By 1789 they were determined to recover what they had signed away, and the best means was to make life unbearable for the settlers. Harmar's federal troops, no blame to him, were poorly fed, scantily clothed, and seldom paid; they deserted in droves. He did manage to send two companies to the Falls of the Ohio to help protect the settlements, but at the same time he was expected to provide troops to guard the surveyors of the *Seven Ranges* (government land) in Ohio. Spare soldiers who could be sent to Mingo Bottom to arrest Lewis Wetzel — well, they were simply not to be found.

### *In Memoriam Lewis Wetzel*

Lydia (Boggs) Cruger, while being interviewed by Draper, had mentioned that, upon the capture of her brother Billy by the Indians in the spring of 1781, his greatest fear was that he would be recognized as one of the men who, with the aid of Lewis Wetzel, had broken into the guardhouse at Wheeling and tomahawked an Indian chief known as Killbuck. Of course he could not have been "recognized", as there were no witnesses among the Indians who would have known who he was or what he had done. If anything. Lydia was not at Wheeling at the time, and the whole story is certainly suspect; Lydia's later reminiscences are often confused [see *Appendix H* for her account of the *Gunpowder Exploit*], but this is not surprising in a woman who was in her eighties, and was recalling events which had happened nearly seventy years before.

Both Boggs and Wetzel were only seventeen years old at the time, and for them to have initiated such an adventure seems unlikely. Nor was the Delaware chief known as Killbuck killed by whites; he is known to have died peacefully in 1811[102], although there may have been other Indians with that moniker. Henry Jolly, another of the early frontiersmen, also mentioned the story of Wetzel tomahawking Killbuck, but one is inclined to believe that he had heard the story from

Mrs. Cruger. Jolly stated that he first became acquainted with the Bonnetts, Wetzel's relatives and neighbors, in 1784, three years after the Killbuck venture, and while he knew Wetzel some years earlier, how well the two young men knew each other is uncertain.

There is, however, a little known but similar incident, in which an Indian captive was tomahawked by a militiaman who broke into the cabin where the Indian was being held. It occurred during Logan's 1786 campaign, after the militia had secured Moluntha's Town. Simon Kenton and Daniel Boone were in charge of the advance on Moluntha's Town, and it was Kenton, being one of the first to enter the village, who personally placed Moluntha and his family under a guard, with orders that no one be allowed to approach them until his return; he then hurried off in pursuit of the fleeing Indians. Many years later Kenton told Judge James:

"McGary claimed to go in, and being an officer was admitted, when he killed him. If I had been there when he struck Moluntha, I would have struck him. McGary was an outbreaking man; he was shy of me, for he knew I could handle him. I knew Moluntha as soon as I saw him, for I had been prisoner with him in 1778. We burnt the Macachac town, and then the Pickaway town where West Liberty is. Here an Indian was taken and confined in a cabin, with his arms pinioned to the wall. After he had been there a day and a night, a man who was rather a particular acquaintance of mine, went in, tomahawked him. I never could forgive such cruelty after deliberation .... We went on, burnt Wapatomica, McKee's Town, Blue Jacket's Town."

Here is a possible explanation of the tale of Lewis Wetzel and William Boggs breaking into the guardhouse at Wheeling in 1781 and tomahawking the chief Killbuck. Although it is probable that Wetzel was a member of Logan's Expedition, and although he may have received the blame (or credit!) for this killing, it was not Lewis Wetzel, it was not a guardhouse, it was not at Wheeling, and it was not Killbuck. But it was an Indian, he was tomahawked while being held inside a building, and after half a century all the little details seemed to run together anyway.

Kenton knew who it was, as he said, a particular acquaintance, but of course Kenton wouldn't name names. He knew the traitor who had brought the warning to the Shawnee the day before Logan's army arrived at Mac-a-chack, but Kenton, even fifty years afterward, wouldn't disclose that name either. This acquaintance was evidently one of the Kentuckians, and perhaps it may have been one of those from the vicinity of Kenton's Station on Lawrence Creek, near present Washington, Kentucky. At least we can be sure that it was not one of the Wetzels, but it is fairly certain that one or more of the Wetzels actually was on this expedition. In the 1830s, then Judge Henry Jolly wrote that Lewis Wetzel "went a volunteer on a campaign from Kentucky, under the command (I believe) of Col. Logan". This would fit in with the Logan Expedition of 1786, just three months after Wetzel's father had been killed by Indians on the Ohio.

Three years later, after Wetzel had escaped from Fort Harmar, where he had been imprisoned for shooting and wounding an Indian, he went downriver to

Kenton's Station, and there, as Kenton's biographer says, "he found ... plenty of sympathy from Kenton's boys, who knew, all of them, all his exploits." Soon thereafter, when Wetzel was illegally apprehended at Limestone and as illegally taken to Cincinnati's Fort Washington, there was talk of raising an army of frontiersmen and descending in a body on the fort, to release Wetzel, by force if necessary. Simon Kenton was one of the leaders of this movement, but Wetzel was released by a federal judge almost as soon as he had reached Cincinnati.

There is no indication that Lewis Wetzel and Kenton ever saw each other again; as Wetzel never went on another military expedition and, as there are no traditions of adventure linking Lewis Wetzel with Simon Kenton, the chances are unlikely that they did. Hence Kenton would not have referred to Lewis Wetzel, forty years later, as the "particular acquaintance" who tomahawked a bound Indian. Nor would that description fit Jacob Wetzel; it is not known whether Jacob was even along on Logan's Campaign, but since that was a Kentucky expedition he was probably not. It was sometime after this that Jacob removed to Kentucky, where he lived for a few years near Kenton's Station, Jacob Wetzel and Simon Kenton becoming a renowned pair of scouts in the last few years of the Indian Wars. But Kenton, we recall, would have killed McGary for the cowardly murder of Moluntha, and he "never could forgive such cruelty" as killing an Indian who was tied; thus he would not have allowed Jacob to accompany him on so many of his expeditions. When Simon Kenton said he never could forgive, that was exactly what he meant. As for the three other Wetzel brothers, George had been killed in 1782, John Jr., was still at home, only sixteen, and Martin did not go on any expeditions after his escape from the Shawnee in 1781.

But just who was this particular acquaintance of Kenton's, after all, who tomahawked the Indian in the cabin? Although it is an obscure fact, the name is known. It was Thomas Kennedy, the same man who had the day before galloped into Moluntha's Town and, avoiding the warriors, had ridden into the midst of a group of squaws, and one captive white girl, slashing at them with his great two-sided claymore as they ran screaming. During the army's retreat from the Shawnee towns, whenever Tom Kennedy was in the vicinity, an occasional voice could be heard calling out jeeringly, "Who hacked the squaws? Who hacked the squaws?".

It is not so unusual for any researcher to find stories such as this, after many of the details of names and dates and places have been all but lost. There are a multitude of stories in existence, for instance the numerous versions of the rescue of the *Forest Rose*, all of which are based on a single event and which have, sometimes intentionally, sometimes not, been altered out of recognition. The story of the "fine looking chief" who was cut down with a tomahawk by a militiaman during Brodhead's Coshocton Expedition is probably nothing more than a cobbled-up version of a militiaman named Hugh McGary killing the Shawnee chief Moluntha, as he was "standing in the street talking to an officer", having been assured that he would not be harmed, during this same Logan's Expedition.

## SEVENTH INTERLUDE: LEWIS WETZEL VS. GEORGE WASHINGTON

*    *    *

For two centuries odium has been heaped upon Lewis Wetzel because, during Brodhead's Expedition he supposedly struck down an Indian from behind (but didn't), because he fired at an Indian who was not on his way to a peace treaty, and because he "once shot an Indian without warning". Lewis Wetzel's marvelous woodcraft, his ability to reload a rifle on the run, his courage, his superb athleticism, his knowledge of his enemy — all these combined to allow him to forsake the usual bungled military expeditions.

Thus, Lewis Wetzel went out after the enemy wherever he could find him, and he went alone because so few others could keep up with him. Not Josh Davis, certainly not Thomas Mills nor the likes of Mike Forshay, nor anyone else, save perhaps such immortals as Simon Kenton, John Slover, and Sam Brady. And perhaps not even them. Lewis Wetzel has been vilified in modern times by those who do not know, simply because he was able to beat the Indians at their own game. These same persons excuse the slaughter of women and children, even babies, by Indian braves, because "that was their custom". There is no evidence that Lewis Wetzel ever killed anyone other than an adult Indian warrior. He never bound any Indian, neither man, woman, nor child, to a stake, and then tortured them for hours for his own pleasure. His father and an older brother were killed by Indians, but this was warfare, and those who engage in war take their chances, or they stay at home. Who among us, living in those bitter times, would not have set out to avenge a mother or father or child, a wife or a sister who had been brutalized by the Indians? Who among us would have stayed at home?

# Chapter XXVI

## Jacob Wetzel

If anyone could be ranked a close second behind Lewis Wetzel as an Indian fighter, his brother Jacob would be one of the main contenders. Little is known of him between the time of his abduction with Lewis in 1777 and his move to Kentucky about 1790, when his renown began to steadily grow. Only one of the earlier stories from the Wheeling Creek homestead is known, as Lewis Bonnett, Jr. described it to Dr. Draper.

It was a common practice of Indians to secret themselves outside the door of a pioneer cabin; at first light, when the man of the house opened the door, all the Indians would fire at him and, with the man killed or seriously wounded, the way was open for the other warriors to charge into the cabin, tomahawks in hand. Sometime in the mid-1780s Jacob made a false man, carving the head out of buckeye wood. With a shirt and pants stuffed with straw and affixed to the dummy head, a woodsman's hat perched on top completed the illusion. One night on the Wetzel farm Jake heard the alarm of the dog and told his younger sister, Susannah, that Indians were about. At daybreak Susannah stood behind the thick plank door; holding the false man away from her body with her left hand, she cautiously opened the door, while Jacob waited, rifle in hand, on the right. As the "man" appeared in the doorway two muskets were fired at it. Susannah let the dummy fall to the floor, where it flopped about with a truly genuine "mortally wounded" appearance, as two Indians raced for the open door of the cabin. They had not covered more than a few feet when the huge form of Jacob Wetzel filled the doorway and fired at the nearer warrior. Stepping back Jacob was already in the act of reloading his rifle as Susannah swung the heavy door to and barred it. With a charge of powder and two balls dropped down the barrel, Jacob stuck the muzzle of the rifle out one of the portholes and fired at the second Indian, bringing him down before he could gain the shelter of the woods. Women on the border, as well as men, were a hardy and adventuresome breed, especially if their name was Wetzel.

Sometime around 1790 Jake had moved to the vicinity of Kenton's Station on Lawrence Creek, near present Washington, Kentucky. There Kenton had assembled a company of frontiersmen and adventurers, who for ten years devoted a goodly portion of their lives to protecting the most endangered area of the Kentucky frontier; of these men the most illustrious was Jacob Wetzel.

One fall Wetzel and Kenton had made plans for a hunt near the mouth of the Kentucky River, but when they arrived at the chosen spot they found numerous Indian sign. The idea of abandoning the hunt and returning home probably did not even occur to them; instead it was a matter of locating the Indians, determining their number, and then deciding how best to attack them. On the second day after their arrival they finally located the Indian camp which contained five warriors. Since it was now nearly dark they agreed to wait until the morning would give them enough light to shoot. Kenton had a *wender*[103] gun, the German term for a swivel-breech rifle, commonly called a double gun, with one barrel superposed above the other. When the upper barrel was fired, the catch was released and the two barrels were swiveled so that the unfired barrel was uppermost, when it could then be fired.

Near the Indian camp was a large fallen tree, and in the branches of this the two frontiersmen stealthily hid themselves to await the dawn. As soon as there was enough light they each selected a target. Kenton shot first; then, as Wetzel fired, Kenton quickly turned the barrels and fired the second round, whereupon both men charged into the camp yelling at the top of their lungs. The two remaining Indians, having heard three shots in rapid succession expected three or more men to be attacking them, and they ran headlong into the forest, with Kenton and Wetzel close on their heels. Kenton soon returned with the scalp of his victim, and only a few moments later Wetzel walked into the camp bearing the scalp of the second Indian.

That two men, alone in the wilderness, would attack a camp of five Indians and kill all five without suffering any harm to themselves, would normally be considered somewhat noteworthy. But not in this instance; although this episode was considered rather daring, it was nothing out of the routine, since the two men involved were Simon Kenton and one of the Wetzel boys.

In the spring of 1791 Jacob Greathouse, brother of the Daniel Greathouse of *Logan's Massacre* infamy, had started down the Ohio with his wife and a large party of movers, intending to settle in Kentucky. At about the same time a company of Harmar's soldiers who had served out their enlistment were returning to Fort Pitt, traveling upstream in a boat, while a party of traders accompanied them walking along the shore. On March 19th, near the mouth of the Scioto, the Indians attacked; several of the soldiers in the boat were killed, but not one of the traders escaped. Five days later the Greathouse party came down the river, and were attacked in almost the same spot, probably by the same band of Indians. One of the boats got through to Limestone with the news, and a party of three hundred men under Alexander Orr went up the river to the scene of the double tragedy. Eight miles above the mouth of the Scioto, on the Kentucky side, they found the remains of the traders, now two weeks dead. A half mile above the river, on the Indian shore, another party of men, including Kenton, Jacob Wetzel, and Joe Lemon, found three dead Indians; they had been thrown into the hole made by the torn-out roots of a fallen tree, then covered over with brush. Although the smell must have been horrific, Lemon went into the hole and scalped them. Three miles below the river the men stumbled across the site of a terrible butchery which had occurred some eight or ten days before.

Kenton had known Jacob Greathouse for years; in the summer of 1771, when Kenton, *alias* Butler, was fleeing his Virginia home with the thought of William Leachman's blood on his hands, he had met Greathouse near Fort Pitt. Along with Bill Grills and two brothers named Mahon, Greathouse was preparing to start out on a hunting trip, and sixteen-year-old Simon was invited to go along. That had been twenty years ago, and they had seen each other several times since, but Kenton had trouble recognizing Greathouse now. He and his wife lay, each at the foot of a small sapling, separated by no more than a few yards. The Indians had developed a novel torture, and after taking them from the boat and stripping them naked they had cut an incision in their abdomens. Reaching in they had pulled out the section of the small intestine connected to the stomach; this they severed and fastened to the sapling. Then with tomahawks heated red hot in the fire they had driven the man and his wife around and around the trees, until both had wound their intestines about them. There they had been left to die, but not before the Indians had turned loose the dozen or so hogs which had been aboard the boat. When Kenton and Wetzel arrived the rummaging hogs and the foraging buzzards had not left much of anything that was still recognizable as human. Several sheep had also been taken from the boat and killed, and apart from the two bodies so grotesquely fastened to the trees there was little else among the remains that could be distinguished between animal and human. Despite the terrible smell the men gathered Greathouse and his wife together and buried them side by side along the shore. But nothing could be done with the refuse of humans and animals mingled together, so one of the men, Luther Calvin, the only one able to bear the stench, went in and shoveled the remains and the filth into the river.

The men had hardly returned home when news came that a large party of Indians, perhaps once again the same group, had descended the river, passed Limestone Creek, and from there had scattered into Kentucky. Then came the report of four large Indian canoes discovered sunk at the mouth of Snag Creek, and Kenton gathered thirty men, among them Fielding Figgans, Jacob Wetzel, Neal Washburn, and Jacob Boone, Daniel's cousin. After traveling about twenty-five miles downstream they came to the mouth of the creek; there they crossed over and hid themselves on the Ohio shore. For the rest of that day they waited, and all the next, and into the next day, until finally a canoe with three Indians was seen crossing over from Kentucky, at the same time swimming seven horses stolen from Kentucky. As the canoe approached the bank the men opened fire, killing two of the Indians outright and wounding the third, who was quickly dispatched with a tomahawk. Jacob Boone, still so enraged over the sights he had witnessed at the Greathouse site, wanted to flay one of the Indians to make a razor strop, but Kenton would not allow it.

The next day three more Indians crossed in another of the canoes they had raised, this time with five horses, and as before they were shot down as they neared the shore. Late the next night the men heard a large party of Indians on the Kentucky shore calling across the river, but receiving no answer they sent over a spy who saw Kenton's camp. When the Kentuckians crossed over next morning they found the Indians gone. Only six Indians had been killed in retaliation for the sixteen whites killed at the mouth of the Scioto, but Kenton's boys could not remain here any longer, they were needed elsewhere.

A year later, in the spring of 1792, following the St. Clair catastrophe, conditions on the frontier had grown worse. All winter it had been open season on Kentucky. Anthony Wayne had been appointed the new army commander, and as he prepared for yet another invasion, there were those in Congress who once again clamored for a peace treaty with the Indians. As a result it was now, in early April, illegal to pursue Indians north of the river, or to embark on campaigns into "Indian Country". The word announcing this prohibition reached Kenton a day or two too late; with nearly forty men he had headed north on April 7th, toward a large Shawnee camp which had been spotted on the Little Miami. Along with Kenton were the usual men, Lemon, Figgans, Calvin, Washburn, Alex McIntire, Samuel Frazee, Jacob Wetzel, and Josh Davis, cousin of the late Thomas Mills from Short Creek.

On the second day out about ten of the men complained that they were too few to accomplish anything against a large encampment and, pretending to go for water for the camp at nightfall, they headed for home and never returned. The thirty now remaining went on undaunted, and the next night the camp was located. Although they did not then know it, it was a major war party, filled with warriors and chiefs like Black Hoof, Black Snake and young Tecumseh. McIntire and Washburn, who had been sent ahead to spy out the camp, reported that it was too large for thirty men to attack in broad daylight, so Kenton called the men together to discuss strategy. Some were for an immediate withdrawal, some wanted to build a breastwork and wait for the Indians to attack, the others wanted to attack at dawn the next day. This last was the plan finally decided upon, and Jacob Wetzel and Sam Frazee were chosen as night spies to creep up to the camp, the better able to observe it at close range from the light of the camp fires, and gain intelligence on the camp's layout in preparation for the next morning's assault. Wetzel got up very close, and as Kenton's biographer described it, upon his return:

"... he reported the camp a very large one, with tents of bark and a large marquee, taken in St. Clairs' defeat and set up for the use of the young Tecumseh to occupy. And again the advisability of retreat was discussed. Wetzel was the one who turned the tide of depression; like a true Wetzelian he said that if no other would go he would go alone and kill at least one. Wood and Whiteman and others spoke up, and it was finally resolved to attack."[104]

They then divided into three groups, with Kenton in charge of the center, and McIntire and Calvin on either side, and began to approach the camp in the darkness. It was still some three hours before daylight, but one of the camp dogs caught the scent of strangers and began barking, whereupon one of the Indians started walking in the direction indicated by the dog. When Calvin heard his men cocking their rifles he shot the Indian coming toward him, and the advantage of surprise was lost.

The engagement continued until near dawn, with sporadic firing back and forth, intermingled with occasional hand-to-hand combat. Suddenly one of the men in front of Calvin was killed, and then, hearing a splashing in the creek behind him, he yelled that they were being surrounded. It was as if he had yelled out the order for retreat; all thirty of the Kentuckians returned to camp, took to their horses, and, two by two, as prearranged, headed back toward the Ohio. Kenton and Lemon were the last two to come in. Two men were casualties, one killed and one missing. Calvin had seen Sam Barr killed, and little "red-headed Aleck" McIntire was the one who never returned. Several years later they learned that he had been taken captive and killed; in the brief engagement the Indians had had seventeen killed or seriously wounded.

*    *    *

Secretary of War Knox's efforts to secure peace were unavailing, and Wayne continued building his army. After their victories over Harmar and St. Clair there was no possibility that the Indians would concede defeat, although the great Miami war chief Little Turtle himself cautioned his warriors that they should treat for peace. They could win one battle after another, he warned, but after each victory the Americans would send another army against them, and then another, and finally the Indians would be defeated. Better by far to get what they could, now, while they held the upper hand in negotiations, than to wait until the Americans had won. The warriors refused to listen to such defeatist talk, and so it was left to Wayne to prove Little Turtle right.

# Chapter XXVII

## Disaster - 1790

They might as well have whistled in the dark as to expect a peace treaty to conclude the Indian Wars. They knew better, of course; they knew that one Indian tribe or another would sign a treaty while the other was sending out war parties to ravage the settlements. By 1790 the greatest fear was of a confederation of Indians, such as had almost been accomplished at the Hurontown conference. But Brant, the organizer, was a Mohawk, an Iroquois, and the Iroquois were no longer the prime mover of the aborigines. It would be twenty years before the phenomenon of Tecumseh would burst upon the scene for his brief flash of glory, the Indian confederation which he welded together once again supported by British military might during the War of 1812.

The principle threat now was the conglomeration of irascible, indefatigable warriors, mainly Miami and Shawnee, and they had a new leader, relatively unknown, the Miami chief Little Turtle. Unknown and unrecognized by his opponents he might have been, but for the next four years he was to lead the Indians in a fashion that even Pontiac would have envied.

Therefore, a military campaign against those western nations was politic, but that raised another concern for the fledgling United States government; those two tribes lived in northwestern Ohio and present-day northeastern Indiana, and a military push against them might be looked upon by the English as a threat against their position on the St. Lawrence River. At whatever cost to the pioneers Congress must avoid even the appearance of belligerence. The St. Lawrence was the key to the interior of the continent; two portages controlled a 2,500 mile waterway from the mouth of the St. Lawrence, through Lake Erie and Lake Michigan, down the Allegheny to Pitt and the Ohio River, and the Wabash, all the way to the mouth of the Mississippi. Those portages were the fourteen-mile crossing at Niagra, and the nine-mile traverse at the Maumee, St. Joseph, and Wabash Rivers.

But conditions on the frontier were in such a state that they must be alleviated, and Washington directed his Secretary of War, Henry Knox, to develop a campaign against the Indians, while at the same time reassuring the British that no offensive measures were intended against them. Final instructions from Knox to Governor St. Clair and General Harmar were sent out on September 14, 1789; it would be in their best interests to build and maintain a fort at the confluence of the St. Marys, St., Joseph, and Maumee Rivers, Knox advised, but that was beyond the present ability of the United States. The purpose of this expedition, therefore, was three-fold: to punish the Miami and Shawnee for their refusal to treat with Congress, as well as for their raids against the frontier, and to demonstrate to them the power of the United States military. In order to avoid the appearance of any possible threat against the English posts, on September 19th Knox wrote to advise Murray, the commandant at Detroit, that an American invasion was being prepared which was aimed solely at the Indians, and the letter specifically informed Murray that the campaign was against none of the possessions currently held by England.

The site selected for attack was known as Kekionga, the area surrounding that nine mile portage connecting the Maumee-St. Joseph with the Wabash, the site of present Fort Wayne, Indiana. This had long been considered the most important strategic point between the Great Lakes and the Ohio, and it was here that the principal villages of the Miami were located. The date set for the assembling of the militia was September 15th, and on that date Harmar began collecting his army; he had a force of three hundred twenty regulars, and so the main body of the army was to be comprised of militia. But the militia was always undependable, and this was not even the militia of ten years earlier. In 1780 a large number of experienced bordermen and battle-hardened frontiersmen would have answered the call to arms, but the enormous influx of easterners in the last ten years had sadly diluted the hardy pioneer stock. Many of the men who showed up at Fort Washington that September were newcomers to the frontier; they had experience neither with the wilderness nor with wild Indians, many of them arrived with broken guns, some showed up with no weapons at all.

Along with the usual problems of obtaining supplies, another potentially more serious problem was the overabundance of militia "officers" who outranked, at least on paper, every single officer of Harmar's First American Regiment, save Harmar himself. The army finally began its march from Fort Washington on September 30th, with Harmar's 320 regulars, and over eleven hundred militia, about four hundred of whom were mounted. The regulars consisted of two battalions, under Majors John Wyllys and John Doughty, the same Major Doughty who the year before had assured Colonel Lee at Cincinnati that Lewis Wetzel had indeed been set free, and that an inquiry was being made into the behavior of Capt. McCurdy's men at Limestone. The regulars were supported by one company of artillery under Capt. William Ferguson, and by one battalion of mounted Kentucky riflemen under Major James Fontaine. The four battalions of Kentucky infantry were under the command of Col. John Hardin, of Kentucky; three from Kentucky commanded by Lt. Col. Trotter, under Majors Hall, McMullen, and Ray, and one battalion of Pennsylvania militia under Lt. Col. Traby, commanded by Major Paul.

Once under way the army moved rapidly along the old trail that had been used by George Rogers Clark in October, 1782, when he led the raid against the Shawnee villages on the Pickaway plains. From Fort Washington the army moved northeast until they reached the Mad River, near present Dayton, where they crossed and swung to the northwest, toward the Miami and the Maumee. Scouts and flankers were continually posted to avoid surprise, always the bane of a slowly-moving army lumbering along through the wilderness, but to their amazement there were no Indians to be seen during the entire two weeks of their advance. Unknowingly, Knox's letter to Murray had completely disheartened the Indians; it was obvious to them that if the Americans were so strong that they could give advance notice of their coming, then they certainly were too strong to oppose, and the Indian threat never materialized. The Miami, whose allies had long since melted into the forest shadows, were forced to withdraw from their villages and watch as Harmar marched in without a single shot being fired. The men set to work quickly, destroying the five major towns and an estimated twenty thousand bushels of corn.

They knew there must be Indians about, however, as so many of the army horses seemed to wander off and not return. Col. Hardin, the most experienced militia officer present, requested and received permission from Harmar to make a reconnaissance with a combined force of regulars and militia, in the hopes of finding the horse thieves. Little Turtle, meanwhile, had been studying the army and had concluded that it was by no means the threat he had been led to believe; he assembled a small band of about a hundred fifty Miami, with a few Shawnee, and awaited his chance. On October 19th Hardin marched out with a hundred eighty men, thirty of whom were regulars under Capt. John Armstrong, and they headed northwest toward Little Turtle's Eel River village. They had covered barely five miles when Hardin called a halt and sent Fontaine and his few cavalry ahead to spy out the ground; almost immediately they reported back to Hardin that a few Indians had been spotted who appeared to be fleeing. Afraid that they would escape Hardin ordered his men forward suddenly, so suddenly in fact that one entire company of militia under Capt. Faulkner, nearly half the militia force, was left behind. As soon as this was noted Hardin incautiously sent back his cavalry to round them up, and what was left to him was strung out for half a mile along a narrow path. This was the moment Little Turtle had been waiting for. He attacked the remnant of Hardin's troops before they could reassemble; a sudden surprise assault by mounted warriors broke the militia, while Indians on foot began encircling the entire force. The regulars stood their ground and were slaughtered; only eight of the thirty made it back to camp that night. The militia ran and were similarly slaughtered; about half of those engaged were killed, Armstrong noting that only nine of the militia remained to fight with his regulars. Once they had fired the single round from their muskets there was no time to reload before the Indians swarmed over them with their deadly tomahawks. The men slowly fought their way back toward Faulkner's slowly advancing company, but even those men became so panic-stricken that they at last refused to go any further, remaining behind trees while the rest of the militia streamed past them. When his command finally collapsed about him Armstrong had hidden himself in a swamp, where with tears in his eyes he watched the last of his brave men being overwhelmed by a total force no larger than Hardin's.

When Hardin made his way back to camp that night and reported, Harmar could not believe his ears. When Armstrong finally stumbled into camp the next morning with the report of the militia's cowardice, Harmar's incredulity turned to rage; he published a general order saying that if the militia ever again behaved in such a shameful manner he would turn the artillery on them. The retreat from Kekionga began on October 21st, but Hardin, discomfited over the behavior of the militia, wanted to lead a detachment back toward Kekionga. There was always the chance that they could catch a few Indians returning to the villages, and a surprise attack against them now, if successful, would recoup the defeat, and would prevent the Indians from harassing the army on its return. Harmar was undecided; the militia had once again proven themselves unworthy of trust, but when scouts brought back word that evening that a group of less than two hundred Indians had indeed returned to Kekionga, he decided to send out a force of regulars to attack. Unfortunately only sixty regulars could be spared; the rest were needed for other work, where dependability was a prerequisite, like guard duty, including the job of guarding the now fast-dwindling supplies from undisciplined militia. In consultation with Hardin and Capt. John Wyllys, an experienced Revolutionary officer from Connecticut, it was decided to send back a force of four hundred, the sixty regulars, with forty mounted horse under Fontaine, and three hundred of the most experienced militia. Hardin would again command the militia, but Wyllys would exercise overall command.

They started the march just after midnight, on October 22nd, and with a clear night advanced to within about two miles of the village, when Wyllys halted and called a meeting of the officers. The plan adopted called for Wyllys and the sixty regulars, accompanied by Fontaine's forty cavalry, to strike directly at Kekionga from the south after crossing the Maumee. At the same time Major Hall, with half the Kentucky militia would move to the west, cross the St. Marys, and then move north before heading back east, where they could cross the shallow St. Joseph and move directly into the village, while Major McMillan, with the hundred fifty Kentucky infantry remaining, would move north, cross the Maumee, then move back to his left toward the village, cutting off the retreat of the Indians in that direction. Hall, with the greatest distance to cover, moved out first, expecting to reach the Indian town just before sunrise. Success was entirely dependent upon surprise and the simultaneous coordination of all three units.

Coordination would be difficult, surprise impossible, since the Indians had been watching Harmar's army constantly, and hours before they had noted the detachment of Wyllys' troops. They assumed that this force was returning to bury the dead which had been abandoned three days earlier. Little Turtle, with barely time to spare, set up his forces in the favorite Indian maneuver, a decoy ambush which would soon disintegrate, and then another ambush when the soldiers ran after the routed decoy. Hall, with Hardin along, had been crossing the St. Marys when they saw an Indian scout. He was fired at by a number of the men, but escaped with his warning, as if the firing of the rifles were not enough to warn the Indians of the soldiers on their right flank.

Wyllys also heard the firing, and angered at this disclosure of the flanking column, pushed his men ahead rapidly. Fontaine led his cavalry as they plunged down the nearly twenty-foot-high embankment of the Maumee, with the regulars following along behind. This late in the year the river was barely a foot deep; some two hundred feet away rose the brush-covered bank opposite. Here the decoy was hidden, and as Fontaine reached mid-stream the hillside erupted in a sheet of flame, and both men and horses went down. Amid the infernal screeching of red men and confused yelling of white men, mixed in with the shrieks of the terrorized horses, the courageous Fontaine shouted for his Kentuckians to charge the enemy, and he spurred his horse toward the bank, his reins clinched in his teeth and a pair of drawn horse pistols in his hands. Firing point-blank into the faces of two warriors, he had just enough time to turn and see that only one man, George Adams, had followed him, then he was riddled by a number of Indian musket balls. Adams, now alone and himself wounded in five places, wheeled his horse and managed to return to the other side.

McMillan had not yet had time to reach the Maumee when he heard the firing; hurriedly he moved the men back and his infantry struck the right flank of the Indian ambush a severe blow. The Indians scattered and ran, straight back to Kekionga, past the village and into a large swampy area north of the town that continued all the way to the St. Joseph. McMillan's Kentuckians and the remnant of Fontaine's horse, now reorganized, pursued them closely. Some distance behind Willys and his regulars followed along, past the ruins of Kekionga, then into a section of the destroyed cornfields.

It could not have been planned better; Little Turtle had not only tricked the militia into chasing his decoys from the river, but now he had caught his most dangerous opponent, badly outnumbered, in the ravaged cornfield which offered no cover. From the edge of that field came a blast of fire and smoke that caught the Americans off guard; they barely had time to recover before the Indians were upon them in hand-to-hand combat. Wyllys, shot in the chest, went down under a flurry of spears and tomahawk blows. His regulars, as always, stood and fought well, and there in the bloody cornfield they died. Those who could escaped through the dense smoke and confusion; the number who survived that battle was only ten, the number who did not was a staggering fifty.

North of the town McMillan's pursuing men, disappointed in finding so few Indians, suddenly heard the battle raging in their rear. Turning back south they soon came upon the few regulars who had escaped, with the Indians close behind. Now the militia outnumbered the Indians, and the warriors slowly gave ground until, nearing the St. Joseph, Hall's force could be seen approaching from the west. At this point the St. Joseph was only a few inches deep and only about twenty feet wide; the Indians streamed down into the river bed and were caught between the two approaching elements of the militia. Out of their potential death trap they charged, through one end of Hall's line, and disappeared into the underbrush. The militiamen looked around and only now realized the battle was over; on the ground about them were scattered the bodies of some forty warriors. But in addition to the forty regulars killed with Wyllys, the Kentuckians had lost sixty-eight men, over a fourth of the total force. At least five of those militiamen had been taken prisoner, and after being interrogated they were put to death.

But from those five Little Turtle had learned that the militia was totally demoralized, that the best of the army had been killed at the ambush in the cornfield, and that provisions for the horses were running low. It was quickly decided to strike again the next day. As soon as Harmar's troops were strung out along the trail Blue Jacket, at the head of nearly seven hundred warriors, Shawnee, Miami, Ottawa, Sauk, and Fox, would attack the militia and scatter them like chickens. Not even Harmar could possibly escape annihilation. But during that beautiful autumn night the full moon, significantly enough the Hunters' Moon of the Indians, shining brightly in a clear sky, suddenly dimmed and darkened, then went out. It was a lunar eclipse, and it lasted only two hours, but the superstitious Indians interpreted it as a portent of evil, and the entire Ottawa contingent, as silently and with as little warning as had the moon, disappeared and were swallowed up by the darkness. Then one by one the other tribes followed, until with the sunrise Blue Jacket was left with only a handful of warriors. That morning Harmar's army began their retreat unmolested, and on November 3rd what was left of his now nearly mutinous force walked into Fort Washington.

The defeat was not Harmar's fault, but being in command he was the one who was blamed. The fault lay in the military system itself, which relied, in spite of its proven and repeated failures, on a system of short-term, untrained, unfed, unpaid, and undisciplined militia. Rather than solve the problem, the remedy was always more of the same. Governor St. Clair, the born politician, left for Philadelphia as soon as word of Harmar's defeat reached him. Huddling together with Washington and Knox, it was decided that St. Clair should replace Harmar, and in March he was appointed a major general in overall military command, while he continued as governor of the territory. Harmar, indignant at this rather shabby treatment, resigned from the service, and thus was lost perhaps the one man most knowledgeable in matters of Indian warfare. Washington's instructions to St. Clair were brief and to the point; speaking as an old soldier who had gained experience when Braddock had stumbled into the Monongahela ambush nearly forty years before, he admonished St. Clair: "... in three words, beware of surprise; trust not the Indian; leave not your arms for the moment; and when you halt for the night be sure to fortify your camp — again and again, General, beware of surprise!". It was sound advice, from one who knew.

# Chapter XXVIII

## March to Catastrophe - 1791

About sundown in the late afternoon of January 2, 1791, a war party of two dozen Wyandot and Delaware crossed the frozen Muskingum to the east side of the river, about thirty miles above Marietta, and entered the settlement known as Big Bottom. This new station consisted of a blockhouse made of green logs, and two small cabins. The nineteen inhabitants were mostly recent immigrants from the east; they had not even finished the blockhouse, and they had posted no sentries. In one of the cabins four men were just sitting down to supper when they suddenly found themselves surrounded by Indians, and as quickly taken prisoner. In the blockhouse ten men and boys, one woman, and two small children were startled as the door was thrown open, then a volley of shots was fired into their midst. Several of the men went down, killed or mortally wounded; the woman struck one of the warriors in the face with a small hand ax, cutting down to his shoulder before she and her two children were tomahawked. One boy climbed to the roof of the blockhouse, begging for his life, when he was shot down by those outside; his brother, hiding under a pile of bedding, was soon discovered and made prisoner. The sound of gunfire alerted the two men in the third cabin, and they bolted into the darkening woods and into the freezing night. Throwing the bodies in a pile inside the blockhouse and setting it afire the Indians moved out of the settlement with their captives. The floor caught fire, but the green logs of the blockhouse refused to burn, and the relief party that arrived two days later found only blackened walls and badly charred bodies. At the expense of one wounded warrior the Indians had killed twelve and taken five prisoners; more importantly, in only a few minutes they had totally wiped out the settlement known as Big Bottom.

Less than twenty miles north of Fort Washington lay Dunlap's Station, containing a couple dozen residents, plus a thirteen-man federal force under the command of Capt. Jacob Kingsbury. On January 8th a party of four surveyors was attacked on the west side of the Miami; one was killed, another, Abner Hunt, was captured, and the other two escaped. They reached Dunlap's on January 9th, but the garrison there assumed that it had been only a small war party that had struck the surveyors, and no action was taken. At sunrise next morning they found the entire stockade surrounded by Blue Jacket's Shawnee warriors, and Abner Hunt called out for the garrison to surrender. Upon Kingsbury's refusal the siege was begun, with occasional parlays throughout the day, Hunt telling them that he would be killed if the fort refused to capitulate.

About midnight a large fire was kindled within two hundred yards of the stockade. Its purpose was not long in doubt; it was the Indians, playing at their old tricks with fire. Abner Hunt, stripped naked, was dragged forward and spread-eagled so near the fire that the heat scorched his skin. At odd times one of the Indians would stab his knife into an arm or leg and thrust a burning coal into the incision in Hunt's body, the Indians dancing about their victim, but their yelling did not drown out the screams of the man in his agony. Eventually the Indians tired of the game, and they kindled a fire on the bare stomach of the still living man. His screams continued to ring in the ears of the men of the garrison until nearly dawn, when they gradually weakened, then ceased altogether.

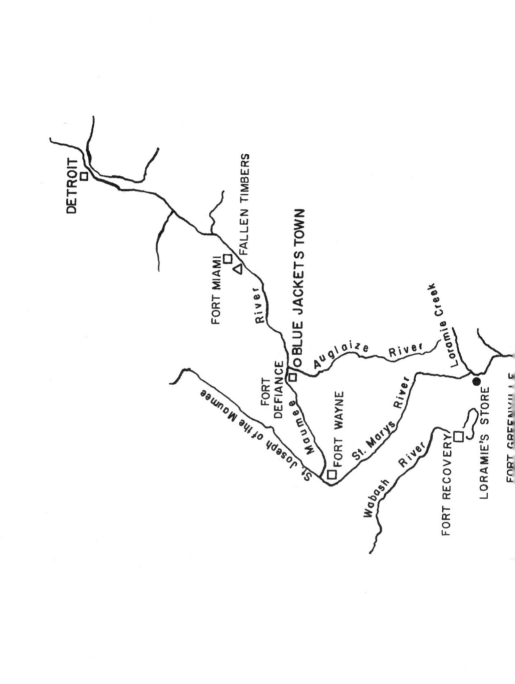

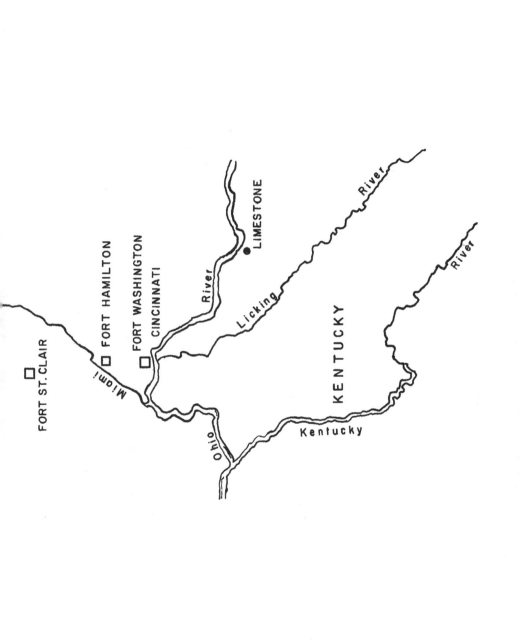

But about ten o'clock that morning, the 11th, the Indians suddenly disappeared, and only a few minutes later a mounted relief party of ninety-six men rode into view from Fort Washington. By chance a hunter had heard the firing coming from Dunlap's Station the day before, and had concluded that they were under attack. His arrival at Fort Washington had resulted in the militia being called out, saving the inhabitants at Dunlap's, but hours too late to save Abner Hunt. The remains of his body were decently buried, and after taking stock of their burned cabins, slaughtered cattle, and destroyed grain, almost all the men decided to abandon the settlement.

It was a matter of tactics outwitting strategy; tactically the two raids had been relatively unimportant, the raid on Dunlap's was actually a failure, but the strategic significance was profound. Before mid-January's Day dawned two settlements in Ohio had been removed from existence as if they had never been. One of those settlements had been only seventeen miles from the largest military post west of the mountains, and if Harmar's defeat had proved to the Indians their invincibility over the American military, so the destruction of Big Bottom and Dunlap's Station proved to them that the American government could never protect its citizens.

The attacks on these two settlements, following Harmar's campaign, finally convinced even the most doubtful skeptics that there could be no westward expansion until the Indian Problem was resolved, and the resolution would not come by treaty. On January 22nd, only eleven days after Abner Hunt had finally gained release from his suffering, Secretary Knox advised Congress that the future of the United States was a matter of considering the cost versus the gain; the solution was pacification of the Wabash Indians, the gain would be the West, and the cost must be borne.

That cost, Knox explained, would entail the establishment of a strongly-fortified post at Kekionga, preceded by a series of smaller supply posts extending from there all the way back to Fort Washington. A year earlier it had been felt to be beyond the capabilities of the government to maintain such a fort at the Maumee, but that was a year ago, and much had happened in that time. Now Knox said that three thousand troops would be mustered. No longer would the United States depend on an armed force of a few dozen men; the army would be expanded to well over two thousand regulars, enlisted non-coms and privates. The balance of the force would be made up of experienced militia and trained rangers.

But developing a plan was not the same as implementing a plan. Money was needed, and money for two thousand full-time soldiers was simply not available. Since the War Department estimated the number of Wabash Indians at about one thousand, plus another thousand allies who could be called upon, a force of three thousand soldiers was deemed sufficient, only a thousand of whom would be regulars. The two thousand additional men needed to fill the role would be six-month recruits, enlisted into the federal service, and subject to officers not elected by the militia. Therefore the military establishment would retain control of the army, but the enlistees could be discharged when their mission had been accomplished.

But talking about soldiers was not the same as obtaining soldiers. Many of the new recruits were men off the streets of cities, or out of prisons, totally unaccustomed to frontier life and even less accustomed to military discipline. In one night alone twenty-five men, led by a sergeant, deserted. St. Clair was so engaged in the logistics of procuring supplies for his army that he did not even return to Fort Washington until September 9th. By that time the first levies, who had arrived on June 14th had already used up nearly half of their six-month time allotment, and still the army was not ready to march. St. Clair had ordered Major Hamtramck, who had arrived from Vincennes in July, to move the advance forces to Ludlow's Station, about five miles north of Cincinnati, if for no other reason than to limit the soldiers' access to liquor, and to begin construction of the first supply post, named Fort Hamilton in honor of the Secretary of the Treasury, another twenty miles further north. But when St. Clair reached the advance units the next day, September 10th, he found that, due to heavy rains, construction of the fort had not even begun. The following day the weather took a decided turn for the worse, the first frost of the season being noted. It was not a particularly good omen.

Other evil omens prevailed, for those who believed in them; only half the Kentucky militia arrived, and when those finally showed up they were heartily jeered by the regulars who had heard the stories of Harmar's militia. The supplies were procured through the contract system, and the materials were incredibly poor; the clothes fell apart in wet weather almost as quickly as the shoes. Knox had decreed that, since the campaign was to be fought in fair fall weather, there was no need to encumber the men with heavy tents, and so only light shelter tents were provided. These had not been properly waterproofed, and the men were soon soaked to the skin in even the lightest rain; even worse, a considerable amount of the gunpowder was ruined by being stored in equally shoddy supply tents. Axes necessary for building the supply posts and for clearing the road were not properly tempered and would not hold an edge. The majority of the horses which had been provided were sickly, underfed animals unfit for military service; the early frosts had killed most of the natural forage, and the horses died by the dozen.

But then the weather improved; from mid-September into October the weather was generally mild, although with intermittent rain, and along with the expectation of a timely advance the spirits of the men improved somewhat. The army began its march from Fort Hamilton on October 4th, but progress was incredibly slow; late in the season though it was, St. Clair insisted that two parallel roads be built, two to three hundred yards apart. The first day the road was advanced less than two miles, the next day only three. On October 12th the men began the construction of the next supply post, Fort Jefferson, five miles south of present Greenville, Ohio. On the 14th the rains began, and when they finally ceased four days later the expedition was as tattered as the inferior clothes the men had been issued. On the 19th St. Clair ordered all excess baggage left behind, so that the remaining horses could be used for provisioning the army of some 2,700 men. Rations were soon cut to a quarter-pound of flour per man per day, and even then the supply ran out, and the horses were sent back for provisions. As was usual with armies of the period, there were a number of camp followers, wives and even children of the soldiers, and they must eat as well.

A few dozen straggling Kentucky militia arrived at the nearly-completed Fort Jefferson on the 22nd, bringing with them a packhorse convoy of flour and a small herd of beeves, but these few new arrivals were not enough to offset the desertions which now seriously threatened the army. Two days later St. Clair left one hundred twenty sickly invalids in charge of the fort and marched his army into the wilderness toward the Miami town. They covered a mere six miles that day; the next day the supplies ran out, and St. Clair ordered the army into temporary bivouac to await the provisions which were expected the next day. Those finally arrived on the 28th, but there was enough only to last the men for four days. On the 29th a few newly-arrived Chickasaw scouts were sent forward on a reconnaissance, and the army set forward once more on the 30th. Word reached the commander that another supply convoy had passed Fort Jefferson, and St. Clair, reasoning that the badly-needed supplies would reach them faster if he halted, stopped after covering seven miles.

Early the next morning he received the alarming news that half of the remaining militia had deserted; they were headed back for that supply train with thoughts of plunder in their heads. Hamtramck was ordered to take the regulars from the First Regiment and pursue the deserters, hopefully saving the supplies as well. But before they could depart it was learned that only about sixty men had left; nearly a third of the militia had originally formed up to march home, but almost all had been persuaded by their officers to remain. Hamtramck was nevertheless sent back to guard the supplies, and the army, now reduced to 1,200 regulars and two hundred fifty Kentucky militia, inexplicably remained in camp on the first of November. On the second they managed to cover eight miles, and the next morning they started out with the ground covered by snow.

Although they were now deep into Indian territory, and in spite of the desertions, St. Clair was still under the delusion that his force would not only outnumber the enemy, but that they were better disciplined. Although a few Indians were seen each day, the officers continued to believe that these were merely random sightings, and the Chickasaw scouts had as yet failed to return with a prisoner. The hostiles were not quite so lax; on October 28th Simon Girty had sent a message to Agent McKee that a battle was imminent. Little Turtle and Blue Jacket had by that time been reinforced by over a thousand warriors from other tribes, and if the American army was slow in coming to them, they would go to meet it.

After covering another six miles in cold weather, across low-lying land, the army came to a ridge where St. Clair ordered a halt for the day. But within minutes scouts came in with a report of a large campground on high land, only two miles ahead, and so it was decided to move on to that area. It was dark by the time the last of the exhausted men made their way into the relocated camp[105], and most were not even aware that they had finally reached the Wabash. They had come about a hundred miles since leaving Fort Washington; it was too dark to erect a defensive perimeter around the camp, even had the men not been too tired. It was still believed that there were no Indians in the vicinity.

It was just another delusion. On the 28th Little Turtle and Blue Jacket had led their thousand warriors-plus, accompanied by Simon Girty, on a leisurely four-day march toward the American army, then encamped about three miles beyond the Wabash, where they waited. When scouts brought in the report of St. Clair's camp-ground, the final arrangements were made. Little Turtle and Blue Jacket would lead their Miami and Shawnee warriors against the center, the Chippewa, Ottawa, and Potawatomi would attack the left, while Girty would advance toward the right with the Wyandot and the few Iroquois. They were all in place before daylight, while St. Clair's men were still asleep.

They were awakened by reveille about a half hour before daylight, then dis-missed to camp, while the outlying sentries, totally oblivious to any enemy pres-ence, were still standing about their campfires when the first shots rang out, and they were quickly overrun by some three hundred painted and screaming warriors. In back of them the entire militia force took to their heels and raced for the shelter of the main camp. Yet only moments after the drum roll sounded throughout camp, bringing officers and men to arms, the wild-eyed and panic-stricken Kentuckians tore through the front line, then through the second, disrupting any attempt at a uni-fied front. Close behind them were the first of the Indian warriors. The pressure on the left quickly became so heavy that Col. Darke ordered a bayonet charge with about three hundred men of the Second Regiment, aided by twenty or so of the cavalry. This maneuver pushed back Girty and his Wyandots several hundred yards, but almost immediately firing was heard from the rear, in the direction from which the men had just come. Hastening back to camp they found that a raiding party had cut their way through to the rear section of the camp; the camp followers, women and children, had been left undefended and had been butchered, some of them cut in two. Some of the warriors had already gained the center of the camp, but in the meantime St. Clair had ordered a detachment of Col. George Gibson's[106] levies to the left, to prevent the entire flank from collapsing. With bayonets fixed the men of Darke's command fought their way through to Gibson's, and the Indians were driven back.

Although the camp was now cleared, the incoming fire still threatened to destroy the army; frightened men who had thrown away their muskets and scurried to camp in the first few minutes of confusion clustered about the center of the camp-ground, so bewildered now that they were incapable of understanding the orders of the officers who tried to reform them. But fewer and fewer officers were available to give orders, as their conspicuous uniforms made them the choice targets for Indian snipers.

The entire camp was now surrounded, and the pressure along the front became so great that the Indians threatened to overrun the men who were still milling in confusion about the center. The army had now disintegrated into a mob, and absolute destruction was only moments away. St. Clair at last ordered a retreat, but the undisciplined men had not the control necessary even to break through the Indian line. Finally cool-headed George Adams, veteran of Harmar's campaign, shouted for some of the men around him to join in clearing a path to the road, just as the warriors finally broke through the line of artillery. Portions of the unarmed militia saw the surge out of the camp and joined in, their sheer numbers aiding in the break-out. One of their last sights was a horde of Indians, busy at their work of slaughtering the last of the women and children; of the entire group of camp followers only three women escaped that day. Of the others, those who were killed were the lucky ones.

Several hundred warriors pursued the headlong flight of the army, but soon the thought of all the plunder lying around the campground lured them back. Nothing else saved the army from total annihilation that day, until several kegs of whiskey were found among the army's stores. When those were opened the escape of the Americans was assured. A band of less than two dozen warriors pursued the fleeing army another four or five miles before giving up, but the panicked men continued their flight all the thirty miles to Fort Jefferson. There they found no relief; there was enough flour there for only one day, and no meat, so the remnant of the army would have to continue on, or starve. With stragglers still coming in St. Clair formed up his exhausted and forlorn soldiers, those who could walk, at ten o'clock that night, November 4th, and marched them through the darkness, over the ice-covered road which he had just built, toward Fort Washington, seventy long and grueling miles away. The first men stumbled into the fort at noon on November 8th, but no provision had been made for a defeated army, and soon the mob, many of them now drunk, were wandering the streets of Cincinnati, in search of food and shelter.

\*     \*     \*

Simon Girty later reported only twenty-one Indians killed, and another forty wounded. Although these numbers were probably low by half, they were as nothing compared to the American loss. When the final count was made it came to six hundred thirty killed; half the men engaged in the battle, however briefly, were dead. What had formerly been considered unthinkable disasters, such as the twenty-one men killed at Foreman's defeat, or even the seventy Kentuckians killed at the Blue Licks only nine years earlier, now paled in comparison. An additional two hundred eighty-three men had been wounded, but survived the battle and the retreat. Altogether, of the thirteen hundred men who had camped on the banks of the Wabash that evening of November 3rd, an unbelievable seventy percent were casualties. It was the worst defeat ever to be suffered by an American army at the hands of Indians. Not even Custer's Last Stand eighty-five years later could come close to equaling it. Catastrophe, indeed.

# Chapter XXIX

## Wayne at the Fallen Timbers

The president was at dinner with guests when the courier arrived; Washington excused himself and listened to the gloomy report, then returned and quietly finished the evening's entertainment. Only until after the last guest had departed could the old warrior contain his rage and frustration. "Here on this very spot I took leave of him," Washington shouted at his private secretary, Tobias Lear. "'Beware of a surprise,' I told him, 'you know how the Indians fight us. Beware of a surprise!' And yet — to suffer that army to be cut to pieces, hacked, butchered, tomahawked by a surprise — the very thing I guarded him against! Oh, God! Oh God, he is worse than a murderer!"

In spite of the nearly seven hundred men killed, the problem was still the same: either concede to the Indians their demands, or solve the problem by military force. But perhaps, after all, one good thing had come from the debacle. The militia system was finished. After those survivors returned to Kentucky with the stories of how they had been starved, how they had suffered from the cold and wet on a near-unbearable march through the wilderness, how they had been issued inferior equipment to fight a dreadful foe, and how the officers had led them to the slaughter without so much as giving them a warning of the presence of the enemy, and once they had returned to Fort Washington how their commanding general had then refused to pay them their wages, telling them it was for their own good, as they would only spend it on whiskey and rum — never again would the militia flock to the army's standard. Washington also used the storm of protest now rising against St. Clair to force Congress into enacting a true military system that would replace the militia. In December he proposed that the United States Army be increased to over *five thousand* men, to serve a term of three years. After a bitter debate in Congress the bill was passed in March, 1792.

The next difficulty was the selection of the man to succeed St. Clair. Washington prepared a list of sixteen names which did not, however, include his personal favorite, his old colleague from Virginia, Henry Lee, Light Horse Harry, noting that Lee could not expect the regular military establishment to serve under a man who had never risen above the rank of colonel. Some of the men on the list were too old, like Lachlin McIntosh. Others were discounted for various reasons: the great leader of the Virginia rifleman, Dan Morgan, was in poor health and he was illiterate; Baron von Steuben was a foreigner; George Scott of Kentucky would have been an able commander, but he was known to be a heavy drinker. In a selection process that in the end came down to choosing the least undesirable, the one name on the list that was finally agreed upon, although not the most impressive, was that of Anthony Wayne.

Although he had secured an admirable record in the Revolution, his problems in civilian life since leaving the army in 1783 had been not only undistinguished, but unsuccessful. Wayne, like U.S. Grant a half century later, had failed at farming and was on the verge of being imprisoned for debt, but also like Grant, he was a true soldier who could demonstrate his abilities only upon the Field of Mars. During the Revolution he had won a reputation as a courageous if sometimes rash fighter, but he was known to be a fine strategist, and perhaps more importantly to the man who would now be in charge of building a strong federal army, he was a stern disciplinarian. In April a commission as major general was issued to the forty-seven year old soldier-farmer-soldier.

In June Wayne reached Pittsburgh, where he began training the first of the recruits which would make up the new United States Army, now known as the Legion of the United States, or, more commonly, the *American Legion*. At the same time attempts were made by Knox to begin peace negotiations, but the St. Clair disaster had, with good reason, given the hostile Indians a sense of invulnerability.

In early April three men were sent out from Fort Washington by Lt. Col. James Wilkinson, bearing a message which invited the chiefs to a council at that post. William May, an enterprising scout from the First Regiment, posing as a deserter, was sent on the trail of the three men. May found their scalped corpses in the woods only hours before he, too, was taken prisoner and carried to Niagra. The next month Major Alexander Trueman was sent to the Miami towns under a flag of truce, bearing a message signed by the President himself, asking for a general council. At the same time Col. John Hardin, of Kentucky and Harmar's Expedition fame, along with a guide, was sent to the Wyandot towns on the Sandusky with a similar message. Like the previous three, none of these five even managed to reach their destinations.

With his servant Will Lynch and an interpreter named Smalley, Trueman, a Revolutionary War veteran and the commander of St. Clair's cavalry, had by the end of May approached to within about fifty miles of the Maumee villages. There he fell in with an Indian hunter and his son who offered to guide the officer, in his resplendent new uniform, the remainder of the distance. The five men traveled north that day, but when evening approached the elder Indian stated that he and his son were leaving, afraid that the white men would overpower them in the night. To show his good will, Trueman offered to tie one of his men to a tree so their numbers would be equal. As soon as Lynch was secured, the Indian, feeling nothing but contempt for such a foolish and weak man, raised his musket and fired point-blank at Trueman. The defenseless Lynch was then calmly tomahawked, and Smalley, who had escaped, was talked into surrendering with the promise that he would not be killed. Col. Hardin and his companion were likewise killed, probably being suspected of spying.

But preparations for war were going on, as well as the failed attempts at peace. Wilkinson, noting that the distance between his outlying posts Fort Hamilton and Fort Jefferson was too great to be covered in one day by a supply convoy, ordered another fort to be built half-way between the two. In March Fort St. Clair[107] was completed, twenty-four miles north of Hamilton and about twenty miles south of Jefferson. The feared Indian attack against the western outposts failed to materialize during 1792 however, in spite of Wilkinson having fewer than 700 privates on the rolls to man his entire six-fort frontier from Cincinnati to Vincennes on the Wabash, at the same time as new recruits were continuing to arrive at Pittsburgh to swell Wayne's American Legion.

In an effort to encourage the Indians to negotiate, Knox ordered all military operations other than purely defensive preparations to cease. On June 11th a war party of about fifty Delaware and Shawnee attacked a party of men out cutting hay near Fort Jefferson; all fifteen men were killed or captured. Four weeks later, on July 7th, a young man named Oliver Spencer was captured on the Ohio; then the Indians seemed to have disappeared for the remainder of the summer. Finally, on September 29th several soldiers were killed, then on November 3rd three more soldiers were captured within sight of Fort Hamilton. The commander sent out a detachment after what was presumed to be nothing more than a small raiding party, but the lieutenant in charge soon brought the men hurrying back with a report of considerable Indian sign.

On November 6th, Wilkinson arrived at Fort Hamilton to take charge of things personally, and he was just in time to hear the latest news personally. Only hours after his arrival three packhorse drivers and a lone militia man staggered into camp with the grim word of the disaster which had occurred at Fort St. Clair two days earlier. In late October Little Turtle had led two hundred Miami and Shawnee warriors southward, reaching Fort Hamilton on November 3rd. From the prisoners they took that day they learned of the supply train that had just gone ahead to Fort Jefferson, and was due to return in a few days. Moving north, Little Turtle considered an ambush for the returning convoy somewhere along the road between Forts St. Clair and Hamilton.

That very evening, however, Indian scouts brought in word that the escort, made up of slightly under one hundred Kentucky militia under Major John Adair, were camped just outside Fort St. Clair, with their horses, over a hundred of them. They were not more than two hundred yards from the walls of the fort, but Little Turtle moved his men into position under darkness of the night of November 5th, and duplicated his feat of the previous November by surrounding the camp on three sides. Just before daylight on November 6th Adair called in the sentries; he was astonished to see a whooping horde of painted Indians following in their footsteps. In only moments the militia had fled in total confusion into the shelter of the nearby darkened woods. Six militia were killed[108] and four were missing, five more were wounded. Bad as that was, the loss of the horses was of a more serious consequence. Of the one hundred-plus animals only twenty-three strays were later rounded up; twenty-six had been killed and ten more severely wounded. All the rest had been captured or driven off, and with winter rapidly moving in, and without horses to carry provisions, the three frontier posts were in danger of starvation or abandonment.

Wayne, meanwhile, had come to the conclusion that a city like Pittsburgh, dirty and filled with too many taverns and too many prostitutes, was no place to train an army. In late November he moved his entire command twenty miles north, to a site named Legionville, and there he continued to instill the necessary order and discipline and to train his recruits in the maneuvers that would enable them to fight an indigenous enemy in a wilderness setting. At the time of the transfer to

Legionville it was anticipated that Wayne would move the army into the war zone, i.e., Fort Washington, as soon as the spring weather of 1793 allowed, and on April 30th Wayne's army embarked on their cruise down the Ohio. By the first week of May most of the army was encamped a mile below Cincinnati, and in order to facilitate operations between the outlying posts he sent Lt. Col. David Strong to build a road connecting the forts, this one to be wide enough for transport wagons. In less than two months the road was finished, extending even six miles beyond Fort Jefferson, and Wayne was set to proceed against the enemy. There was only one obstacle in the way, an insistence by the government on a peace treaty, in spite of the fact that the delegates that had already been sent to the Indians had either been killed or taken captive.

And so the peace negotiations dragged on; three new peace commissioners, distinguished, influential men, had been selected to travel to Detroit via Niagra, where it was expected they would persuade the English to persuade the Indians to accept the 1789 Fort Harmar Treaty Line. England had problems of its own; as of February 1st it was at war with Revolutionary France. The three commissioners were the old war horse of the Revolution, Benjamin Lincoln, along with Timothy Pickering, both from Massachusetts, and Beverly Randolph, of the Virginia Randolphs. But no matter how distinguished and influential these men were in American society, at the Grand Council held at Alex McKee's farm the Indians were so strongly supported by the British, particularly McKee and Simon Girty, that they insisted on a redrawing of the Ohio River boundary, as originally set forth by Sir William Johnson and the Iroquois at Fort Stanwix, nearly a quarter century before. But this could not be, as the United States Government had acquired lands north of the Ohio by both treaty and payment, and had already sold some of those lands to settlers. Finally, in spite of the efforts of Joseph Brant, as the head of the Iroquois delegation, to reach a peaceful settlement, in mid-August the western Indians delivered their final ultimatum: the Ohio River was to be the boundary, and there was the end of the negotiations. The American commissioners quickly packed up and headed for home, and a week later the message was sent to Wayne. "We did not effect a peace."

This was the previously-agreed-upon signal for Wayne to begin offensive operations, while the fine fall weather still held. During June, July and August Wayne had ordered extra troops sent ahead to Fort Jefferson, and provisions for the army for sixty days, more than enough to last through the fall campaign. But because of complaints from the British and the Indians that offensive maneuvers were being undertaken during supposed peace negotiations, Knox was forced to countermand these orders, and Wayne was forced to withdraw nearly two hundred troops from his advanced posts who were considered excessive. Then the army was decimated by attacks of smallpox and influenza, and the auxiliary Kentucky regiment, when it finally arrived, was found to be seriously understrength. Nonetheless Wayne moved his army out of Cincinnati on October 7th and reached Fort Jefferson only six days later, having averaged better than seven miles per day. There he received another shock; the supply of provisions for the campaign was only a fourth of what had been ordered. But that was a moot point since, even had the full amount arrived, there were so few horses and wagons that it could not have been transported.

Wayne had no choice but to halt while provisions and the necessary transport was brought up. But four days later, a few miles north of Fort St. Clair, the supply convoy of twenty wagons, with the teamsters and handlers, and escorted by nearly a hundred infantry under the command of Lt. John Lowry, was suddenly attacked by a band of forty Ottawa under Little Otter. The supply train was strung out in a disorganized column, and in spite of outnumbering the Indians by nearly three to one, when the Ottawa warriors struck only about two dozen soldiers stood with Lt. Lowry to fight, and every single one was killed or captured; the rest of the detachment fled in typical panic. Fifteen men were killed, including Lowry, ten more were taken prisoner, and the entire herd of seventy horses was removed from the wagons and driven off.

If nothing else this one sortie proved to Wayne the logistical difficulty of an overextended supply system; accordingly he went into winter quarters at his encampment six miles north of Fort Jefferson, named Greeneville[109] in honor of Wayne's colleague in the Revolution, Nathaniel Greene. On November 13th now Brigadier General Wilkinson was sent back to Fort Washington with every available horse and over five hundred men as an armed escort. They reached their destination safely and returned to Greeneville on December 2nd, but it was necessary to repeat the journey if the men were to remain at their advanced post until spring. On December 22nd eight hundred packhorses laden with the needed provisions arrived, as well as eight hundred head of cattle.

But there was more to do than sit idly in camp waiting for favorable weather, especially for a man of Wayne's capabilities. Twenty-three miles to the north was the site of St. Clair's defeat, and Wayne was determined to occupy that ground before spring. There were two valid and compelling reasons that he should do so: it would establish a forward supply post from which to begin operations the next spring, but more importantly it would give the Americans a definite psychological advantage over the Indians if they took possession of the ground on which the Indians had won such a decisive victory. Accordingly on December 23rd Wayne, discounting the comforts of an established post, led eight companies of infantry forward; on Christmas Day the men pitched their tents on the skeleton-strewn battlefield. There were so many bones on the field that the men had to shove them out of the way before they could put up their tents. On the following day all the remains were gathered together, including some five hundred skulls, and ceremoniously interred. The small fort which was built here, enclosed by a fifteen foot high stockade, had a feature seldom found on frontier forts — embrasures for three pieces of artillery. Will May, the daring scout who had been sent to find the three peace emissaries dispatched by Wilkinson, had passed through the battlefield during his Indian captivity; the Indians had told him of the eight cannon left hidden nearby, and with May's help three of these were located and installed in the fort, which had been given the title *Fort Recovery* by Wayne himself.

Nor were the Americans the only ones preparing for war; since an attack on Detroit appeared imminent, the British Lieutenant Governor of Canada, John Simcoe, ordered a new defensive installation built along the south bank of the Maumee, to replace the fort which had been dismantled after the treaty of 1783. In April, 1794, Simcoe, determined that the fort should be completed before Wayne began his advance, personally directed the initial construction of the fort, named Fort Miami. It was an obvious act of aggression, this building of a fort on American property[110], but aside from writing scathing letters denouncing the violation of the Paris Treaty, there was little that could be done until Wayne began his advance. This was originally scheduled for April 1st, but the army, however streamlined, was still dependent on the old system of provisioning from private contractors, and those private contractors, safe back at Cincinnati, were more interested in their profits than in the army's advance. Because of the shortage of provisions the advance was postponed to April 15th, then to May 1st, and then it was postponed indefinitely.

In response to the build-up of the American force, the Indians were not only provisioned by the English, but also assured by them that when the Americans approached the Indians and British would fight side-by-side. A council of war was called on June 16th to determine strategy, at which it was determined that all whites present, including Indian Agent McKee's subordinate, Matthew Elliot, as well as a British officer and several traders, all join the ranks of the war party, dressed as Indians, to show their support. It was generally agreed that the Indians would avoid the forts, concentrating instead on disrupting the supply routes which fed Wayne's army. Nearly twelve hundred warriors left the encampment on June 20th, and reached the general rendezvous site on the 23rd, halting there for three days as they waited for the other contingents to come up. After three days word was received that some of the warriors had not yet started, and the Ottawas and other northern tribes, determined to take command of the expedition, insisted that rather than waiting while the Americans developed their strength, the Indians should attack each fort in succession and reduce it by direct assault. Forty Wyandots arrived on June 29th, and they were ready to strike the nearest fort, Fort Recovery, only fifteen miles away.

On that very evening an immense convoy had arrived at Recovery. Major McMahon, with an escort of fifty dragoons, and Captain Hartshorne, with nearly a hundred picked riflemen, led in three hundred sixty packhorses carrying over a thousand kegs of flour. Since there was insufficient space inside the walls of the fort, the escort set up camp about a hundred yards from the walls of the fort. The next morning the drovers began moving their herd back along the road to Greeneville; they had gone less than a mile when those in the fort heard sporadic firing. McMahon rushed toward the sound of the firing with his dragoons, while Hartshorne and the riflemen followed close behind. The Indians had still been in the process of setting up their ambush when the horse herd arrived. Typically unable to resist the prospect of easy trophies, the closest warriors had fired, killing two men and taking three captive. Suddenly the dragoons rushed into the midst of the Indians and were cut to pieces in minutes; the remainder turned and raced back through the ranks of Hartshorne's approaching riflemen.

Inside the fort the commander, Capt. Alexander Gibson, hurriedly sent Lt. Samuel Drake with every man available to reinforce the men caught outside. Drake's men had gone only a few hundred yards when they met the remnants of the soldiers and Indians, all mixed together. Firing only a single volley, Drake's men turned and followed the others back to the safety of the fort. They had suffered a loss of about forty men, and were now completely surrounded by an overwhelming force, obviously intending a protracted siege; to make a bad situation worse, they were short on powder for both the muskets and the cannon. Amazingly, a large body of Indians now charged the fort, dodging from tree stump to tree stump, but unable to close with those in the fort, or to inflict any damage. The firing kept up until darkness fell. At daybreak the next morning, July 1st, after a few shots had been fired on both sides, silence prevailed, and a few hours later a scouting party left the fort to locate the Indians. Soon they reported back that they had seen long columns of warriors — heading north! The Indians were short of ammunition and short of food; many were angered over the foolish springing of the trap by a few before the others were in place. The original plan calling for disruption of strung-out supply convoys along a narrow road was practicable, but the reduction of a fortified position held by artillery was too much for the Indians. On July 2nd, much to the disgust of the English advisors present, the entire Indian army broke up into dissatisfied segments and headed for home.

In mid-July Wayne received notice from the old Kentucky veteran, Brigadier General Charles Scott, that he was on his way with over seven hundred Kentucky Volunteers. On the morning of July 28th Wayne's American Legion, with only five days' provisions and twenty-four rounds of ammunition per man, began the march north to battle. On August 1st the army halted for two days to build another temporary supply station, named Fort Adams in honor of the vice-president, on the banks of the St. Marys. Here they were met on August 3rd by the Second Regiment of Kentucky Volunteers with a substantial supply of provisions, and at dawn the next morning the army was on the move again. Three days and thirty miles later they encamped on a tributary of the Auglaize, only twelve miles from the new Blue Jacket's Town at the confluence of the Auglaize and the Maumee. A number of Indian villages were in the vicinity, and a quick reconnaissance on the 7th conducted by Wayne in person convinced him that the Indians had deserted not only their towns, but their valuable and now-ripening crops; more proof, if more were needed, that the enemy was disorganized and disinclined to fight. The next morning the army moved forward again, and soon it came upon one of the most impressive sights any of the men had seen. All the way to the Maumee, still several miles away, stretched cornfields, on both sides of the river, as far as the eye could see; it was the Indians' *Commissary of the West*, and it had been abandoned to Wayne and his American Legion.

Wayne ordered another major fort built here, and soon fatigue parties were busily erecting the fifteen foot high stockade wall, timbers a minimum twelve inches in diameter, and with a blockhouse at each corner. Wayne aptly named it Fort Defiance. But intelligence was still lacking, because the scouts had as yet been unable to bring in prisoners for interrogation; indeed; the army was amazed at how few Indians had been seen at all. Finally William Wells, Robert McClelland and four other scouts were sent out on August 10th, with a promise of a $100 reward if they could bring in but one warrior. On the 11th they took a Shawnee warrior, but not content with only one, they soon discovered a hunting camp of about fifteen Delaware. Leaving their prisoner with the other four, Wells and McClelland, boldly riding in, engaged them in conversation, but the warriors grew suspicious, and suddenly seizing their muskets fired at the two men. Both were wounded, Wells in the wrist and McClelland in the shoulder, but both escaped and made their way back to the others. On the 12th they returned with the Shawnee, who said that seven hundred warriors were already on the ground, with six hundred more, mostly Wyandot and Ottawa, expected momentarily, and that the English had assured them that they would fight alongside their red brothers. At dawn on the 15th the Legion crossed to the northern shore of the Maumee, on the final leg of their offensive. Behind them smoke filled the air; the Commissary of the West was a ruin, storehouses burned, cornfields destroyed, and then the cattle and horses had been turned loose in the fields to forage.

The Indians were in near-panic, men, women, and children retreating toward the Miami Rapids, the site of Fort Miami. After the Fort Recovery debacle a serious attempt had been made to woo back the disaffected Wyandot and Ottawa, and on the 13th Alexander McKee reported a thousand warriors present at the Miami Rapids. But this did little more than make a bad situation worse, with several thousand starving refugees crowding about the gates of the fort, and no supplies to feed them. McKee, knowing that the Indians were vital to British control of the area, personally assured the chiefs that the British militia from Detroit was on its way, and he hinted that perhaps even British regulars would join them in their destruction of the American army. The Indians were greatly encouraged when the schooner *Chippewa* sailed up to the gates of Fort Miami and dislodged Major William Campbell and two companies of infantry from the Twenty-Fourth Regiment, along with a fresh supply of gunpowder and a hundred barrels of provisions for the Indians.

Suddenly on August 14th Christopher Miller rode into the Indian camp with the Shawnee prisoner, and delivered Wayne's offer for a negotiated settlement. A grand council was called; Little Turtle, doubting the sincerity of McKee, Elliott, and Girty, with their promises of British military aid, and knowing only too well that his warriors were badly outnumbered by an army commanded by a "chief who never sleeps", urged that a delegation of chiefs meet with Wayne. The other moderate chiefs also urged negotiation, but this ran directly counter to the defiant war spirit of the others. Declaring for war they sent a message to Wayne, telling him to remain where he was, and in a few days they would send representatives from all the tribes to meet him.

Miller returned to camp with this message on the 15th, but also with the warning that the Indians were preparing for battle; on the 17th the army moved ahead, and on the 18th arrived at Roche de Bout, just south of Fort Miami on the Maumee. Bad news awaited Wayne there, however. His detachment of scouts, some miles ahead of the column, had ridden into an ambush and been scattered; even worse, William May, the intrepid scout, had been captured by the Indians, and his fate was certain. Already crippled by the loss of Wells and McClelland, this further weakened the army's intelligence system. It was also the first serious indication of the Indians' willingness to fight, and accordingly Wayne directed that a fortified camp be established. All excess baggage would be left here, to enable the army to move forward into battle unhindered. August 19th was devoted to the building of this station, known as Camp Deposit, and that afternoon Major Price's battalion of mounted Kentuckians scouted to within two miles of the British fort, withdrawing after observing a large number of warriors arrayed in line of battle. As soon as there was sufficient light the next morning, the fateful August 20th, Wayne's American Legion would move forward.

The Indians were ready and waiting. When Will May had been brought into camp on the 18th he had been interrogated; from him the British and Indians had learned that Wayne would advance on either the 19th or 20th, depending on how long the army spent building their supply repository. Early the next morning May was stripped, tied to a large oak tree near the fort and, after a mark had been made on his chest, the Indians competed to see who could shoot closest to the mark.

McKee's influence had caused the leadership of the Indian force to be passed from Little Turtle to Blue Jacket, war chief of the Shawnee, and Blue Jacket was not the strategist that the Miami chieftain was. Although he was a courageous warrior and of commanding presence, Blue Jacket was also noted for his arrogance as well as his intemperance. Some thirteen hundred warriors were under his command and about seventy Canadian militia, painted and dressed as Indians were also on the field, while McKee, Elliott, and Girty would serve as observers. Since Wayne was advancing up the Maumee toward Fort Miami, the Indians ensconced themselves along the river about five miles south of the fort, in an area of heavy undergrowth and fallen trees which had been produced by a tornado some years before. This "fallen timbers" extended nearly a mile, from the Maumee on the northeast to Sugar Creek on the southwest, and it varied from two hundred to four hundred yards in depth. Impenetrable to horsemen, the army would have to push its way on foot through this natural abatis in order to approach the warriors. Here the Indians waited, throughout the 18th and 19th and into the 20th. As was their usual custom they had fasted, in order that there would be no food in their bodies; in case they were shot in the stomach the chance of recovery would be improved.

The appointed hour for the Legion's advance was five o'clock on the morning of the 20th, but an intermittent rain delayed the start until seven. Then the army moved out and advanced rapidly, unhampered by excess baggage, carrying only a single blanket with two days' provisions, and their muskets and ammunition. Two privates of Price's one hundred fifty man Kentucky Battalion, Sherman Moore and William Steele, had volunteered to lead the advance into the trees. A quarter-mile behind Price were Cook's two companies, about seventy men, and behind them the Legionnaires advanced in supporting columns, ready to move to whichever portion of the field they were needed. Amongst the timber the high underbrush limited visibility; Price's two Kentuckians had advanced only a hundred yards into the thicket when suddenly a roar of musket fire erupted from the timber, and both Moore and Steele fell. Price's men turned to the left, angling away from the ambush, but were immediately hit by another volley, this time at almost point-blank range, and the men scattered. Behind them the Indians poured from their ambush, while Cook's front guard delivered a volley at Price's Kentuckians, now streaming back toward them, then turned and fled. Then the attack stalled.

By dawn of the 20th many of the Indians were entering their third day of fasting; the rain seemed to indicate that Wayne's army would not advance that day, and about half the warriors had left the ambush site and returned to Fort Miami. Even when the gunfire erupted, it lasted so briefly that those Indians believed it was only a minor skirmish, and remained about the fort. The vanguard of Wayne's army had walked into the very center of the ambush, as expected, and the Ottawa and Pottawatomi who held that position, the same warriors who had mismanaged the Fort Recovery attack, had rushed out of the protection of the downed timber, some armed only with their tomahawks and scalping knives, and now they came face-to-face with the Legionnaires in an open field. Here they halted, only about five hundred warriors total, to test the Americans' new line. Since the other Indians had remained in proper alignment, these advanced warriors were now badly out of position.

Lieutenant William Henry Harrison, Wayne's aide-de-camp and future president, asked for orders, and he received them bluntly: "Charge the damned rascals with the bayonet!" Wayne roared. Immediately a small group of dragoons under Captain Campbell charged, but too soon; they were unsupported and they were cut down. Wilkinson's men were coming up behind them, however, and when the outnumbered Ottawa saw this line approaching, they turned and ran, so precipitately in fact that Wilkinson feared that it was the typical Indian tactic of decoy and second ambush. On the left Hamtramck's two sublegions engaged the Wyandot and Delaware, who were closely supported by the Canadian militia. Although the fighting here was intense for a few minutes, Todd's dismounted Kentucky militia soon came up and moved into position on the Indians' flank, causing the entire wing to collapse. On the right Wilkinson's men moved ahead, practically unresisted, pushing the Indians at the point of the bayonet. Many of the warriors tried to swim the Maumee but were shot down in mid-stream by the Kentucky riflemen. One "Indian", found hiding along the riverbank, was taken captive, but he was immediately discovered to be a white man dressed as an Indian, a French trader named Antoinne Lasselle.

The assault suddenly halted, as Wayne's legionnaires poured out onto an open field on the high ground and saw the remnants of the Indian army fleeing ahead of them. And there, across a wide ravine, the high ground continued, running along a ridge, atop which the Americans also saw the British Fort Miami. The Indians were massed about the fort, clamoring for admittance, but to their total amazement and utter frustration the fort's gates remained tightly closed. When the commander, Major William Campbell, had seen streams of Indians retreating northward from out of the woods he had the chevaux de frise placed about the fort and the gates were barred. Now completely demoralized the warriors continued on for another mile, to the villages where the women and children were camped. Only a few minutes later, at 11:05, Wayne had the recall sounded; the battle of Fallen Timbers had lasted only a few minutes more than an hour. Some of the officers could still scarcely believe that it was over, some of them thought it little more than a skirmish, not worthy of being termed a battle. Altogether only about forty Indians had been killed, while the Legion had lost thirty-three men, all but two of whom were regulars, and a hundred more had been wounded.

Although they sent several messages back and forth, demanding and refusing surrender, both Wayne and Campbell knew that any act of belligerence on their part would initiate an international war. After destroying all the property in the vicinity, Wayne paraded his men in full sight of the fort on the morning of the 23rd, and then withdrew. The army, now beginning to run short of provisions, reached Fort Defiance on the 27th, and from there moved westward to the Miami villages on the Maumee, where another fort was established; this had been the principal objective of St. Clair, and finally, three years late, it was completed on October 22, 1794. This one was named by its commander, Major Hamtramck, in honor of the commanding general, Fort Wayne.

Governor Simcoe arrived at Fort Miami on September 27th and, in an effort to rally the discouraged Indians, called for a grand conference to be held at the Wyandot village known as Brownstown, near the mouth of the Detroit River, which was to begin on October 11th. But Joseph Brant, belatedly appearing, took command of the conference, and demanded a definite commitment from Simcoe for British support in attacking one of the American posts; since Simcoe could not possibly comply, Brant called an end to the conference on October 14th.

At Fort Wayne a message had been received in late September from the Wyandots on the Sandusky River, asking Wayne for terms of peace. Wayne replied that the conditions which had been agreed upon at the 1789 Fort Harmar Treaty must be observed. Two weeks later Antoine Lasselle's brother Francois showed up with three American prisoners, to exchange for his brother. He also brought word that Blue Jacket, feared war chief of the Shawnee, was interested in peace. Wayne allowed Antoine to return to Detroit, taking with him word that peace was desired, and that only the English stood in the way. On November 15th Lasselle left Detroit with a sizeable contingent of Indian leaders and, picking up scattered delegations along the way, arrived at Fort Wayne in mid-January, 1795. The first of a series of preliminary peace negotiations began on January 19th, with Wayne announcing that a general council would be held at Fort Greeneville, commencing on June 15th. When Blue Jacket, accompanied by about fifty Shawnee and Delaware, arrived at Fort Defiance on January 29th, the British stranglehold over the Indians was at last broken.

# Chapter XXX

## The Greeneville Treaty, 1795

So then, the British army had been defeated by the Americans, and in 1783 there was a general peace between the English and the Americans. Now the Indians had been defeated by the Americans, so there was to be a general peace between the white man and the red man, who would live together as brothers, so the Indians said. But one thing was not forgotten, nor forgiven. It had not been the British army that had raided wilderness cabins in Kentucky and butchered women and children; it had not been Lobsterbacks who had driven tomahawks into the heads of wounded soldiers at St. Clair's Defeat, until their arms were weary; it was not English redcoats who had howled with delight as their captives at the stake suffered hideous agonies with fire. The Indians had chosen the English as their allies, and the Americans had defeated them and the English had deserted them. The Indian chiefs now assured Wayne that they were ready to bury the hatchet and build a peace that would last forever, but they were only deluding themselves.

For an entire peoples' lifetime the frontier had been a place in which one lived in dread of the Indian war whoop, the Indian ambush, and the Indian torture stake. Forty years earlier the Indians had played the French against the English, then chosen the side of the French, and the French had lost. Twenty years later they had played the English against the Americans, then chosen the side of the English, and the English had lost. But the situation had changed while they were deliberating; now it was not a matter of choosing the side of the Americans. They were no longer allies of any nation, now they were a defeated and a despised enemy. The Americans had become embittered toward them through year after grim year of brutal war, and now the Indian nations represented no more than an obstacle to the westward progress of civilization.

The grand council at Greeneville was set to open on June 15th, but by that date only a few Indians had assembled; a party of Delaware came in on the 21st, and Little Turtle arrived with his Miami on the 23rd. Still the Shawnee had not appeared by July 12th, when a large party of Wyandot came in, whereupon Wayne told the assembled nations that they could now set the date for preliminary talks, the 15th being agreed upon. Wayne delivered the terms of peace, describing the new boundary that was required, based on the Fort Harmar/Fort McIntosh treaty line, and gave the Indians three days to deliberate. The new line, designated as the Greeneville Treaty Line, followed the Cuyahoga River south, then to the Tuscarawas; turning west-southwest it ran in a straight line to Fort Recovery on the Wabash, thence southward to the mouth of the Kentucky River on the Ohio.

To this most of the Indian nations acquiesced, the notable holdout being Little Turtle and the Miami; his position was the same old time-worn argument, that since the Miami had not attended those treaties the Americans had no claim to lands which other Indians had granted the Americans. On the 23rd Wayne quashed this assertion by stating that at least six other Indian tribes, besides the Miami, had claims to this land, that the Miami had refused to come to earlier treaties to negotiate because they had chosen the English over the Americans, and the English had been defeated.

But even before the Battle of Fallen Timbers John Jay had traveled to London to meet secretly with the British government; the English being immensely relieved to find that Jay wished to discuss a peaceful resolution of the problems. They had secretly feared, indeed they had been almost certain, that the Americans were about to join their old ally, the French, in the war against England, and at the moment things were not going well for British forces on the continent. Even before Jay's arrival the British ministers had decided to evacuate the disputed posts, exclusive of Detroit. Jay's treaty had been ratified by the Senate on June 24, 1795, and Wayne read to the gathered Indians the significant portions of the Treaty of Paris and Jay's Treaty which dealt with those lands. He concluded by stating that the Indians had already been paid twice for this land, at the time of the two previous treaties, but now the United States would pay for it a third time.

Wayne then called for a voice vote to ratify the articles of the treaty, and one by one the Indian nations were called and, with all hope of British support now having evaporated like mist, one by one they voted in favor of the terms, unanimously, even the Miami. While the treaty was being written out for the formal signatures, a feast and celebration was held until, on August 3rd, each chief made his mark in the designated place. Conspicuous by its absence, however, was the name of Little Turtle; one of the village chiefs, Jean Baptiste Richardville, signed for the Miami. Tarhe, the great Wyandot chief, then gave the concluding speech for the Indian confederation, and the presents and annuities were distributed. Finally, on August 12th, at a private conference with Wayne, Little Turtle agreed to the treaty, and his name was added to complete the list of names.

*    *    *

But this was a treaty unlike the treaties of the past, wherein some tribes had signed away lands while others refused even to attend the negotiations. By the Treaty of Greeneville, fully accredited representatives of all twelve major Indian nations of the northwest had finally accepted the fact that the war had been lost, irretrievably lost, and the only alternative to emigration across the Mississippi was peaceful submission to the victorious Americans. Of course there would still be the isolated raids by the few disaffected Indians who would never give up, but one of the articles of the treaty agreed upon was that any contemplated instances of hostility were required to be immediately reported to the nearest post commander.

Now the immigration into the west was unstoppable; in 1795 more than ten thousand new settlers arrived in Kentucky, in one month alone, as Kentucky's population neared 200,000. Kentucky had already entered the Union in 1792 as the fifteenth state, and then in 1796 Tennessee became the sixteenth; in fewer than ten years Ohio would become the seventeenth. On July 11th, 1796, with drums rolling and flags flapping in the breeze, the United States garrisons took formal possession of Detroit.

But of all the aspects of the Greeneville Treaty, the one most important to the thousands of pioneers in the west was that the threat of Indian attack upon their isolated cabins had now been lifted. The specter of that horrible fate, which had loomed over them for two score years, like all phantoms eventually, had faded away into nothingness. The Border Wars were over.

### Final Interlude
### A Last Sadness: the Murder of the Tush Family
### September 6, 1794

But all was not peace and quiet on the frontier, not yet. The battle at the Fallen Timbers was not just a battle lost for the Indians. They had lost the war, the Border Wars of the Upper Ohio were indeed over, finally, but no one knew it, not yet. Not the settlers in their isolated cabins scattered throughout the wilderness, least of all the Indians themselves. True, they had lost a battle, but they had lost battles before; some of those warriors who had gone with Little Turtle to face Wayne in the fallen timbers, and lost, were the same warriors who had faced Andrew Lewis, twenty years before and 250 miles to the south, at Point Pleasant, in 1774. Then they had been led by the great Shawnee, Cornstalk, and they had lost that day too, but the war had continued, continued for their entire lifetimes. Their chiefs would have to go to Greenville the next year to make peace, but that was next year, and now it was September. It was still prime time for raiding parties to cross the Ohio in search of plunder, scalps, trophies, and prisoners for torture.

George Tush lived on Wheeling Creek, not far distant from the Wetzel property, with his wife and six children, at least four of whom were young girls; in order of age the daughters were Polly, Nancy, Susan, and the infant, Mary, still in her crib just outside the door, where it was cooler than in the cabin on this late afternoon of September 6, 1794. A seventh child was on the way when, anticipating no danger, George Tush went outside to feed the hogs. Resting his arms on the rails of the pig pen, a sudden volley of shots was fired at him by Indians in ambush; one of the balls struck him in the chest but somehow did not seriously disable him. Quickly he grabbed up Susan, who was also in the yard with the two older girls, and ran into the house, Polly and Nancy close behind. Only when he reached up to take down his rifle from its hook did Tush realize that the ball which had struck him in the chest had done little damage only because it had first passed through his arm, breaking it. Unable to defend himself or his family, he again ran outside and, distracted, abandoned his family to its fate. Running at full speed he eventually reached the Wetzel cabin. The Indians, now unopposed, entered the cabin and began their slaughter. The baby, Mary, was snatched from her crib and swung by her heels against a tree, then thrown to the ground. Polly, Nancy, and Susan were tomahawked, scalped, and mutilated, as were the other two children. This was not murder for profit; the British were no longer paying a bounty on scalps. These small children were killed for revenge, because they were white.

The next day, the 7th, George Tush returned to his cabin, accompanied by Martin and Jacob Wetzel, their cousin, Lewis Bonnett, Jr., Moses Shepherd, and two other men. They expected to find no one alive, but were amazed to discover that the baby, Mary, had not been killed; sometime after the Indians had left she had revived and had crawled back into the cabin, where she was found lying asleep with her head on her sister Susan's breast. Nor was that all; Susan herself, though scalped and suffering a terrible wound, was still breathing. The other bodies had been horribly mutilated by the Indians, but ravaged even worse by the hogs. There was no sign of Mrs. Tush, and it was assumed that she had been taken prisoner. Unfortunately for her, she had. There was little else for the men to do except bury the dead, and Martin Wetzel must surely have been reminded of that day, nearly twenty years earlier, when he had returned to the Narrows to help bury the dead of the Foreman Massacre. There were fewer of them on this day, but Wetzel was now a father, and he was helping to bury little children who had been killed and mutilated by Indians.

Little Susan survived her wound throughout the winter, but in March of 1795 she succumbed at last, and was buried beside her sisters. Mrs. Tush had been in an advanced stage of pregnancy, expecting their next child, and was unable to travel rapidly. After putting some distance between themselves and any possible pursuit the Indians tomahawked and scalped her, after they had finished with her. Two years later her remains were found, on a branch of Wheeling Creek nine miles distant. Like Susan the spring before, she was buried with the other members of her butchered family.

# *Afterword:*
## *And Life Goes On*

Little Mary Tush had not been killed; she not only survived, but when she grew up she fell in love with a young man named George Goodrich, the first-born son of Nathan and Susan Goodrich. After they were married and the western Virginia frontier was fading, the Goodrich family decided it was time to move further west. George, with his wife Mary and his father and mother, moved to Indiana, not quite as far west, but shy by only about twenty-five miles, of the location where Jacob Wetzel had moved his family just a year or two before.

And that was good because, although not often, it was still possible for the two families to visit occasionally, Jacob and Ruhama Wetzel, and Nathan and Susan Goodrich, with their son George and his wife, Mary. Mary Tush, the baby girl who had been swung by her heels against a tree by the Indians and left for dead, had survived to become the daughter-in-law of Susannah Wetzel Goodrich, younger sister of the mighty Wetzel brothers.

# END

GRAVE OF SIMON KENTON—Drawn by Henry Howe in 1846.

Simon Kenton's original grave site, Zanesfield, OH
Kenton's original grave at Zanesfield, Ohio, as drawn by Henry
Howe in 1846, for Howe's Historical Collections of Ohio.

# The
# Final
# Resting Places

The Blue Licks Marker, Blue Lick Springs, KY

Samuel Brady, West Liberty, WV

Daniel Boone, Frankfort, KY

The Foreman Marker, Moundsville, WV

Simon Kenton, Original Marker, Urbana, OH

Simon Kenton, Urbana, OH

Samuel McColloch, Van Meter's Fort site, Ohio County, WV

Tarhe, Wyandot County, OH

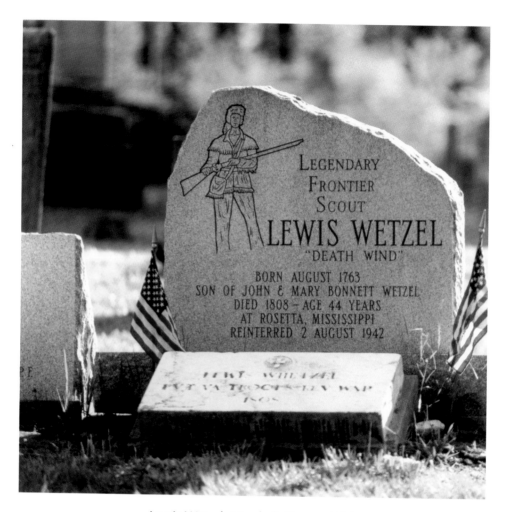

Lewis Wetzel, Marshall County, WV

Ebenezer Zane and Jonathan Zane, Martins Ferry, OH

Elizabeth (Betty) Zane McLaughlin Clark, Martins Ferry, OH

Elizabeth (Betty) Zane Memorial, Walnut Grove Cemetery, Martins Ferry, OH

City Cemetery, Wilkes-Barre, PA
(Within the area shown here is the unmarked grave
of Capt. John Combs, of Sullivan's 1779 Campaign).

Isaac Zane and Myeerah Marker, Zanesfield, OH

Crawford Monument, Wyandot County, OH

*A Sketchbook of...*

# The Border Wars

# of the Upper Ohio Valley:

# 1769-1794

*Conflicts and Resolutions*

# Appendices

# contents:

# Appendix A:
## *A Wetzel Genealogy*

In 1939 C.B. Allman, a descendant of Capt. John Wetzel, published his *Life and Times of Lewis Wetzel*, later reprinted as *Lewis Wetzel, Indian Fighter*. In the *Introduction* to this book Allman provided considerable genealogical material on the family; the following paragraph is a general summary of that information concerning the ancestry of Lewis Wetzel:

> In 1747 the *Palatine Imported* left England for North America carrying 300 emigrants, among whom were two teenage boys, Martin and John Wetzel, accompanied by their mother and stepfather. The mother died during the crossing, however, and upon their arrival in Philadelphia the two boys were indentured to pay their passage, and the stepfather disappeared from history. About 1754, upon completion of their servitude, both young men moved northwest to Berks County, Pennsylvania; within a year John had met and married Mary Bonnet, the daughter of Huguenot emigrants from France. Soon after they moved to Rockingham County, Virginia, where their first child, a son named Martin, was born in 1757. In 1759 a daughter, Christiana, was born, and George, the second son, appeared on the scene two years later. It was at about this time that John moved his family back to Pennsylvania, but a little further west, settling in Lancaster County about 1762. In August of 1763 the third son, Lewis Wetzel, was born, followed by Jacob in 1765 and Susannah in 1767. After the opening up of the western Virginia lands John moved his family to the Monongahela country (in the vicinity of Redstone Old Fort, Catfish Camp, or Dunkard Creek) sometime about 1769. From there he selected a homestead on Wheeling Creek, 14 miles from its mouth on the Ohio, and in 1770 moved his family to that site, just before or just after the birth of their seventh and last child, the fifth of the Wetzel boys, John, Jr.

Allman also listed a Hans Martin Wetzel as coming to America in 1731, but stated that he did not know his relation to the noted Indian fighter of western Virginia, Lewis Wetzel. However, later research has shown that it was this man, Martin Wetzel, who was the grandfather of Lewis Wetzel. The parents of Capt. John Wetzel, Sr., the father of Lewis Wetzel, were Hans Martin Wetzel, Sr. (1700-1760) and Maria Barbara Wetzel (1698-?). They arrived in Philadelphia on September 21, 1731, aboard the *Britannia*, from Rotterdam, by way of Cowes, England. With them were their three children, Hans Martin, Jr. (1725), Nicholaus (1727), and Katherina (1728). The Wetzels had come with a company of 269 Germans led by a Lutheran Pastor named Rieger. The Wetzel family eventually settled on a farm adjoining that of John Jacob and Anna Maria (Dereux) Bonnett, in Frederick Co., Maryland, where they lived from

1741 to 1752. In that year the two families, together, moved to adjacent farms about fifteen miles southwest of Winchester, Shenandoah County, Virginia. Here Hans Martin, Sr., died in August, 1760, and his will is recorded in Winchester, Virginia.

The children of Hans Martin and Maria Wetzel were:
Hans Martin, Jr. (1725), m. – Bartolet; ten children.
Nicholaus (1727).
Katherina (1728), never married[111].
Henry (1731), m. Catherine -; 7 children.
John (1733-1786) m. Mary Bonnett (1735-1805)
[the parents of Lewis Wetzel].

Contrary to long-held belief, John Wetzel, Lewis father, was a native American citizen born in North America, as was his older brother Henry, and not a German, Dutchman, or Swiss, as has formerly been stated. In 1760, upon the death of the elder Wetzel, Henry inherited the Wetzel property, being the oldest son then living at home.

John Jacob [Jean Jacques] Bonnett (1701) and his wife Anna Maria Bonnett (1701) were French Huguenots who arrived at Philadelphia on August 27, 1733, aboard the *Elizabeth*, with their children Margaret Catherine (1725; m. John Syckes, or *Sickes*) and John Simon (1731; m. Mary Bickley). Two other daughters, Christiana and Susanna, born in France, had died aboard ship during the voyage. The three Bonnett children born in North America were Mary[112] (1735; m. John Wetzel), Lewis, Sr. (1737; m. Elizabeth Waggoner), and Samuel (ca. 1740; m. Mary Elizabeth -).

# Appendix B:
## *A Zane Chronology*

| | |
|---|---|
| 1673 | Robert Zane, of Denmark, emigrates to Salem, New Jersey, via Dublin, Ireland. |
| 1675 | Robert's first son, Nathaniel, born in Salem. |
| 1677 | Robert moves to Philadelphia. |
| 1679 | Marries Alice Alday. |
| *ca.* 1685 | Marries Elizabeth Willis. |
| 1694 | Dies in Philadelphia leaving wife Elizabeth, and seven children all under 20 years of age. |
| 1697 | Nathaniel Zane marries Grace Rakestraw, of Philadelphia. |
| 1712 | Nathaniel's son William born in Philadelphia. |
| *ca.* 1740 | William Zane moves to the South Branch[113] of the Potomac River. |
| 1745-53 | William's sons Silas (1745), Ebenezer (1747), Jonathan (1749), Andrew (l751), and Isaac (1753) are born on the South Branch. |
| 1762 | Indian raid on the Zane home; William and his five sons are taken captive. [William 50; Silas 17; Ebenezer 15; Jonathan 13; Andrew 11; Isaac 9]. |
| *ca.* 1763-64 | William and the four oldest sons (all but Isaac) are ransomed in Detroit and return to the South Branch. Isaac remains a captive. |
| 1766 | William Zane's only daughter Elizabeth (Betsy, or Betty Zane) is born. |
| *ca.* 1768 | Ebenezer Zane marries Elizabeth McColloch. |
| 1769 | Silas (24), Ebenezer (22), and Jonathan (20) explore west to Wheeling Creek. |
| 1770 | Ebenezer Zane begins his settlement on Wheeling Creek. |
| 1772 | Isaac Zane escapes from the Indians, but is recaptured; some time thereafter he marries Myeerah, daughter of the Wyandot chief Tarhe, the Crane. |
| 1777 | William Zane visits Wheeling, probably after the death of his wife; after sending Betty to live with an aunt in Philadelphia, he resides at Wheeling for some time. |
| 1777 | First Siege of Fort Henry, September 1st. Ebenezer Zane builds his blockhouse. |
| *ca.* 1780 | Andrew, about thirty years of age, is killed by Indians. |
| *ca.* 1781 | William Zane marries for the second time. He and his new wife, along with Betty, move to Wheeling Creek. |
| 1781 | Indian attack on Fort Henry, September 3rd. |
| *ca.* 1782 | William dies at age seventy, probably at Wheeling. |
| 1782 | Second Siege of Fort Henry, September 11th-13th. |
| 1785 | Silas, forty years old, is killed by Indians on the Scioto River in Ohio. |
| 1798 | Ebenezer tears down the blockhouse and builds his stone mansion. |
| 1812 | Ebenezer dies at Wheeling on November 9th. |
| 1814 | In January Elizabeth McColloch Zane dies at Wheeling. |

| | |
|---|---|
| 1816 | Isaac and Myeerah die at present Zanesfield, Ohio. |
| 1824 | Jonathan Zane dies at Wheeling. |
| 1828 | Elizabeth (Betty) Zane McLaughlin Clark dies at Martins Ferry, Ohio. |
| 1860 | Daniel, thirteenth and last child of Ebenezer and Elizabeth Zane, dies at Wheeling. |

# Appendix C:
## *On the Causes of Dunmore's War;*
## *the Sappington Narrative, Clark's Letter,*
## *the Caldwell Affidavit, & the Zane Letter*

The following four narratives give the clearest and most accurate picture of those events which immediately preceded Lord Dunmore's War, and which may be said to be the precipitating factors for that conflict, the first major conflict between the white and red men in ten years, since the conclusion of Pontiac's Rebellion. These two letters, a narrative, and an affidavit were written by four of the men who were there at the time and who were actively involved in the various incidents. One of them, John Sappington, was the man who fired the first shot which signaled the beginning of the massacre of Logan's family at Yellow Creek on that fateful April day in 1774.

George Rogers Clark was one of the members of Captain Cresap's party, and Cresap was living at the Wheeling residence of John Caldwell at the time of the Yellow Creek massacre. Cresap returned to Wheeling shortly after the killing of the Indians at Pipe Creek, and at that time he surely discussed with Caldwell what had transpired. Col. Zane was the founder of Wheeling, and was well acquainted with the events which occurred in that vicinity.

The original purpose of each of these documents, written a quarter century after the death of Michael Cresap, was to absolve him of the blame of instigating the murder of Logan's family at Baker's Bottom, a crime which he had been accused of in Logan's famous Lament. The documents below speak for themselves.

### I - The Sappington Narrative

*I, John Sappington, declare myself to be intimately acquainted with all the circumstances respecting the destruction of Logan's family, and do give in the following narrative, a true statement of that affair.*

*Logan's family (if it was his family) was not killed by Cresap, nor with his knowledge, nor by his consent, but by the Greathouses and their associates. They were killed 30 miles above Wheeling, near the mouth of Yellow creek. Logan's camp was on one side of the river Ohio, and the house where the murder was committed opposite to it on the other side. They had encamped there only four or five days, and during that time had lived peaceably and neighborly with the whites on the opposite side, until the very day the affair happened. A little before the period alluded to, letters had been received by the inhabitants from a man of great influence in that country, and who was then, I believe, at Captina, informing them that war was at hand,*

*and desiring them to be on their guard. In consequence of those letters and other rumors of the same import, almost all the inhabitants fled for safety into the settlements. It was at the house of one Baker the murder was committed. Baker was a man who sold rum, and the Indians had made frequent visits at his house, induced probably by their fondness for that liquor. He had been particularly desired by Cresap to remove and take away his rum, and he was actually preparing to move at the time of the murder. The evening before a squaw came over to Baker's house, and by her crying seemed to be in great distress. The cause of her uneasiness being asked, she refused to tell; but getting Baker's wife alone, she told her, that the Indians were going to kill her and all her family the next day, that she loved her, did not wish her to be killed, and therefore told her what was intended, that she might save herself. In consequence of this information Baker got a number of men to the amount of twenty-one to come to his house, and they were all there before morning. A council was held and it was determined that the men should lie concealed in a back apartment; that if the Indians did come and behave themselves peaceably, they should not be molested; but if not, the men were to show themselves and act accordingly. Early in the morning seven Indians, four men and three squaws, came over. Logan's brother was one of them. They immediately got rum, and all, except Logan's brother, became much intoxicated. At this time all the men were concealed, except the man of the house, Baker, and two others who staid [sic] out with him. These Indians came unarmed. After some time Logan's brother took down a coat and hat belonging to Baker's brother-in-law, who lived with him, and put them on, and setting his arms akimbo began to strut about, till at length coming up to one of the men, he attempted to strike him, saying "white man, son of a bitch". The white man, whom he treated thus, kept out of his way for some time; but growing irritated he jumped to his gun, and shot the Indian as he was making to the door with the coat and hat on him. The men who lay concealed then rushed out, and killed the whole of them, excepting one child which I believe is alive yet. But before this happened, one canoe with two, another with 5 Indians, all naked, painted and armed completely for war, were discovered to start from the shore on which Logan's camp was.*

*Had it not been for this circumstance, the white men would not have acted as they did; but this confirmed what the squaw had told before. The white men, having killed as aforesaid the Indians in the house, ranged themselves along the bank of the river, to receive the canoes. The canoe with two Indians came near, being the foremost. Our men fired upon them and killed them both. The other canoe then went back. After this two other canoes started, the one contained eleven, the other seven Indians, painted and armed as the first. They attempted to land below our men; but were fired upon, had one killed, and retreated, at the same time firing back. To the best of my recollection there were three of the Greathouses engaged in this business. This is a true representation of the affair from beginning to end. I was intimately acquainted with Cresap, and know he had no hand in that transaction. He told me himself afterwards at Redstone Old Fort, that the day before*

Logan's people were killed, he, with a small party, had an engagement with a party of Indians on Capteener, about 44 miles lower down. Logan's people were killed at the mouth of Yellow creek on the 24th of May, 1774, and on the 23rd, the day before, Cresap was engaged as already stated. I know likewise that he was generally blamed for it, and believed by all who were not acquainted with circumstances, to have been the perpetrator of it. I knew that he despised and hated the Greathouses ever afterwards on account of it. I was intimately acquainted with General Gibson, and served under him during the late war, and I have a discharge from him now lying in the land office at Richmond, to which I refer any person for my character, who might be disposed to scruple my veracity. I was likewise at the treaty held by Lord Dunmore with the Indians at Chelicothe. As for the speech said to have been delivered by Logan on that occasion, it might have been, or might not, for anything I know, as I never heard of it till long afterwards. I do not believe that Logan had any relations killed, except one brother. Neither of the squaws who were killed was his wife. Two of them were old women, and the third, with her child which was saved, I have the best reason in the world to believe was the wife and child of General Gibson. I know he educated the child, and took care of it, as if it had been his own. Whether Logan had a wife or not I can't say; but it is probable that as he was a chief, he considered them all as his people. All this I am ready to be qualified to at any time.

John Sappington

Attest: Samuel M'Kee, Jun.

Madison County, Feb. 13, 1800.

I do certify further that the above named John Sappington told me, at the same time and place at which he gave me the above narrative, that he himself was the man who shot the brother of Logan in the house as above related, and that he likewise killed one of the Indians in one of the canoes, which came over from the opposite shore.

He likewise told me that Cresap never said an angry word to him about the matter, although he was frequently in company with Cresap, and indeed had been, and continued to be, in habits of intimacy with that gentleman, and was always befriended by him on every occasion. He further told me, that after they had perpetrated the murder, and were flying in the settlements, he met with Cresap (if I recollect right, at Redstone Old Fort,) and gave him a scalp, a very large fine one as he expressed it, and adorned with silver. This scalp I think he told me, was the scalp of Logan's brother; though as to this I am not absolutely certain.

Certified by
Samuel M'Kee, Jun.

## II - A Letter from General George Rogers Clark to Dr. Samuel Brown, 1798

*This country was explored in 1773. A resolution was formed to make a settlement the spring following, and the mouth of the Little Kanawha was appointed the place of general rendezvous, in order to descend the river from thence in a body. Early in the spring the Indians had done some mischief. Reports from their towns were alarming, which deterred many. About eighty or ninety men only met at the appointed rendezvous, where we lay for some days.*

*A small party of hunters, that lay about ten miles below us, were fired upon by the Indians, whom the hunters beat back, and returned to camp. This and many other circumstances led us to believe that the Indians were determined on war. The whole party was enrolled and determined to execute their project of forming a settlement in Kentucky, as we had every necessary store that could be thought of. An Indian town called the Horsehead bottom, on the Scioto and near its mouth, lay nearly in our way. The determination was to cross the country and surprise it. "Who was to command?" was the question. There were but few among us that had experience in Indian warfare, and they were such that we did not choose to be commanded by. We knew of Captain Cresap being on the river about fifteen miles above us, with some hands, settling a plantation; and that he had concluded to follow us to Kentucky as soon as he had fixed there his people. We also knew that he had been experienced in a former war. He was proposed; and it [was] unanimously agreed to send for him to command the party. Messengers were dispatched, and in half an hour returned with Cresap. He had heard of our resolution by some of his hunters, that had fallen in with ours, and had set out to come to us.*

*We now thought our army, as we called it, complete, and the destruction of the Indians sure. A council was called, and, to our astonishment, our intended Commander-in-Chief was the person who dissuaded us from the enterprise. He said that appearances were very suspicious, but there was no certainty of a war. That if we made the attempt proposed, he had no doubt of success, but a war would, at any rate, be the result, and that we should be blamed for it; and perhaps justly. But if we were determined to proceed, he would lay aside all considerations, send to his camp for his people, and share our fortunes.*

*He was then asked what he would advise. His answer was, that we should return to Wheeling, as a convenient post, to hear what was going forward. That a few weeks would determine. As it was early in the spring, if we found the Indians were not disposed to war, we should have full time to return, and make our establishment in Kentucky. This was adopted, and in two hours the whole were under way. As we ascended the river we met Killbuck, an Indian chief, with a small party. We had a long conference with him, but received little satisfaction as to the disposition of the Indians. It was observed that Cresap did not come to this conference, but kept on the opposite side of the river. He said that he was afraid to trust himself with the Indians. That Killbuck had frequently attempted to waylay his father to kill him. That if he crossed the river, perhaps his fortitude might fail him, and that he might put Killbuck to death. On our arrival at Wheeling, (the country being pretty well settled thereabouts), the whole of the inhabitants appeared to be alarmed. They flocked to our camp from every direction; and all that we could say could not keep them from under our wings. We offered to cover their neighborhood with scouts, until further information, if they would return to their plantations; but nothing would prevail. By this time we had got to be a formidable party. All the hunters, men without families, etc., in that quarter, had joined our party.*

*Our arrival at Wheeling was soon known at Pittsburgh. The whole of that country, at that time, being under the jurisdiction of Virginia, Dr. Connelly had been appointed by Dunmore, captain commandant of the District, which was called West Augusta. He, learning of us, sent a message addressed to the party, letting us know that a war was to be apprehended, and requesting that we would keep our position for a few days, as messages had been sent to the Indians, and a few days would determine the doubt. The answer he got was, that we had no inclination to quit our quarters for some time. That during our stay we should be careful that the enemy should not harass the neighborhood that we lay in. But before this answer could reach Pittsburgh, he sent a second express, addressed to Capt. Cresap, as the most influential man amongst us, informing him that the messages had returned from the Indians, that war was inevitable, and begging him to use his influence with the party, to get them to cover the country by scouts until the inhabitants could fortify themselves. The reception of this letter was the epoch of open hostilities with the Indians. A war post was planted, a conference was called, and the letter read by Cresap, all the Indian traders being summoned on so important an occasion. Action was had, and war declared in the most solemn manner; and the same evening two scalps were brought into camp.*

*The next day some canoes of Indians was discovered on the river, keeping the advantage of an island to cover themselves from our view. They were chased fifteen miles down the river and driven ashore. A battle ensued; a few were wounded on both sides; one Indian was taken prisoner. On examining their canoes we found a considerable quantity of ammunition and other warlike stores. On our return to camp a resolution was adopted to march the next day and attack Logan's camp, on the Ohio, about thirty miles above Wheeling. We did march about five miles, and then halted to take some refreshments. Here the impropriety of executing the projected enterprise was argued. The conversation was brought forward by Cresap himself. It was generally agreed those Indians had no hostile intentions, as they were hunting, and their party was composed of men, women and children, with all their stuff with them. This we knew, as I, myself, and others present had been in their camp about four weeks past on our descending the river from Pittsburgh. In short, every person seemed to detest the resolution we had set out with. We returned in the evening, decamped, and took the road to Redstone.*

*It was two days after this that Logan's family was killed. And, from the manner in which it was done, it was viewed as a horrid murder. From Logan's hearing of Cresap being at the head of this party on the river, it is no wonder that he supposed he had a hand in the destruction of his family.*

*What I have related is fact. I was intimate with Cresap. Logan I was better acquainted with at that time than any other Indian in the Western country. Cresap's conduct was as I have related it.*

### III - Caldwell's Affidavit

The following affidavit of John Caldwell, one of the early residents of Wheeling, was rewritten in 1839 by a Wheeling lawyer, Daniel M. Edgington:

Caldwell states: *That in the year 1774 he emigrated from Baltimore, Md., to the western country, and settled at the mouth of Wheeling creek, on the Ohio, in what was known as the District of West Augusta, and afterwards and now as Ohio County, Virginia. That he was well and intimately acquainted with the late Captain Michael Cresap, of Frederick county, Md., in 1774, and for some time before, and afterwards till his death. At the time last mentioned the section of the country in which affiant resided was frequently disturbed by the Indians, (as well for several years previous to 1774, as for many years afterwards) who were in the habit of stealing horses from the white inhabitants on the frontier, and committing other depredations. Horses were stolen from William McMahon and Joseph Tomlinson and others in 1774. Much ill feeling at all times existed among the white people of the frontier against the Indians on account of their depredations and the murders which they had at different times committed among the settlements. In 1774 several Indians who had dwelt on the west side of the Ohio, at or near the mouth of Yellow creek, crossed over the river to what was then known as Baker's bottom, opposite, or nearly opposite the mouth of said creek, and were killed by the whites at that place, as the affiant always understood and well believes, from feelings of animosity, growing out of the causes aforesaid against the Indians generally. The Indians so killed were said to have been, and affiant believes such was the fact, the relatives or family of the chief, Logan, with whose massacre the said Captain Cresap is charged in Jefferson's Notes on Virginia, Dr. Doddridge's Notes, etc. At the time said Indians were killed, Captain Cresap made his home at the house of the affiant, at the mouth of Wheeling creek, but was generally absent, further down the river, with a party of men in his employ, making improvements on lands he had taken up near Middle Island creek. Shortly before, and at the time of the massacre of Logan's relatives, there was a general apprehension on the frontiers from various indications, that there was to be a general outbreaking of the Indians upon the settlements, and much alarm prevailed. Captain Cresap and his men came up the river to affiant's house, and affiant well remembers that he, Captain Cresap, was there on the day the Indians referred to were killed at Baker's bottom, and that he remained there for some days afterwards, and until the news of their being killed reached Wheeling. Affiant further states that Baker's bottom was situated forty or fifty miles above his residence, immediately on the Ohio river; that on the evening of the day the report reached Wheeling, that the Indians had been killed, affiant started down the river to Middle Island creek, where he also had some hands engaged in making improvements, to warn them of the danger apprehended by the people above, and to bring them home; and that when he left home Captain Cresap was at his house.*

*Affiant further states that he was called on, some years ago, by some person, whose name he does not now remember, but who was understood to be the agent, or as acting under the direction of Mr. Jefferson, for his (affiant's) testimony in relation to the murder of Logan's family, and that he then gave his affidavit, which, in substance, was the same as the foregoing. Affiant further says it was well understood and believed on the frontier at that time that the persons principally engaged in killing said Indians were John Sappington, Nathaniel Tomlinson, Daniel Greathouse, and perhaps, others; and that Captain Cresap was never charged or implicated in the report, in any manner, so far as he knows or believes, in this country, until after the publication of Jefferson's Notes on Virginia.*

### IV - A Letter from Col. Ebenezer Zane to (Kentucky) Senator the Honorable John H. Brown

*I was myself, with many others, in the practice of making improvements on lands upon the Ohio, for the purpose of acquiring rights to the same. Being on the Ohio, at the mouth of Sandy creek, in company with many others, news circulated that the Indians had robbed some of the land-jobbers. This news induced the people generally to ascend the Ohio. I was among the number. On our arrival at Wheeling, being informed that there were two Indians with some traders near and above Wheeling, a proposition was made by the then Captain, Michael Cresap, to waylay and kill the Indians upon the river. This measure I opposed with much violence, alleging that the killing of those Indians might involve the country in a war. But the opposite party prevailed, and proceeded up the Ohio with Captain Cresap at their head.*

*In a short time the party returned, and also the traders, in a canoe; but there were no Indians in the company. I inquired what had become of the Indians, and was informed by the traders and Cresap's party that they had fallen overboard. I* examined the canoe, and saw much fresh blood and some bullet-holes in the canoe. This fully convinced me that the party had killed the two Indians and thrown them into the river.

On the afternoon of the day this action happened, a report prevailed that there was a camp or party of Indians on the Ohio below and near Wheeling. In consequence of this information, Captain Cresap with his party, joined by a number of recruits, proceeded immediately down the Ohio, for the purpose, as was then generally understood, of destroying the Indians above mentioned. On the succeeding day Captain Cresap and his party returned to Wheeling, and it was generally reported by the party that they had killed a number of Indians. Of the truth of this report I had no doubt, as one of Cresap's party was badly wounded, and the party had a fresh scalp and a quantity of property, which they called Indian plunder. At the time of the last mentioned transaction, it was generally reported that the party of Indians down the Ohio were Logan and his family; but I have reason to believe that this report was unfounded.

Within a few days after the transaction above mentioned, a party of Indians were killed at Yellow creek. But I must do the memory of Captain Cresap the justice to say that I do not believe that he was present at the killing of the Indians at Yellow creek. But there is not the least doubt in my mind, that the massacre at Yellow creek was brought on by the two transactions first stated.

All the transactions, which I have related, happened the latter end of April, 1774; and there can scarcely be a doubt that they were the cause of the war which immediately followed, commonly called Dunmore's war.

I am with much esteem, yours, &c.
Ebenezer Zane
Wheeling, February 4, 1800

## Appendix D:
### *The Roster of the Foreman Expedition, September 27, 1777*

Captain William Foreman, and 24 men;
Captain Joseph Ogle, and 10 men;
Captain William Linn, and 9 men.

Of the forty-six men who made up the Foreman Expedition, Thwaites & Kellogg assembled a list of twenty-five names from the Draper Manuscripts, while DeHass gave twenty-one names, fifteen of which are not on the Thwaites & Kellogg roster. Following are the names of forty of the forty-six participants. Of those forty-six twenty-two were killed, one was captured, and twenty-three escaped.

Thirteen of the men named here are listed as killed in action, one captured, and twelve escaped. Of the other twenty men on the expedition nine were killed and eleven escaped. Of those twenty-two men who were killed almost all were of the twenty-five which comprised Foreman's company, including Foreman himself, and either two or three of his sons.

Among those killed Thwaites & Kellogg listed *Jacob Greathouse*, but this is incorrect, as Jacob's death in 1791 is well documented[114]. At least three of those (besides Nathan Foreman) on the DeHass list, probably more, were also killed. Only one man, Jonathan Pugh, was taken captive; all the others were either killed on the spot or escaped, although some of the latter were wounded.

*From Thwaites & Kellogg[115]:*

Killed: (12)
1. *Foreman, William, Capt.
2. Avery, George
3. Brazier, Thomas
4. Clark, Hugh
5. *Foreman, Hamilton
6. Greathouse, Jacob [this is incorrect]
7. Hedges, Ezekiel
8. Lawson, Moses
9. *Ogle, Jacob
10. Polk, John
11. Shens, William
12. Williams, William

Captured: (1)
1. Pugh, Jonathan

Escaped: (12)
1. Castleman, Harry
2. Chambers, John
3. Cullins (probably *Collins*), John
4. *Engle (or *Ingle*), William
5. Harkness, Robert
6. Harrod, William
7. *Jones, Solomon
8. Linn, William, Capt.
9. McLain, Daniel
10. Ogle, Joseph, Capt.
11. *Vincent, John
12. Wetzel, Martin


*Additional names from DeHass, not listed by Thwaites:*

1. Foreman, Nathan (killed)[116]
2. Greene, James
3. Harris, Isaac
4. Johnston, Samuel
5. Lowry, Samuel
6. McGrew, Robert
7. Miller, Anthony
8. Peterson, Edward
9. Pew [Pugh], Jacob
10. Powell, Abraham
11. Powell, Benjamin
12. Riser, Henry
13. Shivers, Elisha
14. Viney, Bartholomew
15. Wilson, John

# Appendix E:
## *Mingo Bottom — Mingo Town*

Confusion has arisen in the past few years regarding the location of the often-mentioned *Mingo Bottom*, although the site is quite definitely established as being on the Virginia shore. This, note, in spite of a popular modern authority on the Border Wars who, willy-nilly, places Mingo Bottom on both sides of the river, and in spite of another author who recently wrote of Col. Crawford assembling his army, in May of 1782, at Mingo Bottom, *Pennsylvania*! The problem has arisen both from a confusion in speech, and from a misunderstanding.

During the French & Indian War a Mingo Indian village was established where the town of Mingo Junction, Ohio, now stands, about 20 miles north of Wheeling, and just below Steubenville, Ohio. This village, called Mingo Town, was described as being on a high bank (hardly a *bottom*) on the north shore (i.e., the right shore, as one descends the river). During Washington's tour of the Ohio in 1770 he spoke of the Mingo Town as having about 20 cabins, with some 70 inhabitants. The towns-people and the locale were notorious, however, with a reputation for raiding and plundering passing canoes. It was to some extent this activity that brought about Lord Dunmore's War in 1774; the first two Indians killed by Capt. Michael Cresap and his men, on April 27th, were probably residents of this village, whose goods, offered to some passing traders, caused Cresap's party to head north in a canoe from Wheeling, returning later with the traders, sans Indians, but with bullet holes in their canoe, and the explanation, Daniel Boone-like, that the Indians had "fallen overboard".

At about this time the inhabitants of Mingo Town removed to the headwaters of the Scioto River, although the area around the creek continued to retain the old name. An important Indian trail lead westward from Mingo Town toward the Indian villages on the Muskingum, around Coshocton, and as the eastern terminus of this road Mingo Town was an important site.

*Mingo Bottom* is a large, relatively flat and open area [commonly referred to as bottomland] on the (West) Virginia shore; it derived its name solely from the fact that it was situated opposite the Mingo Town — it was never the site of an Indian village. In 1777 Gen. Hand was ordered to station a lieutenant and 18 men at the post there, and because of its particular qualities, as well as because of the well-defined trail just across the river which lead to the Indian towns, it served as an ideal gathering place for campaigns against the Indians. In 1782 both Williamson and Crawford used the location as a staging area for their expeditions, and it was to Mingo Bottom that the stragglers of Crawford's Expedition returned.

In 1796 a map drawn by Victor Collet for the French ambassador clearly showed and identified both locations. Mingo Town still retained its name more than twenty years after the village had been abandoned, and Mingo Bottom was correctly shown as being on the Virginia side. It is important to remark, however, that one may find the term Mingo Bottom still being applied to both locations.

# Appendix F:
## *The Search for the Crawford Burn Site*

Col. Crawford, after his capture in June, 1782, was not burned at (new) Pipe's Town, but rather about three-quarters of a mile to the west, at the bend in Tymochtee Creek where the squaws and children had been taken for safe-keeping upon the approach of Crawford's army. But for two hundred years the precise location of Crawford's death has been a source of dispute among local historians, and only recently has substantial evidence been presented which clearly locates the torture site. Commonly referred to as the *burn site*, it is about a half-mile east of the community of Crawford, Ohio, on the north side of County Highway 29, about a quarter mile from that road, and just to the north of the farmhouse that presently occupies the ground.

After several years of patient research (and frustration) the Reverend Dr. Parker B. Brown was finally rewarded by locating the site where Col. William Crawford was burned by the Delaware Indians. The trail of papers and documents led westward, from Pennsylvania to Ohio, Wisconsin, Nebraska and Kansas; of particular importance were the extensive but widely-scattered manuscript collections of Consul Willshire Butterfield, the lawyer-historian who had published the definitive work on the Crawford Expedition[117]. Brown's study of some of those documents, quoted and unquoted in Butterfield's book, indicated that another major source of documents was yet to be found.

The clues offered by Butterfield in his book as to the location of the burn site along Tymochtee Creek were four: the distance from Pipe's Town to the torture stake, the 1830 brick house of Daniel Hodges, the ford where the Indian trail crossed the creek, and a grove of white oak trees. None of these, by themselves or in combination, were sufficient to precisely locate the site, and Butterfield himself could only place it somewhere within a particular half-section of land; "the *precise* spot I do not attempt to locate," he wrote. It was just somewhere within those three hundred twenty acres. After another hundred years had passed, or two hundred years after Crawford's death, Pipe's Town no longer existed, the Indian trail might now be covered by underbrush, the brick house may have been torn down (it was!), and the grove of white oaks is more likely someone's cultivated cornfield.

Starting over again in Columbus, Ohio, Dr. Brown's perseverance paid off in 1983 when he found a librarian's receipt to Butterfield's daughter, which in turn led him to a large manuscript collection, fifty-five dusty scrapbooks in the basement vault of the Western Reserve Historical Society in Cleveland. Among those were found the most important documents, the papers written by Governor William Walker, the Wyandot leader who was a native of Upper Sandusky, and later governor of Nebraska Territory.

Dr. Knight, the expedition's surgeon, after being forced to watch Crawford's sufferings, was then led to the lodge of the Delaware war chief Pipe, at the newly established Pipe's Town. This, according to Knight, was three-quarters of a mile distant from the torture site. With the former site of Pipe's Town known, an approximate distance of twelve to fourteen hundred yards could be measured toward and along Tymochtee Creek.

One of Butterfield's informants was Joseph McCutcheon, an innkeeper and state senator, who wrote that he had often visited the burn site; it was located on the east side of the creek, on property owned by Hodge's heirs (William Ritchey), with a fine grove of white oaks nearby. But Henry Howe, while preparing his *Historical Collections of Ohio*, had interviewed Colonel John Johnston, an Indian agent in the first decade of the nineteenth century at Fort Wayne, Indiana, and Piqua, Ohio. Johnston claimed that the torture had taken place on the west side of Tymochtee Creek, on low ground, and on the right hand side of the trail going west, but all three of these citations conflicted with almost all other testimony. Several other early sources had commented on the grove of white oak trees which surrounded the site, and such trees do not grow on low, marshy land.

But there was no indication that Johnston had ever been on the ground, and in the end it was Walker's testimony which was decisive. He gave, to the delight of future historians, two alternate sets of directions to the site. To Butterfield he wrote:

"Find a brick house built in early times by Daniel Hodge.... proceed, a little north of west, nearly a quarter of a mile to a piece of rising ground, near the east bank of the Tymochtee creek.... surrounded with (or was then) a grove of young white-\oaks."

"When I first visited the place in the spring of 1814 ... on disturbing the surface, ashes and charcoal appeared. The spot was pointed out to me by a Wyandot of high respectability who was present when Crawford was tied to the stake, and was present in the engagement at Battle Island."

Walker had earlier been interviewed by Dr. Draper, to whom he further elucidated:

"*Crawford's Burning Spot* — He was burned on the east side of Tymochtee creek, the eighth of a mile from the stream on a rise of some ten feet to a level oak grove table land: on a farm since owned by D.C. Hodges."

Unfortunately this interview was buried among the Draper Manuscripts [11U:73, dated July 6, 1868], and Butterfield was unaware of its existence. Along with the other evidence these two descriptions should serve to identify the location; in addition the site of the Hodges House could be definitely located with the aid of county atlases, and with the help of a descendent of Daniel Hodges.

The problem is in Walker's statement, that from the Hodges House one should go a little north of west, nearly a quarter of a mile to a piece of rising ground, near the east bank of the creek. But when one leaves the site of the house, there is no rising ground anywhere to the north or west, and going in that direction one soon descends the bluff to cross to the west side of the creek. The difficulty was solved by Dr. Brown's deduction that Walker was suffering from vision problems caused by old age, being in his seventies, and only shortly before his death, when he wrote this letter to Butterfield. Instead of a little *north* of west, he had meant to write a little *south* of west, and he had not caught the error before sending the letter to Butterfield.

With this information in hand, one can walk from the site of the Hodges House, a quarter mile *southwest* to a piece of rising ground, near the east bank of the Tymochtee creek; or, alternatively, one may cross the creek from the north, go about an eighth of a mile (about two hundred yards) south, and after climbing a slight elevation the searcher finds himself on a level tableland, on the east side of the creek, and in the same spot as when approaching from the Hodges House site. The map shown here, compiled from Dr. Brown's research, gives the relevant points and locates the burn site within a relatively small area.

\*     \*     \*

In 1877 a monument[118] to Col. Crawford was dedicated by the Pioneer Association of Wyandot County; an eight foot pillar of grey sandstone rises on the bluff just northeast of the spot where Crawford endured such agony. For over a hundred years the monument was a well-known site, and the area was often frequented by visitors interested in the history of the Indian Wars. The monument and the burn site itself are located just northeast of the actual burn site, some distance west of the Ritchey Cemetery shown on the map. But both the monument and the burn site are on private land, and in recent years the owners of the property have unfortunately seen fit to deny public access to the burn site and the monument. In order to rectify that situation a new monument was therefore recently erected on public land by the Wyandot County Historical Association, on the southern edge of the Ritchey Cemetery. The new monument is an exact duplicate of the original, except for the requisite change in the inscription. The distance from this monument to the burn site is greater than from the original monument, but access to the monument and the cemetery is not restricted.

\*     \*     \*

But in spite of all the interest in the Border Wars, and the defeat of Crawford's army and his terrible sufferings at the hands of the Delaware, one important element has been sadly overlooked, as is so often the case — the suffering of those who were left behind. In this regard no one ever thinks of the bereaved widow, Hannah

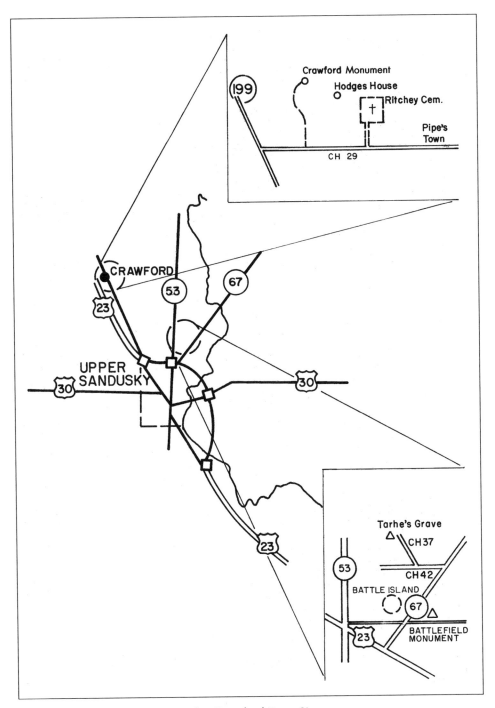

The Crawford Burn Site

Crawford, who had been, as Dr. Brown said, deprived of the consolation of Christian interment for her husband, and who waited in vain for the man who would never return.

Dr. Brown told of a Virginia lawyer, Charles Johnston, who had been abducted by the Shawnee in 1790, and who had lived at Upper Sandusky for five weeks, during which time he was guided to the spot where Crawford had been burned. Then, as Dr. Brown concluded:

"Nor was this the last American visit recorded during the presettlement period of Wyandot County. In 1806, nearly twenty-five years after her husband failed to return home, Hannah Crawford came. For years she lived impoverished in the log house beside the Youghiogheny River. Deprived the consolation of a Christian burial for her husband, Hannah mourned heavily and mourned long. As a grandson was to remember her, she mounted her horse one day, seated him as a child behind her, crossed the river, and rode to a moss-covered log. Sitting on it, she wept. 'Here,' she lamented, 'here I parted with your grandfather.'

"Now, at the advanced age of eighty-four, she approached the Tymochtee on a plodding horse. Her escort from Pennsylvania was a grandnephew, Billy. Guiding them the final miles most likely were some Wyandots. Back home afterwards it became known that the burn site was barren. No grass would grow upon it."[119]

## Appendix G:
### *Betty Zane, Molly Scott, And Lydia Boggs:*
### *The Gunpowder Exploit at Fort Henry*

About noon on the 12th of September, 1782, some 250 Indians and 40 British Rangers watched in amazement as the gates of the fort they were besieging swung open, allowing a teenage girl to slip out. Still watching intently, they saw the girl run quickly across the open field, where she disappeared into an adjacent cabin which stood about sixty yards from the southeastern corner of the fort. Only a few minutes passed before they saw this same girl emerge from the cabin, but now she carried a large bundle wrapped in the apron about her waist. Suddenly realizing, nearly too late, that in her apron this girl was carrying several pounds of gunpowder to the fort, the Indians opened fire on her during the short time that their target was in view. Fortunately for the lives of those settlers in that western Virginia fort, the girl sped up the slight incline to the fort with such fleetness of foot that she was able to reach her destination unharmed, carrying her precious cargo of powder. And with that powder the fort continued to hold off the attackers until the following morning, when, losing heart, the enemy lifted the siege and departed. One group of them moved off to attack another, much smaller fort fifteen miles distant — Rice's Fort (near present Bethany, Brooke Co., WV); once again they were frustrated in their plans, as they were unable to capture the half-dozen defenders of that stockade.

The 16-year-old girl who performed that courageous feat was Elizabeth Zane, and the fort which was saved by her daring was Fort Henry, located in what is now the downtown business district of Wheeling, West Virginia. The adjacent cabin from which she obtained the gunpowder was that of her brother, who, in an effort to provide a cross-fire for the fort, was occupying his own cabin-blockhouse during that siege. Betty's brother was the founder and defender of that stately little city of Wheeling, the 34-year-old pioneer, Colonel Ebenezer Zane, and this was the third time within the last five years that a large body of Indians had attacked his settlement, and the second time that the Indians had conducted an extensive siege of this fort.

This *Gunpowder Exploit* became one of the standard tales of the heroism of the pioneers during the long and bloody Indian Wars along the Western Border; so much so that by the latter part of the Nineteenth Century the author of any work on the history of the United States could find it sufficient to state that it was unnecessary to give an account of this story, as it was "known to every schoolboy". In 1903 Zane Grey, the outstanding author of western novels (and himself a descendent of the illustrious Zane family), published a fictionalized account of the story, and at that time titled his novel simply *Betty Zane*, secure in the knowledge that every reader would already be familiar with the basic theme of his novel. Unfortunately, during the last half-century or so, the heroes and heroines of American history, and the bravery of our pioneer ancestors, along with their incredible hardships and struggles, have seldom been given more than grudging notice, at best, in most standard school texts.

That Betty Zane's *Powder Exploit* might not be as well-known as could otherwise be wished may be due in part, however, to an incident which occurred in 1849, 67 years after the event. In November of that year one of the last surviving adult eye-witnesses of that siege of Fort Henry, an 83-year-old woman named Lydia Boggs Shepherd Cruger, swore out an affidavit to the effect that it had not been Betty Zane who had run with the powder; she stated instead that the true heroine of Fort Henry was a young woman named Molly Scott. In addition, she stated that it was not the men in the fort who had run out of powder; Molly Scott had run from Col. Zane's cabin to the fort, where she obtained the powder (with Lydia's assistance), and had then returned to the Zane cabin. Furthermore, according to Lydia, it was not such a feat of daring, as Molly Scott had been in no danger of being harmed, since the Indians were so distant from the fort that they did not even shoot at her. Most incredible of all, she claimed that Betty Zane had not even been at the fort during that siege!

The controversy stirred up by Mrs. Cruger's account was immediate, intense, and bitter. For two-thirds of a century the people of the western parts of Virginia had gloried in the fame attached to this tale of heroism; this story of a local girl, an ordinary teenager, performing the act of a real-life heroine, of which any participant of the Heroic Age could have been proud! And suddenly an actual eye-witness to that event had not only discredited Betty Zane, but gave such a totally different account of what had happened during that siege as to utterly confound everyone. Not only the local residents, but professional historians as well, debated whether, in the face of long-established tradition, it was possible that the heroine had indeed been Molly Scott. As an actual eyewitness to the siege, how could Mrs. Cruger's word be doubted? But, on the other hand, how could all the other people there have been so mistaken about not only the girl's identity, but all the other details as well? Was perhaps this old woman's memory so befuddled, so many years afterward, that she was merely confused? Granting that it might have been Molly Scott, how could Lydia possibly have remembered, so many years afterward, that Betty Zane had not even been present during the siege? And had it really been the men in the Zane cabin who had run out of powder, rather than those in the fort, as Lydia proclaimed — so that it was necessary for an inmate of that cabin to run to the fort, where there was a more than sufficient supply of powder? And were all the Indians really so far away that the heroine, whoever she may have been, was not even fired upon?

The conclusions which historians have generally drawn are that:

1) Lydia was mistaken — the credit was properly given to Betty Zane;

2) Lydia was correct — Molly Scott was the true heroine;

3) There were *two* Gunpowder Exploits, one of them (perhaps in 1777) with Molly Scott as the heroine, and the other in 1782 with Betty Zane.

*     *     *

Anyone who has read the "standard accounts" of the Border Wars, such as those by Withers and De Hass, is well aware of the two Sieges of Fort Henry, the first occurring in September, 1777, the Year of the Bloody Sevens, and the second, five years later in that same month, in 1782. And they are also likely aware of the controversy surrounding the identity of the "true" heroine of Fort Henry's famous *Gunpowder Exploit*, Lydia's 1849 affidavit having been published for the first time in De Hass. But most people who do know this are probably unaware of Lydia's *Narrative of 1846*, which indirectly contains the solution to the entire riddle.

In 1846, more than sixty years after the siege, the preeminent historian of the Trans-Allegheny frontier, Lyman C. Draper, interviewed Mrs. Cruger concerning those bitter times, and his notes of that interview make up the *Narrative of Lydia Boggs Shepherd Cruger*, recently published by Jared Lobdell in his *Indian Warfare*. During that interview, Draper, already quite familiar with the details of the Gunpowder Exploit, must have been absolutely astounded as he sat listening to Lydia blithely speak of helping Molly Scott get powder to take to Col. Zane's cabin, and of Silas Zane being in Col. Zane's cabin, and of Betty Zane not even being at Fort Henry during the siege. Draper surely questioned her on this, as he then noted: "Mrs. Cruger in this says she couldn't be mistaken."

There are five major discrepancies in Lydia's account of this siege, as given in her affidavit, and as told to Dr. Draper:

**1)  that it was the men in Col. Zane's cabin who had run out of powder:**

All other accounts state that the men in the fort had run out of powder; it was the imminent loss of the lives of those in the fort that caused such concern. If the men in the cabin were out of powder, and the Indians were too far away to have shot with any effect, then why would not one of those men in the cabin have gone for powder? He would have been able to carry an entire keg upon his shoulder, rather than just an apronful; Lydia herself stated that he would have been in no danger of being shot by the Indians. And if those in the cabin had run out of powder, and there were only a half-dozen men and one woman there, then why could not all of them have walked over to the safety of the fort, where Lydia says there was plenty of powder for all?

**2)  that it was Molly Scott who ran with the powder:**

Everyone else said that it was Betty (or Betsy) Zane, the 16-year-old sister of the commander of the settlement. How could everyone else have been so blind during this episode that they were unable to differentiate between a Betty Zane and a Molly Scott?

### 3) that Molly ran from Col. Zane's cabin to the fort, and then back to the cabin:

All the other witnesses said that Betty ran from the fort to the Zane cabin, and then back to the fort with the powder. Everyone present could not have been so confused that, after having seen someone run towards them from Col. Zane's, and then watching as she ran back to his cabin, they now believed she was safely inside the fort, with or without the powder.

### 4) that Col. Zane's brother, Silas, was one of the men helping to defend the Zane cabin:

It has been definitely established that Silas Zane was in command of Fort Henry during the siege; the nominal commander, Captain John Boggs (Lydia's father), had been sent for reinforcements, while Col. Zane was defending his fortified cabin/blockhouse.

### 5) that the Indians did not fire at her, as they were too far away:

Admittedly, the Indians did not fire at Betty as she was running toward the Zane cabin, but upon her return to the fort they fired a volley at her! It is really quite difficult to believe that all the Indians, while besieging a fort, would have remained so distant from it that they could not have fired at it with the hope of hitting anyone.

But perhaps the most astonishing discrepancy in this interview is that after 1782 a legend will develop of the courage of Betty Zane running with the powder. But then, why had these pioneers, who themselves were not unaccustomed to acts of bravery, marveled so at this deed if the Indians really were too far away to have fired at her? What was it, then, that had required such supreme valor on anyone's part?

Lydia definitely remembered giving the powder to none other than Molly Scott, and, as she stated in her affidavit, she —

> remembers with perfect distinctness every circumstance connected with the incident. She saw Molly Scott enter the fort, assisted her in getting the powder, and saw her leave, and avers most positively that she, and she alone, accomplished the feat referred to, and deserves all the credit there may be attached to it.

She had watched as Molly ran back to Col. Zane's cabin, with the Indians firing not one single shot at her. Lydia knew she was right, and after all is said and done, quite surprisingly, she was! But there is a twist to her correctness. In her affidavit Lydia stated: *The undersigned... will now state without the fear of contradiction, that the powder was given to Molly Scott, and not to Elizabeth Zane.* She was certainly correct in her claim of "without fear of contradiction". Who was there left alive, in 1849, who could contradict her? Betty had been dead for over twenty years, and Molly Scott herself for ten. Sixty-seven years after the event there was only one adult eye-witness still living, a Mrs. Mary Burkitt, who was then quite elderly.

The first sentence of Lydia's 1849 affidavit begins: *The undersigned, having been applied to for a statement of facts respecting... the "Gunpowder Exploit"....* It must have been Dr. Draper, of course, who had applied to Lydia for a statement of facts, only three years after his interview with her. But it seems odd that someone would ask her for a statement about the Gunpowder Exploit only. From Lydia's affidavit — *"those within the stockade observed a female leave the residence of Col. Zane, and advance with rapid movements towards the fort... she entered [the fort] in safety. That person was none other than Molly Scott, and the object of her mission was to procure powder for those who defended the dwelling of Col. Zane."*

Then follow the details of how Lydia's mother (!) had instructed Lydia to give the powder to Molly Scott, etc., and — *Elizabeth Zane... was at that time at the residence of her father near the present town of Washington, Pa...* What an incredible memory, after a lapse of nearly 70 years, to be able to recall where someone, who was not there, was at that particular time.

But here is Lydia, only three years previously, talking to Dr. Draper in 1846:

> "Near mid-day [of September 12th], having exhausted the powder at Zane's house, Molly Scott ran over from Zane's to the Fort, sixty yards, for a supply. Captain Boggs had charge of the magazine, and in his absence the magazine was open, and I went in with her and poured out some tenths [?] into Molly's tow apron, and she ran back. She was not fired at going or returning. The Indians were on the hillside and elsewhere too far to have shot with any effect".

The major contradiction in the affidavit is in her statement that it was the men in Col. Zane's cabin who ran out of powder. But from official letters, it cannot be disputed that the militia's entire supply of powder for the defense of the fort was stored in Col. Zane's cabin, having been sent downriver that summer by General Irvine, the military commandant at Fort Pitt. Nor did anyone have time, from the warning of the Indians' approach until the beginning of the siege, to move the powder from the cabin to the fort; nor would those few men in the cabin have been able to burn up all that powder in a month, much less in only twenty hours.

The major dilemma presented in this episode, which cannot be explained away, is that Molly Scott herself often related the events of that Siege of 1782 to members of her own immediate family, as well as to friends and neighbors, and she repeatedly told all of them that she herself had watched *Betsy Zane* run to Col. Zane's cabin for powder, and return with it to the fort. In a written statement by James F. Scott, Molly Scott's grandson, he related how he had heard "from her own lips" numerous times —

> *about the exploit of Betsy Zane carrying powder in her apron from Col. Zane's dwelling to the fort, during the siege... as well as the narrow escape she had from the bullets of the Indians.... She [Molly Scott] never gave any other name than Elizabeth or Betsy Zane, as she called her, as the one who carried the powder. She never claimed the credit for herself.*

Lydia, in her affidavit, claimed that it had been Molly Scott who had carried the powder, that Molly carried it from the fort to Col. Zane's cabin, that the Indians did not fire at her, and that Betty Zane had not even been at Fort Henry. But Molly Scott herself contradicted all four of Lydia's statements. It is no longer sufficient to say that Lydia was an eye-witness, therefore her word cannot be doubted; Molly Scott was just as much an eye-witness, and she said she did not run with the powder — it was Betsy Zane, and she ought to have known!

Was Lydia, then, just an out-and-out liar, trying to get even with Betty Zane, perhaps because of some long-standing personal jealousy? Or was she so senile that, in her confusion, she interchanged Molly Scott with Betty Zane, and reversed the direction of the run? Both of these have been offered as explanations for the discrepancies in the affidavit, but neither of them seems to be acceptable.

According to the "standard tradition", the men in the fort ran out of powder, and since the men in Col. Zane's cabin had more than sufficient for their own needs, Silas Zane, in command of the fort during Capt. Boggs' absence, allowed his sister, 16-year-old Betty, to risk running to their brother's cabin, where she obtained a quantity of powder in her apron, and returned to the fort under a hail of bullets from the Indians. It is quite possible that at the time this occurred, Lydia Boggs was busy doing something else, somewhere else in the fort, and did not see this event take place.

*   *   *

Despite all that has been written above, it is still possible to maintain:

1)  that Lydia Boggs did help Molly Scott put some powder in her apron, under her father's (not her mother's) instructions, since Captain Boggs was there in the fort;

2)  that Molly Scott did run to Col. Zane's cabin with that powder, since the men there were low on powder;

3) that the Indians did not shoot at Molly, because they were too far away — on the hillside and elsewhere, to have shot with any effect;

4) that Silas Zane was in Col. Zane's cabin;

5) and that Betty Zane was not even there, at all!

How then, is it possible to reconcile all these discrepancies in *Lydia vs. the Frontier People*? It has been suggested that there were perhaps two gunpowder exploits: that Molly Scott, helped by Lydia, ran with powder from the fort to Col. Zane's cabin at the first Siege of Fort Henry in 1777, and that Betty Zane ran from the Zane cabin to the fort at the second siege in 1782. But this clearly won't work, as there was no one in Col. Zane's cabin during the 1777 siege; certainly fortunate, as the Indians burned it to the ground. And Lydia couldn't have helped Molly Scott with any gunpowder during that siege, because Lydia was not there in 1777. By her own admission she didn't arrive at Fort Henry until four years later.

But almost all of the writers on this period of frontier history have been totally unaware of (or have chosen to ignore) another very important fact. There was another siege, other than the two famous sieges. It was technically more of an Indian attack than a siege, being of only a few hours duration, and it took place, once again in the month of September — but this was in September of *1781*.

Just after dawn on an early September day, about eighty Indians, led by the Delaware Chief Pekillon, appeared within sight of Fort Henry. Having been previously warned by David Zeisberger, the Moravian missionary, that a large body of Indians was moving to attack the frontier settlements, the settlers at the fort were prepared for them. Commanding the fort was Capt. John Boggs, who only a month previously had moved to Wheeling with his family. Unable to take the fort by surprise as they had hoped, the Indians found three boys outside the fort. They killed one boy and took another captive, while the third, wounded through the wrist, escaped into the fort. Having accomplished so little in this attack, in Lydia's own words — *"they [the Indians] then ran off instantly"*. Nothing else of consequence happened during this attack; very few shots were fired at the fort, as the majority of the Indians were too far away.

But if Capt. Boggs was in command of the fort, then where were Colonel Zane and his brother Silas? They were both in Col. Zane's cabin, defending it from the Indians, Silas having only recently returned from the Eastern Front. The Colonel's cabin had been burned to the ground during the Siege of 1777, four years previously, whereupon the colonel had built a new home in the form of a blockhouse, with every intention of occupying it in the event of another Indian attack. There is no reason to believe that he would have built his cabin in that form, with that intention, in 1777, and then not have occupied it after having been warned of the impending attack in 1781. He was in his cabin during two attacks; in 1781 for only a few hours, and again the next year for nearly 48 hours, during the Siege of 1782.

Knowing of the approach of the Indians in 1781, he had requested some gunpowder from the militia stores in the fort, for the use of those men who would be defending the Zane blockhouse. Capt. Boggs had complied, instructing his wife (probably) to tell their daughter Lydia to assist the messenger from Col. Zane's cabin, a young woman named Molly Scott. Lydia helped her obtain a quantity of powder from the magazine for the defense of the Zane cabin, as that was also a military operation, and vital to the defense of the fort. Lydia then watched as Molly Scott ran back to the Zane cabin with the powder in her apron; she was not fired on by the Indians, who at that time *were on the hillside, and elsewhere* (on the island, on the opposite side of the fort) and certainly *too far to have shot with any effect* at anyone between the fort and the Zane cabin.

Lydia had indeed been involved in Molly Scott's run with powder back to the Zane cabin, but Lydia thought *that* was the gunpowder exploit that everyone had talked about all these years. That particular incident, however, had occurred in 1781, and it had not seemed especially hazardous to her at the time, since the Indians were so far away; 68 years later she stated in her affidavit: "*At the time of its occurrence, the achievement was not considered very extraordinary*".

It was *this* Gunpowder Exploit that Lydia remembered in such precise detail. And at that time Betty Zane *was* living with her father at Catfish Camp (present Washington), PA. Until a year or so before Lydia herself had been living there, and had lived there since before 1777. The two girls were probably close friends; being 15-year-old girls on the Indian frontier would naturally have brought them together, and there could not have been a great many other unmarried girls in their mid-teens on the western border at that time. So, in the fall of 1781 Lydia knew quite well that Betty was living there with her father, while the Zane brothers were here at their settlement on Wheeling Creek.

Sometime around 1780 Captain Boggs had moved his family to Buffalo Creek, near (present) Wellsburg, West Virginia, about 20 miles north of Wheeling. Then, in August of 1781, he had been ordered to the command of Fort Henry, and of course he had taken along his family, including Lydia. In her affidavit, Lydia stated that Elizabeth Zane was one of her earliest acquaintances; that was how Lydia knew exactly where Betty had been during that attack on Fort Henry. Lydia had been at the fort only a single month herself, and this was her very first Indian attack. All the details were indelibly impressed upon her, and 68 years later there would be absolutely no doubt in her mind as to whom she had given the powder; it had certainly not been Betty Zane.

A year later the Indians were back, three times as many of them, with the aid of forty British Rangers from Detroit, and as before, Colonel Zane defended his cabin, where the militia's supply of gunpowder was being stored. But, unlike the last attack, this time there had been only a few minutes warning before that large number of the enemy appeared. Captain Boggs had immediately been sent for reinforcements, but as he subsequently stated, he had gone only a mile and a half on horseback when he heard the fort's cannon being fired. There had not been time to transfer the powder from Col. Zane's cabin to the fort, nor was there any definite indication that they would even need to do so. The famous Siege of 1777, only five years before, had lasted less than a day; the Indians successfully ambushed three separate parties of men on the morning of September 1, 1777, all before noon, and then, satisfied with their destruction, they withdrew to attack other forts. At the previous attack in September of 1781, the Indians had been unable to surprise the fort, and had departed after only a few hours. Might they not do so again this time, since they had once again been unsuccessful in their effort to surprise the fort?

It was certainly an exception for Indians to besiege a fort; if they could not capture it by surprise or stratagem, they almost always gave up and moved on to another fort which offered a promise of more gain with less risk. And that was exactly what they had done during their attack the year before. Being unsuccessful at Fort Henry, they had left there almost immediately and headed for Jacob Link's blockhouse on Middle Wheeling Creek, fourteen miles from Fort Henry, which they attacked with success, taking the blockhouse and killing Link and at least one other man. With the advantage of hindsight, we know that the Indians would lay siege to the fort for two full days in September of 1782, from the afternoon of the 11th until about noon of the 13th. But the defenders inside the fort had no possible way of knowing how long the Indians would persist. It was probably only at the insistence of the British officer who was present (Captain Bradt) with his Rangers that they remained as long as they did. It was then, on the second day of *this* siege, on September 12th, 1782, with no indication that the Indians were about to withdraw, that Betty Zane ran from the fort to her brother's cabin, and returned to the fort with her apron full of gunpowder.

So Lydia did indeed remember helping Molly Scott get gunpowder during an Indian attack, and she remembered Molly running back to the Zane cabin with it, and she knew that her good friend, Betty Zane, was missing out on all the excitement, because she had remained behind at Catfish Camp. But Lydia had not seen Betty run with the powder during the prolonged siege of the following year, and two-thirds of a century later, when people wanted to know about *"Betty Zane Running with the Powder during the Siege of Fort Henry"* — Lydia didn't remember anything about that. All she remembered was that, while there were Indians outside the fort, she was in the fort helping Molly Scott get gunpowder for the men in Col. Zane's cabin. How could she remember whether that incident had happened 67 years ago or 68 years ago? It happened when she was a teenager, at Fort Henry, when the Indians were attacking. And when asked about these events by Dr. Draper in 1846, she combined elements of both Indian attacks into one. She remembered with great clarity details which had occurred sixty-eight years before; she was being asked about an event which had taken place a year later.

And perhaps the single most astonishing thing about the entire episode is that there was nothing wrong with Lydia's memory. Everything that she said is absolutely correct. But – a prime requisite in the solution of this problem is the separation of those events which occurred in the 1781 Attack from those which took place during the 1782 Siege. And then everything falls neatly into place.

Lydia said: "*Molly Scott ran over from the Zane cabin to the fort, got some powder with my assistance, and ran back.*" That is correct. That happened in 1781, when the Indians first appeared on the hillside and elsewhere too far away.

Lydia said: "*My father was absent*". Also correct, but that was in 1782; Captain Boggs had been sent for reinforcements, and Silas Zane was in charge of the fort.

Lydia said: "*Betty Zane was living with her father at Catfish Camp*". In September of 1781 Lydia knew quite well where Betty was living, having previously resided there herself. Sometime after the attack of 1781, but well before the Siege of 1782, Betty, her father, and her new step-mother moved to the Wheeling settlement, to be near the Zane brothers; their father had recently married for a second time.

Lydia said: "*Scouts gave warning of approach of Indians about 3 o'clock in the afternoon*". That was 1782; in 1781 the Indians had appeared early in the morning, about an hour after sunrise.

Lydia said: "*The Indians did not shoot at Molly Scott going or returning*". Correct for 1781. The Indians on the hillside were not close enough to the fort to have fired at anyone with any effect, while those on the island could not even have seen anyone running from the fort to the cabin.

Lydia said: "*About mid-day, on the second day of the Siege, a girl ran between the fort and the Zane cabin, with some powder*". But that *second day of the Siege* could have referred only to the Siege of 1782, as there had been no second day of the siege in either 1777 or 1781, and the girl must therefore have been Betty Zane, Molly Scott having been the courier the year before.

Lydia said: "*The siege commenced sun an hour high, Monday, September 11th*". Both times and dates are correct, but only alternately. In 1782 the 11th of

September fell not on a Monday but on a Wednesday. However, the 3rd of September *was* a Monday in 1781, and it is more likely that Lydia would correctly recall the day of the week than the date of the month. Perhaps she remembered attending church on a Sunday (September 2nd) and then the Indians were seen, just after sunrise on the very next morning — in 1781.

In her affidavit she stated: *"On Monday afternoon, September 11, 1782, a body of about 300 Indians, and 50 British soldiers... appeared in front of the fort..."*. She had earlier told Draper that the siege began sometime after about 3:00 o'clock in the afternoon, when scouts gave the alarm of the approach of the Indians. The Indian Attack of 1781, however, began early in the morning, within an hour or so after sunrise. And, during the progress of the interview with Draper, she described the activities of several men from the fort, who were out and moving about during the morning hours of that day — in 1782.

Lydia must have known that everyone said that the Siege of 1782 began on a Wednesday, September 11th, but for some reason she persisted in remembering it as being a Monday. The exact date of that Indian attack of 1781 has never been exactly determined — until now. Doddridge gave it as the seventh or eighth of September, but if Lydia was correct, and it was a Monday, then it must have been Monday, September 3, 1781[120]. *"The Siege commenced about sun an hour high, Monday"* is therefore correct, for 1781.

*   *   *

Her two conflicting statements: *"the Siege commenced about sun an hour high"*, and *"about 3 o'clock in the afternoon"* — should have been a clue to researchers, since both statements could have been false, but both could not possibly be true. Evidently those historians were not aware, however, that Lydia was speaking of two separate events, a year apart.

Lydia told Draper that the: *"Siege commenced about sun an hour high, Monday, September 11th"* — at all events, the 11th. But during the course of the interview, she also told him that as a warning of the first approach of the Indians, the scouts discharged their weapons *"about 3 o'clock in the afternoon"*. Since she could not have been speaking of this same event, then she must have been referring to two different events, at both of which she had been present. Somehow, in the notes taken by Draper, either Lydia mixed up two different sets of recollections in her own mind, or else Draper himself failed to distinguish between her comments on two different forays by the Indians against Fort Henry, or else somewhere in the transcription and cataloging of these "notes" this confusion concerning the times of the approach of the Indians has occurred. Since there is no doubt that at the Siege of 1782 the Indians appeared sometime in the latter part of the afternoon, then Lydia's comments about the scouts' warning of the approach of the Indians at three o'clock in the afternoon can refer *only* to that siege. Therefore, her other remark concerning the appearance of the Indians, *"Siege commenced about sun an hour high"*, must be a reference to the Indians' appearance in 1781. And her *"Monday, September 11th"* (1782) would then be that Monday which was September 3, 1781.

It is also interesting to note her use of the phrase: *"Monday, September 11th" — at all events, the 11th*. Why did she add *"at all events"*? Had she previously mentioned that the siege had begun on a Monday, and been corrected by someone insisting that September 11th was a Wednesday? Was there a particular reason for her remembering and specifically insisting, both in her interview with Draper in 1846 and again in her affidavit three years later, that the siege commenced on a Monday?

In 1782 (Wednesday, September 11th) the Indians appeared around three o'clock in the afternoon. This would have allowed plenty of time for the following events, from Lydia's timetable: *"On the morning of the 11th, a damp morning, Stephen Burkam and one Wright"* began their journey *"from the Fort to Washington"* (Pennsylvania), and for them to travel about *"three or four miles"*, where they found sign of Indians, whereupon they *"returned to the fort and reported"*; as well as allowing time for the various activities of the other men that morning that Lydia described.

It is basically a problem of Lydia's faulty memory confusing two separate events; events that had not concerned her for nearly seventy years, and the details of which had occupied neither much prominence nor much importance in her thoughts for two-thirds of a century. When questioned about it, she was convinced of the accuracy of her recollections, especially when she was able to remember certain details so vividly, specifically helping none other than Molly Scott get powder for those men in the Zane cabin. There is no doubt that there was some confusion in her mind about these particular events; when interviewed by Draper in 1846, she said that Molly Scott was not fired upon either coming over to the fort or returning to the Zane cabin, as the Indians were on the hillside and elsewhere too far to have shot with any effect. However, three years later, evidently having been involved in disputes about the nature of this episode, as a result of Draper's interviews, she revised her statement somewhat, saying that on the second day of the siege, *Tuesday, September 12th* (September 12th in 1782 was a Thursday): *"the enemy, having temporarily withdrawn from the attack, but occupying a position within gunshot of the fort, those within observed a female leave the residence of Colonel Zane, and advance with rapid movements towards the fort..."*.

So now the Indians are no longer *too far away to shoot*; they have only *temporarily withdrawn from the attack*, but they are still *within gunshot of the fort*. In other words, they were close enough to shoot at her, but for some reason failed to do so. However, in his official report of the siege, which he wrote on the day following the conclusion of the 1782 siege, Col. Zane specifically stated that during the second day *"the enemy kept a continual fire the whole day."*

The Indians and the British troops kept up a continuous fire on the fort all day long. They were not *"on the hillside and elsewhere too far away"* to shoot at the fort, or at anyone running between the fort and the cabin. They did not move back up on the hillside, so that Molly Scott would be allowed to run unhindered with a load of powder from the fort over to the Zane cabin. Nor does anything appear in Lydia's affidavit about Silas Zane being in the Zane cabin in 1782. It seems certain that she did correctly remember, when she helped Molly get the powder in 1781, that Silas Zane *was* with his brother in his cabin. But too many people insisted that Silas was commander of the fort (in 1782) and so Lydia remained silent on that.

In spite of numerous self-proclaimed authorities throwing up their hands with the remark that: "it is now, at this late date, impossible to determine the truth of the matter" — it seems that certain conclusions are fairly obvious. The Indians attacked Fort Henry on three separate occasions: in 1777, in 1781, and again in 1782. During one of these Lydia Boggs helped Molly Scott get powder from the fort to take to the men (including Silas Zane) in the Zane cabin, at a time when the Indians were too far away to shoot with any effect, and when Betty Zane was not at Wheeling. This could have been neither 1777 (Lydia was not there that year) nor 1782 (because Betty *was* there, and the Indians kept up a continuous fire on the fort all day). Therefore, *that* event must have occurred in 1781. Again, during one of these sieges Betty Zane ran from the fort to her brother's cabin and back again, with her apron full of powder, on the second day. That could have been neither 1777 nor 1781, as there was no "second day" in those two years, and Betty did not arrive at Fort Henry until 1782. Therefore, this must have occurred at the siege of 1782.

There was one other early spectator to this debate, but his evidence seems to have been as generally neglected as that of Jim Scott's. In the early 1830s George S. McKierman became interested in the history of the border wars, at a time when there were still several survivors of those times. Between 1832 and 1836 he interviewed a number of those pioneers, among whom was Lydia Boggs Cruger. In his observations he stated:

> *"When I first knew Mrs. Cruger she was [as] bright and sparkling as a young woman. In her later days her memory became confused. She assured Mr. Draper, for instance, in 1846, that John McColloch was the hero of the leap over Wheeling hill, instead of his brother, Sam.... From the interesting nature of the incident of carrying the powder, I made it the subject of inquiry in my interviews with all those persons, and I am quite*

*certain that Mrs. Cruger did not attribute the powder exploit to Molly Scott or to anyone but Betsy Zane, neither did any other of the old inhabitants. There is not the shadow of a doubt in my mind that she and not Molly Scott was the heroine of the powder keg. In fact, I never heard any of the old pioneers mention the name of Molly Scott. They were unanimous in giving the honor to Miss Zane."*

Yet how could Lydia be so completely positive, and yet so totally wrong? The answer, once seen, is like the answer to many complex problems: not only is it absurdly simple, but it was even stated (or rather *misstated*) by several others, many years before. Lydia was indeed confusing details which had occurred in two separate events, but not the two events which had been postulated by others as their solution: not the Sieges of 1777 and 1782, but rather the Attack of 1781 and the Siege of 1782.

\*　　\*　　\*

The author has the greatest respect for Lydia, as he has for all our pioneer ancestors. Theirs was an unbelievably arduous life; a life so incredibly difficult that it is no longer possible for us moderns even to begin to comprehend the difficulties. Mere survival itself required an almost Herculean effort, and many failed to survive those rigorous times. My purpose has not been to denigrate an estimable lady, who, born a loyal subject of George III, lived through those terrible days of revolution and horrific Indian warfare as a teenager. She was well into her forties when Abraham Lincoln was born in Kentucky, and she survived to see the end of a civil war and the assassination of President Lincoln. Rather, the purpose of this essay is to do what seems right and proper, and what Lydia herself once deemed imperative: *"But undersigned does not wish to detract any from the heroism of that feat, she only desires to correct a gross error — to give honor to whom honor is due. This she deems imperative, that the truth and justice of history may be maintained."* (Cruger Affidavit, November 28, 1849)

Honor to whom honor is due, that the truth and justice of history may be maintained, and the honor is most certainly due to Betty Zane. As the illustrious Colonel Zane, speaking through his descendent, Zane Grey, might well have said:

*We should stop a moment to think of the heroes who have gone before... we who worked, fought, bled beside them, who saw them die for those they left behind, will render them all justice, honor and love. To them we give the victory.... They were true: then let us... likewise be true in memory of them....*

[See page 364 for Lydia Boggs Cruger's "Sketch Map of Fort Hentry"]

# Appendix H:
## *A Brief Wetzel-Harmar Chronology*

ca. July 5, 1789:
Lewis Wetzel, perhaps in the company of Vachel/Veach Dickerson, shoots and wounds Que-shaw-sey, a Delaware Indian known as George Washington.

July 9, 1789:
General Harmar writes to Secretary of War Henry Knox concerning the shooting of George Washington, by one Lewis Whitsell.

ca. mid-July, 1789:
Wetzel is placed under arrest by Judge Parsons at Marietta and, for want of a jail, is confined at the garrison at Fort Harmar; Wetzel soon escapes.

ca. August 20, 1789:
In Limestone Wetzel is apprehended by Sgt. Lollor, at the home of a friend. He is taken to Cincinnati.

August 26, 1789:
Judge John Cleves Symmes deposes: Lewis Weitsel, having escaped from Fort Harmar, and having been retaken into custody at Limestone, Kentucky, by Capt. McCurdy; Wetzel has this day been delivered into the custody of the civil authority by McCurdy.

September 10, 1789:
A letter of this date to the editor of the *Kentucky Gazette* (Lexington) is printed (September 26) which states that a free citizen (Wetzel) was taken from the house of a friend by a military officer (McCurdy) and his soldiers, placed in custody, and confined in a military garrison.

ca. mid-October, 1789:
Col. Henry Lee, county lieutenant of Mason County, Kentucky, goes to Fort Washington (Cincinnati), where Major Doughty is commanding. Doughty informs Lee that Wetzel had been accused of the murder of an Indian, but the Indian had recovered, and the only witness against Wetzel had left the country; also that Doughty had instructed McCurdy to deliver Wetzel to Judge Symmes, which he had done, whereupon Wetzel was released.

October 24, 1789:
In the *Kentucky Gazette* appears a letter from Col. Lee, who feels that the military authority has exceeded the

civil. He states that not only was Wetzel unlawfully seized and detained, but that McCurdy's men stole goods and looted the town.

October 25, 1789: Gen. Harmar writes to Major Hamtramck to make the necessary enquiry into the McCurdy affair.

December 3, 1789: Hamtramck writes to Harmar that he has made an enquiry about McCurdy, in which any plundering by the men under McCurdy is denied.

January 13, 1790: Harmar writes to Hamtramck that all Kentucky is in an uproar about the disorderly behavior of McCurdy and his company; that he has received another letter from Lee, who seems determined to prosecute the matter. Harmar orders McCurdy placed under arrest, and that he should report to headquarters [Cincinnati] in the spring to stand trial. No mention of Wetzel.

January 23, 1790: Harmar writes to Lee informing him that he has ordered McCurdy arrested.

April 20, 1790: Hamtramck writes to Harmar that Captain Beatty will give him the money which was taken from Wetzel at Limestone.

ca. May, 1790: McCurdy arrives at Fort Washington.

August 27, 1790: Harmar writes to Hamtramck to inform him that Captain McCurdy has been acquitted by the Court Martial.

# Appendix I:
## *The Forts at Wheeling, and the Forts Randolph*

In the latter part of the last century, and extending well into this one, a debate was carried on as to the exact location of Wheeling's Fort Henry. On one side were those who placed it at the site of present 10th and Main Streets, while others insisted just as strongly that it had been located a half mile further south, at the juncture formed by the mouth of Wheeling Creek and the Ohio River. Both sides could point to documentary evidence as well as oral testimony that the fort had been at the locale of their designated choice.

Actually, surprisingly, it did not matter whose choice was selected, nor which of the locations was being pointed out. There had been *two* forts at Wheeling, from 1774 until well into the early part of the 1800s, and they stood, separated by a half mile, at the two sites indicated. But only one of those was designated Fort Henry, and that was the only one ever to withstand a siege; the other fort still remains basically unknown.

That there should have been a debate in the first place is hardly surprising, knowledge of history being so quickly lost. Only forty years after the last siege of Fort Henry, the Reverend Joseph Doddridge visited the city while finishing up his monumental *Notes*:

> Should you visit Wheeling, you would make the visit with the impression of its being regarded, by the whole country as classic ground, on account of the memorable events, which have taken place there. No such thing. In the town itself you might inquire of a dozen people, where Fort Henry stood, without receiving any other answers, than that they knew nothing about it.
>
> *The Russian Spy*[121] *No. XXI*

[Published in *The Supporter and Scioto Gazette*, Chillicothe, Ohio, July 13, 1826.]

And yet, there was really no need for this dispute, except perhaps for the inaccessibility of the Draper Manuscripts; probably few if any of the disputants in this case were aware that Dr. Draper had interviewed Lydia (Boggs Shepherd) Cruger in 1846. But during that interview she had talked about the two forts at Wheeling, although without identifying the second by name, and not only had she mentioned them, she had also given the exact locations of each.

Fort Henry, the old lady had explained, was:

"directly on the river bank — half a mile above the mouth of Wheeling Creek."

"Do you mean right down on the river bank itself?" Draper must have asked.

"No, no!" said Lydia, "it was up higher" —
           "on the second bank."

meaning on the bluff, overlooking the river. Then, "after 1786," she continued —

"the old fort decayed, and a new fort was erected near the mouth of Wheeling Creek."

Why had Lydia chosen that particular year to say that the old fort decayed? Obviously because it was in that year of 1786, or shortly afterward, that the new fort, named Fort Randolph in honor of the current governor of the state[122], was built. It was probably also at about this time that the old fort, Fort Henry, was dismantled and the logs were recycled, as was the common practice. At any rate Fort Henry was no longer in evidence in 1803, when the Reverend Mr. Harris made his *Tour into the Territory Northwest of the Allegheny Mountains*, the Journal of which was published in 1805. Arriving in Wheeling in April of 1803, he wrote a description of the town of Wheeling, in which he mentions the old fort [actually this was the "new" fort], which stood:

"below the town, at the point of land formed by the junction of Wheeling Creek and the river."

According to G.L. Cranmer (*History of Wheeling City & Ohio County*), this was a fort which had been built by the federal government in the latter part of the eighteenth century. Constructed of logs and occupying the site of the B&O railroad depot, it stood in decaying condition for many years. To quote Cranmer on its eventual demise:

It stood in fair repair until a time when an unruly ox, being led by John Wiseralls and Henry Sockman, butchers, started to run from them.... Sockman held on to the steer with a rope until he reached the fort, when he took a hitch with the rope on the end of a projecting log. The log was pulled out and soon afterward the fort was all a ruin.

Additional supplementary evidence of the construction of a second fort at Wheeling, in or shortly after 1786, can be found in a new book on the Upper Ohio Frontier: *Elusive Empires: Constructing Colonialism in the Ohio Valley 1673-1800*, by Eric Hinderaker[123]. Although Fort Randolph is not mentioned by name, and even though there are no specific references to a fort at Wheeling, there is no doubt that a new fort must have been erected in the early part of General Harmar's administration.

Writing on the "Indian Problem" after the end of the Revolutionary War, he tells of Lt. Col. (later General) Josiah Harmar being sent west "late in 1784". Following that is a paragraph on George Rogers Clark's raid against the Mad River Indian villages in 1786, and then:

*"After 1786 the Ohio Indians were primarily confined to a corridor to the south and west of Lake Erie... on the Sandusky, Maumee, and Wabash Rivers. Harmar dispatched two companies of federal troops to Louisville .... at the same time, responding to reports of violence, Congress raised additional troops to send to the Ohio Valley. Soon they were posted at forts along most of the length of the river: at Venango on the Allegheny, Fort Pitt, Fort McIntosh at the mouth of the Beaver River, at Wheeling, Fort Harmar on the Muskingum, Fort Steuben opposite Louisville, and in Vincennes, where the Americans were just establishing themselves." (pp. 239-241)* [124]

But where were these additional [government] troops garrisoned whilst they were *at Wheeling*? In 1786 Fort Henry was still standing, of course, but decaying, and probably no longer habitable. There were the other forts — Pitt, McIntosh (Beaver, PA), Venango (Franklin, PA), Harmar (Marietta, OH), and the fort at Louisville (actually at present Clarksville, IN) and Fort Knox at Vincennes, Indiana. But Lydia had said that the fort was decaying by 1786; so it was in that year that a new fort had to be constructed at Wheeling for the use of Harmar's troops, few as they were, and widely scattered. Not on ground owned by the Zane Family, but rather at the mouth of the creek. This was the new fort, *Fort Randolph.*

In Collet's 1796 survey of the Ohio River [125], the settlement at Wheeling is denoted as *Wheeling Island, Town, and Fort*, with the fort situated next to the mouth of Wheeling Creek. Obviously the Fort shown there must be Fort Randolph, as Fort Henry had been described as "decayed" ten years earlier. Fort Randolph, then, was still standing some ten years after it had been built. Years later Fort Randolph, unused, was also falling down, until such time as a cantankerous ox finally accomplished what successive bands of painted Indians could not — the destruction of a government fort in *Wheeling Town.*

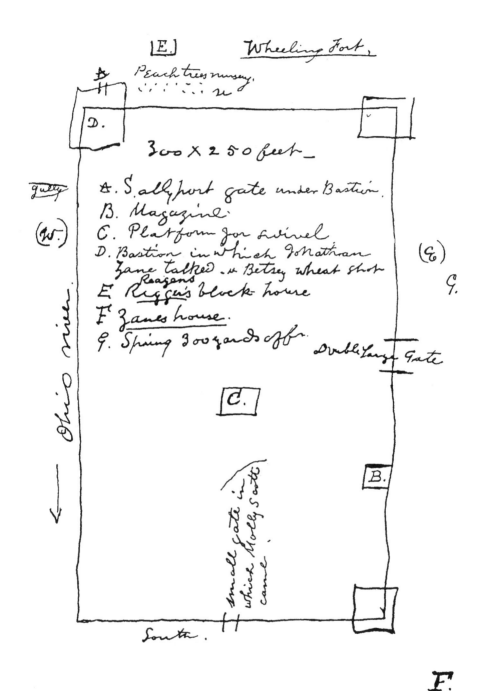

Lydia's "Sketch Map of Fort Henry"

# Footnotes

## Prologue

[1] *Favour, Alpheus, Old Bill Williams, Mountain Man, Norman, OK, University of Oklahoma Press, 1936, pp 79-80.*

[2] *By far the best account of the French and Indian War, as well as the subsequent events leading up to the American Revolution, can be found in Dale Van Every's magnificent Forth to the Wilderness: The First American Frontier, 1754-1774, New York, William Morrow & Co., 1961.*

## Chapter One

[3] *Right and left banks of a river are determined as one descends the river; therefore Ohio (to the west) is on the right bank of the Ohio, (West) Virginia and Kentucky are on the left.*

## Chapter Two

[4] *In 1775, when Boone was leading his extended "family" along the Wilderness Road into Kentucky, one of the men found a skeleton in a hollow sycamore. The rifle was missing, but the powder horn was still there, with the initials J.S. on it.*

## Chapter Three

[5] *In 1903 Zane Grey, the well-known author of westerns, and the great-grandson of Ebenezer Zane, wrote in the preface to his first novel, Betty Zane, that he was in possession of the long-lost journal of Col. Ebenezer Zane. Although Betty Zane was a novel, Grey said that he had taken the main facts of his story from "its faded and time-worn pages". Since this "journal" has once again been lost, there are many who deny its existence, claiming that Grey was merely making up a little fiction in order to lend credence and personal interest to his story. But there is more than just a slight chance that those faded and time-worn pages that Zane Grey once held in his hands were not from his great-grandfather's long-lost journal, but rather that they were the materials that Noah Zane had collected in preparation for the biography of Col. Zane, and for the history of the Wheeling settlement.*

[6] *In 1770 George Washington made a tour of the Ohio River; although he did not see Williams or the Zanes, as he approached the mouth of Buffalo Creek he observed in his diary that it had been reported to him that all the land from that point southward for a dozen miles had been claimed by three adventurers from Virginia.*

7 *Another of the unsung heroines of the pioneer days, Rebecca Williams (b. February 14, 1754) was the daughter of Joseph Tomlinson, founder of Tomlinson's Station at the Grave Creek Flats in 1771, the first white settlement in present Marshall County, West Virginia. Her first husband, John Martin, was an Indian trader in the late 1760's, until he and a man named Hartness, one of Rebecca's uncles, were killed by Shawnee Indians on the Hocking River in 1770. The sixteen-year-old widow had then lived with her brothers at Moundsville until she married Isaac Williams, in October, 1775. Like Mrs. Zane she gained considerable renown for her skill as a pioneer surgeon and doctor.*

# Chapter Four

8 *The fact that Logan was a peacful, inoffensive Indian is not to say that all the other Indian men in his camp were quite so peaceful and inoffensive.*

9 *It has been stated that Logan's father was also one of those killed, but this is incorrect; Shickalamy had died years before, in 1749, at his village at the forks of the Susquehanna.*

10 *Valentine Crawford's reference to the Little Kanawha was in error; the correct location was the mouth of Pipe Creek. The infant son of Col. John Gibson, an Indian trader and American patriot, and his Indian wife, Logan's sister, was taken from the Greathouse party by William Crawford after its mother had been killed; Crawford then gave the baby to John Neville, who later had it delivered to its father.*

11 *The reference to Coneestoga: in 1763 a mob of border ruffians known as the Paxton Boys killed twenty peaceable Mingo (Conestoga) Indians.*

# Chapter Five

12 *The fort at Wheeling was originally named Fort Fincastle, in honor of the governor, but in 1776 the name was changed from Fincastle to Henry to honor the new governor of the State of Virginia, Patrick Henry. Although its size has been described as anywhere from one-tenth of an acre (!) to several acres, it was probably about the same size as other frontier government installations of the time, i.e., about 160-180 feet wide by 220-240 feet long, encompassing overall just slightly less than one acre. The palisade fence was of squared timbers of white oak, sunk three feet deep, and standing approximately twelve to fourteen feet in height, with bastions, or blockhouses, at each of the four corners. Cabins were built along the inside wall, with the doors opening out onto the central area. There was also the commandant's cabin, a powder magazine, and a corral for the livestock. In 1781 a double pen, or two story log structure, was built near the front gate, on which the French cannon*

*was placed. There exists a mistaken impression that, since George Rogers Clark was at Wheeling at this time, he must have been the man who designed and was in charge of the construction of Fort Henry. Not so; although he would soon receive his commision as captain, in June of 1774 Clark was no more than a 22-year-old subaltern in Michael Cresap's militia company, while McDonald, not only a colonel but an army engineer as well, chose the ground, designed the fort, and supervised the construction.*

[13] *Andrew Montour had accompanied George Washington and Christopher Gist on their famed trip in 1753 to the French on Lake Erie, where Washington delivered Governor Dinwiddie's order to vacate.*

[14] *There were several Shawnee towns known by the name Chillicothe. One was three miles north of present Xenia, another was at Frankfort in Ross County, and this village, fifteen miles north of present Chillicothe, Ohio.*

[15] *Logan could speak English, and on a later occasion he related his anguish to another person in that language. But in talking with Gibson he almost certainly spoke in the Iroquois tongue.*

[16] *Logstown, originally the site of a Shawnee village, was an important location for many years. It was situated on the right side of the Ohio, eighteen miles below Fort Pitt. An important treaty was concluded at Logstown in 1748, and Washington stopped there on his journey for Governor Dinwiddie to the French posts in 1753. He mentions it again in his travels of 1770. The site was eventually abandoned after the close of the Revolution.*

# Chapter Six

[17] *The Treaty of Pittsburgh was considered so important by the early 20th-century researchers, Thwaites and Kellogg, that they devoted over 100 pages to the complete negotiation process in the second book of their series on the Trans-Appalachian frontier, The Revolution on the Upper Ohio, 1775-1777, pp. 25-127.*

[18] *Walker had been the first white man through the Cumberland Gap, which he had discovered in April, 1750, and named in honor of the Duke of Cumberland. This was the "gap" through the mountains into Kentucky; under Boone, a quarter century later, it was to become a part of the Wilderness Road.*

[19] *Fort Blair was built immediately following the Battle of Point Pleasant. After it was burned in October, 1775, a new fort, Randolph, was built the next year, commanded by Captain Matthew Arbuckle, and named in honor of the president of the First*

Continental Congress, Peyton Randolph. This was not the same Fort Randolph which was built a decade later at the mouth of Wheeling Creek, during Harmar's reign, to replace the decaying Fort Henry.

## Chapter Seven

[20] This camp was near present Winchester, Kentucky.

## Chapter Eight

[21] This name was the inspiration for Zane Grey's Village of Peace, in Ohio, in his novel, The Spirit of the Border; this "Village of Peace", however, was in Pennsylvania.

[22] This is the Christian Indian settlement that Zane Grey refers to as the "Village of Peace".

[23] The site of Schoenbrunn was purchased by the Ohio Historical Society in 1923; the first cabin reconstruction was completed in 1927, the meeting house and schoolhouse were rebuilt in 1928. Restored Schoenbrunn is now a state park, maintained by the state historical society.

## Chapter Nine

[24] The Kittanning was the name given to an area on the east side of the Allegheny river, about fifty miles northeast of Pittsburgh, at the present town of that name. In 1756 it consisted of several Delaware villages, which had located there since about 1730. At the beginning of the French and Indian War Kittanning was a rendevous for the tribes, numerous raiding parties against the frontier issuing from there.

## Chapter Ten

[25] Ohio County, (West) Virginia, had been formed from the older District of West Augusta in October, 1776.

[26] Lewis Bonnett (1778-1850) was interviewed by Draper in 1845.

## Chapter Eleven

[27] This was the killing of Thomas Ryan.

[28] Shepherd had come out to the Wheeling area about 1773, and had purchased the Silas Zane improvement six miles east of Wheeling, present Elm Grove, West

*Virginia, where he built Shepherd's Fort. The site is now occupied by the stone mansion known as Monument Place. In January of 1777 Shepherd had been chosen Ohio County lieutenant, an office which he held until his death in 1795. In March, 1777, he had written to Governor Patrick Henry that in the estimation of the men on the border it would be necessary to post fifty men at Wheeling, fifty more at Grave Creek a dozen miles to the south, and twenty-five at Beech Bottom Fort a dozen miles to the north. Shepherd was at Fort Henry during the siege of 1777, and he also commanded a regiment in Brodhead's Coshocton Expedition of 1781.*

[29] *According to the account book kept by Francis Duke, deputy commisary of Ohio County.*

[30] *This according to Shepherd's official report to General Hand, dated Sept 15, 1777.*

[31] *Francis Duke (1751-1777) had married Sarah, the oldest daughter of David Shepherd, in Berkeley Co., VA, in 1773. They came west to Wheeling about that time, and Duke was appointed, by Col. Shepherd (his father-in-law) to be deputy commisary; as such he was stationed at Beech Bottom Fort. This fort, occupied only during 1777, was located three miles below Wellsburg, and twelve miles above Wheeling.*

[32] *In 1777 Col. Zane and Sam Mason had laid out the road to the forks of Wheeling Creek, at Shepherd's Fort.*

[33] *Matthew Arbuckle was one of the most experienced Indian fighters of his time. In 1765 he had explored the length of the Kanawha Valley all the way to the Ohio River. No other white man, Indian captives like Mary Ingles excepted, had ever passed that way. It was as a result of this experience that he was chosen during Dunmore's War as captain of a company of scouts for Lewis's army. Because of his great experience in the region he was placed in command of Fort Randolph (Point Pleasant) in 1776, where he served for three years. In a strange twist of fate this talented and capable woodsman and soldier was killed during a severe storm in 1781 by an unseen and unsuspected enemy, a falling tree.*

[34] *Present Henderson, Kentucky*

[35] *New Madrid remained a military post and frontier settlement under Spanish control until 1804, when it was transferred to the Americans as a result of Jefferson's Louisiana Purchase.*

# Chapter Twelve

[36] In 1771 Joseph Tomlinson had built the first cabin in present Marshall County, on the Grave Creek Flats, at the site of the present Moundsville Middle School. A marker in front of that school commemorates his settlement.

[37] Thwaites and Kellogg, in their Frontier Defense on the Upper Ohio, 1777-1778, also list Jacob Greathouse as having been killed in this affair. This, however, is incorrect, as Jacob Greathouse, along with his wife, was most brutally murdered by the Indians in 1791.

[38] There has been some dispute both as to the number of men involved in Foreman's Expedition, and the number killed. The correct numbers are forty-six, of whom twenty-one were killed, and one (Jonathan Pugh) captured. For the Foreman Roster see Appendix E.

[39] Along with Cornstalk and his son Elinipisco, others at the Battle of Point Pleasant had included Chiksikah, Red Hawk, and the chiefs Blue Jacket, Black Hoof, and Puckeshinewa, the only chief killed there, and the father of Chiksikah and Tecumseh.

[40] Dale Van Every, A Company of Heroes, The American Frontier 1775-1783, New York, William Morrow & Co., 1962, pp. 116-117.

# Chapter Thirteen

[41] Old Chillicothe was located on the Little Miami River, about three miles north of present Xenia, Ohio.

# Chapter Fourteen

[42] The Western Christian Advocate, Cincinnati, Ohio, March 29 – April 26, 1839.

# Chapter Fifteen

[43] Kaskaskia was the oldest French post in the west, having been founded about the year 1700, and it had been in continuous existence since, being transferred to British control in 1765. After its capture by Clark in 1778 the entire district became the Illinois County of Virginia until 1787, when it became a part of the old Northwest Territory. Kaskaskia remained the capital of the Illinois Territory until after the War of 1812 when, in 1819, the capital was moved to Vandalia.

[44] George Clark was no relation to George Rogers Clark.

# Chapter Sixteen

45 Silas Harlan was one of the men who had come out with Jim Harrod in 1774, before the outbreak of Dunmore's War.

46 Col. Daniel Brodhead (1736-1809) was born in Ulster County, New York, his family moving to Pennsylvania soon after his birth. At the outbreak of the Revolution he raised a company of riflemen and joined Washington. In March, 1777, he was promoted to command of the 8th Pennsylvania Regiment, and in August of 1778 he marched west with his regiment to Fort Pitt, where he replaced Gen. Lachlin McIntosh as commander of the Western Department, in April, 1779. Brodhead would lead two expeditions against the Indians; in September, 1779, and again in April, 1781. In January, 1781, he was made Colonel of the First Pennsylvania Regiment, but during the course of that year he became involved in a controversy with John Gibson, who replaced Brodhead as commander in September. After the Revolution Brodhead was promoted to brigadier-general, and later served as the Pennsylvania's surveyor-general.

47 The officer in charge of that lead division cutting the road through to Wyoming, present Wilkes-Barre, Pennsylvania, was Captain John Combs, of New Jersey. Captain Combs, the author's fourth-great-grandfather, now lies in an unmarked grave in the sadly neglected City Cemetery of Wilkes-Barre.

48 Many of the Indians had probably never seen a cannon in close-range combat action before. There is a world of difference in watching a cannon demonstration on a parade ground from a safe distance, and being in a wooded area, with the cannon pouring shot and shell, canister and grape, in your direction, shells bursting in the woods around you, shattering trees, starting fires, and creating general havoc.

49 Canadasego was a mile and a half northwest of present Geneva, New York; it consisted of about sixty log homes. A stockade fort had been built around the town during the French and Indian War, and John Butler had a trading post there. The only person found in the town was a three-year-old white captive, abandoned when the Indians had fled.

50 An Indian village on the Allegheny, near the New York border, in present Warren County, Pennsylvania.

51 Hendricks had run away from home at the age of fourteen and joined Boone's expedition to Kentucky. After his capture with the saltmakers he was adopted into a Shawnee family in one of the Pickaway towns. That summer he escaped, while the Indians were gone to Boonesborough, but was recaptured by a party of returning and decidedly unhappy warriors. Nearly killed, he was rescued at the last possible

*moment by a group of Kickapoo, who took him to the Wabash. Some time later he was ransomed by Isaac Zane, and having worked for Zane until he had repaid his purchase price, he was permitted to return to Kentucky. He later moved to the Illinois country, and died there in 1799.*

## Chapter Seventeen

52 *This was not the William Crawford who commanded the Sandusky Campaign in May, 1782.*

53 *Upon the organization of Westmoreland County, Pennsylvania, in 1773, Col. Archibald Lochry (sometimes Laughery) was chosen county lieutenant, a post he held until his death. In June of 1781, just after Brodhead's return, the county officers met and proposed that Lochry be placed in command of a body of volunteer Pennsylvania militia to join George Rogers Clark in the planned expedition against Detroit. Clark wrote to Col. Shepherd that he had selected Wheeling as the site of the rendezvous, and set the date at July 15th, or as soon thereafter as possible.*

54 *March 29-April 26, 1839. The issue referring to Martin Wetzel was that of April 5th.*

55 *Mistakes abound, certainly not an uncommon characteristic of oral tradition, but McDonald shows his ignorance of the specifics involved. The year was 1781; Coshocton was not the name of a river, but rather the Indian village; the Muskingum River is formed at Coshocton by the confluence of the Walhonding and Tuscarawas Rivers; Martin Wetzel was not on this expedition; the army consisted of slightly under 300 men.*

56 *Lewis Bonnett, Jr's. father, Lewis, Sr., was the brother of Mary Bonnett Wetzel.*

57 *For a detailed analysis of this episode, see the Seventh Interlude, Lewis Wetzel vs. George Washington.*

## Chapter Eighteen

58 *Where his grave may still be seen, the first Christian burial in Ohio.*

59 *Following the 1795 Treaty of Greeneville Simon Girty crossed the river into Canada, where he resided until his death in 1818.*

## Chapter Nineteen

60 *Although the exact relationships are uncertain, this Billy Ryan who was killed during the Attack of 1781 was either a son or a younger brother of that same Thomas*

Ryan who had been killed by Indians in the spring of 1777, while working in his fields, not long before Lewis and Jacob Wetzel had been abducted. Davy Glenn was just as likely a son or younger brother of the Thomas Glenn who had been killed just outside the gates of Fort Henry during the siege in that same year of 1777. Orphans were common on the frontier.

61 The site of Fort Henry is on Main Street in downtown Wheeling, at approximately Tenth Street.

62 There are occasional references to Col. Zane's wife, Elizabeth (McColloch) Zane remaining in the blockhouse with her husband, but this is not correct. Her services as a surgeon would have been of much greater value inside the fort, the principal point of attack.

63 Some researchers have given his name as Jonathan, but Jacob appears to be correct.

64 Presley Peek was taken to Detroit, along with young William Boggs, where they were exchanged, and eventually both reached home, after a captivity of a year and a half.

65 So much for the modern delusion that the hostile Indians were outraged the next spring, when Williamson's militia massacred ninety of these same Christian Indians.

66 The two boys were taken to Sandusky, where the elder died. The younger boy was then sold to the Wyandots, from whom his father was finally successful in recovering him in the fall of 1784.

67 There is good reason to suppose that the returning war parties purposely led their pursuers back to Gnadenhatten, and as purposely left incriminating evidence there, such as a few horses and Mrs. Wallace's dress. If the militia took the time to search the village, they would easily find the items which had been left. Thus, a few hours delay, at the expense of the detested Christian Indians, would give the raiders just that much more time to evade pursuit.

Only two of the intended victims escaped; a boy of about fourteen had been knocked on the head and scalped, but regaining consciousness some time later, crept toward the door, and observing that it was nearly dark, cautiously crept from the mission house and, notwithstanding his wound, managed to gain the woods. Another boy, somewhat younger, who had been shut up with the women in the cooper's house, managed to pry up one of the floorboards and drop down into the cellar. As darkness approached he was able to make his way out of a window, or airhole, and thus escape.

The two most reliable researchers of the border wars of the Upper Ohio, R.G. Thwaites and C.W. Butterfield, both agree that several of the men killed were hostiles, who had returned to Gnadenhutten after raiding the settlements, and had been taken prisoner along with the Christian Indians. It is even possible that some of the Delaware who had brutalized Mrs. Wallace were still among them. Heckewelder later wrote: "... on the 4th or 5th of March the Warriors told one of our People [then at Gnadenhutten] — They had the greatest reason to expect a party of Virginians here Shortly, for that they (the Warriors) had been over the Ohio, robbed the house of a Gentleman (named Wallis or Wallace) & taken his Wife & Child Prisoners: That after crossing the Ohio to this side they had murdered the woman & child, & that they believed undoubtedly to be followed, within a short time."

## Chapter Twenty

[68] The massacre was almost universally condemned in the east, and a number of the leaders in the west also deplored the killings, but the common attitude of those on the border, of those who had suffered most from the Indians, was that the Moravians got no more than what they had deserved.

[69] Their villages were located on the banks of the Sandusky River, in present Wyandot County, Ohio; these towns were sometimes referred to as Upper Sandusky to distinguish them from the other Sandusky, Lower Sandusky, present Sandusky, Ohio, on the southwestern shore of Lake Erie. These two sites have since caused considerable confusion in regard to the destination of Crawford's army; Upper Sandusky was also the site of the Moravian Captives' Town.

[70] For a description of Mingo Bottom and the corresponding Mingo Town on the Ohio side, see Appendix E.

[71] Although Nicholson is now the least-known of the three guides, as a result of the subsequent exploits of Zane and Slover, at the time of this expedition he was probably the best known; he was certainly one of the most experienced scouts on the border. It was he who had guided McDonald's expedition eight years earlier, in the summer of 1774, after which he served as scout and interpreter for Lord Dunmore. Joseph Nicholson, his brother, also acted as a scout on many expeditions.

[72] The Delaware chief Pomoacan, known as the Half King, originally had his village just south of Detroit, but upon the outbreak of the Revolution he had moved southward to the Sandusky, present Upper Sandusky, Ohio. This was the village known to Slover and Zane, but at the time of Crawford's Expedition that site had been deserted a year or more, and Half King had taken up residence eight miles northeast of Upper Sandusky. Pipe's Town was located west of that, about eight miles northwest of present Upper Sandusky, just east of the present community of Crawford.

73 *An island, in border terminology, did not refer to a piece of land surrounded by water, but rather any wooded area surrounded on all sides by an open, fairly level plain. The site of Battle Island is now marked by a monument, and the location of the island is still visible.*

74 *Crawford's son, John, escaped with the remainder of the army and returned home; Col. Crawford's nephew, William Crawford, and his son-in-law, Major William Harrison, were both captured by the Indians, and both were killed. While a captive at Wapatomica John Slover saw and recognized their bodies. It was the nephew William, not the son John, who was the "young Crawford" reported as being killed.*

75 *Near present Leesville, Ohio.*

76 *Many commentators insist that the pursuit of Williamson's force and the other stragglers continued for days, not ending until the Indians reached the banks of the Ohio, and the last man had finally crossed the river. This is incorrect, although there certainly were other bands of warriors constantly on the prowl [see the following chapter for an adventure of Lewis Wetzel and Thomas Mills]. But the last hostile shot fired at the militia was near present Crestline, Ohio; after that neither Indian nor Ranger was seen by any of Williamson's men.*

77 *Withers implies that this was Benjamin Biggs, but the correct name is John. He had served as a captain in Brodhead's Coshocton Expedition the year before. Benjamin Biggs, who was probably a brother, was not present on this campaign; he later commanded Fort Henry, and after the Revolution became a brigadier-general of militia.*

78 *There has been some confusion as to the exact date of Crawford's torture; the correct date is Tuesday, June 11th, 1782; this according to the narrative given by Dr. Knight after his return, and he was there.*

79 *The information regarding the terrible agonies inflicted upon Col. Crawford came from Dr. Knight's Narrative, which was published in 1783 by Hugh Brackenridge, a Pittsburgh lawyer. In recent years efforts have been made to downplay the atrocities, by casting doubt on the authorship of the narrative, claiming that Brackenridge made major alterations in the manuscript for his own purposes; viz., to infuriate the frontier people to exterminate the Indian, and to cast Simon Girty as the arch-villain who could laugh at the sufferings of his old friend. Brackenridge may have altered some words or phrases here and there, but there seems no basis, other than political correctness, for claiming that the Narrative did not appear basically as it had been written by Knight himself, immediately after his return to Fort Pitt. The original*

printing did not include Slover's Narrative, which was published in subsequent editions. Slover was illiterate and, according to Brackenridge, he took down the story of his captivity and escape from Slover himself. Of course neither narrative contains any information on the army's retreat, and only Knight's contains the description of the horrific tortures suffered by Crawford. C.W. Butterfield, after an exhaustive study of the Sandusky Expedition, in which he compared all the known documents of the survivors with the statements given by Knight and Slover, came to the conclusion that there was no reason to doubt the truthfulness of the Narratives.

[80] Slover's home on the New River had been attacked by Miami Indians in 1761, during the French and Indian War, when John was eight years old. His father had been killed, one brother escaped, but John, his mother, and two sisters were taken captive. The two girls died on the journey to western Ohio, and the mother was exchanged and returned home, but died soon afterwards. John remained with the Miami six years, until he was traded to the Shawnee in 1767. After another six years captivity, he accompanied some of the Shawnee to Fort Pitt in 1773, where he was recognized and persuaded to remain.

[81] This despite the semantic labyrinth of some modern cultural anthropologists who insist that any human society is a "civilization", and thus meets the criteria of being "civilized".

[82] c.f., the modern practice of exorcism.

# Chapter Twenty-One

[83] The name is sometimes given as John Mills, but most authors say Thomas; possibly the confusion arose from the fact that there was a John Mills residing in the area.

[84] In Wetzel's time this site was called the Indian Springs; it has since come to be known as Wetzels Spring. Formerly a well-known local landmark at St. Clairsville, Ohio, Wetzels Spring was located eleven miles west of Wheeling along U.S. 40/Interstate 70. In a typically common act of destruction of an historic site, the spring was destroyed some years ago during the construction of a motel, which now sits atop the spring.

[85] Not to be confused with Grave Creek, seven miles to the north, at Moundsville.

[86] This interview took place at the residence of Lydia (Boggs) Cruger, at her mansion in present Elm Grove, West Virginia. John Wetzel was called "Old John", not because of advanced age, he was barely into his fifties when he was killed, but rather from the common practice of distinquishing a father, John, Senior, from a son, Junior, "Young John". The Miller referred to may have been Jacob Miller, who will

*be mentioned later as a defender of Rice's Fort in 1782.*

# Chapter Twenty-Three

[87] *There is some confusion regarding who was in the Zane Blockhouse during the Attack of 1781 and the Siege of 1782; the lists of names given here are considered the most reliable. Andy and Molly Scott were surely there in 1781, and were certainly there in 1782. Some commentators have placed Jonathan Zane in the Zane Blockhouse during one or both of those assaults, but Lydia Cruger said she remembered him being in the northeast bastion of the fort in 1781, which at least is reasonable, as that was the most vulnerable point, but in 1782 he may have been in the Blockhouse. Others have placed Martin Wetzel in the Blockhouse, but this is incorrect, as both he and his brother Lewis were at Beeler's Station, some miles south of Wheeling. As mentioned earlier, it has also been reported that the Colonel's wife remained with her husband, but this is highly unlikely, as her skill as a surgeon would have been much more effectively utilized inside the fort. A contributing factor in the confusion has been that several of the early writers mixed events of the various assaults, including Lydia Cruger's confusing Molly Scott's gunpowder run in 1781 with Betty Zane's in 1782, for which see Appendix G. Both Newton and Cranmer copy De Hass in placing the death of Francis Duke in 1782, when it was actually 1777; all three say that when word reached Shepherd's Fort a relief expedition started out from there with Duke at its head. This was not possible for the year 1782, of course, as Shepherd's Fort had been abandoned after the Siege of 1777 and the Foreman Massacre, and it was then burned by the Indians.*

*One of the most common errors concerning the two sieges of Fort Henry (discounting the short-lived attack of 1781) is the placement of Simon Girty at one or the other, or both. Of course he was still employed at Fort Pitt in 1777, so he would not have been at Wheeling then. He deserted from Pitt in 1778, but in 1782 he had only just returned to Wapatomica from the Blue Licks, about three weeks before the siege began on September 11th. He returned home from an arduous campaign that had extended for some six weeks of wilderness travel, culminating in a grand victory over the Kentuckians; by the time he arrived home the Wheeling-bound party had already left, and if he were to arrive at Wheeling in time to demand the surrender of Fort Henry he would have to hurry to overtake them. His brother George had accompanied the Kentucky expedition, and the same reasons for Simon apply to George as well. It is not so much that they could not have been there, but rather that they would not have been there. Since both Simon and George had been on the Kentucky Campaign, then what was Brother Jim doing?*

*So many other mistakes have been made by so many writers that it has resulted in more confusion regarding those heroic events at Fort Henry between 1777 and 1782 than those of any other installation. Withers, for example, begins his account of the 1782 siege with:*

In the first of September John Lynn (a celebrated spy and the same who had been with Capt. Foreman at the time of the fatal ambuscade at Grave Creek) being engaged in watching the warriors paths, northwest of the Ohio, discovered the Indians marching with great expedition for Wheeling....

But the 1782 date was September 11th; September 1st is correct for 1777. It was William Linn, not John, who had been with Foreman in 1777; William had been killed in 1781. De Hass next says that Cope Sullivan, who had arrived at Fort Henry on the very day of the attack in 1782, had been placed in charge of the fort, although it was actually Silas Zane, ad infinitum.

[88] The "French" cannon was so called because it came from Fort Duquesne. Upon the approach of Forbes's army in 1758, the French had spiked the cannon and thrown it in the river, before burning the fort and departing. It had been found there by Lt. Benjamin Neilly while swimming in the river, and it was brought to Fort Henry by Neilly when he arrived there to take command from Capt. Benjamin Biggs, in June, 1781. Neilly was then relieved the next month by Capt. John Boggs, but Neilly left his cannon there, as he thought it might prove useful. The cannon was a small "swivel gun", easily mounted in a frontier fort for defense; it had a bore of about two inches, throwing a one pound ball, and during the Siege of 1782 it was under the direction of John Tate, who had served in the artillery during the Revolution.

[89] In spite of statements to the effect that there were only a dozen or so defenders in the fort, the actual number was closer to fifty; that figure includes some forty men, and ten to twelve women and older boys who could handle a rifle. Altogether, men, women, and children, there were nearly a hundred inmates of the fort.

[90] That night, Thursday, the 12th, two men who had been held captive for some years managed to escape from the Indians. They arrived at Catfish Camp on the 14th and gave particulars as to the size of the army attacking Fort Henry, as well as the encouraging news of the fort's ability to withstand the assault.

[91] *The peace treaty was not officially signed by Great Britain and the United States until nine months later, on September 3, 1783. On November 3rd, General Washington disbanded the army, and the United States Congress ratified the treaty on January 14, 1784.

# Chapter Twenty-Four

[92] McGary was court-martialed for this violation of orders, but the only punishment was a temporary reduction in rank. For more on the cowardly behavior of Kennedy and McGary, see: In Memoriam Lewis Wetzel, following the Seventh Interlude.

93 *Isaac Williams was the son-in-law of Joseph Tomlinson.*

94 *Baker's Station, also known as Cresap's Fort, is not to be confused with Baker's Bottom at Yellow Creek, site of the massacre of Logan's family in 1774. It was built by Captain John Baker in 1782, at the head of Cresap's Bottom, Marshall County, West Virginia.*

# Chapter Twenty-Five

95 *This competition is adapted from a letter by Isaac Leffler (1788-1866), eldest son of the Jacob Leffler, alluded to by Doddridge in his Notes (Attack on Rice's Fort, pp. 217-221), and was written in response to Draper's letter of inquiry, May 19, 1862. The letter is dated Chariton, Iowa, May 27, 1862.*

96 *A few authors have endeavored to make a good story even better, by expanding the incident into a truly remarkable story involving ghostly apparitions and unearthly noises in the night, and by having Wetzel kill the Indian only in order to save the sweetheart of his widowed mother. All such details can be considered purely fictitious.*

97 *the mouth of Virginia Short Creek; i.e., where Short Creek on the (West) Virginia side enters the Ohio River, as opposed to Indian Short Creek or Ohio Short Creek on the opposite (Ohio) shore.*

98 *But that was evidently a misprint.*

99 *After his father's death Lewis had gone to live with his uncle, Lewis Bonnett, Sr. [see Appendix A for the Wetzel genealogy], three miles north of the Wetzel Homestead, where he resided for about two years. Lewis's cousin, Lewis Bonnett, Jr., later told Dr. Draper that the scalp which Wetzel collected during this expedition hung in Lewis's upstairs room of his father's house.*

100 *like the steam from the scape-pipe = the escape pipe, or relief valve, on a steamboat.*

101 *had originally been arrested by Judge Parsons — so the story that Harmar had Wetzel arrested and placed in irons at Fort Harmar is another fiction.*

102 *Killbuck was baptized by the Moravians in 1788 under the name of William Henry, and lived in their settlement at Goshen, Ohio, until his death. He is buried in Goshen, just a few feet from the grave of David Zeisberger.*

# Chapter Twenty-Six

[103] *from the German wenden, to turn.*

[104] *Kenton, Edna, Simon Kenton, His Life and Period, pp. 219-220*

# Chapter Twenty-Eight

[105] *at present Fort Recovery, Ohio.*

[106] *Col. George Gibson was the brother of John Gibson. After serving in the Jersey campaigns with Washington during the Revolution, he retired to Cumberland County, Pennsylvania, acting as county lieutenant. In that capacity he led a regiment under St. Clair, and was one of the many officers killed in the battle.*

# Chapter Twenty-Nine

[107] *about two miles southwest of present Eaton, Ohio.*

[108] *The six militia were buried just outside the walls of the fort, where their graves may still be seen today.*

[109] *Present Greenville, Ohio.*

[110] *Just north of present Maumee, Ohio.*

# Appendix

[111] *When Lewis Wetzel's brother Martin escaped from Indian captivity in 1781, he returned to the old family home in Virginia, where he visited his relatives. It was during this visit here that he met and married Mary Coffield, before returning with his new bride to his family on Wheeling Creek.*

[112] *Mary Bonnett Wetzel was later to name her two daughters, Christiana and Susannah, in honor of her two older sisters who had died before reaching America.*

[113] *The Zane home was located in present Moorefield, Hardy County, West Virginia.*

[114] *One of the early pioneers, George Edgington, stated that Daniel Greathouse died of the measles in 1775, the year following the Yellow Creek massacre. There was a third Greathouse brother (see the Sappington Narrative), and this may have been the Greathouse who was killed on this expedition.*

[115] *The six names marked with an asterisk are those that were duplicated on the DeHass list; Jacob Ogle was the brother of Capt. Joseph Ogle.*

[116] *A.S. Withers says that Captain William Foreman and his two sons were killed.*

[117] *An Historical Account of the Expedition against Sandusky under Col. Crawford in 1782, Cincinnati, 1873.*

[118] *Not to be confused with the later memorial to Col. Crawford established more recently at the eastern edge of Crawford, Ohio, on Ohio 199.*

[119] *Rev. Brown's article was published by the Historical Society of Western Pennsylvania, in the Western Pennsylvania Historical Magazine, January, 1985 (v. 68, n. 1).*

[120] *Additional corroboration of this date is found in the writings of the Moravian missionary John Heckewelder.*

[121] *The Russian Spy was a short-lived publication of Doddridge's, originally begun in 1825; Doddridge died on November 9, 1826, at 57 years of age, only a few months after this letter was published.*

[122] *Edmund Jennings Randolph, Governor of Virginia from 1786 to 1788. The Fort Randolph built at Point Pleasant to replace the burned Fort Blair, in 1775, the year after Dunmore's War, was named in honor of Peyton Randolph, president of the First Continental Congress (1774), who presided over the Virginia House of Burgesses until his death in October, 1775.*

[123] *Cambridge University Press, 1997.*

[124] *From letters of Josiah Harmar to the Secretary of War, dated 15 November, 1786, and 7 June, 1787.*

[125] *See Appendix E.*

# Bibliography

The following is not intended as an inclusive list of all the books pertaining to the Border Wars of the Upper Ohio Valley; instead, these are what the author considers to be the most informative *and* the most reliable. Personal bias and mistakes abound in all of them, however, and the reader is well advised to be wary of accepting any independent statement without adequate cross-references.

And this *caveat* applies to the present work, as well.

Allman, C.B. *Lewis Wetzel, Indian Fighter.* 1961 (originally published as *The Life and Times of Lewis Wetzel*, 1939).

Bakeless, John. *Daniel Boone.* 1939.

Butterfield, Consul Willshire. *An Historical Account of the Expedition against Sandusky under Col. William Crawford in 1782.* 1873.

—— *History of the Girtys.* 1890.

Cranmer, Gibson L. *History of Wheeling City and Ohio County, West Virginia.* 1902.

De Hass, Wills. *History of the Settlement and Indian Wars of Western Virginia.* 1851.

Doddridge, Joseph. *Notes on the Settlement and Indian Wars of the Western Parts of Virginia and Pennsylvania from 1763 to 1783.* 1824.

Faragher, John Mack. *Daniel Boone.* 1992.

Hartley, Cecil B. *The Life and Adventures of Lewis Wetzel, the Virginia Ranger.* 1860.

Hintzen, William. *The True Wetzelian*, v. I & II. 1997–1998.

Kellogg, Louise Phelps. *Frontier Advance on the Upper Ohio.* 1916.

—— *Frontier Retreat on the Upper Ohio.* 1917.

Kenton, Edna. *Simon Kenton, His Life and Period.* 1930.

Lobdell, Jared (ed.) *Further Adventures of Lewis Wetzel and the Upper Ohio Frontier.* 1994.

—— *Indian Warfare in Western Pennsylvania and North West Virginia*, 1992.

—— *Recollections of Lewis Bonnett, Jr.* 1991.

Newton, J.H., et al. *History of the Pan-Handle of West Virginia.* 1879.

Sword, Wiley. *President Washington's Indian War.* 1985.

Thwaites, Reuben Gold, *Daniel Boone*, 1902.

Thwaites, Reuben Gold, and Kellogg, L.P., (eds.) *Documentary History of Dunmore's War, 1774.* 1905.

—— *The Revolution on the Upper Ohio.* 1908.

—— *Frontier Defense on the Upper Ohio.* 1912.

Van Every, Dale. *A Company of Heroes.* 1962.

—— *Ark of Empire.* 1963.

Wallace, Paul A.W. *Thirty Thousand Miles with John Heckewelder.* 1958.

Withers, Alexander Scott. *Chronicles of Border Warfare.* 1831.

## *Peripherals:*

There are many other works related to the Border Wars which contain various items of information on the frontier; a great many of those bits and pieces are unavailable elsewhere. Unfortunately many of the earlier books are almost impossible to find outside of rare book libraries. Among these are Archibald Loudon's *Indian Narratives* (1808 & 1811), John McClung's *Sketches of Western Adventure* (1832), Timothy Flint's *Indian Wars of the West* (1833), Samuel Kercheval's *History of the Valley of Virginia* (1833), Joseph Pritts' *Incidents of Border Life* (1839), and Samuel P. Hildreth's *Pioneer History ... of the Ohio Valley* (1848).

Dale Van Every's introductory volume[1] to his *American Frontier* series is *Forth to the Wilderness*, by far the most accurate general history of the French & Indian War, and it provides not only an excellent background for all the later events which occurred on the Western Border, but it also gives considerable insight into *why* those events occurred. His earlier *Men of the Western Waters* covers the history of the long hunters of the North Carolina-Tennessee-Kentucky region. Otto Rothert's *The Outlaws of Cave-in-Rock* contains the best history of the subsequent career of Samuel Mason after his departure from Fort Henry, including his relationship with the Harpes; Paul I. Wellman's *Spawn of Evil* is an excellent history of the Natchez Trace land pirates, beginning with those terrible Harpes.

Allan W. Eckert's *The Frontiersmen*, based on the life of Simon Kenton, is a very readable, overall view of the Indian Wars on the frontier, by a modern author. In the same vein are many of the late nineteenth century works on the western frontier; of these probably the most reliable is Charles McKnight's *Our Western Border, One Hundred Years Ago*. In addition there is E.G. Cattermole's *Famous Frontiersmen, Pioneers, and Scouts*, Augustus L. Mason's *The Romance and Tragedy of Pioneer Life*, and Walter Spooner's *The Back-Woodsmen, or Tales of the Borders*.

---

[1] *The second and third volumes are A Company of Heroes and Ark of Empire, listed above; the final volume is entitled The Final Challenge. This four-volume set covers the middle states' frontier from 1754 to 1815.*

# Index